Japanese Technology Reviews

Section A: Electronics

Volume 2

MMIC-Monolithic Microwave Integrated Circuits

Yasuo Mitsui

Volume 4

Bulk Crystal Growth Technology

Shin-ichi Akai, Keiichiro Fujita, Masamichi Yokogawa, Mikio Morioko and Kazuhisa Matsumoto

Volume 8

Semiconductor Heterostructure Devices

Masayuki Abe and Naoki Yokoyama

Volume 11

Development of Optical Fibers in Japan

Hiroshi Murata

Volume 12

High-Performance BiCMOS Technology and Its Applications to VLSIs

Ikuro Masuda and Hideo Maejima

Volume 13

Semiconductor Devices for Electronic Tuners

Seiichi Watanabe

Volume 19

Amorphous Silicon Solar Cells

Yukinori Kuwano

Volume 20

High Density Magnetic Recording for Home VTR: Heads and Media

Kazunori Ozawa

Please see the back of this book for other titles in the Japanese Technology Reviews series

MEGA-BIT MEMORY TECHNOLOGY

From Mega-Bit to Giga-Bit

GENERAL INFORMATION

Aims and Scope

Japanese Technology Reviews is a series of tracts which examines the status and future prospects for Japanese technology.

MEGA-BIT MEMORY TECHNOLOGY

From Mega-Bit to Giga-Bit

Hiroyuki Tango

Tokyo Institute of Polytechnics
Kanagawa, Japan

CRC Press is an imprint of the
Taylor & Francis Group, an **informa** business

First published 1998 by Gordon and Breach Science Publishers

Published 2018 by CRC Press
Taylor & Francis Group
6000 Broken Sound Parkway NW, Suite 300
Boca Raton, FL 33487-2742

ISBN-13: 978-90-5699-098-5 (pbk)
ISBN-13: 978-1-138-41395-5 (hbk)

Visit the Taylor & Francis Web site at
http://www.taylorandfrancis.com

and the CRC Press Web site at
http://www.crcpress.com

British Library Cataloguing in Publication Data

Mega-bit memory technology: from mega-bit to giga-bit.
(Japanese technology reviews; v.32)
1. Random access memory 2. Integrated circuits - Ultra large scale integration
I. Tango, Hiroyuki
621.3'973

Contents

Preface to the Series

Modern technology has a great impact on both industry and society. New technology is first created by pioneering work in science. Eventually, a major industry is born, and it grows to have an impact on society in general. International cooperation in science and technology is necessary and desirable as a matter of public policy. As development progresses, international cooperation changes to international competition and competition further accelerates techological progress.

Japan is in a very competitive position relative to other developed countries in many high-technology fields. In some fields, Japan is in a leading position: for example, manufacturing technology and micro-electronics, especially semiconductor LSIs and optoelectronic devices. Japanese industries lead in the applicaiton of new materials such as composites and fine ceramics, although many of these new materials were first developed in the United States and Europe. The United States, Europe and Japan are working intensively, both competitively and cooperatively, on the research and development of high-critical-temperature superconductors. Computers and communications are now a combined field that plays a key role in the present and future of human society. In the next century, biotechnology will grow, and it may become a major segment of industry. While Japan does not play a major role in all areas of biotechnology, in some areas such as fermentation (the traditional technology for making sake), Japanese research is of primary importance.

Today, tracking Japanese progress in high-technology areas is both a necessary and rewarding process. Japanese academic institutions are very active; consequently, their results are published in scientific and technical journals and are presented at numerous meetings where more than 20,000 technical papers are presented orally every year. However, due principally to the language barrier, the results of academic research in Japan are not well-known overseas. Many in the United States and in Europe are thus surprised by the sudden appearence of Japanese high-technology products. The products are admired and enjoyed, but some are astonished at how suddenly these products appear.

With the series Japanese Technology Reviews, we present state-of-the-art Japanese technology in five fields:

Electronics
Computers and Communications
New Materials
Manufacturing Engineering
Biotechnology

Each tract deals with one topic within each of these five fields and reviews both the present status and future prospects of the technology, mainly as seen from the Japanese perspective. Each author is an outstanding scientist or engineer actively engaged in relevant research and development.

The editors are confident that this series will not only give a deep insight into Japanese technology but will also be useful for developing new technology of interest in our readers.

As editor-in-chief, I would like to sincerely thank the members of the editorial board and the authors for their contributions to this series.

TOSHIAKI IKOMA

Preface

This book is one of the series of Japanese Technology Reviews. Dr. Toshiaki Ikoma, Guest Professor of University of Tokyo, and also Representative Director and President of Texas Instruments Japan Limited, is Section Editor of the electronics section and Editor in Chief of the series. This book describes LSI process technology. It focuses on the rapid progress of state-of-the-art dynamic random access memory (DRAM) process technologies – the longstanding Technology driver of Si ULSI – as they advance from the 1 Kbit to the Gbit DRAM era.

The book is organized into two parts. The first part, Chapters 1 and 2, provides an overview of recent progress and trends in device technology in general. To deal with the field of process technology and by way of introduction to subsequent chapters, the scaling of MOSFETs is briefly described in Chapter 1, and in Chapter 2 an overview is provided of DRAM memory cell structures as a typical device technology combining various process technologies, and which is a key technology to high-density DRAMs. The second part, Chapters 3 through 9, deals with each process technology from lithography to Si wafer technology. We present the theoretical and practical aspects of LSI fabrication steps with an emphasis on DRAM devices. Additionally, process-device simulation technology and SOI (Silicon-On-Insulator) technology are described in Chapters 10 and 11, respectively. These technologies are important from the viewpoint of quick device fabrication on the computer instead of in the clean room and as the most promising device technology in future scaled MOSLSIs, respectively.

This book is intended for engineers, scientists, and managers engaged in the field of LSI processes and device technology. Graduate students and faculty will also find it worthwhile as a reference book.

Each chapter is written by experts involved in the R&D of ULSI process technology at TOSHIBA Corporation.

As the editor of this book, I would like to thank Professor Ikoma for providing us with the opportunity to publish this book, and the authors for their contributions.

Hiroyuki Tango

Contributors

Hiroyuki Tango (Chapter 1, 2)
Tokyo Institute of Polytechnics
Department of Image Engineering
1583, Iiyama, Atsugi-city, Kanagawa-pref. 243-02, Japan

Masataka Miyamura (Chapter 3)
Toshiba Chemical Corporation
New Product Development Center, Kawaguchi Works
5-14-25, Ryoke, Kawaguchi-city
Saitama-pref. 332, Japan

Makoto Sekine (Chapter 4)
Toshiba Corporation
Microelectronics Engineering Laboratory
ULSI Process Engineering Laboratory
8, Sinsugita-cho, Isogo-ku, Yokohama 235, Japan

Kikuo Yamabe (Chapter 5, 6)
Institute of Materials Science
University of Tsukuba
Tsukuba, Ibaraki 305, Japan

Kyoichi Suguro (Chapter 7)
Toshiba Corporation
Microelectronics Engineering Laboratory
ULSI Process Engineering Laboratory
8, Shinsugita-cho, Isogo-ku, Yokohama 235, Japan

Nobuo Hayasaka (Chapter 8)
Toshiba Corporation
Microelectronics Engineering Laboratory
ULSI Process Engineering Laboratory
8, Shinsugita-cho, Isogo-ku, Yokohama 235, Japan

Yoshiaki Matsusita (Chapter 9)
Toshiba Ceramics Co., Ltd
Technical Department, Silicon Division
30, Soya, Hadano-shi, Kanagawa-pref. 257, Japan

Tetsunori Wada (Chapter 10)
Semiconductor Leading Edge Technologies, Inc.
Advanced Technology Research Dept.
292, Yoshida-cho, Tosuka-ku, Yokohama 244, Japan

Makoto Yoshimi (Chapter 11)
Toshiba Corporation
Research and Development Center
Advanced Semiconductor Device Research Laboratories
1, Komukai Toshiba-cho, Saiwai-ku, Kawasaki 210, Japan

CHAPTER 1

MOS Device Technology

1.1. Introduction

Over the last quarter century, the bit density of DRAMs has been increasing by a factor of four every three years and the design rule has been scaling down by a factor of 0.64 every generation[1] as shown in Table 1.1. According to this trend, commercial 1Gbit DRAMs are expected to appear in 2000.

However, below $\sim 1.0\,\mu m$ feature sizes (1Mbit-4Mbit DRAM), the large number of processing steps and the complexity of the DRAM cell have gradually emerged as a big problem from the viewpoints of chip price and technology[2,3]. "The π Rule"[4], which describes the trend of the average price of packaged DRAM chips as a function of time, states that bit cost of DRAMs is reduced to one fourth every generation, and the price decline approaches 1 U.S. dollar per year at a price level of π U.S. dollars. This price level corresponds to the peak volume of DRAM shipment as well as the maximum return on the DRAM investment. "The π Rule" was applicable to DRAMs up to 256 Kbit. "The Bi Rule"[5], named for its prediction that bit cost will be reduced by one half with each succeeding DRAM generation has been proposed for 1Mbit DRAMs and above, considering the chip price increase due to the increase of process steps, chip-size, equipment cost (throughput), development cost, decrease of yield, etc. (Fig. 1.1).

In order to keep the chip price under "the Bi-rule", great efforts have been made and many kinds of new technologies have been introduced for each generation of DRAM devices[3,22].

In this chapter, we describe the evolutional device technology introduced in Mbit DRAM generation, and forecast technology trends for 1Gbit DRAMs and beyond.

Table 1.1 Process and device technology trend in MOS-LSIs.

Production Start		1970	1975		1980		1985	1990		1995		2000	2005	2010
Feature Size (μm)		12	8	5	3	2	1.3	0.8	0.5	0.35	0.25	0.15	0.10	0.07
DRAM (Bit)		1K	4K	16K	64K	256K	1M	4M	16M	64M	256M	1G	4G	16G
Memory Cell	Structure	3T	1T•Planar				Stack/Trench (3D)						(Planar/ Highε,•••)	
	Insulator Thick. (nm)	120	100	50	35	20	10	8	5 (Stack) / 4 (Trench)			0.4/4	0.3/3	0.2/3
Device	Power Supply (V)	~20	12		5 (Int. 3.3)					3.3	3.3~1.5			1.2
	Transistor	pMOS	nMOS				CMOS						(CMOS/SOI)	
	Drain Structure	SD					LDD					(Improved)		
	Oxide Thick. (nm)	120	100	75	50	35	25	20	15	12	10	8	6	4.5
	Channel Length (μm)	~8	5	3	2	1.3	0.8	0.8	0.5	0.3	0.2	0.15	0.10	0.07
	Junction Depth (μm)	~1.5	0.8	0.5	0.35	0.3	0.25	0.2	0.15	0.12	0.1	0.08	0.06	0.05
Process	Lithography	Contact			1/1PJ	1/10PJ	1/5PJ,g	i			KrF		ArF/EB/Xray	
	Ecthing	Solution				Plasma, RIE			ECR, Magnetron					
	Isolation	Planar	LOCOS						(Improved)			STI		
	Gate Material	Al	p-Si	Double p-Si		Polycide			(Al-Shunt)			Refractory		
	Metallization	Al		Al-Si			Al-Si-Cu (Barrier)			Multi-Level				
	Wafer Size	2	2.5	3	4	5	6	6~8	8	8~10			12"ϕ	

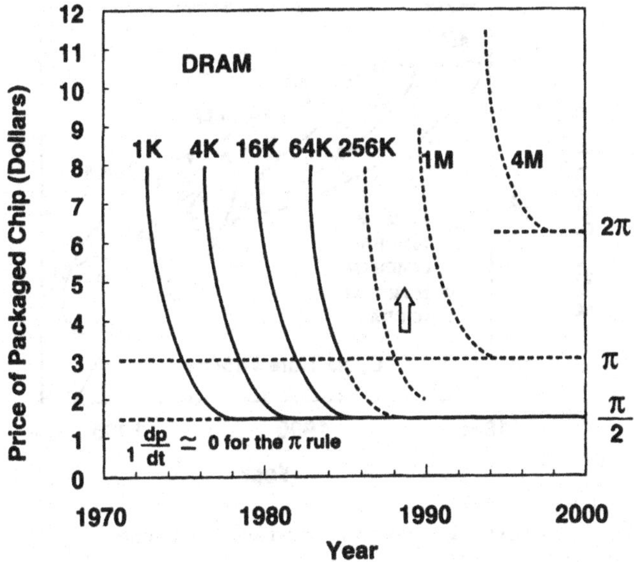

Figure 1.1 "The π rule" predicts that the price stabilizes $\pi/2$ dollars. It also predicts that for larger-scale generation of DRAMs (1Mbit and above), the stabilizing price will double each generation[5].

1.2. MOS Device Technology

Several evolutional device technologies have been introduced with the fine patterning technology to increase memory capacity. The use of CMOS instead of the traditional NMOS circuit reduced power dissipation of 1 Mbit DRAM to one half of that of NMOS due to the reduced peripheral circuit current[6], which results from CMOS peripheral circuits and CMOS decoders. With the downsizing of computer and communication systems for portable multimedia applications, low power DRAMs have become indispensable for battery-powered equipment. As shown in Figure 1.2, active power of 4Mbit-256Mbit DRAM gradually decrease from 1 W to 100 mW with increasing memory capacities due to the decrease of power supply voltage[7].

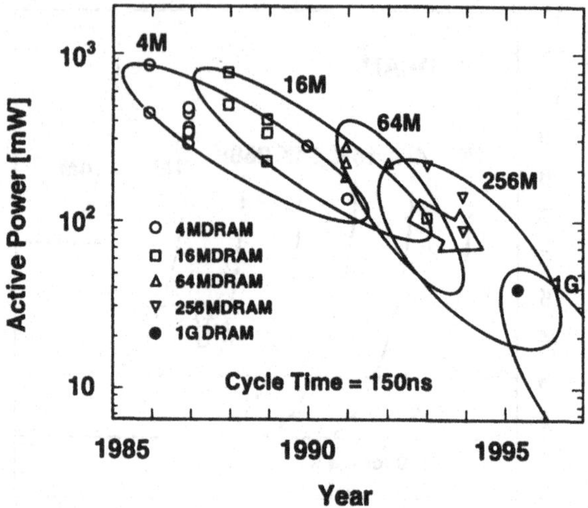

Figure 1.2 Active power trend for LSI memories.

Although the device structure was downscaled following the traditional scaling law[8], supply voltage of 5 V was not scaled and persisted until 1 μm generation devices, causing the significant problem of hot-electron induced degradation in the traditional SD (Single Drain) structured MOSFETs. The LDD (Lightly Doped Drain) transistor[9,10] introduced firstly in the 1 Mbit generation, which spreads the high field at the drain pinch-off region resulting in the reduction of the maximum field intensity (Fig. 1.3), solved the hot-electron problem in the 1 μm generation devices. Subsequently, "the drain engineering", which deals with the optimum impurity profile design near the drain region, has been investigated to improve the current drivability, breakdown voltage, and hot-carrier immunity of MOSFETs used in each generation. As a 0.5 μm generation (16 Mbit generation) MOSFET, the gate over-lapped LDD structure has been reported[11,12,33] (Fig. 1.4). It can improve, while maintaining the hot-carrier immunity, the transconductance (Gm) degradation due to series resistance in the lightly doped *n*-LDD region, caused by the depletion by hot-carrier induced trapped charge on top of the lightly doped *n*-LDD region.

Three-dimensional (trench or stacked) capacitor to increase the storage capacitance in the DRAM cell has been introduced from the

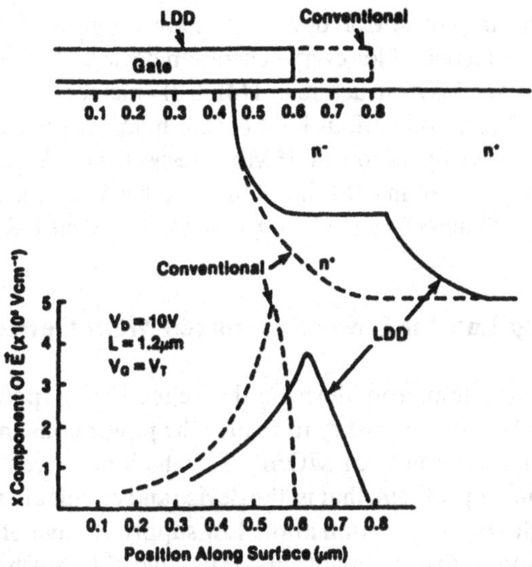

Figure 1.3 Magnitude of the electric field at the Si-SiO_2 interface of L_{DD} transistor as a function of distance; $L = 1.2\,\mu m$, $V_{DS} = 8.5\,V$, $V_{GS} = V_T$[1C].

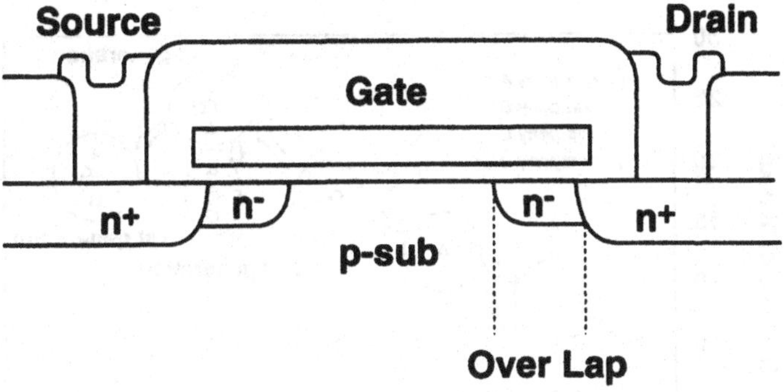

Figure 1.4 Schematic cross section of gate overlap L_{DD} structure.

4 Mbit generation with the decreasing of insulator thickness, which will be described in detail in Chapter 2.

In order to suppress the increasing of cost of manufacturing processing, efforts on the reducing of the number of masks have began from the development stage of 64Mbit devices. As shown Figure 1.5, the number of masks used increased for every generation devices. This is due to the introduction of CMOS structure in 1Mbit, 3D memory cell and double layer Al in 4Mbit, and various kind of threshold voltage transistors to make high speed operation in 16Mbit, respectively. As a result, the number of masks used in 64Mbit DRAMs has been reduced to the same level, around 20 masks, as the first generation of 4Mbit DRAMs[16].

1.3. Scaling Law for Lower Sub-micron MOS Devices

In the lower submicron devices, the reduction of power supply voltage has become necessary to reduce the power consumption and maintain high reliability of MOSFETs, which has given rise to the most significant problem, that is, the device and circuit are required to achieve high-speed operation at the low supply voltage of 1.5–3.3 V. In proportion to the scaling of supply voltage, the threshold voltage scaling is necessary to obtain the high-speed operation.

A scaling guideline for optimum power-supply voltage and process/device parameters for half-micron and lower submicron CMOS

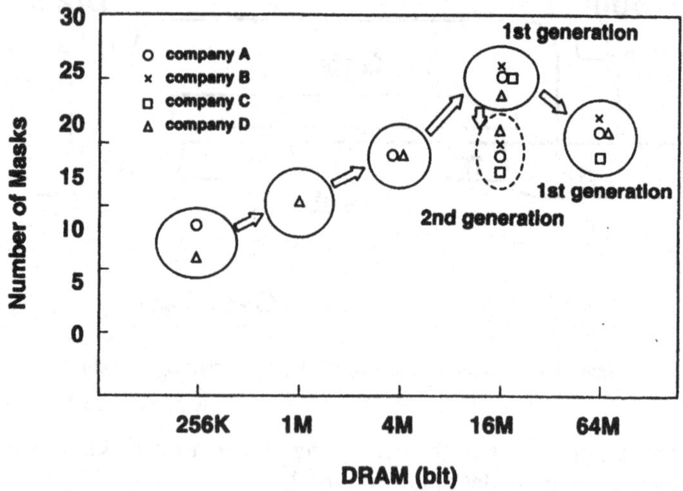

Figure 1.5 Number of masks used in every DRAM generation[16].

devices down to the 0.3 μm design rule, has been proposed[13]. This guideline achieves high circuit performance while maintaining MOS device reliability. As shown Figure 1.6, the optimum voltage reduction obtained follows the square root of the design rule, which has been experimentally verified over a wide range of gate oxide thickness (7–45nm) and gate length (0.3–2.0 μm). Relationships of $V_{DD} = 6.1 \times (L/2)^{1/2}$ for conventional structure and $V_{DD} = 8.2 \times (L/2)^{1/2}$ for LDD structure were obtained.

Another approach is the method based on "the substrate engineering" which deals with the optimum design of substrate impurity doping[14,15]. An empirical relationship between the possible minimum channel length, $L_{ef.mini}$, and a parameter $(N_s + N_j)/2$ is obtained. N_s and N_j are Si surface and substrate doping doses at source-drain junction depth X_j, respectively. $(N_s + N_j)/2$ implies the average doping level at 0.05–0.1 μm depth, calculated by 2 dimensional process simulator, as follows;

$$\text{Lef.min} \propto [(N_s + N_j)/\ 2]^{1/2} \tag{1.1}$$

Eq. (1.1) is independent of threshold voltage (V_{th}) at any given T_{ox}, X_j, and substrate doping, resulting in a guideline for scaling down V_{th} without punch-through by reducing N_s and increasing $(N_s + N_j)/2$ at 0.05 ~ 0.1 μm depth, can be obtained.

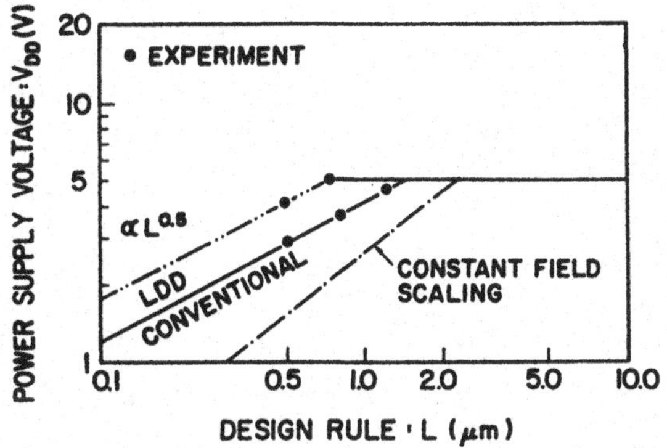

Figure 1.6 Most optimum power supply voltage at various design rules[13].

In the submicron regime, the prolonged DRAM generation (3–5 years per generation) and difficulties with fine patterning have led to reconsideration of the traditional scaling factor of 0.64 per generation. That is, the traditional generation of 3 years has been divided into two or three steps, "step-to-step scaling".[3] DRAMs of three or four generations coexist in a market at any time, and, as an example, the original 4Mbit DRAM (0.8 μm-rule, the 1st generation) is scaled down stepwise to 0.7 μm (the 2nd generation) to 0.6 μm (the 3rd generation) and 0.5 μm. As a result, at the last step, the older generation DRAM (4Mbit) is produced using the newer generation (16Mbit) technology which is called the cut-down version[3]. Figure 1.7 shows the sample delivering time of the 1st and the 2nd generations for every DRAM generation[16].

1.4. Toward Gbit and Beyond

Experimental 1Gbit DRAMs[17,18,35,36] and 4Gbit DRAM[37] also have already been reported. Commercial 1Gbit devices will appear in the market at the beginning of the 21st century. To realize the Gbit memory and beyond as commercial ULSIs, requires not only the

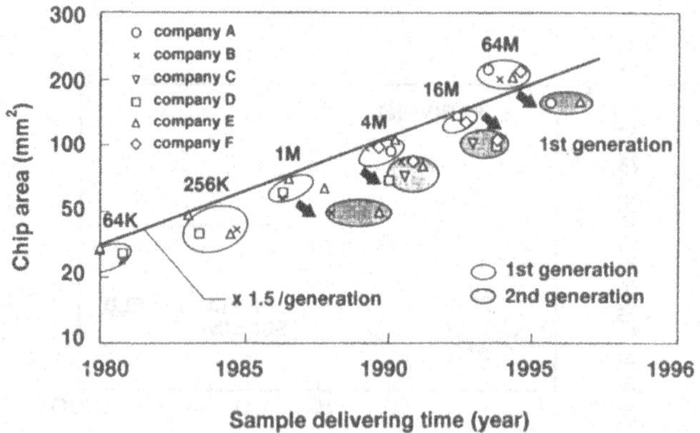

Figure 1.7 Sample delivering time of the 1st and the 2nd generations for every DRAM generation[16].

pursuit the limits of technologies and materials, but also the low-cost manufacturing technology and the value-added chips to create new markets.

The requirement for LSIs from downsizing systems are small size, value-added, low voltage, low power dissipation, large integration, high reliability (hot carrier effect, α-particle immunity), high speed, and low cost. Without a scaling scenario, it is extremely difficult to satisfy these requirements. A new scaling scenario toward 0.1 μm and below, has to be developed.

Efforts have been made to advance device technologies toward 0.1 μm and below. A 40 nm gate length *n*-MOSFET which operate in pentode characteristics at room temperature as shown in Figure 1.8, has been realized[19]. To fabricate 10 nm source and drain junction depth, two novel techniques has been used, that is, the resist thinning technique using isotropic oxygen plasma ashing and solid phase diffusion technique from phosphorus-doped silicate glass (PSG).

The performance fluctuations of MOSFETs caused by the statistical fluctuation of the channel dopant number is one of the most serious concerns in future gigabit-scale LSIs[20,21]. It has been shown that V_{th} distribution is given by the Gaussian function and its fluctuation is mainly caused by depletion layer charge fluctuation due

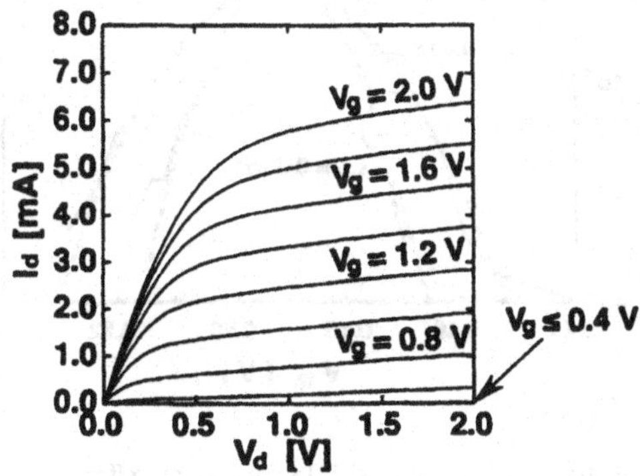

Figure 1.8 I_D-V_G characteristics of a 40 nm n-MOSFET at room temperature[19].

to statistical fluctuation of the channel dopant number, and the channel dopant number in small dimensional MOSFET's can be given by the Gaussian distribution (Fig. 1.9). To suppress the V_{th} fluctuation, lower surface impurity concentration, which can adjust to low threshold voltage simultaneously, is needed. This approach leads to SOI MOSFETs with fully depleted thin SOI layer and undoped epitaxial channel MOSFETs[13,29,30]. Further investigation of the scaling law regarding these device structures is necessary toward 0.01 μm.

1.5. Si Quantum Devices

As the device feature size scales downward to below 0.01 μm, quantum effects appear even in Si devices. The research on Si quantum effects has begun to identify a new phenomena related to device reliability, such as single electron trapping in gate oxide causing drain current fluctuation[23,24] and velocity overshoot causing the drain current increase[25]; however, the recent research has been directed

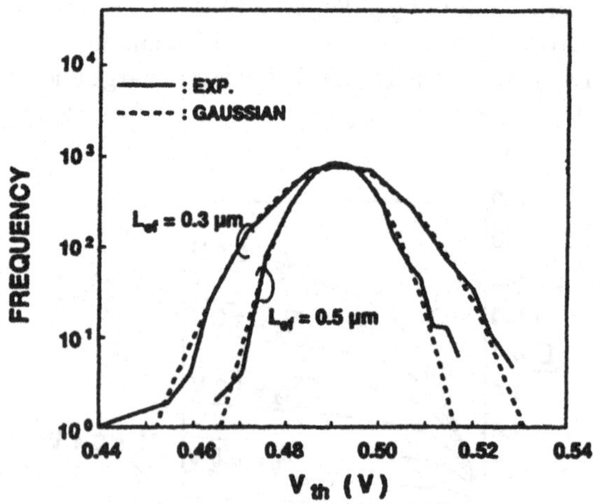

Figure 1.9 V_{th} distribution of 8k-NMOS array at effective channel length (L_{ef}) = 0.5 μm and 0.3 μm, with oxide thickness (T_{ox}) of 11 nm and average p-well concentration (N_a) of 7.1×10^{16} cm^{-3} [21].

toward the new quantum devices[26,27,31,32,38]. Figure 1.10 shows a single-electron memory structure[28]. It operates at room temperature as a non-volatile RAM. In the poly-Si TFTs with 4 nm thickness and 10 nm grain size, a single electron is stored (or "written") with every 15 v gate voltage increase, and the number of stored electrons is counted (or "read") by the quantized threshold voltage shift. Figure 1.11(a) shows the cross-sectional view of a single-electron transisitor (SET) fabricated by converting a one-dimensional Si wire on a SIMOX (separation by implanted oxygen) substrate, which has a small Si island with a tunneling barrier at each end[39]. Figure 1.11(b) shows the equivalent circuit. The Si island is surrounded by the gate electrode, substrate Si under the SiO_2 layer, and source and drain regions. Figure 1.12 shows the conductance characteristics at various temperature for a SET's[39]. Conductance oscillations, which are due to Coulomb blockade by tunnel barriers with very small capacitance formed at the constrictions, are observed even at room temperature. Figure 1.13 shows schematic cross section of edge quantum wire MOSFET fabricated on SOI substrate. The SOI film thickness is less than 15nm and the channel length is around 3.5 μm. Using this MOSFET, Coulomb Oscillation of channel current with gate voltage sweeping was observed[34].

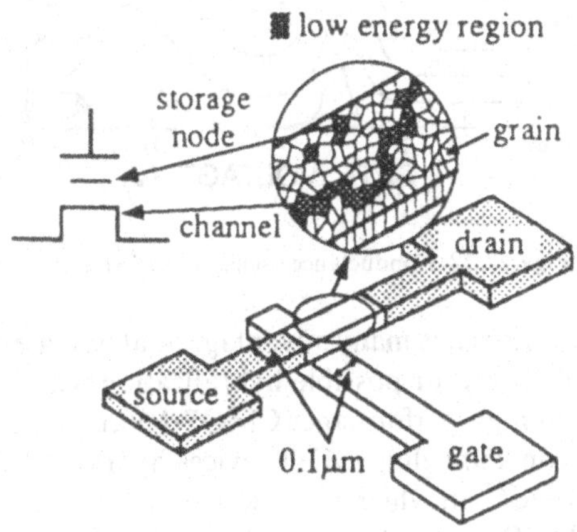

Figure 1.10 Single electron memory structure[28].

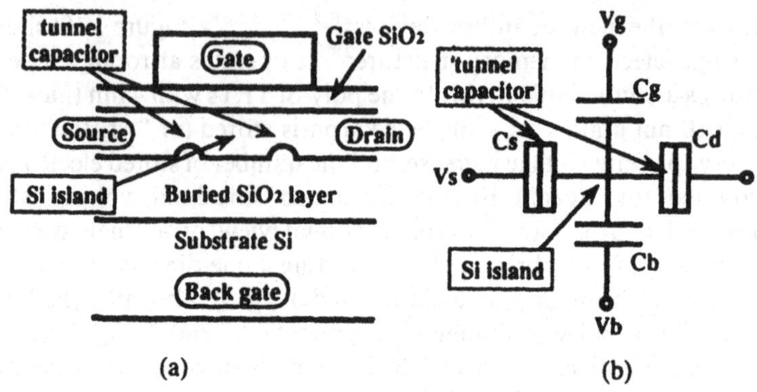

Figure 1.11 (a) cross-sectional view of the SET, (b) equivalent circuit of the SET[39].

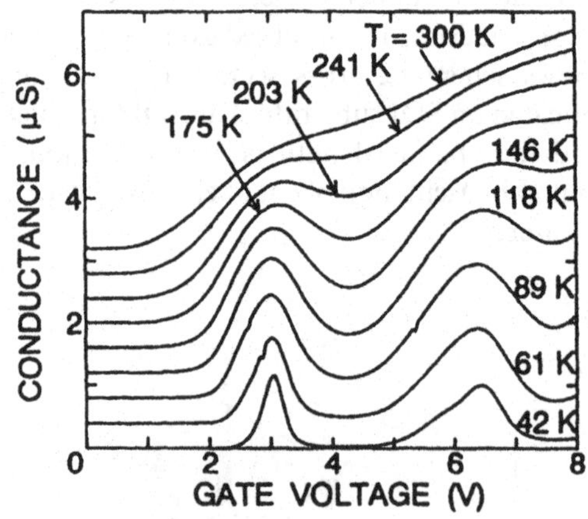

Figure 1.12 Conductance oscillations of SET's[39].

Si quantum devices has many advantage, that is, material stability, process controllability, or possible hybridization with conventional Si devices such as high-performance CMOS devices[34]. The concept of Si Single Electron Tunneling (SET) devices hybridized with CMOS has been proposed[27], in which the external system accesses the SET devices via CMOS circuits, and the low gain SET devices will be compensated by conventional CMOS performance.

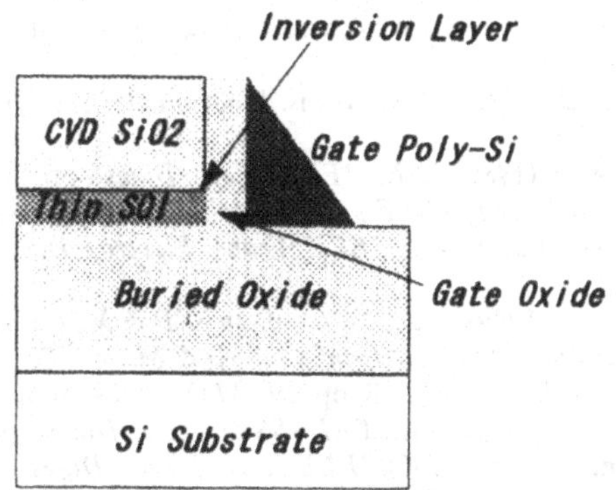

Figure 1.13 Shematic cross section of edge quantum wire SOI MOSFET[34].

If single electron devices are realized based on innovative research in pursuit of simple and manufacturable structures to which advanced Si ULSI production technologies can be applied, they may enable realization of future LSIs free from the problems posed by huge increases in power dissipation and number of transistors.

In this chapter, we have briefly described the historical trend and forecast of the progress of device technology from Mbit to Gbit DRAM era and beyond. Having staked out the territory, in the following chapters each process technology is discussed.

References

1. Sunami, H. (1994). *Tech. Proceedings SEMI Technology Symp.*, pp. 29–38.
2. Komiya, H. (1993). *IEEE ISSCC Tech. Digest*, pp. 16–19.
3. Ogirima, M. (1993). *Symp. on VLSI Technology, Tech. Digest*, pp. 1–5.
4. Lepselter, M. P. *et al.* (1985). *IEEE Circuits and Devices: Magazine*, January, pp. 53–54.
5. Tarui, Y. *et al.* (1991). *IEEE Circuits and Devices: Magazine*, March, pp. 44–45 and also *IEEE Circuits and Devices: Magazine*, July, pp. 37 (1991).
6. Itoh, K. *IEEE Trans. Electron Devices*, ED-25, No. 3, pp. 778–789.
7. Takada, M. (1994). *Tech. Proceedings SEMI Technology Symp.*, pp. 29–38.
8. Dennard, R. H. *et al.* (1974). *IEEE J. Solid-State Circuits*, vol. SC-9, 256–268.

9. Saito, K. (1978). Densi-Joho-Tsusin Gakkai Kenkyukai, SSD78-37 (in Japanese).
10. Ogura, S. *et al.* (1980). *IEEE Trans. Electron Devices*, ED-27, pp. 1359–1367.
11. Huang, T. *et al.* (1986). *IEEE IEDM Tech. Digest*, pp. 742–745.
12. Izawa, R. *et al.* (1987). *IEEE IEDM Tech. Digest*, pp. 38–41.
13. Kakumu, M. *et al.* (1990). *IEEE Trans. Electron Devices*, ED-37, pp. 1334–1342.
14. Izawa, R. *et al.* (1989). *The 21st Conf. on SSD & M*, pp. 121–124.
15. Takeda, E. (1989). *The 21st Conf. on SSD & M*, pp. 521–524.
16. NIKKEI MICRODEVICES, pp. 29–37 (Nov. 1993) (in Japanese).
17. Horiguchi, M. *et al.* (1995). *IEEE ISSCC Tech. Digest*, pp. 252–253.
18. Sugibayashi, T. *et al.* (1995). *IEEE ISSCC Tech. Digest*, pp. 234–235.
19. Ono, M. *et al.* (1995). *IEEE Trans. Electron Devices*, ED-42, pp. 1822–1830.
20. Keyes, R. W. (1975). *Proc. IEEE*, **63**, 740–767.
21. Mizuno, T. *et al.* (1994). *IEEE Trans. Electron Devices*, ED-41, pp. 2216–2221.
22. Kohyama, S. (1994). *Symp. on VLSI Technology, Tech. Digest*, pp. 5–8.
23. Skocpol, W. J. (1986). *et al.*, *Phys. Rev. Lett.*, **56**, 2865–2868.
24. Ralls, K. S. (1986). *et al.*, *Phys. Rev. Lett.*, **52**, 228–231.
25. Chou, S. Y. *et al.* (1985). *IEEE Electron device Letters*, EDL-6, pp. 665–667.
26. Takahashi, Y. *et al.* (1994). *IEEE IEDM Tech. Digest*, pp. 938–940.
27. Toriumi, A. *et al.* (1995). *Abstract of 14th symposium on Future Electron Devices*, Oct. Tokyo, pp. 67–72.
28. Yano, K. *et al.* (1993). *IEEE IEDM Tech. Digest*, pp. 541–544.
29. Yan, R. H. *et al.* (1991). *Appl. Phys. Lett.*, **59**(25), 3315–3317.
30. Noda, K. *et al.* (1994). *Symp. on VLSI Technology, Tech. Digest*, pp. 19–20.
31. Morimoto, K. *et al.* (1993). *International Conf. on SSD & M*, pp. 344–346, 1993.
32. Ishikuro, H. *et al.* (1996). 43rd Spring Meeting, The Japan Society of Applied Physics and Related Societies, 26-P-ZA-12 (in Japanese).
33. Ko, P. K. *et al.* (1986). *IEEE IEDM Tech. Digest*, pp. 292–295.
34. Ohata, A. *et al.* (1996). *International Conf. on SSD & M*, pp. 455–457 1996.
35. Nitta, Y. *et al.* (1996). *IEEE ISSCC Tech. Digest*, pp. 376–377.
36. Yoo, J. H. *et al.* (1996). *IEEE ISSCC Tech. Digest*, pp. 378–379.
37. Muratani, T. *et al.* (1997). *IEEE ISSCC Tech. Digest*, pp. 74–75.
38. Grabert, H. and Devoret, M. H. (1992). ed. NATO ASI Series (Plenum press, New York).
39. Takahashi, Y. *et al.* (1996). *IEEE Trans. Electron Devices*, ED-43, pp. 1213–1217.

CHAPTER 2

Memory Cell Technology

2.1. Memory Cell Technology Trend

In the first semiconductor memory, the 1Kbit DRAM, which debuted in 1970, three transistor memory cell was used. The single transistor cell (1 MOSFET + 1 capacitor) using single layer poly-Si, which was invented by Dennard[1], became the mainstream for the 4Kbit DRAM[2,3,4]. To obtain higher performance and packing density, the 1T cell using double level poly-Si was used in the 16Kbit DRAM, and triple level poly-Si structure appeared in 256kbit devices[5].

Although other approaches, such as gain-cell, have been proposed in which the amplification function is included in the cell, there have been no memory cells except the 1T cell due to its simplicity of structure and fabrication procedure, and performance.

The 1T cell is composed of a storage capacitor and a switching transistor for reading or writing the charge. The storage capacitance of the memory cells is affected by the sensitivity of sense amplifier, the noises (such as α-particle induced soft error and the generated noise in the memory circuit) and the stored charge leakage. With larger scale memory integration, the memory cells have become smaller, resulting in the decrease of signal storage capacitance (C_s), which adversely affects the signal to noise ratio (S/N).

Figure 2.1 shows the trend of DRAM cell. To maintain the stored charge at around 30fF, as cell area downward-scaling proceeds in Mbit DRAMs regime (cell area decreases of 36% with each success generation), the following capacitor parameters have been pursued[6];

- Dielectric Film Thickness
- Dielectric Constant
- Stored Voltage
- Effective Capacitor Area

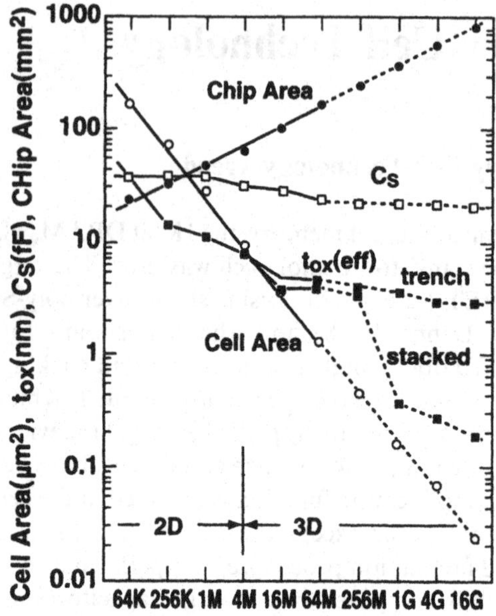

Figure 2.1 Trend of DRAM cell.

Research efforts have been focused on decreasing the dielectric film thickness while keeping the stored voltage constant of 5V. As shown in Table 1.1, around 120 nm thick SiO_2 films for 1Kbit, and 20 nm for 256Kbit were used as the memory cell insulator films. Composed insulating films, such as ONO(SiO_2(top oxide)/Si_3N_4(nitride)/SiO_2 (bottom oxide)), ON(Si_3N_4/SiO_2(bottom oxide)), began to be used from the 1Mbit generation onward as alternative dielectrics to thin SiO_2 films because of the increase of pin hole density of thinner SiO_2 films and the requirement of high dielectric materials.

Typical process steps of ONO multilayer films are as follows. The bottom-oxide is grown by thermal oxidation of Si substrates. The top-oxide is thermally grown on the nitride deposited by the LP(Low Pressure)-CVD method. The top SiO_2 layer is considered to reduce an electron trapping in the stacked films and improve intrinsic breakdown properties. The intrinsic breakdown properties of the stacked films are determined by the SiO_2 layer, and Si_3N_4 layers reduce the random failures of the films which is caused by the weak spots dotted homogeneously in accordance with Poisson's distribution in bottom-oxide layers[7].

The ON dielectrics used in the 4 and 16Mbit generations, as well as the oxide equivalent insulator thickness (t_{ox}) of 8nm for 4Mbit and 5nm for 16Mbit DRAMs, provide capacitance values of 6–7 fF/μm^2 for 3.3V internal supply voltage devices, which has been combined with the use of 3-dimentional (3D) memory cells such as trench and stacked cells, which will be described in the following section. Thinner films of these dielectrics will be used in 64Mbit and 256Mbit devices.

To build gigabit DRAMs, considerably higher capacitance values are needed to keep the cell structures simple and manufacturable while maintaining the storage capacitance of around 30fF. High dielectric constant (high ε) films and ferroelectric films, which are the most promising materials, are described in section 2.4. in this chapter and Chapter 8.

As for the power supply voltage (V_{cc}), 5V power supply has prevailed from 16Kbit devices to 4Mbit DRAMs. However, the reliability of MOSFET gate insulator and power consumption have become major concerns in pursuing high-volume DRAMs. To assure the hot-electron reliability of 0.5 μm MOS transistors and to reduce the power dissipation, internal voltage of 4V or 3.3V with external supply voltage of 5V, has been used in the 16Mbit devices. Furthermore, since a low-power-dissipation system and high device reliability are required, 3.3V for both internal and external voltage in the 64Mbit DRAM, and, in the gigabit devices, lower supply voltage such as 1.5V and 1.2V will be used, as shown Table 1.1. As a low power system application, battery-based 1.5 V DRAM has been reported[8].

The use of thinner dielectric films in cell capacitors is limited by dielectric film breakdown caused by electric field dependent Fowler-Noldheim tunneling. To avoid the tunneling current, a 1/2 plate voltage method[9,10], in which a half of the power supply voltage (1/2 V_{cc}) is applied to the cell plate , began to be used with 1Mbit devices with 10nm thick films. Furthermore, 1/4 V_{cc} bitline swing architecture has been proposed aiming at 4Gbit DRAM and beyond[11].

To provide the larger capacitance area of megabit DRAMs on the rapidly-decreasing surface cell area, three-dimensional (3D) trench[12] and stacked capacitor(STC)[13] structures have been proposed

(Fig. 2.2). A great deal of research have been devoted to developing the new types of trench and the STC cells, and these cells have been mainly used from 4Mbit devices in mass production instead of planar cell. In the next section characteristics of trench capacitor cells are discussed and compared with those of STC cells.

2.2. Trench Capacitor Cells

The trench capacitor cell was first proposed in 1982[12,14]. The trench capacitor shown in Figure 2.2(b) stores the charge along the outside walls of the trench. Compared with the stacked capacitor, the trench capacitor has the following advantages:

(1) smooth chip-surface topography which reduces photograhic issues over the capacitor surface,
(2) higher capacitance in limited cell area by deeper trench etching.

However, for scaled memory cells, the trench capacitor suffers from these disadvantages:

(1) leakage or punch-through current between two adjacent trenches, which is enhanced with the downscaling of the cell size
(2) α-particle soft error immunity
(3) leakage occurs and highly reliable dielectric thin films are required on the etched sidewalls of trench surface,

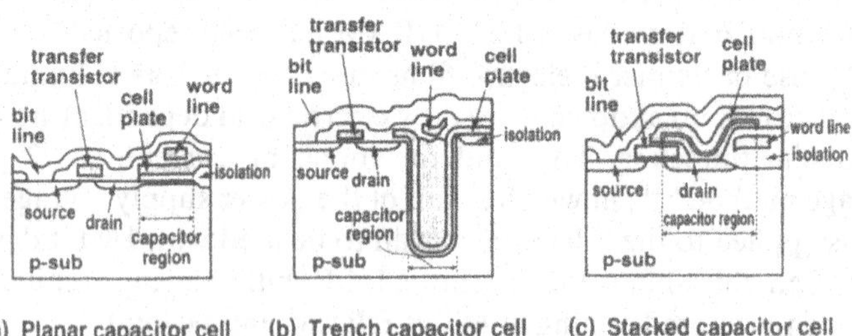

Figure 2.2 Cross-sectional view of a planar (a), a trench (b), and a stacked capacitor (c) cells.

Considerable research efforts have been made to solve these problems for each generation. One approach to suppress the leakage or punch-through and α-particle soft error is to store the charge on the inside wall of the trench and to use the outer region of the trench as the capacitor plate as shown in Figure 2.3(b). The outside regions of the trench are heavily doped p^+ substrate and the charge is stored on the poly-Si plate inside the trench. The outside substrate is connected to a power supply and is an electrically common node.

4Mbit generation

To suppress the punch-through or leakage current between neighboring trenches and the soft-error problem, Hi-C(high-capacitance) trench structure, which forms n^+-p^+ structure on the outside of the trench sidewalls (Fig. 2.4) has been reported and discussed in regard to the p^+ concentration dependency of punch-through, breakdown voltage and soft error rate[15]. Another proposed structure is buried trench in the doped *p*-well which maintains the acceptable avalanche breakdown voltage[16,17,18] (Fig. 2.5). This cell stores the charge along the outside walls of the trenches. Using this trench cell with a trench depth of around 3 μm in a doped *p*-well, high immunity of α-particle

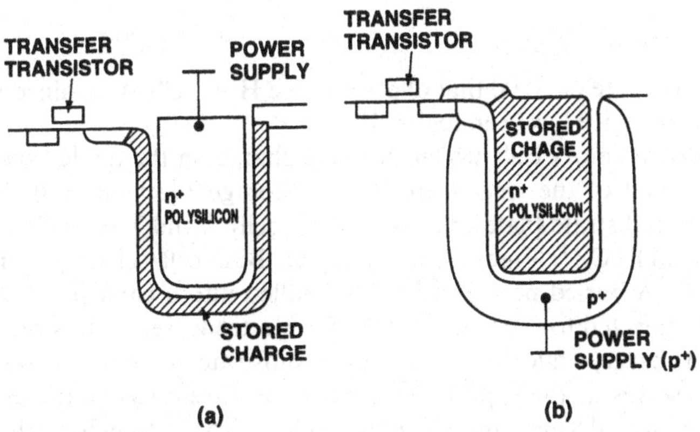

Figure 2.3 Concept of oxide isolated charge storage. Trench outside (a) and inside (b) charge storage.

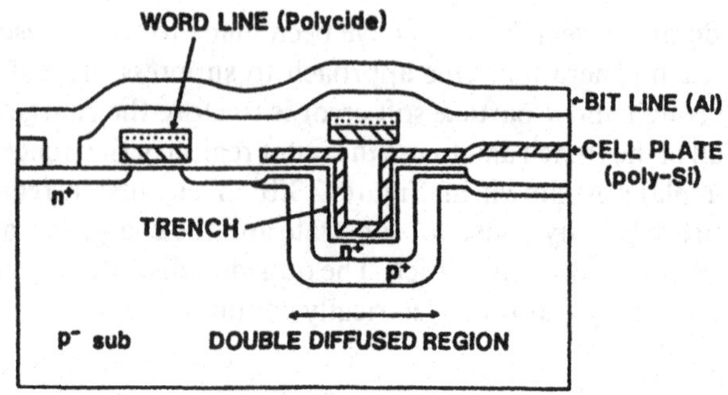

Figure 2.4 Cross-sectional view of Hi-C trench structure[15].

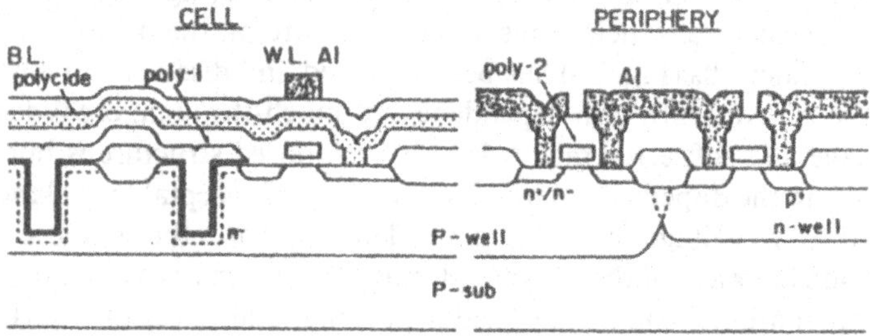

Figure 2.5 Schematic cross section of trench cell in the *p*-well and MOS transistors[16].

soft error rate of 1/200 that of planar type Hi-C cells is obtained and a 4Mbit device has been realized[17,18].

Other memory cells which store the charge on the oxide isolated inside wall of the trench are Buried Storage Electrode cell (BSE Cell)[19], Substrate Plate Trench cell (SPT cell)[20], and Trench Transistor Cell(TTC)[21]. Figure 2.6 shows the BSE cell schematic cross section. A buried poly-Si electrode, refilled into a capacitor trench and connected to a transfer MOSFET electrode, serves to store the signal charge, while the heavily doped substrate of a p/p^{++} epitaxial wafer serves as the capacitor plate. The BSE cell was fabricated at 8.8 μm^2 with 0.8 μm minimum design rule with 5 μm trench depth and the storage capacitance of 35fF was obtained. Figure 2.7 shows SPT cell[20], where a *p*-channel transistor is used as a transfer gate MOS-

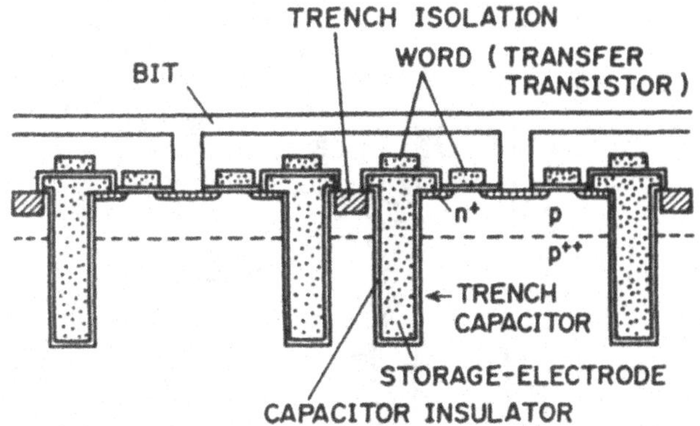

Figure 2.6 Schematic cross section of Buried Storage Electrode Cell[19].

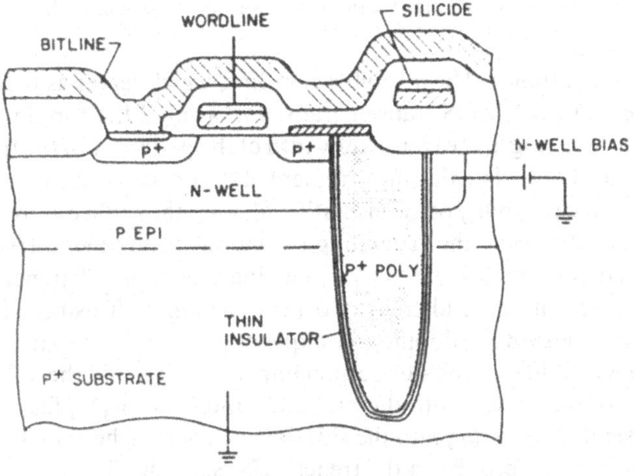

Figure 2.7 Schematic of the STP cell cross-section[20].

FET and the capacitor is further isolated from the transfer transistor by the *n*-well in *p*-type epitaxial layer on p^+ substrate.

The Trench Transistor Cell (TTC)[21], shown in Figure 2.8, lays out as a cross point array in 9 μm^2 using 1 μm design rule and features both the capacitor and the transfer transistor on the sidewalls of the

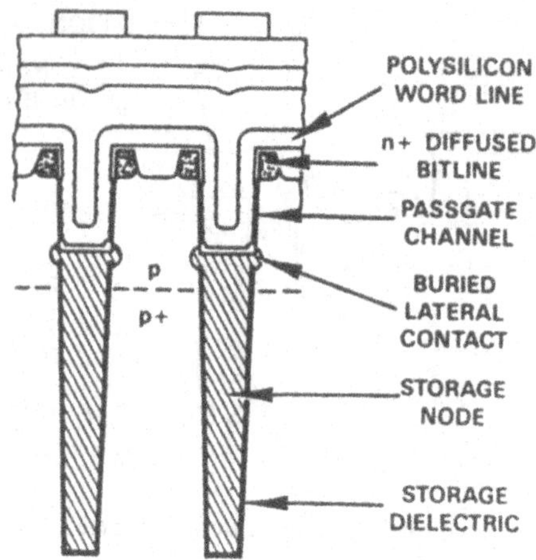

Figure 2.8 Schematic of the TTC layout and cross-section[21].

8 μm depth trench. The n^+ diffused bitline, which serves as the drain of the vertical NMOS transfer transistor, around the top lip of the trench, resulting in the transistor width of the perimeter of the trench.

Studies focused on the improvement of the breakdown characteristics and the reliability of the insulating films on the surface of trenches. These studies were the "rounding oxidation" technique of trenched top and bottom edges[22,23,24,25], etching technique of trenched Si surface smoothing and trench corners rounding-off using CF_4/O_2 downflow etching[26], doping technique of the trench sidewall doping using AsSG films[22] and oblique ion implantation[27] and the use of the insulators combined with thermal SiO_2 and CVD Si_3N_4 films.

Arsenic (As) doping into the sidewalls of the trenches in the *p*-well has been a key process in the trench cell technique. Table 2.1 shows a typical process sequence of a trench capacitor made in the heavily doped *p*-well, developed for 4Mbit DRAM[22]. After the LOCOS isolation process, deep trenches having typical sizes of 1 μm width and 3 μm depth are etched using the RIE technique, where CVD SiO_2 films are used as an etching mask. The trench surfaces are then slightly etched in order to eliminate damage near the Si surfaces. Arsenic (As) doped SiO_2 (AsSG) films, in which typical As concentration is $8 \times 10^{20} cm^{-3}$, are deposited on the trench vertical and bottom

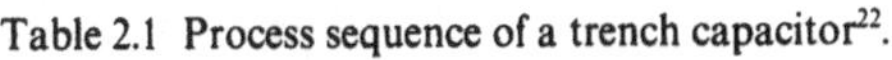

Table 2.1 Process sequence of a trench capacitor[22].

1. TRENCH RIE
2. DEPOSITION OF LPCVD AsSG
3. As DRIVE IN
4. AsSG REMOVAL
5. ROUND OXIDATION
6. GATE OXIDATION
7. CONVENTIONAL PROCESS FOR MOS CAPACITORS

surface. Then, the shallow n^+ layer is formed by solid phase diffusion from AsSG at 1000 C for 60min in N_2 ambient. The typical surface As concentration in Si is 7×10^{19} cm^{-3} after diffusion. The junction depth of 0.15 μm is obtained. After removing of AsSG films, the SiO_2 films of about 50 nm thickness are firstly grown and then striped in diluted HF. This oxidation is done to round both the top convex and the bottom concave corners at the trench Si edges. Secondly, the gate oxide is thermally grown in H_2O diluted with argon at 900 C. Poly-Si films are filled into the trenches, which serve as capacitor electrodes.

16Mbit generation

As the trenches are brought closer to downscale the size of 16Mbit generation cell, large body effect of transistor in peripheral circuit due to the increase of well doping concentration has to be suppressed. Triple-well structure, as shown Figure 2.9, consists of two types of *p*-well (*p*-well-1 and *p*-well-2) in *n*-type substrate and *n*-well which is formed in *p*-well[28]. The surface concentration of *p*-well is lower than that of *p*-well-2. By adopting this triple-well structure, one can supply independent bias voltage for each well and substrate, and the threshold voltage (V_{th}) of transistor in each well is adjusted at each bias voltage. As a result, body effect of transistor in *p*-well-2 can be improved and high performance transistor can be obtained. The distance between the neighboring trenches of 0.7 μm is achieved in the case of 7.3×10^{16}cm^{-3} surface concentration under the actual operating bias condition.

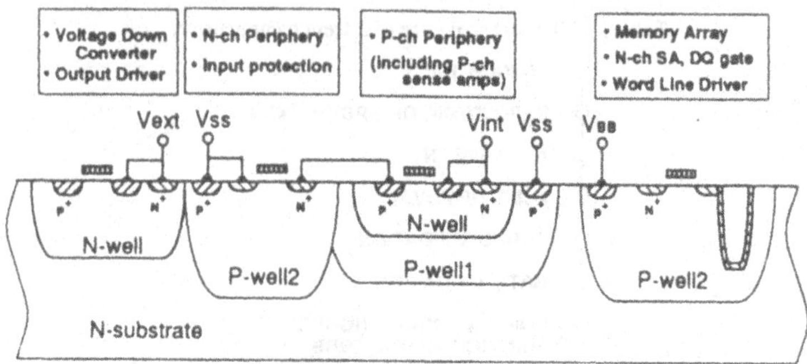

Figure 2.9 Schematic cross section of triple well structure[28].

64Mbit generation

For 64Mbit devices, buried-plate type trench cells which retained the advantages of the substrate plate trench (STP) cell such as the charge leakage and the soft error rate, have been developed[29,30,31]. The trench consists of two regions, that is, the upper part in the *p*-well for transfer NMOSFETs and the lower portion in the *n*-type diffused region, as shown in Figure 2.10. All *n*-type diffused regions in the

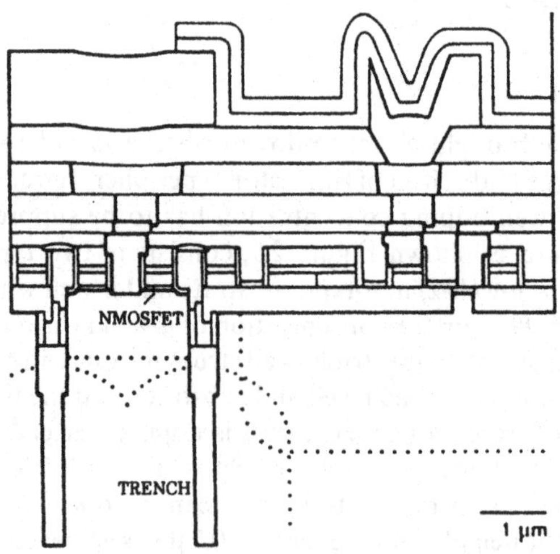

Figure 2.10 Schematic cross section of buried plate trench cell[29].

array coalesce to become continuous, while the buried *n*-type plate is contacted by a strap at the edge of the array. Effective oxide thickness of 10 nm ONO dielectric films is used for the capacitor and the trenches are filled with N^+ poly-Si[29]. A total depth of trench is 7.0 μm and a nominal capacitance is 47 fF.

Another buried plate cell has been reported[31]. A cell size of 1.48 μm^2, the trench size of 0.62 μm × 0.48 μm, and the depth of trenches of 5 μm were obtained. The equivalent oxide thickness of cell dielectrics is 5nm, and cell capacitance is around 30fF.

256Mbit generation, and 1Gbit and beyond

A trench cell with a self-aligned BuriEd STrap (BEST) for a 256M-bit DRAM has been proposed (Fig. 2.11). The cell area of 0.605 μm^2 at 0.25 μm design rule has been obtained[32,33]. This cell is a self-aligned buried strap which forms at the intersection of the storage trench and the junction of the array devices. Arsenic from the n^+ poly-Si in the storage trench out-diffuses into the substrate to electrically connected storage node and the junction of the array device. To avoid the impact of the strap outdiffusion on the array device, arsenic is used as the

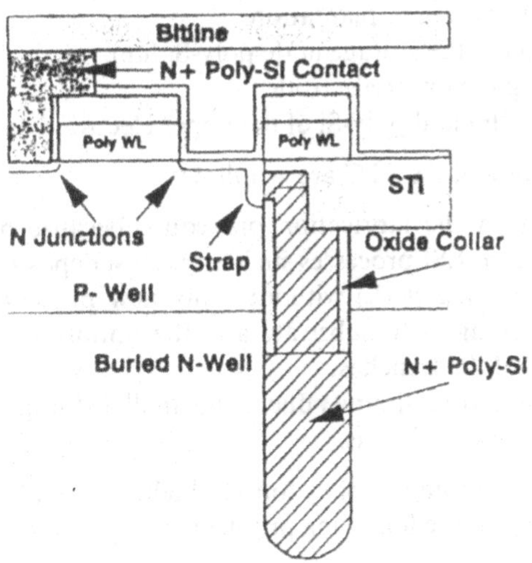

Figure 2.11 Schematic cross section of the BEST cell[32].

outdiffusing dopant from the storage trench. In addition, the thermal budget and the arsenic concentration in the trench poly-Si are controlled so that the strap outdiffusion does not exceed 0.1 μm from the side of the trench. Moreover, a substrate-plate-trench cell scheme applying to gigabit devices has been reported[34]. Small cell area of 0.29 μm^2 for a 0.2 μm design rule was obtained by using a Si lateral selective epitaxial growth (SEG) technique to reduce connection formation between the capacitor and transistor to one fabrication step, and also reduce a distance between the trench and the gate.

2.3. Stacked Capacitor Cell

Stacked Capacitor Cell (STC) was first proposed in 1978[21], which provides cell area reduction and/or an increase in storage capacitance by stacking the main portion of the storage capacitor on the transfer transistor. Fundamental structure of STC is shown in Figure 2.2(c). Typical process steps of the STC cell are as follows[81]:

(1) opening contact window for the lower electrode of the stacked capacitor,
(2) deposition of poly-Si film of the lower electrode of the stacked capacitor and ion implantation,
(3) deposition of the storage node poly-Si film,
(4) patterning the lower electrode,
(5) dielectric film and poly-Si of the upper electrode deposition

The advantages of the STC are as follows:

(1) simplicity in the fabrication procedure because of the use of conventional LSI processes such as poly-Si deposition and reactive ion etching (RIE) without using new process such as the trench etching of Si substrate and the impurity doping to the sidewalls of the trenches.
(2) higher soft error immunity due to the smaller storage diffused area than that of trench cells.

However, regarding application for higher density DRAMs, the STC is subject to the following problems:

(1) difficulty of obtaining sufficient storage capacitance in a small area,

(2) larger step-height of the memory cell, which results in the difficulty of the delineation of fine patterns over the storage capacitor.

To overcome these problems, much effort has been extended for each generation of DRAMs.

1Mbit and 4Mbit generation

Although 1Mbit DRAMs mainly used planar cell, some commercial 1Mbit DRAM devices employed STC[35]. The cell capacitance of 35–55fF using 26.46 μm^2 cells with 1.4 μm design rule was obtained by utilizing the curvature and sidewall of second layer poly-Si. Equivalent oxide thickness of 10nm was used. This STC cell was scaled for 4Mbit devices with cell area of 7.5 μm^2 with 0.7 μm design rule[36]. STC cells came into wider use with 4Mbit generation[36,37].

16Mbit generation

With the scaling of the STC memory cell, research was focused on the enlargement of the storage capacitance, giving rise to a fin-structured stacked cell[38,39], and a core storage node (thick storage node type) STC cell[76], as shown in Figure 2.12 (a), (b). The storage node of the fin-structured stacked cell is formed by two poly-Si layers (in case of two-fin structure). Dielectric film of the capacitor surrounds the

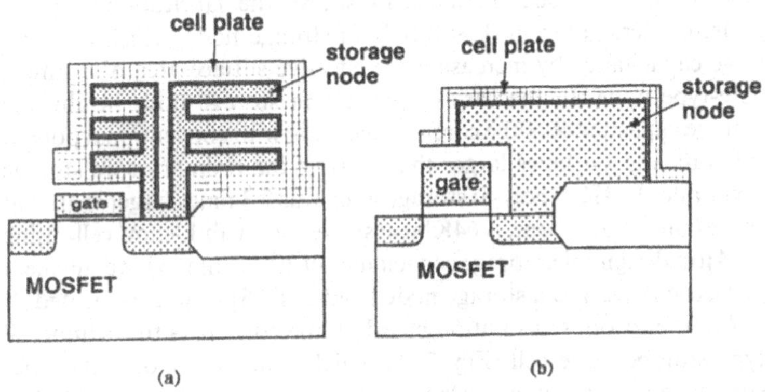

Figure 2.12 Schematic cross section of (a) fin-structured STC cell, (b) core storage node STC cell.

whole surface of the fins, and cell plate poly-Si not only surrounds the whole surface of the fins but also fills each gap between the fins. The number of fins can be increased without using extra mask to form fin structure, and in comparison with conventional STC cell, storage capacitance increase of 170% and 300% have been obtained in case of one-fin and two-fin structured cell, respectively[39]. One-fin structured cell was firstly used in the commercial second-generation 4Mbit DRAM, and has continued to be use in the first-generation of 16Mbit DRAM with the cell size of 4.64 μm^2 and the cell capacitance of 30fF. Two-fins stacked cell capacitor will be used for 64Mbit devices with the cell size and the cell capacitance of around 2 μm^2, and 25fF, respectively[40,41].

64Mbit generation

For the 64Mbit generation and beyond, a new conceptual cell structure has appeared, which attains both the storage capacitance enlargement and the step-height reduction of the STC cells for the delineation of fine patterns over the capacitor. In this structure the storage capacitor is formed over the bitline in an arrangement as shown in Figure 2.13 (b) (in case of core storage node), called DASH (Diagonal Active Stacked capacitor cell with a Highly-packed storage node[42]), COB(Capacitor-Over-Bitline[43]) and fin-structured cell with this conceptual structure[39].

Based on this concept, new STC memory cells for 64Mbit devices have been developed. Figure 2.14 shows the fabrication steps of a Hemispherical-Grain (HSG) poly-Si storage node, which provides large capacitance by increasing the effective surface area of a simple core-type node. In the case of the 0.6 μm storage node height, the storage capacitance of the core storage node with conventional poly-Si sidewall was 1.4 times larger than that of the ordinary core storage node, and the HGS poly-Si storage node was 2.3 times larger than that of the conventional one. A 64Kbit-test memory with 1.8 μm^2 cells using a 0.4 μm design rule, storage capacitance of 30fF, 7nm oxide equivalent dielectric films, and a storage node height of 0.5 μm was fabricated[43].

Another proposed solution based on the concept is the cylindrical type storage node cell (Fig. 2.15) which utilizes not only its inner surface but also outer surface as the storage capacitor[44,45]. The thickness of dielectric film was 5nm of SiO_2 equivalent thickness and

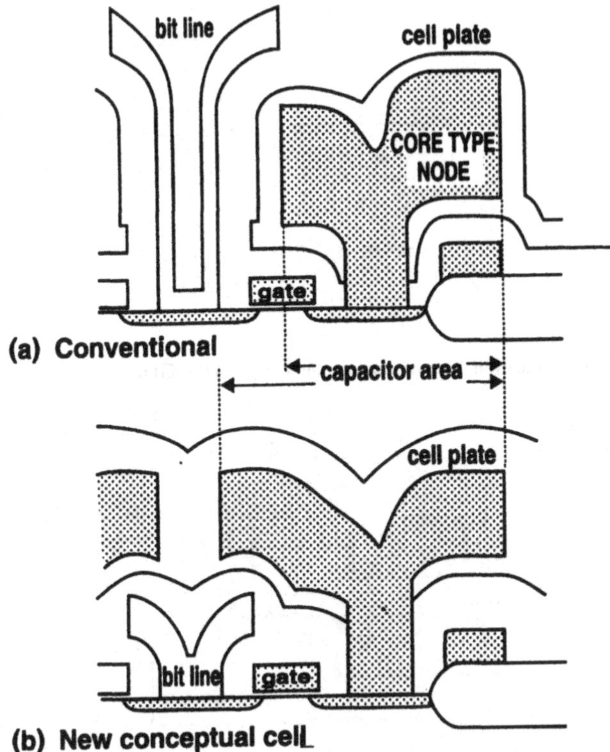

Figure 2.13 Schematic new conceptual cell. (a) conventional cell, (b) new conceptual cell; bit lines are formed before storage capacitors, so other patterning after storage electrode is not necessary.

the estimated storage capacitance of more than 30fF in 1.5 μm^2 cell with 1.5 μm storage node height was obtained[44].

256Mbit generation

For enlargement of the storage capacitance required for the 256Mbit generation, multilayered vertical stacked capacitor has been developed[46,86] (Fig. 2.16). This multilayered cylindrical cell with cell capacitor above bitline, was estimated to have 25fF cell capacitance on a area of 0.5 μm^2 using a dielectric (ONO) with 7.5nm equivalent oxide thickness, and with a surface topology of less than 0.7 μm.

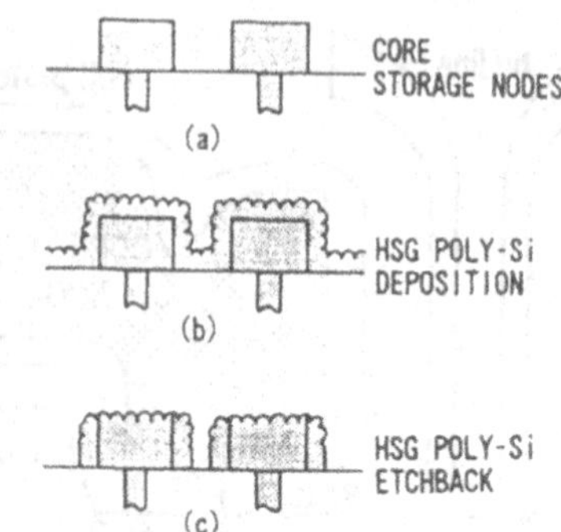

Figure 2.14 Fabrication steps of a hemispherical-grain (HSG) poly-Si storage nodes[43].

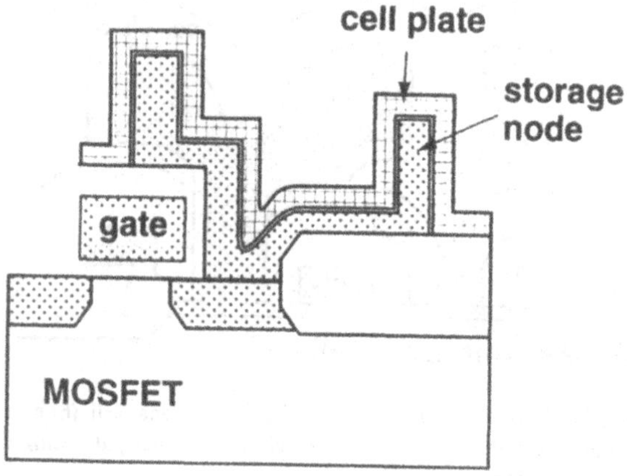

Figure 2.15 Schematic cross section of cylindrical storage node cell.

The rugged poly-Si cylindrical monolayer electrode cell is also a candidate for 256Mbit devices. This is a combination of high dielectric constant material (10 to 15 nm thick CVD-Ta_2O_5) with a rugged HemiSpherical Grain poly-Si electrode, and high capacitance value of 20fF/μm^2 has been obtained[87].

Experimental 256Mbit DRAM chips using HSG cylindrical STC cells[47], double cylindrical STC cell[48,49,50,53], planar STC cell using high ε films[51], 5-fin structured cell[52], and STC cell[77] have been reported, and delivery of samples has begun.

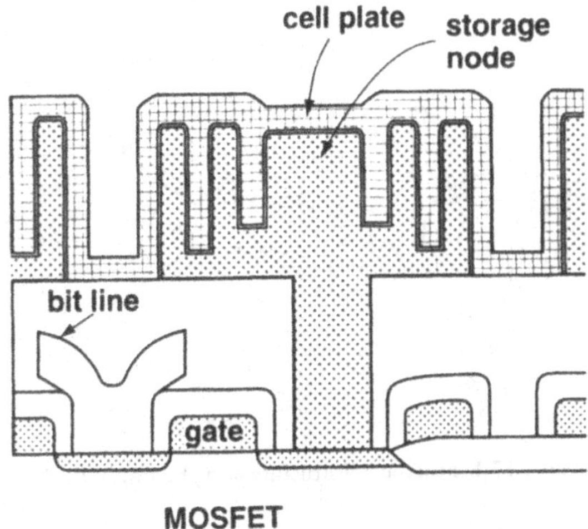

Figure 2.16 Schematic cross section of multilayered vertical stacked capacitor.

1Gbit generation and beyond

For the 1Gbit generation, high ε films will be necessary to maintain the storage capacitance in the limited cell area, and will be used with the combination of HSG cylindrical STC, and multi-cylindrical STC, which will be used in the commercial 256M-bit devices.

For gigabit DRAMs, an STC cell using vertical ultrathin SOI MOSFET (DELTA, fully DEpleted Lean-channel TrAnsistor) has been proposed[54,55]. Figure 2.17 shows the schematic cell structure using SOI MOSFET. Since the ultrathin fully depleted SOI structure provides the reduction of short channel effects, minimized subthreshold swing and high noise immunity, and can operate under low supply voltage of 1.5–2.0 V, DRAM cells using thin film SOI MOSFET will be one of the structures most likely to be used for the gigabit generations.

Experimental 1G-bit DRAM chips using a 0.29 μm^2 STC cell fabricated by 0.16 μm CMOS technology with power supply of 1.5 V[56], a 0.54 μm^2 cell fabricated by 0.25 μm CMOS technology with power supply of 2.0–2.5 V[57], a 0.29 μm^2 cell fabricated by 0.15 μm CMOS technology with power supply of 1.8 V (peripheral) and 1.2

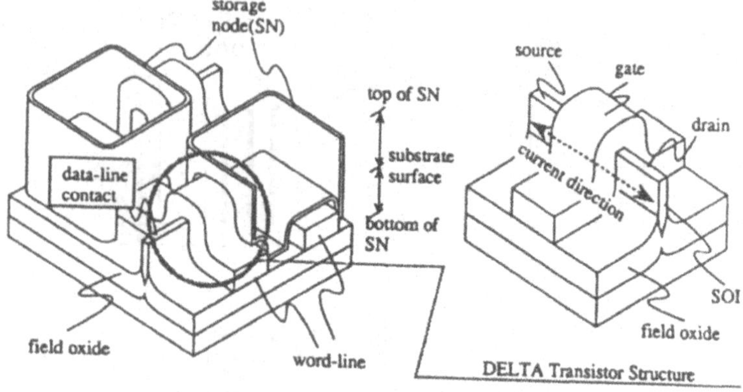

Figure 2.17 Schematic cell structure using SOI MOSFET[55].

V (array)[88], and a 0.33 μm^2 cell fabricated by 0.16 μm CMOS technology with power supply of 2.0 V (peripheral) and 1.8 V (array)[89] have already reported. Experimental 4G-bit DRAM has also already reported[96]. 4-level storage circuit technology was used to reduce the effective cell size. The cell size was 0.23 μm^2 using 0.15 μm CMOS technology with power supply voltage of 2.5–2.0 V. To maintain the same signal level as that of conventional 2-level storage, three times larger storage capacitance was needed in the 4-level storage. High ε material $(Ba_xSr_{1-x})TiO_3$ (BST) was used.

Another technique to reduce the memory cell area for future high density DRAMs is the use of the NAND-structured cell[58,59], in which a unit of NAND-structured cell is composed of 4 stacked capacitor cells connected in series (Fig. 2.18). This has only one bitline contact per 8 stacked cells corresponding to 2 units, reducing bitline contact area per cell to one-fourth. There are no isolation areas between the adjacent cells in a unit, resulting in the cell area of 0.962 μm^2 for 256M-bit devices using relaxed 0.4 μm design rule, which is 37% below that of a folded structure[59,60].

2.4. High ε and Ferroelectric Films for the Gigabit Generation

For the gigabit generations, research is being vigorously conducted in pursuit of high quality, ultrathin dielectric films. Candidates are ON

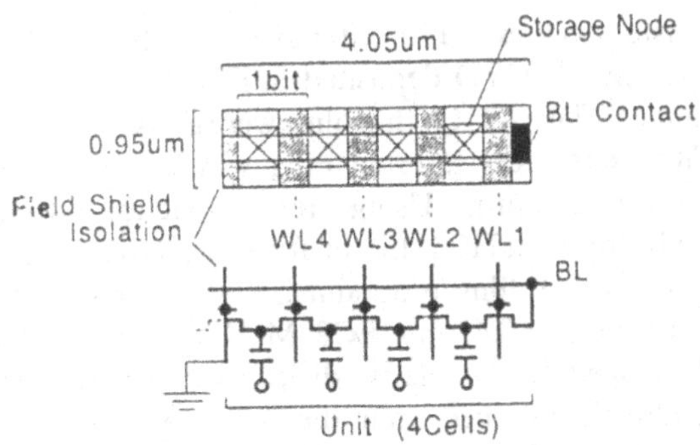

Figure 2.18 Top view and equivalent circuit of NAND structured cell[59].

films on rugged poly-Si stacked capacitor bottom electrode[61,62,63], ON films on the cylindrical stacked capacitor[82], high dielectric constant (high ε) films on the stacked capacitor such as Ta_2O_5 films ($\varepsilon = 20-30$) [45,64,65,66,67,68,79,87,92,93], $SrTiO_3$ films ($\varepsilon = 140-210$)[69,78], (Ba_xSr_{1-x}) TiO_3(BST)[70,80,84,85], and ferroelectric films such as PZT($Pb(Z_r,T_i)O_3$: Lead Zirconate Titanate) films ($\varepsilon \sim 1000$)[71,72,77,94], PLZT (Lanthanum-doped PZT) films ($\varepsilon = 870-1000$)[73,83], and $BaTiO_3$ films[74].

Since the SiO_2 layer formed between the Ta_2O_5 film Si electrode decreases the storage capacitance, an ultrathin Si_3N_4 layer, which has larger dielectric constant than SiO_2, is made on the surface of poly-Si electrode by rapid thermal nitridation (RTN). Thickness of Ta_2O_5 films is around 2.5 nm[92]. Step coverage of the low pressure CVD Ta_2O_5 is superior to that of a sputtered film, however, as-deposited CVD Ta_2O_5 has a large leakage current caused from the oxygen vacancy in the films. To improve the leakage current, several treatments of Ta_2O_5 films such as the two step annealing, that is UV-O_3 annealing (annealing under ultra violet radiation) followed by dry-O_2 annealing[64], RTA (Rapid Thermal Annealing) dry-O_2 treatment[68,87,92] and O_2 plasma treatment[79,91] have been reported. Since Ta_2O_5 chemically reacts with poly-Si, a reactive sputtered or CVD TiN films are deposited on the Ta_2O_5 films[67,87,92].

Sputter deposited $SrTiO_3$ thin films have been reported. Using the metal barriers, that is Pt/Ti or Pt/Ta double layer barrier in the thin film capacitor structure of $SrTiO_3$/barrier layers/Si substrate, dielectric constant values of 140–210 have been obtained for 150 nm thick $SrTiO_3$ films[69]. CVD deposited $SrTiO_3$ thin film capacitors have been made[78]. The $SrTiO_3$ thin films were grown on 1.0wt.% Nd-doped $SrTiO_3$ single crystal substrate, which makes the grown $SrTiO_3$ surface smooth. Using the capacitor structure of Pt/$SrTiO_3$/Nb-doped $SrTiO_3$, the relative dielectric constant of 87 for 10 nm thick $SrTiO_3$ films is obtained, which corresponds to SiO_2 equivalent thickness of 0.48 nm. ECR MOCVD $SrTiO_3$ films have also been developed[95]. The relative dielectric constant of 150 for 40 nm $SrTiO_3$ films is obtained using the capacitor structure of poly-Si/TiN barrier/0.5 μm RuO_2/$SrTiO_3$/TiN/Al. As thick Pt is not suitable for RIE fine patterning of Giga-bit generation devices, a RuO_2/TiN structure is alternatively used. TiN is used as a barrier to oxygen and Si diffusion, and prevents the SiO_2 layer formation when depositing RuO_2 directly on Si[95].

A stacked capacitor cell with $(Ba_xSr_{1-x})TiO_3$ Film by RF sputtering has been fabricated[70,84,85]. A large unit area capacitance of 40fF/μm^2 and a low leakage current of 10–16A/cm^2 by a combination of a thin $(Ba_{0.5}Sr_{0.5})TiO_3$ film having an equivalent SiO_2 thickness of 8A and a capacitor structure of TiN/$(Ba_{0.5}Sr_{0.5})TiO_3$/Pt/Ta/Si[70]. CVD deposition method of $(Ba_xSr_{1-x})TiO_3$ thin film has also been reported focusing on the conformal deposition technique and the composition control technique of Ba/Sr composition ratio (x in $(Ba_xSr_{1-x})TiO_3$) and Ti/(Ba + Sr) stoichiometry, both of which are important for the electrical properties of $(Ba_xSr_{1-x})TiO_3$ thin films[80].

PZT thin films have been made on Pt/SiO_2/Si substrate by rf-magnetron sputtering method[72]. It was found that Pb content in a PZT films strongly affects its electrical properties. The highest value of dielectric constant value of 1180 has been obtained in the films whose Pb content in the ratio Pb/(Zr + Ti) is 1. An MOCVD method using metalorganic source has been proposed[94]. Using Pt/PZT/Pt capacitor structure, it has been shown that a smaller Pb content gives less leakage current and weaker ferroelectricity to the MOCVD-PZT films.

The electrical properties of sol-gel derived PLZT thin films has been investigated[73,83]. With less than 10 mol % lanthanum contents, dielectric constant of more than 870 and has been obtained using the sol-gel deposited PLZT films on platinum coated Si wafers[73].

Figure 2.19 shows the maximum charge density vs various kinds of thin film dielectric constant. The maximum charge density (defined as the product of the relative dielectric constant by maximum field of leakage current of 1 $\mu A/cm^2$) increases in proportion to the square root of the dielectric constant of thin films (ε 1/2)[75].

In spite of research into high materials for DRAM cells, a lot of problems still remain unsolved regarding the thin film formation techniques (sputtering and Chemical Vapor Deposited (CVD)), cell structure, stoichiometric control, and dielectric break-down (leakage current), etc.[76]. For the gigabit generation, it is necessary to solve the problems of cell complexity and cost.

In this chapter, by way of introduction to the following chapters, we have reviewed the trend of DRAM cell technology from the megabit era to the gigabit era. Conventional wisdom has it that the answer to the question "Which cell should be chosen ?" is strongly dependent on the manufacturer's accumulated experience and favorite technologies, and it is also clear that simple and the manufacturable storage cell structures have to be pursued from the viewpoint of economy, especially in the gigabit generations.

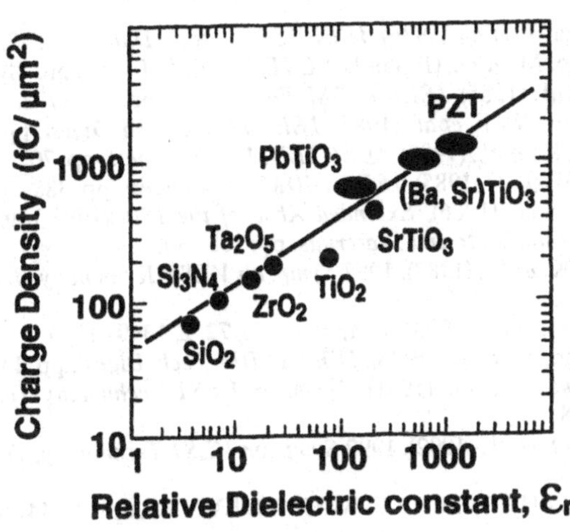

Figure 2.19 Maximum charge density vs various kind of thin film dielectric constant[75].

References

1. Dennard, R. H. *U. S. Patent*, 3387286, June 4, 1968.
2. Engeler, W. E. *et al.*, (1972). *IEEE J. of Solid-State Circuits*, SC-7, pp. 330–335.
3. Stein, K. V. *et al.*, (1970). *IEEE J. of Solid-State Circuits*, SC-7, pp. 336–340.
4. Rideout, V. L. (1979). *IEEE Trans. Electron Devices*, ED-26, pp. 839–852.
5. Sunami, H. (1985). *IEEE IEDM Tech. Digest*, pp. 694–697.
6. Chattejeer, P. *et al.*, (1986). *IEEE IEDM Tech. Digest*, pp. 128–131.
7. Mitsuhashi, J. *et al.*, (1985). *Extended Abst. of the 17th Conf. on Solid State and Materials*, pp. 267–270.
8. Aoki, M. *et al.*, (1989). *IEEE ISSCC Tech. Digest*, pp. 238–239.
9. Shimotori, K. *et al.*, (1983). *IEEE ISSCC Tech. Digest*, pp. 228–300.
10. Kumanoya, M. *et al.*, (1985). *IEEE ISSCC Tech. Digest*, pp. 240–242.
11. Inaba, T. *et al.*, (1995). 1995 *Symp. on VLSI Circuits, Tech. Digest*, pp. 99–100.
12. Sunami, H. *et al.*, (1982). *IEEE IEDM Tech. Digest*, pp. 806–808.
13. Koyanagi, M. *et al.*, (1978). *IEEE IEDM Tech. Digest*, pp. 348–351.
14. Morie, T. *et al.*, (1982). Japan Society of Applied Physics, Fall Meeting (Domestic), Abst. No. 30p-Q-6.
15. Yoneda, M. *et al.*, (1986). 1986 *Symp. on VLSI Technology, Tech. Digest*, pp. 77–78.
16. Ishiuchi, H. *et al.*, (1985). *IEEE IEDM Tech. Digest*, pp. 706–709.
17. Furuyama, T. *et al.*, (1986). *IEEE J. Solid-State Circuit*, SC-21, pp. 605–611.
18. Furuyama, T. *et al.*, (1986). *IEEE ISSCC Tech. Digest*, pp. 272–273.
19. Sakamoto, M. *et al.*, (1985). *IEEE IEDM Tech. Digest*, pp. 710–713.
20. Lu, N. *et al.*, (1985). *IEEE IEDM Tech. Digest*, pp. 771–772.
21. Richardson, W. F. *et al.*, (1985). *IEEE IEDM Tech. Digest*, pp. 714–717.
22. Yamada, K. *et al.*, (1985). *IEEE IEDM Tech. Digest*, pp. 702–705.
23. Kao, D. B. *et al.*, (1985). *IEEE IEDM Tech. Digest*, pp. 388–391.
24. Imai, K. *et al.*, (1986). *Extended Abst. of the 18th* (1986 International) *Conf. on Solid State and Materials*, pp. 303–306.
25. Yoneda, K. *et al.*, (1987). 1987 *Symp. on VLSI Technology, Tech. Digest*, pp. 95–96.
26. Nishino, H. *et al.*, (1993). *J. Appl. Phys.*, **72**, 2, 1349–1353.
27. Nagatomo, M. *et al.*, (1986). *IEEE IEDM Tech. Digest*, pp. 144–147.
28. Yoshikawa, S. *et al.*, (1981). *Symp. on VLSI Technology Tech. Digest*, pp. 67–68.
29. Kenney, D. *et al.*, (1992). 1992 *Symp. on VLSI Technology, Tech. Digest*, pp. 14–15.
30. Isaac, R. D. (1993). NIKKEI MICRODEVICES, pp. 38–44 (Nov., 1993) (in Japanese).
31. Kaneko, T. *et al.*, (1994). TOSHOBA REVIEW, **49**, 771–774.

32. Nesbit, L. *et al.*, (1993). *IEEE IEDM Tech. Digest*, pp. 627–630.
33. Bronner, G. *et al.*, (1995). 1995 *Symp. on VLSI Technology, Tech. Digest*, pp. 15–16.
34. Noguchi, M. *et al.*, (1995). 1995 *Symp. on VLSI Technology, Tech. Digest*,pp. 137–138.
35. Takamae, Y. *et al.*, (1985). *IEEE ISSCC Tech. Digest*, pp. 250–251.
36. Mochizuki, H. *et al.*, (1987). *IEEE ISSCC Tech. Digest*, pp. 284–285.
37. Shimohigashi, K. *et al.*, (1987). *IEEE ISSCC Tech. Digest*, pp. 18–19.
38. Kisu, T. *et al.*, (1988). Extended Abst. of the 20th (1988 International) *Conf. On Solid State and Materials*, pp. 581–584.
39. Ema, T. *et al.*, (1988). *IEEE IEDM Tech. Digest*, pp. 592–595.
40. Taguchi, M. *et al.*, (1991). *ISSCC IEDM Tech. Digest*, pp. 112–113.
41. NIKKEI MICRODEVICES, pp. 29–37 (Nov., 1993) (in Japanese).
42. Kimura, S. *et al.*, (1988). *IEEE IEDM Tech. Digest*, pp. 596–599.
43. Sakao, M. *et al.*, (1990). *IEEE IEDM Tech. Digest*, pp. 655–658.
44. Wakamiya, W. *et al.*, (1989). 1989 *Symp. on VLSI Technology, Tech. Digest*, pp. 69–70.
45. Kawamoto, Y. *et al.*, (1990). 1990 *Symp. on VLSI Technology, Tech. Digest*, pp. 13–14.
46. Temmler, D. (1991). 1991 *Symp. on VLSI Technology, Tech. Digest*, pp. 13–14.
47. Sugibayashi, T. *et al.*, (1993). *IEEE ISSCC Tech. Digest*, pp. 50–51.
48. Kitsukawa, G. *et al.*, (1993). *IEEE ISSCC Tech. Digest*, pp. 48–49.
49. Kotani, H. *et al.*, (1994). *IEEE ISSCC Tech. Digest*, pp. 142–143.
50. Yoo, H.-J. *et al.*, (1995). *IEEE ISSCC Tech. Digest*, pp. 250–251.
51. Asakura, M. *et al.*, (1994). *IEEE ISSCC Tech. Digest*, pp. 140–141.
52. Taguchi, M. *et al.*, *Tech. Report of The Institute of Elec. Information and Communication Eng.*, SDM92–138, pp. 7–14 (1993–01). (in Japanese).
53. Yoo, S.-M. *et al.*, (1994). 1994 *Symp. on VLSI Circuits, Tech. Digest*, pp. 85–86.
54. Hisamoto, D. *et al.*, *IEEE IEDM Tech. Digest*, pp. 833–836.
55. Hisamoto, D. *et al.*, (1991). *IEEE IEDM Tech. Digest*, pp. 959–961.
56. Horiguchi, M. *et al.*, (1995). *IEEE ISSCC Tech. Digest*, pp. 252–253.
57. Sugibayashi, T. *et al.*, (1995). *IEEE ISSCC Tech. Digest*, pp. 234–235.
58. Kimura, K. *et al.*, (1991). *IEEE ISSCC Tech. Digest*, pp. 106–107.
59. Hasegawa, T. *et al.*, (1993). *IEEE ISSCC Tech. Digest*, pp. 46–47.
60. Hamamoto, T. *et al.*, (1993). *IEEE IEDM Tech. Digest*, pp. 643–646.
61. Sakao, M. *et al.*, (1990). *IEEE IEDM Tech. Digest*, pp. 655–658.
62. Yoshimaru, M. *et al.*, (1990). *IEEE IEDM Tech. Digest*, pp. 655–658.
63. Fasan, P. C. *et al.*, (1990). *IEEE IEDM Tech. Digest*, pp. 663–666.
64. Shinriki, H. *et al.*, (1991). *IEEE Trans. Electron Devices*, ED-38, pp. 455–462.
65. Kaga, T. *et al.*, (1991). *IEEE Trans. Electron Devices*, ED-38, pp. 255–261.
66. Shinriki, H. *et al.*, (1990). *IEEE Trans. Electron Devices*, ED-37, pp. 1939–1947.

67. Kamiyama, S. *et al.*, (1991). *IEEE IEDM Tech. Digest*, pp. 827–830.
68. Kwon, K. W. *et al.*, (1994). *IEEE IEDM Tech. Digest*, pp. 835–838.
69. Sakuma, T. *et al.*, (1990). *Appl. Phys. Lett.*, **57**, 2431–2433.
70. Koyama, K. *et al.*, (1991). *IEEE IEDM Tech. Digest*, pp. 823–826.
71. Moazzami, R. (1990). *IEEE IEDM Tech. Digest*, pp. 417–420.
72. Torii, K. *et al.*, (1991). *Extended Abst. of the 1991 international Conf. On Solid State Devices and Materials*, pp. 195–197.
73. Okudaira, T. *et al.*, (1991). *Extended Abst. of the 1991 international Conf. on Solid State Devices and Materials*, 204–206.
74. Li, P. *et al.*, (1991). *Appl. Phys. Lett.*, **58**, pp. 2639–2641.
75. Tukahara, K. (1993). Proc. of spring meeting Electronics Group of The Inst. of Elect. Information and Com. Eng. p.1–9 (in Japanese).
76. Ogirima, M. (1993). 1993 *Symp. on VLSI Technology, Tech. Digest*, pp. 1–5.
77. Abt, N. *et al.*, (1991). 1994 Extended Abst. of the 1991 international Conf. on Solid State Devices and Materials, pp.189–191.
78. Kiyotoshi, M. *et al.*, (1995). *Appl. Phys. Lett.*, **67**, 2468–2470.
79. Aoyama, T. (1996). *J. Electrochem. Soc.*, **143**, 977–983.
80. Eguchi, K. *et al.*, to be published in *Integrated Ferroelectronics.*
81. Watanabe, H. *et al.*, (1988). *IEEE IEDM Tech. Digest*, pp. 600–602.
82. Aoki, M. *et al.*, (1993). 1993 *Symp. on VLSI Technology, Tech. Digest*, pp. 1–5.
83. Kim, J. *et al.*, (1994). 1993 *Symp. on VLSI Technology, Tech. Digest*, pp. 151–152.
84. Ohno, Y. *et al.*, (1994). 1994 *Symp. on VLSI Technology, Tech. Digest*, pp. 149–150.
85. Park, S. O. *et al.*, (1996). 1996 *Symp. on VLSI Technology, Tech. Digest*, pp. 24–25.
86. Iguchi, K. *et al.*, (1991). 1991 *Symp. on VLSI Technology, Tech. Digest*, pp. 11–12.
87. Fasan, P. C. *et al.*, (1992). *IEEE IEDM Tech. Digest*, pp. 263–266.
88. Nitta, Y. *et al.*, (1996). *IEEE ISSCC Tech. Digest*, pp. 376–377.
89. Yoo, J. H. *et al.*, (1996). *IEEE ISSCC Tech. Digest*, pp. 378–379.
90. Yamaguchi, H. *et al.*, (1996). *IEEE IEDM Tech. Digest*, pp. 675–678.
91. Kamiyama, S. *et al.*, (1994). *J. Electrochem. Soc.*, **141**, pp. 1246–1251.
92. Takaishi, Y. *et al.*, (1994). *IEEE IEDM Tech. Digest*, pp. 839–842.
93. Kaga, T. *et al.*, (1994). *IEEE IEDM Tech. Digest*, pp. 927–929.
94. Itoh, H. *et al*, (1991). *IEEE IEDM Tech. Digest*, pp. 831–834.
95. Lesaicherre, P.-Y. *et al.*, (1994). *IEEE IEDM Tech. Digest*, pp. 831–834.
96. Murotani, T. *et al.*, (1997). *IEEE ISSCC Tech. Digest*, pp. 74–75.

CHAPTER 3

Lithography

3.1. Introduction

To fabricate the fine pattern of half micron size for LSI devices, many kinds of technologies have been developed. 0.25 μm pattern will be needed for 256 Mbit DRAM and design rule of 1Gbit DRAM will be 0.15–0.2 μm.

3.2. Photolithography

3.2.1 Step and Repeat Type Projection Exposure System (Stepper)

Since the adoptation of the stepper for 64 Kbit DRAM mass-production line, it has stepper have been used for photolithography of LSI.

3.2.1.1. *g*-line Stepper

The early stepper featured 10 reduction lenses with a numerical aperture (N.A.) of 0.28. High N.A. lens have been developed and resist pattern size of less than the wavelength of light is obtained with the most recent exposure system. Eguchi *et al.*[1] investigated a high numerical aperture, 0.6, *g*-line (wavelength; 436 nm) stepper and achieved 0.45 μm line and space for resist thickness of 1.2 μm.

The focus depth for 0.5 μm pattern was ± 0.4 μm. Nikon's groups[2] have developed a *g*-line stepper machine, the NSR-1505G6E, N.A. of 0.54 and *g*-line lens for half-micron lithography. The 5 reduction type projection lens has 15 mm by 15 mm field size. Canon's groups[3] have developed a high N.A. *g*-line stepper having 5 reduction lenses with a numerical aperture of 0.45 and field size of 20 mm square (28.2 mm dia.).

3.2.1.2. *i*-line Stepper

The *i*-line stepper has been used for 1 Mbit DRAM mass-production. Nakamura *et al.*[4] have manufactured an extremely high numerical aperture (N.A) *i*-line (wavelength ; 365 nm) lens in order to study the capability of *i*-line lithography. Table 3.1 shows the specification of the lens.

They have evaluated the resolution and the depth of focus by using TSMR-365*i* and NPR-Sigma18SH1 resist. They obtained minimum resolution of 0.325 μm L/S and 1.0 μm depth of focus for 0.4 μm L/S by using NPR-Sigma18SH1 resist (resist thickness 1.2 μm). Furthermore, they examined the resolution and the depth of focus in the case of the thinner resist thickness (0.6 μm). Resist pattern profiles and depth of focus at 0.35 μm L/S were improved compared with the case of 1.2 μm resist thickness. They obtained 0.3 μm L/S resolution and 1.4 μm depth of focus for 0.4 μm L/S and confirmed that thinner resist has an advantage over thick resist in terms of both resolution and depth of focus. Hitachi's groups[5] have developed a new *i*-line stepper, the LD-5010*i* having 5 reduction lenses with numerical aperture of 0.4 and field size of 21.2 mm diameter and this has facilitated for the CEL process and the FLEX method (see Section 3.2.1.5).

3.2.1.3. DUV Stepper

A. KrF Stepper Nakase *et al.*[6,7] have developed a KrF excimer (wavelength; 248 nm) stepper (Fig. 3.1) which employs an achromatic lens of numerical aperture, 0.37. They achieved 0.3 μm resolution with the tri-level resist, PMGI(polydimethylglutarimide)/SOG (spin on glass)/ OFPR-500 (novolak photoresist), process.

Sasago *et al.*[8] and K. Ogawa *et al.*[9] have developed a KrF stepper by using PCR (Polarizing Beam Resonator) band pass narrowing. Specification of these KrF excimer steppers are shown in the Table 3.2.

Table 3.1 Specification of high NA *i*-line lens.

Wavelength (nm)	365
N. A.	0.65
Magnification	1/10
Field Size (mm)	5 × 5

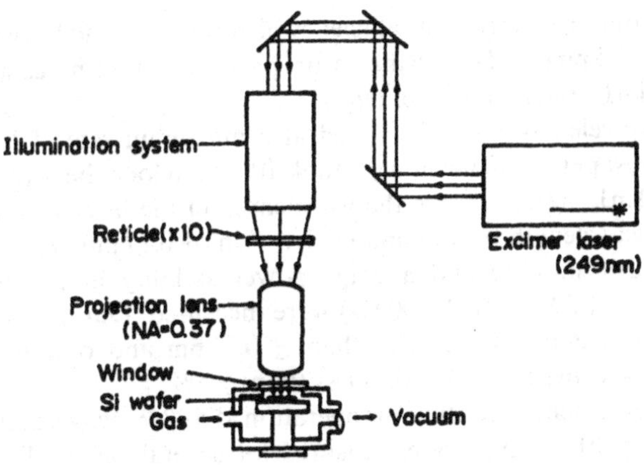

Figure 3.1 KrF excimer laser exposure system[6,7]

Table 3.2 Specification of KrF excimer steppers.

	Toshiba (Nakase)	Matsushita (Sasago)
N. A.	0.37	0.36
Magnification	1/10	1/5
Coherence Factor	0.7	–
Field Size (mm)	5 × 5	15 × 15

B. Excimer Laser Line narrowing of KrF excimer laser is positioned as stepper system light source for higher density DRAM production. Several narrow band excimer lasers for DUV lithography have been developed by Sengupta *et al.*[10], Sandstrom,[11], Lokai *et al.*[12], Brimacombe *et al.*[13], Furuya *et al.*[14], Saito *et al.*[15], Shimada *et al.*[16], McKee,[17] and Wakabayashi *et al.*[18]. The line narrowing methods employed by these lasers are the intra-cavity etalons method and a Littrow grating with the beam expansion method. Wakabayashi *et al.* (Komatsu Ltd.) have investigated the narrowing methods of KrF excimer laser by the hybrid method of an etalon and a Littrow grating with beam expansion. The etalon was used for fine narrowing and the grating for coarse narrowing in order to obtain the thermal stabilization and minimization of wavelength drift.

They obtained narrowing efficiency of about 30% and linewidth of less than 2.5 pm(FWHM) using an air spaced etalon with free spectral range of 41.7 pm and fines of ten.

The wavelength could be tuned at a maximum rate of 16 pm/s. After a rest period of one hour, it took 100 ms to lock the wavelength (8 W; 20 mJ, 400 Hz). Once the wavelength of the laser was locked, output wavelength was maintained within ±0.17 pm. The typical wavelength stability and average power stability in intermittent operation at 8 W (20 mJ, 400 Hz) were measured. During the operation, wavelength drifted less than ±0.25 pm and output power stability was maintained within less than ±5%.

In intermittent or continuous operation at 5–8 W, wavelength drift and linewidth change were measured for several weeks. They obtained long term wavelength stability of less than ±0.5 pm and linewidth of less than 2.5 pm(FWHM) (Table 3.3).

3.2.1.4. V UV Exposure System

Sasago *et al.*[19,20] have developed ArF stepper and resist process. The ArF stepper employed a catagyoptric optical system and had high NA of 0.45. It featured a 5X-type projection lens and 12.5 mm by 12.5 mm field size. Ozaki *et al.*[21] studied a projection exposure system using four kinds of spherical lens: monochromatic lens, achromatic lens with separate lens, achromatic lens with cemented elements and partially achromatized lens. They found the partially achromatized lens to be best from the viewpoint of current technology limit of bandwidth narrowing of ArF excimer laser. 0.18 μm resolution was

Table 3.3 Characteristics of the hybrid method KrF excimer laser.

	Specification
Average Power (W)	8
Repetition Rate (Hz)	400
Pulse Energy (mJ)	20
Linewidth (FWHM) (ppm)	<2.5
Wavelength Stability (ppm)	< ±0.5
Beam Dimension (V*H; mm)	25 × 5
Beam Divergency (V*H; m rad)	2.92 × 0.43 ($1/e^2$)

confirmed using the Ag/Se-Ge inorganic resist process. Mutoh *et al.*[22] studied vacuum UV lithography by using D2 lamp and three layer resist process, PMMA(0.1 μm)/Si/polyimide. A polyimide linewidth of 0.1 μm was obtained for 0.15 μm line and 0.25 m space patterns of the photomask.

3.2.1.5. FLEX

To increase the DOF of hole pattern, Fukuda *et al.*[23,24] have developed multiple exposures in several different focal planes at the same wafer x and y position, a system known as FLEX (Focus Latitude Enhancement Exposure). Figure 3.2 shows the principal of FLEX. FLEX was found to be more effective for isolated transparent patterns such as contact holes than for other pattern such as L/S's. For the conventional exposure method with a single focal plane, the area image of the mask pattern can only be formed within a small focal range along the light axis. FLEX enhances the depth of focus by extending this small image distribution in the direction of the light

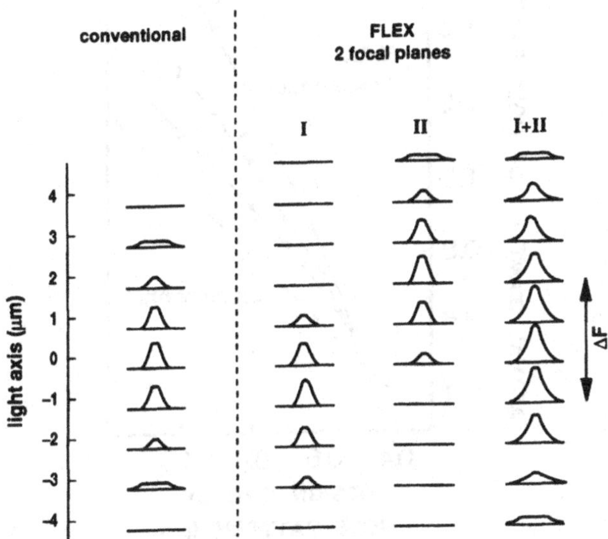

Figure 3.2 Principle of FLEX[23,24].

axis. Several focal planes are created at different positions along the light axis and exposures are made using each focal plane. The relations between the design feature size of the mask pattern and the resist pattern size obtained after exposure and development were examined for the conventional method and FLEX (Fig. 3.3). They found that the greater the number of focal planes, the larger the degradation in linearity.

3.2.1.6. Annular Illumination System

To improve the DOF and the resolution limit, Horiuchi *et al.*[25] and Fehrs *et al.*[26] proposed to use the annular illumination of optical aligner. Kamon *et al.*[27] have reported the sub-half-micron capability of this method theoretically and experimentally. The contrast de-

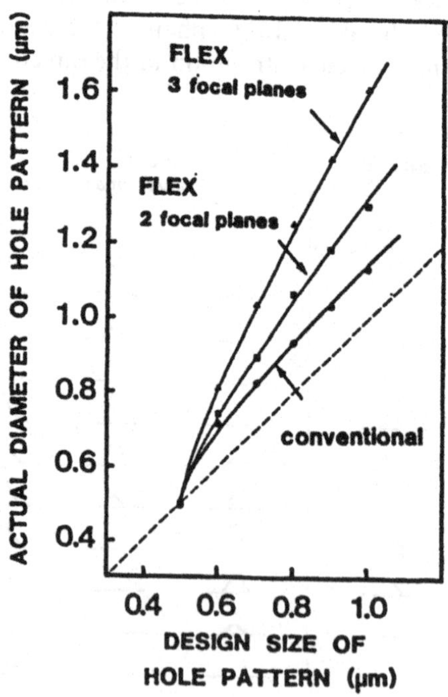

Figure 3.3 Design size of hole pattern versus resist pattern size[23,24].

pendence on the light shielding area (Fig. 3.4 and 3.5) has been calculated by using the MULSS (Multi Layer Shape Simulator) simulator.

As sigma*b increases, the contrast of the small pattern, < ramda/2NA, is improved. The practical DOF enlarges as sigma*b increases (Fig. 3.6). These simulation results were confirmed experimentally.

However, they found this method to have the following drawbacks: the exposure latitude is small and dose uniformity within one shot decreases due to the decrease in the number of effective flyeye lenses.

Shiraishi *et al.*[28] proposed SHRINC "Super High Resolution by Illumi-Nation Control" in which a spherical aperture stop is positioned at the exit surface of flyeye lens (Fig. 3.7). Light illuminates the reticle pattern only at the specific incidence angles, off center from the optical axis, allowed by the transmissive portions of the SHRINC aperture. They concluded that the resolution, DOF and mask linearity (pattern width versus reticle width) were superior to that of conventional system. However, SHRINC has no significant effect in

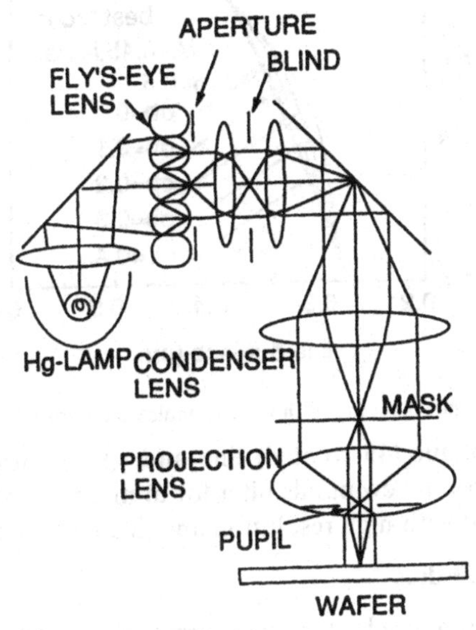

Figure 3.4 Annular illumination type step and repeat exposure system[27].

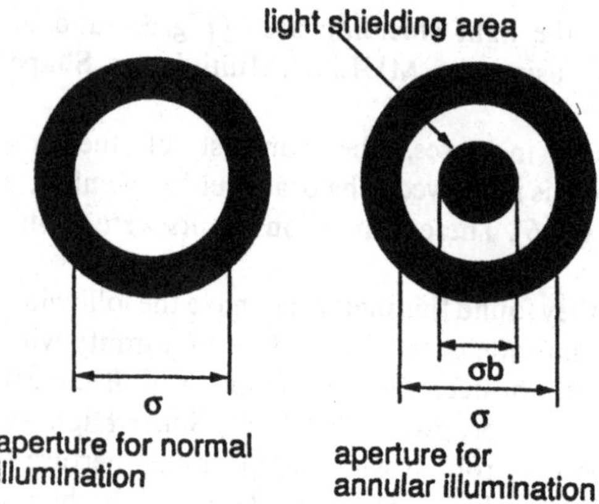

Figure 3.5 The top of view of the aperture for normal and annular illumination[27].

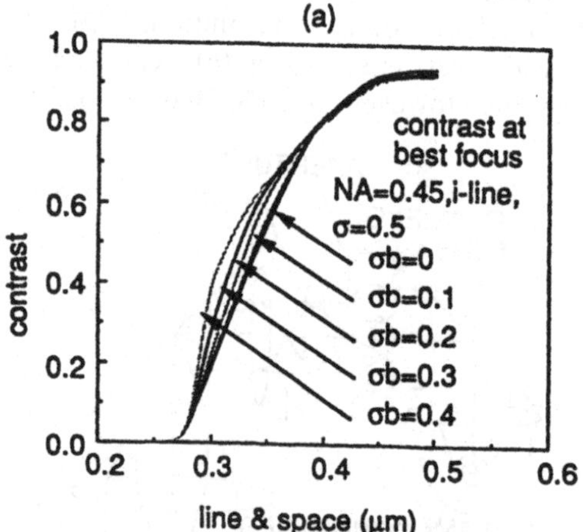

Figure 3.6 Linewidth versus simulated contrast.[27].

the case of oblique (45 rotated) line and space patterns. Fukuda *et al.*[29] developed a new pupils filter for annular illumination which can be achieved with high resolution and deep focal depth.

3.2.1.7. Pellicle Films

Pellicle film composed of nitrocellulose was used as protection against the dust adhesion on the mask for *g*-line stepper. However,

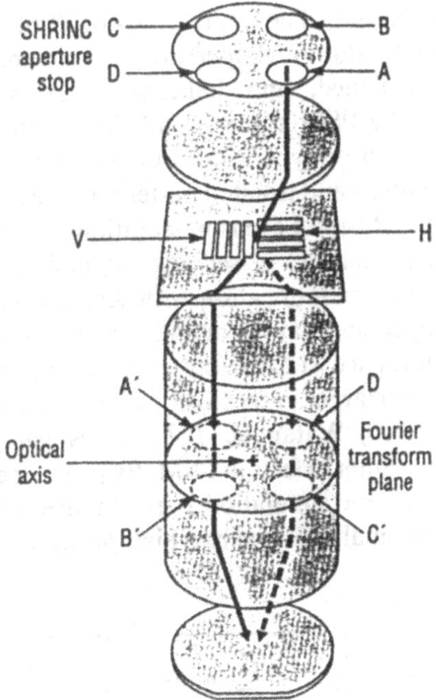

Figure 3.7 SHIRINC exposure system[28].

nitrocellulose film sustained damage with *i*-line exposure and optical transmittance and membrane stress decreased. Nakagawa,[30] developed stable pellicle for *i*-line exposure which was composed of modified nitrocellulose.

3.2.2 Phase Shifting Mask(PSM)

3.2.2.1. Phase Shifting Mask

The PSM method was developed by Shibuya in 1982[31]. At the same time, but independently, Levenson *et al.*[32,33] proposed the use of a PSM to improve the resolution of photolithography. On the other hand, Yamakoshi *et al.*[34] proposed high resolution X-ray lithography using a phase mask constructed by arranging two kinds of material, Si_3N_4 (1.9 μm) and Cu (0.19 μm) for a 10 A wavelength. Somemura *et al.*[35] proposed the use of an X-ray PSM to expand the proximity gap condition. The many kinds of PSM systems-among them the Levenson, additional aperture, transparent, edge contrast enhanced or selfaligned, and halftone types were developed. Figure 3.8 shows the PSM systems and their structures. It is well known that the Levenson type PSM dose not improve resolution in the case of hole pattern and isolated pattern. Inoue *et al.*[36] simulated the optimization PSM-the Levenson, additional aperture, transparent, edge contrast enhanced or self-aligned, and halftone types-for 0.25 μm isolated pattern fabrication with KrF stepper (N.A. = 0.45, sigma = 0.3). They found that the main linewidth of any isolated line mask and the main space width of any isolated space mask need to be designed smaller and larger, respectively, than the desired feature size (Fig. 3.9 and Fig. 3.10). Watanabe *et al.*[37] investigated the detection and printability of shifter defects in PSM. By printing experiments for programmed defects and simulation, they obtained following results. A defect located in small features had high printability.

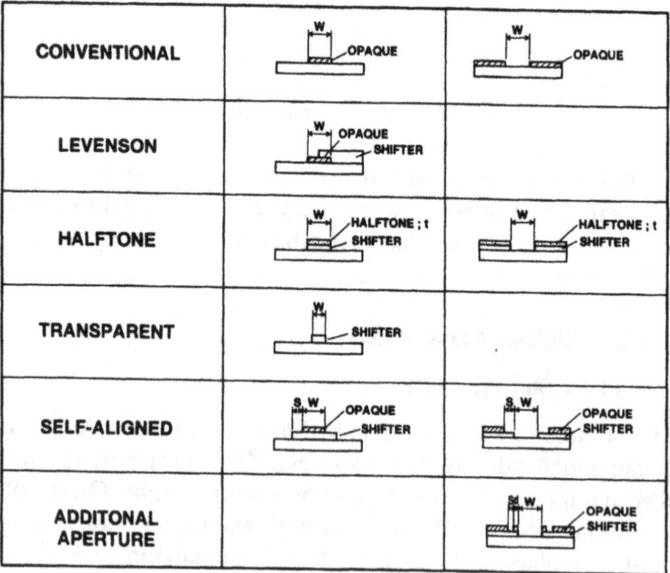

Figure 3.8 Phase Shift Mask (PSM).

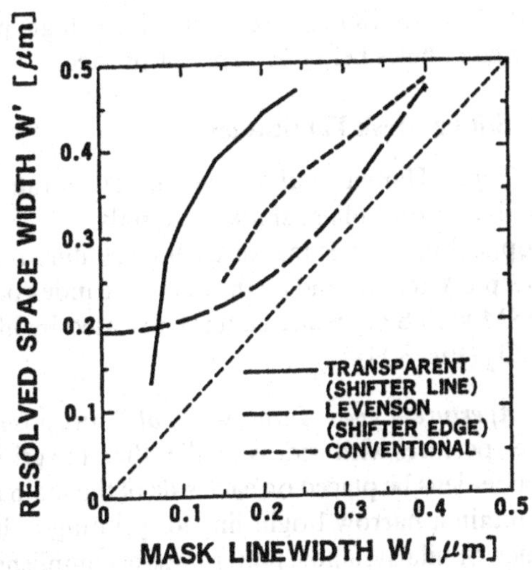

Figure 3.9 Resolve space widthlinearity for isolated line masks[36].

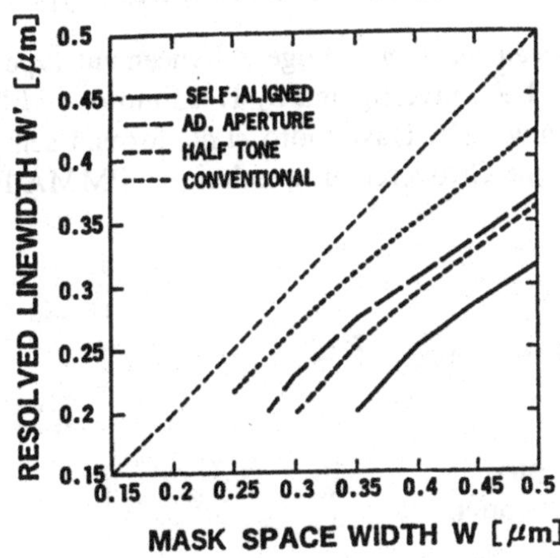

Figure 3.10 Line width linearity for isolated space mask[36].

Defects with 120° to 180° phase angles have high printability. Defects with phase angles below 90° are not printed.

3.2.2.2. Phase Sifting Mask Fabrication

A. Levenson Type Hanyu *et al.*[38] tried to evaporate SiO_2 and plasma CVD SiN films as phase shifter materials.

From the optical properties measurement, (1) film absorbance in the UV and deep UV region, and (2) the refractive index of films, they proposed a PSM with SiO_2 phase shifter fabricated by lift-off of the evaporated SiO_2 (Fig. 3.11).

B. Additional Aperture Type Terasawa *et al.*[39] proposed that two additional line apertures with widths smaller than the critical dimension of the stepper lens be placed on each side of the main aperture of the mask to obtain a narrow bright line for printing a fine isolated space on a wafer. Similarly, a hole pattern was accomplished by using a main aperture surrounded by four additional apertures. They obtained 0.3 μm isolated space and 0.4 μm hole pattern by using *i*-line stepper (NA = 0.45) with the additional aperture type PSM.

C. Edge Enhancement Type Edge enhancement type (self-aligned type) PSM has been investigated by Hashimoto *et al.*[40], Watanabe *et al.*[41] and Ishiwata[42]. Hashimoto *et al.*, formed self aligned type PSM by using the Cr overetching technique. PMMA EB resist was

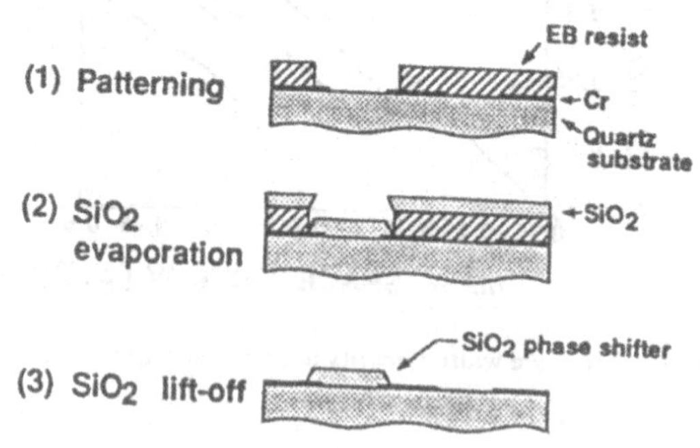

Figure 3.11 PSM fabrication process by evaporated SiO_2 lit-off[38].

used as the PSM material. Ishiwata *et al.*[43] investigated the fabrication of edge-enhancement type PSM with a self-aligned process. Phase shifting region was formed by Cr the overetching technique. They obtained the shifter depth accuracy of 0.015 μm (3σ) and the shifter width accuracy of 0.07 μm (3σ) by using this process. Yanagishita *et al.*[44] reported to application of the edge enhancement type PSM mask fabrication of IC pattern.

D. Halftone Type Inoue *et al.*[45] discussed the halftone type PSM. This PSM consists of a transparent substrate and the 180° phase shifter with a halftone layer whose amplitude transmissivity is t. The light wave, weakened and phase shifted by passing through the halftone layer, affords the edge sharpness of the intensity profile.

E. Transparent Type Yamanaka *et al.*[46] and Nakagawa *et al.*[47] investigated the transparent type PSM consisting of a transparent substrate and a 180° phase shifter. The destructive interference at both edges of the phase shifter results in one dark line in the case where the shifter linewidth is under the resolution limit for optical tools. Yamanaka *et al.*, applied the transparent type PSM to the narrow space fabrication of SRAM cell.

F. Shifter Materials Imai *et al.*[48] developed the PSM process by using spin-on-glass (SOG) technology which is sensitive to electron beam exposure (negative-type EB resist). They applied this material to PSM fabrications. Watanabe *et al.*[49] prepared the transparent type PSM by using two kinds of shifter materials; (1)polymethylmethacrylate, PMMA and (2) inorganic layer, SiN_x. A 3700 A thick PMMA was coated onto the mask substrate. A 2300 A SiN_x film was deposited onto the antistatic coating mask substrate.

Hanyu *et al.*[50] proposed using Al_2O_3 for the etch-stop layer in the PSM process. Oxygen ion-beam assisted evaporated Al_2O_3 films had high transparency at *i*-line and KrF wavelength, and etching selectivity of 270° for SiO_2 films. They proposed to ease the repair defective PSM which were two types, chipped phase shifter and shifter material remaining on non-shifted aperture.

3.3. Resist and Resist Process

3.3.1 Novolak Photoresist

3.3.1.1. *g*-Line resist

Hanabata *et al.*[51,52,53,54] studied the relationship between novolak molecular structure and resist performance. The optimum value of ortho-ortho bonding content was found to exist in terms of resist sensitivity. Heat resistivity of the photoresist decreases but the resolution capability is improved greatly when high-ortho novolak resins are used. These results indicate that the azocoupling reaction between novolak resins and quinonediazide compounds (Fig. 3.12) are concerns with the image formation mechanism in high-ortho novolak resin-quinonediazide systems. The influence of molecular weight distribution (Mw/Mn) of novolak resins on the performance of positive photoresist was investigated. The resist sensitivity is improved with the increase in Mw/Mn value. The film thickness retention, heat resistance and resolution capability are improved with the increase of the quinonediazide. These results are explained in terms of a simple model for positive photoresist development, the "stone wall model". On the other hand, Sugimoto *et al.*[55,56] measured the photoactive and development parameters of commercially available photoresists, OFPR800, OFPR5000,TSMR8900 and TSMR-V3. From the

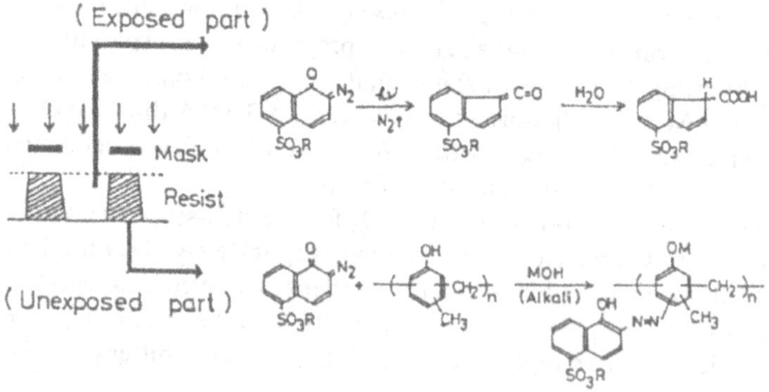

Figure 3.12 Image formation mechanism of naphthoquinonediazide-novolak positive photoresist[51,52,53,54].

simulated and experimental line widthlinearity data, they found that the photoactive parameters have little effect on the resolution power (linearity limit and optical parameters A, B, C[57]) of photoresist, while the development parameters (dissolution rate characteristics) greatly affect the resolution power.

Two new indicates, which can be used to accurately characterize the resolution power of photoresists, were extracted from the dissolution rate characteristics curves (Fig. 3.13). One is Cd, which is the contrast of the dissolution rate and the other is Rd, which is the range of the dissolution rate. These indices are closely related to the resist resolution power. A large Cd or Rd gives a higher resolution power to the photoresist (Fig. 3.14). The necessary value of Cd × Rd for the 0.5 μm feature size photolithography process was derived from experimental data under the present highest NA (= 0.55) *g*-line stepper for mass production and Cd × Rd must be larger than 39. Both Cd

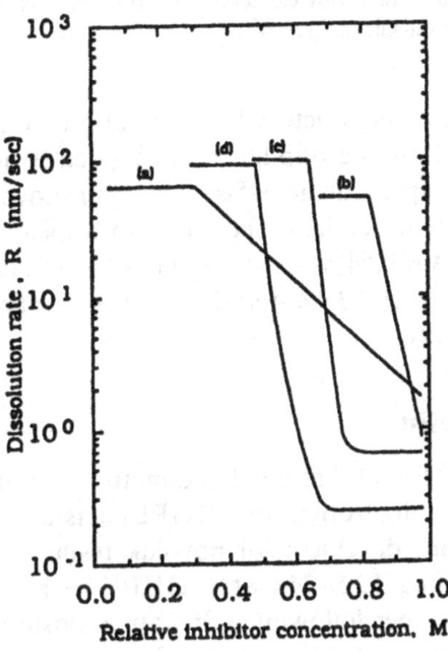

Figure 3.13 Dissolution rate curves of commercial resist.. (a) OFPR 800, (b) OFPR 5000, (c) TSMR 8900, (d) TSMR V3 [57].

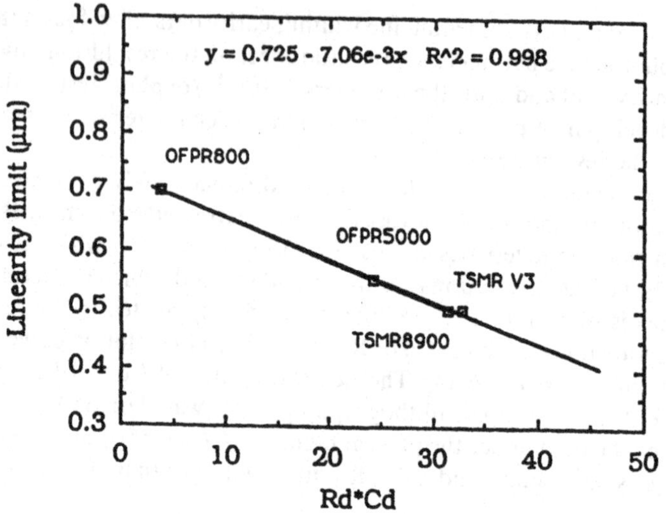

Figure 3.14 The product of Rd/by Cd versus linearity limit. (N. A.: 0.55, sigma: 0.6, ramda: 436 nm, resist thickness: 1.3 μm)[57].

and Rd are useful parameters for estimation of the photoresist resolution power. Fuji's group have investigated structural effects of NAC-5(1, 2-diazonaphthoquinone-5-sulfonyl ester)/novolak resin[58,59,60]. A new photoresist which had a potential to resolve 0.4 μm line and space pattern (NA = 0.54) was developed by Sato[61]. Ichikawa *et al.*[62] found that NAC-5 of 2.3.4.4'-tetrahydroxybenzophenone had high resolution sensitizer.

3.3.1.2. *i*-Line Resist

Yamaoka *et al.*[63] found that the 2, 6-dimethyl-3, 5-dicarboxyl-4-(2'-nitrophenyl)-1, 4-dihydropyridine (DHPE) acts as a dissolution inhibitor for alkaline developer for novolak resin. The DHPE resist prepared by adding 12.5–24.6 wt% DHPE to novolak resin was dissolved in developer following a 365 nm exposure of 100mJ/cm^2 and fabricated the fine positive pattern. Nemoto *et al.*[64] investigated the structural effects of NAC-5/novolak resin. JSR's groups have investigated structural effects between the novolak resin composite and photosensitizers. Kajita *et al.*[65] found resin containing 3,5-dimethyl phenol to be effective for increasing the ratio of intra-/inter-molecular hydrogen bonds. To clarify the characteristics of the novolak resin, they have defined an "I-Value" based on 13C-NMR spectroscopic analysis of the methylene coupling carbons. A resin with a large I-value formed a high degree of intramolecular hydrogen bonding among neighboring phenolic hydroxy groups. Figure 3.15 shows the I-value with copolymerized *m*-cresol novolak resin. They attribute this behavior to the effectiveness of the phenol with alkyl-substituents at both meta positions are effective in increasing the I-value. From the results, they estimated (Fig. 3.16) that a "pseudo-cyclophane" host-guest complex in the novolak-quinondiazide mixture was composed of a NAC-5 moiety and cavity or channel formed with the aggregation of several o-o linked units. Oki and Fuji Chemical Industry groups have reported[66] to the examination of LMR-UV resist (Low Molecular weight Resist for UV lithography; see Section 3.3.3.2.D) for *i*-line exposure. It resolves isolated 0.3 μm space and 0.35 μm hole patterns of 1.0 μm thickness by using *i*-line reduction projection aligner (NA = 0.42).

3.3.1.3. DUV Resist

The following novel azido polymers with alkaline developability and plasma etching resistance were synthesized by Koseki *et al.*[67]: the

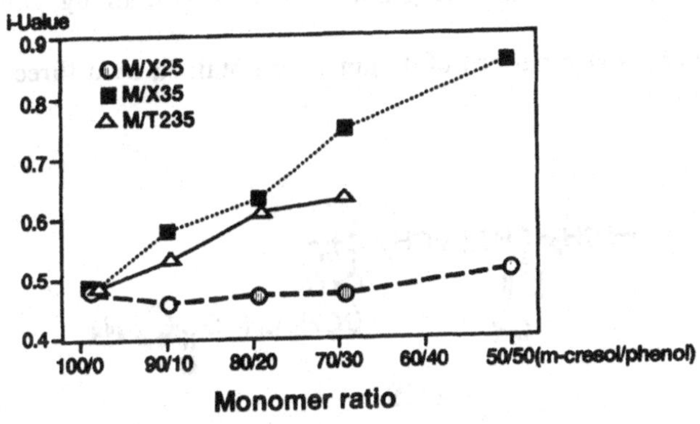

Figure 3.15 The I-value versus molar ratio of m-cresol.[65]

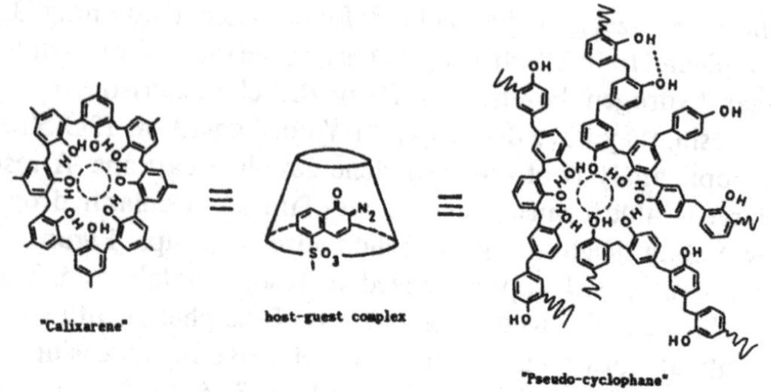

"Calixarene" ≡ host-guest complex ≡ "Pseudo-cyclophane"

Figure 3.16 Model structure of phenol and quinonediazide compounds[65].

copolymer of 2-(*p*-azidobenzoyloxy)ethyl methacrylate (AZMA) (Fig. 3.17) and *p*-hydroxystylene (PHS). The copolymers which contained above 60mol% of PHS unit were developable with aqueous alkaline solution. The copolymer (AZHS) with optimal resist characteristics was obtained by copolymerizing 70 mol% AZMA and 30 mol% PHS. The AZHS showed high sensitivity to deep UV light (11 mJ/cm^2 at 254 nm) with a resolution of 0.5 μm and high resistance to CF4 plasma etching (174 A/min.). Horiguchi *et al.* (68) have examined negative tone KrF resist by using diazo-*b*-diketone compounds. They have investigated the photo reaction of diazo-*b*-ketone and found that these sensitizers decomposed by photo irradiation, and prepared ester compounds with OH group in phenol containing polymer matrix.

Line and space pattern of 0.3 μm were obtained by a three-layer resist process.

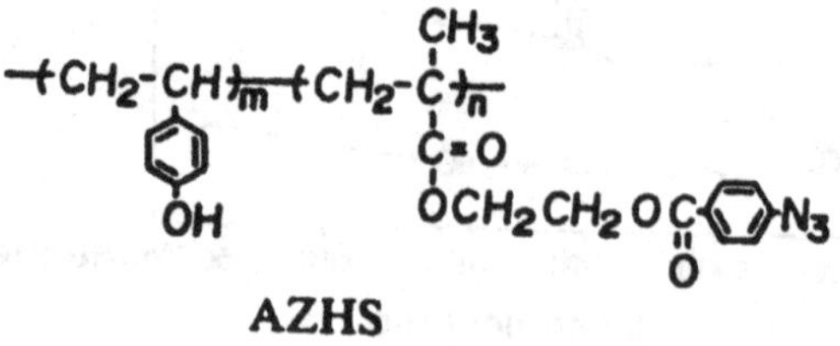

AZHS

Figure 3.17 AZHS resist.[67].

3.3.1.4. VUV Resist

Kudo *et al.*[69] studied hydrogen discharge source and PMMA resist parameters, such as spectral sensitivity and absorption coefficient, in the vacuum UV region.

The spectral distribution of the H2 light source was divided three regions: L1 = 115–125 nm, L2 = 125–170 nm, L3 = 170–300 nm, by using optical filter. Figure 3.18 shows sensitivity curves of PMMA resist for three spectral regions. They obtained 0.2 μm line and space pattern produced by the L2 region of H_2 light source. Kajimoto *et al.*[70] developed a new resist comprising alicyclic the copolymer of adamantylmethacrylate and *t*-butylmethacrylate with photoacid generator which has high transparency at ArF wavelengths and dry etch resistance.

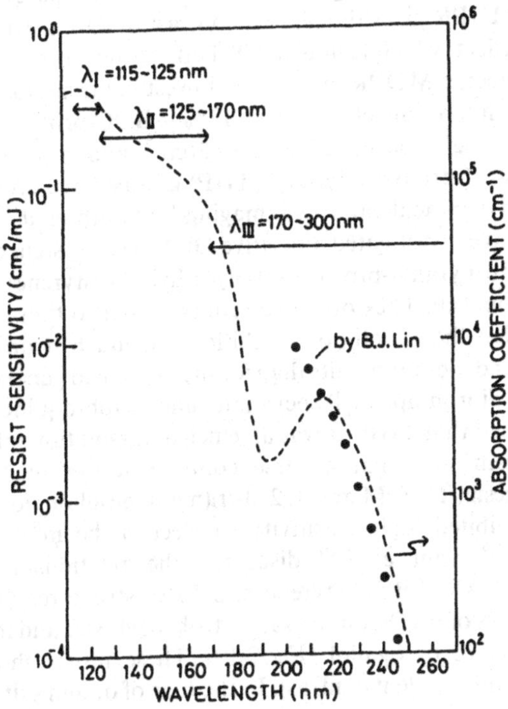

Figure 3.18 PMMA resist sensitivity in the VUV region[69].

3.3.2 Chemically Amplified Resist (CAR)

3.3.2.1. CAR Materials

The CAR system have been proposed by Ito[71] to break the deadlock of resolution and sensitivity improvement.

A Posi CAR System Kawai *et al.*[72] developed a chemically amplified monodisperse poly-hydroxystyrene-based positive resist (MDPR) composed of partially *t*-butyloxycarbonyl-protected PHS (*t*-BOC-PHS), a *t*-BOC-protected bisphenol A (BPAB) as a dissolution inhibitor, and diphenyl (*p*-thiophenoxy phenyl) sulfonium hexafluoro antimonate as a photo acid generator (PAG). A *t*-BOC-PHS with a weight average molecular weight (Mw) of 13,000 and molecular weight distribution (Mw/Mn) of 1.29 was used. As *t*-BOC-protected ratio increases, gamma value increases. The 29% *t*-BOC-protected MDPR gives the highest contrast due to a strong surface inhibition effect, which results in "T-Top" pattern profiles. The 9% *t*-BOC-protected MDPR yielded the lowest contrast due to a poor dissolution inhibition effects. The 17% *t*-BOC-protected MDPR provided a high sensitivity of 50 mJ/cm^2 and a high contrast (gamma = 4). Tetrahydropyranyl (THP) groups have been reported to be effective in acid-catalyzed imaging by Smith *et al.*[73]. Hayashi *et al.*[74,75] have investigated a positive DUV resist system containing of tetrahydropyranyl-protected poly(*p*-hydroxystyrene) (THP-M) and an onium salt. They obtained results similar to those of Ito and Floress[76] that the dissolution inhibition was much stronger for the sulfonium and iodonium salts than for the other acid generators, such as tri(2, 3-dibromopropyl)isocyanate and naphtoquinonediazide. They reported that THP-M was an efficient dissolution inhibitor for novolak resin, and that a three component system comprising a novolak resin, THP-M and 1, 2, 3-tri(methanesulfonyloxy)benzene (MeSB) exhibited high sensitivity to electron beam[77] and DUV exposure[78,79] Tani *et al.*[80] discussed the relationship between stability of CAR, *t*-BOC styrene and PAG structure. They investigated 3 types of PAGs: onium salt, nitrobenzyl ester and methansulfonyl triester of pyrogallol (Fig. 3.19). These resists showed high sensitivity and excellent contrast. In the case of onium salt sensitizer,

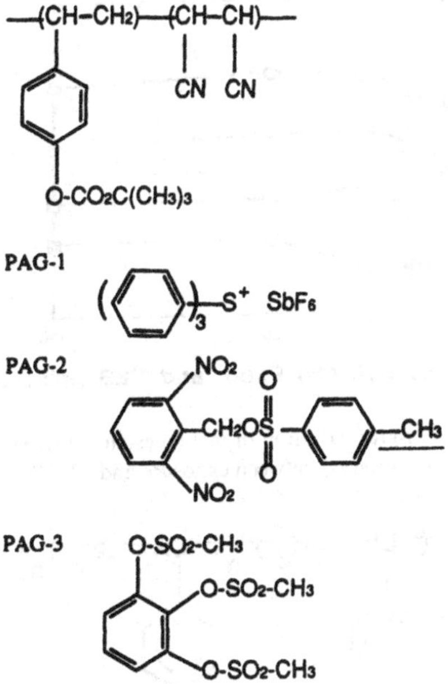

—(CH–CH2)—(CH–CH)—
CN CN
O-CO2C(CH3)3

PAG-1

(C_6H_5)$_3$–S$^+$ SbF_6

PAG-2

NO2 O CH2OS CH3 O NO2

PAG-3

O-SO2-CH3
O-SO2-CH3
O-SO2-CH3

Figure 3.19 The chemical structure of acid sensitive polymer and photo acid generators[80].

a hard surface insoluble layer was observed. However, other sensitizers showed vertical pattern profile up to 0.35 μm L/S.

The resist using methansulfonyl triester of pyrogallol sensitizer could maintain initial sensitivity. Figure 3.20 shows the linewidth variation of methansulfonyl triester of pyrogallol for the time interval between exposure and PEB. This resist could keep initial width in the first 20 min. delay. After 30 min. delay, the linewidth shift depended on the delay time and beccame saturated after more than 1 hour delay. They concluded that excess strong high-efficiency PAGs with high efficiency are not needed for the CAR material for KrF excimer lithography.

Onishi *et al.*[81] have investigated the new dissolution inhibiting polymer, partially *t*-butoxycarbonylmethylated poly(*p*-hydroxystyrene); (BOCM-PVP; Fig. 3.21). The dissolution inhibiting effects of BOCM-PVP showed greater than *t*-BOC-PHS. They obtained

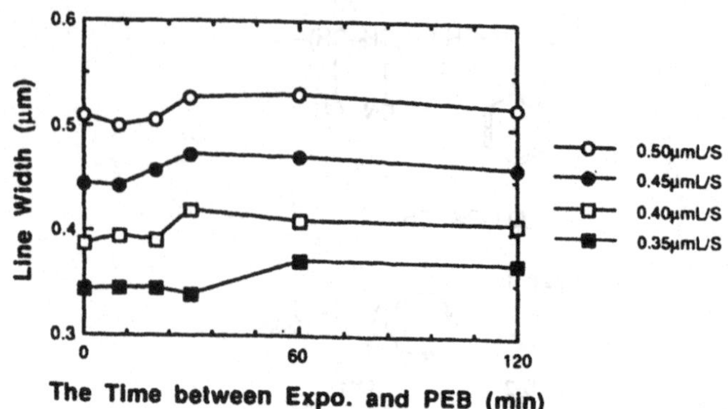

Figure 3.20 The line width variation of methanesulfonyl triester of pyrogallol sensitizer for the delay time interval between exposure and PEB[80]

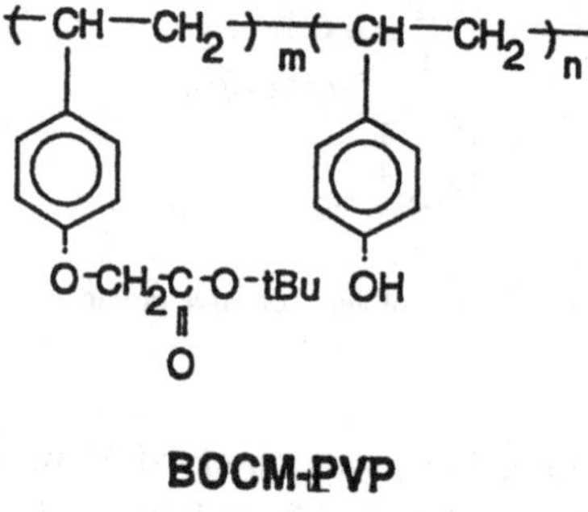

BOCM-PVP

Figure 3.21 Chemical structure of BOCM-PVP[21].

0.31 µm line and space pattern using BOCM-PVP and triphenylsulfonium trifluoromethanesulfonate sensitizer at 32 µmJ/cm^2 exposure doses of KrF excimer laser. Hayase *et al.*[82] investigated positive CAR using 1, 2-naphtoquinonediazide-4-sulfonate ester (NAC-4) which prepared sulfonic acid by UV irradiation[83]. Kobayashi *et al.*[84] investigated a new resist comprising silylated polyhydroxystyrene and photoacid generator. They obtained 0.26 µm line and space pattern in a 0.7 µm thick film by using KrF excimer laser stepper (NA = 0.45) with sensitivity of 48 mJ/cm^2.

B. Nega CAR System Tada *et al.*[85] found negative work CAR system composed of novolak resin, pinacol and onium salt. Oie *et al.*[86] investigated the reactivity of photo acid generator and cross-linking agent. From the experimental results, they proposed three photochemical reaction mechanisms: C-alkylation, O-alkylation and self condensation (Fig. 3.22).

3.3.2.2. Mechanism of CAR System

(1) *Diffusion Mechanism of Acid in Resist Polymer*

A. Posi Resist: The exposed area in the CAR is changed to an alkaline developable molecular structure by acid catalyzed reaction during the PEB process. Nakamura *et al.*[87] estimated the acid diffusion length in the polymer by using X-ray exposure system (Fig. 3.23). From the results, the diffusion coefficient of photogenerated acid was $1 \times 10 - 13\ cm^2/S$ under the 65°C PEB condition. They[88] have investigated the diffusion of acid in the three component resist. They considered the rate equation for acid-catalyzed reaction. The diffu-

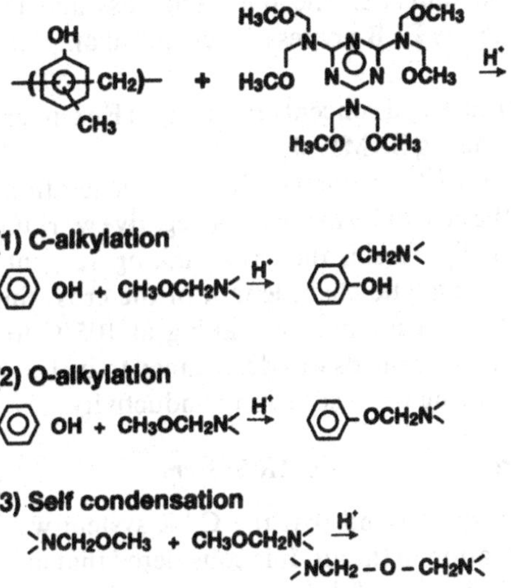

(1) C-alkylation

$\text{Ph-OH} + CH_3OCH_2N\!< \xrightarrow{H^+} \text{(}CH_2N\!<\text{)-Ph-OH}$

(2) O-alkylation

$\text{Ph-OH} + CH_3OCH_2N\!< \xrightarrow{H^+} \text{Ph-}OCH_2N\!<$

(3) Self condensation

$>\!NCH_2OCH_3 + CH_3OCH_2N\!< \xrightarrow{H^+} >\!NCH_2-O-CH_2N\!<$

Figure 3.22 Reaction mechanism of negative working CAR[86].

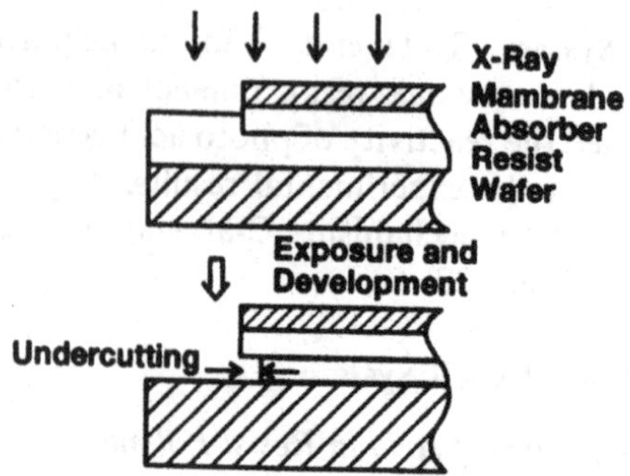

Figure 3.23 Acid diffusion length measurement method.[87].

sion coefficients of catalytic acids in some CAR range from 0.1 to $100\,nm^2/S$. The acid diffusion coefficients of EXP resist[89] are $15\,nm^2/S$ at 55°C and $50\,nm^2/S$ at 65°C. Asakawa[90] measured the diffusion range of acid in the CAR system with PAG separation method.

B. Nega resist: Yoshino *et al.*[91] proposed a new model which included the acid diffusion, the bulk acid loss and the crosslinking reaction during the PEB process for chemical amplification reaction resist.

Photogenerated acid concentration for KrF excimer laser exposure was calculated using SAMPLE.

Nakamura *et al.*[92] evaluated the acid generation, the catalytic reaction and the acid diffusion using a negative working CAR consisting of the novolak resin, the cross-linking reagent and the acid generator. The catalytic chain length of the cross-linking reactions was about 30 for post exposure baking at 105°C for 120 sec. The diffusion coefficient of acids was determined to be $1 \times 10^{-12}\,cm^2/S$ at 105°C by measuring the resist's ion conductivity.

(2) *Atmosphere Influences of CAR System*

MacDonald *et al.*[93] found that the CAR system was influenced by ppm contamination in the air. It is considered that air contamination induced to inactivation of the photogenerated acid. From the results, T-shaped resist and the effect of delay time on the developing process were induced. Naramasu *et al.*[94] reported that the T-shaped positive CAR resist is prepared by alkaline gas, too. To protect alkaline from contamination gas, several methods have been reported. Mori *et al.*[95] investigated with FT-IR and XPS the diffusing behavior of hexamethyldisilazane (HMDS). They concluded that the insoluble surface residues were caused by formation of Si-O bond in the resist films. On the other hand, Kumada *et al.*[96] investigated over-top coating materials to solve the T-top chemically amplified resist profile. They proposed to use the over-top coating materials containing organic acid compounds on the CAR films.

They reported that the pattern profiles did not change with the process delay time by using polyacrylic acid containing 5 wt% of low molecular weight poly(2-acrylamido-2-methylpropanesulfonic acid) (PAMPS) over-top coating films.

3.3.3 Resist Process

Less than wavelength resolution without critical dimension variations over topography is difficult to achieve with the conventional resist process, even if higher NA lens is being used. Various resist processes are introduced in this section.

3.3.3.1. UV Hardening

Endo *et al.*[97] reported deep UV irradiation to a NAC-5/novolak photoresist. Deep UV irradiation caused crosslinking of the low molecular weight cresol novolak resin and ester bond formation between the resin and irradiated diazonaphtoquinone ester. Thermal resistance of the resist was improved by the deep UV exposure after pattern formation, and the resist pattern was resistant to thermal deformation at 160°C, while no change in the plasma resistance was observed.

3.3.3.2. Multilayer Process and Surface Imaging

A. Inorganic Resist and Silicon Containing Resist Kudo *et al.*[98,99] found that amorphous polytungstic acids containing peroxo groups (O-O) provided a negative type inorganic resist. They synthesized two kinds amorphoustungstic acid which were isopolytungstic acid (experimental formula $12WO_3$ $7H_2O_2$ nH_2O; IPA) and heteropolytungstic acid (experimental formula CO_2 $12WO_3$ $7H_2O_2$ nH_2O;HPA). Both materials had the same properties, high sensitivity for deep UV, electron beam and X-ray (Fig. 3.24) and high O_2 reactive ion etching resistance *et al.*[100]. The sensitivity curve with the KrF exposure is shown in Fig. 3.25. Sensitivity of Nb-doped HPA is six times higher than that of the nondoped one. The exposure dose at a normalized resist thickness of 0.5 is 100 mJ/cm^2. The reason of the sensitivity enhancement is that polymerization reaction for Nb-doped HPA

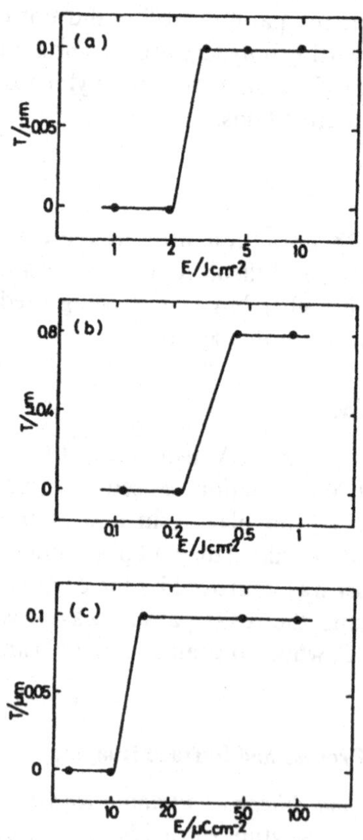

Figure 3.24 Sensitivity curves of IPA resist. (a) UV, (b) EB, (c) X-ray[98,99].

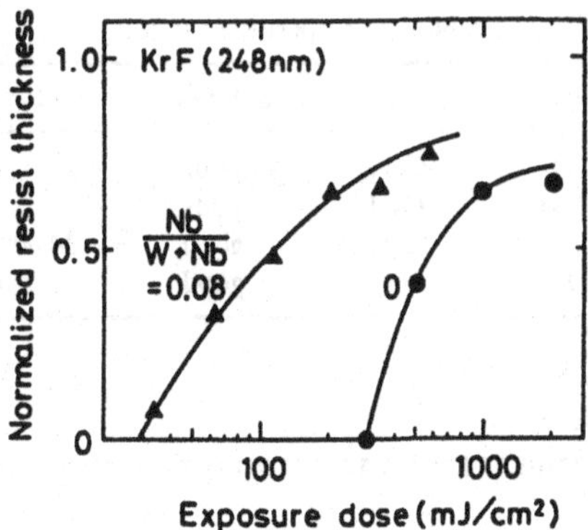

Figure 3.25 Sensitivity curves of Nb doped HPA resist for KrF excimer exposure[98,99].

proceeds easily compared with the reaction for the nondoped one. Nb-doped polyanion is unstable because incorporation of NbO_6 octahedral causes a distortion of the polyanion structure. Moreover, they found reciprocity failure effect of KrF laser pulse energy on the Nb doped HPA resist. The dependence on sensitivity is small in the energy region less than 16 mJ/cm^2-pulse. They obtained a good profile sub-half micron pattern with an aspect ratio of 3 by using KrF excimer stepper (NA 0.35) through the tow-layer resist process of Nb-doped HPA and polyimide (PIQ).

Organosilicon resists have been reported to show resistance against oxygen plasma, and to be able to act as the top imaging layer in the multilayer resist system. Ishikawa *et al.*[101] have investigated the photochemical reaction of polymeric organosilicon compounds containing disilanyl unit. Nate *et al.*[102] have prepared poly(p-disilanylenephenylene:PDSP) and examined some features of their photochemical behavior for top imaging layer in multilayer resist systems (Tab. 3.4).

PDSP-EM acted as a positive photoresist, but after development a residue was observed in the exposure region. It appeared that a recombination reaction occurred in parallel with the degradation reaction. The addition of radical trap agents, such as 2, 6-di-*t*-butyl-*p*-cresol, was studied to prevent residue formation and enhance sensitivity. Fig. 3.26 shows exposure characteristics of PDSP-MHP.

Table 3.4 Properties of PDSP.

Polymer	R_1	R_2	Solubility	Mw	mp(°C)
PDSP-MM	CH_3	CH_3	poor	–	–
PSDP-EE	C_2H_5	C_2H_5	poor	–	203–206
PDSP-EM	CH_3	C_2H_5	good	34,000	186–189
PDSP-MPH	CH_3	Ph	good	31,000	155–163

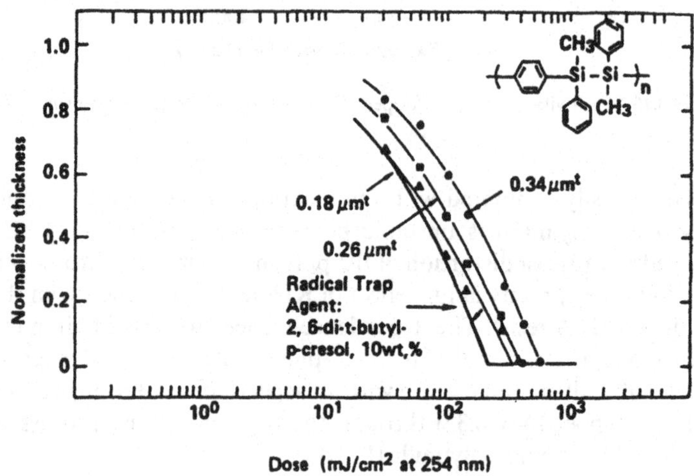

Figure 3.26 Characteristics of PDSP-MHP resist[101].

To investigate the mechanism of the its photodegradation, UV spectra of PDSP-MPH were measured. The absorption attributed to the conjugation of the Si-Si bond and phenylene group was greatly decreased after UV irradiation. This indicates that PDSP induced the radical scission of Si-Si bonds by deep UV irradiation. The O_2-reactive ion etching rate of PDSP, PIQ, photoresist(AZ-1350J) and siloxane(KJR-618) were measured under the following experimental conditions: RF power, 0.64 W/cm^2 (7 MHz); O_2 pressure, 3 mToor; and cathode bias voltage, − 120 to 100 Volts. PDSP had oxygen plasma etching resistance about 30 times that of PIQ and AZ-1350J (Fig. 3.27). Tomura *et al.*[103], Ueno *et al.*[104] and Hayashi *et al.*[105] found that a low molecular weight poly(phenylsilsesquioxane) was compatible with commercially available positive photoresist and that *cis*-(1, 3, 5, 7-tetrahydroxy)-1, 3, 5, 7-tetraphenylcyclotetrasiloxane ($T_4(OH)_4$) was soluble in aqueous alkaline solution. On the basis of this finding, they have developed new positive *g*-line sensitive photoresist containing silicon (ASTRO) as a top-layer resist for two-layer resist system. Table 3.5 shows composition of ASTRO and the resist properties.

The loss in resist thickness at the lower dose was about 0.04 μm for each sample. The contrast depended upon PAG concentration and sample-3 showed better contrast than the OFPR-800 resist. The sensitivity of ASTRO resist was 50 mJ/cm^2. The etch rates for O_2 RIE of ASTRO resist were measured. The proportion of GR-950 to phenyl $T_4(OH)_4$ does not affect the etch rate. The etch rate depends upon the silicon content of resist materials. Tanaka *et al.*[106,107] and S. Imamura *et al.*[108] have developed a novel silicon-based positive photoresist (SPP) composed of acetylated polyphenylsilsequioxane

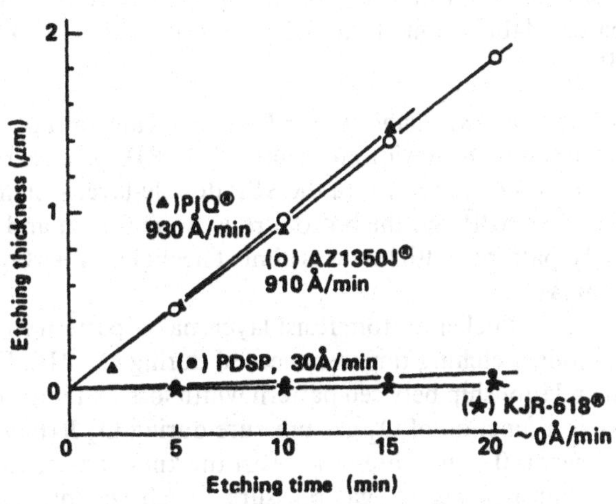

Figure 3.27 Etching rate of PDSP resist by O_2 RIE[101].

Table 3.5 Composition of ASTRO and the resist properties.

No	Novolak (%)	PAG (%)	GR-950 (%)	T4(OH)4 (%)	γ (%)	Dev. Time (sec.)
1	100	0	45	30	0.6	27
2	83	17	45	30	1.25	19
3	77	23	45	30	1.32	20
4	71	29	45	30	0.95	31
OFPR-800	–	–	–	–	98	24

*PAG: Photo Active Generator; 2,3,4-tri-(1,2-o I naphtoquinonediazide-5-sulfonyloxy)-benzophenone
*Novolak: PSF-2803; Gun-ei Chemical INC. Limit. Cresol Novolak Type Resin
*GR-950: Owens-Illinois Co.; Poly(phenylsilsesquioxane)
*OFPR-800: Tokyo Ohka Kogyo Co.; g-line sensitive resist

(APSQ) and NAC-5 compounds as a photosensitizer. SPP resist has high sensitivity of the short wavelength such as 248 nm, 365 nm and 436 nm. However, resist contrast (Gamma value) become worse. A fine SPP pattern below 0.5 μm was obtained using a *g*-line stepper equipped with a high NA reduction lens (NA = 0.6). The etching rate of SPP was −3.5 nm/min, whereas that of the AZ-type resist was higher than 80 nm/min (Fig. 3.28). The O_2 RIE resistance allowed the pattern fabrication of the AZ-type resist with a mask of very thin SPP.

B. Multi-layer Process Double-Layer Process Tanaka *et al.*[106] have investigated the pattern width loss during O_2 RIE process by using SPP resist and AZ-type resist. In the SPP double-layer system where the thickness of SPP and the bottom resist were 0.1 μm and 0.6 μm, respectively, pattern width loss was almost negligible after O_2 RIE of the bottom layer.

However, the thicker bottom resist layer makes pattern width loss large as a longer etching time was needed during O_2 RIE. Fig. 3.29 shows the relationship between pattern width loss and bottom resist thickness as a function of O_2 gas pressure during O_2 RIE when the SPP thickness is 0.1 μm. Threshold resist thickness was measured. It was thicker at a higher O_2 gas pressure, which was preferable for a decrease in pattern width loss. However, the undercut of the bottom

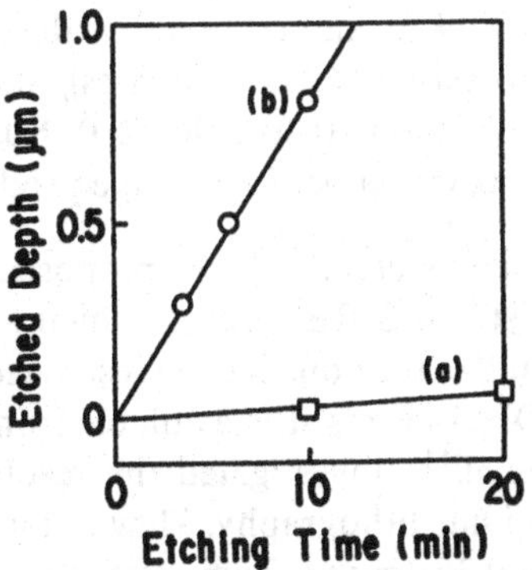

Figure 3.28 O_2 RIE characteristics of SPP resist and hard baked AZ-type resist. condition; O_2 flow: 50 sccm, O_2 pressure: 1.3 Pa, RF power: 0.1 W/cm^2, Bias voltage: 500 V

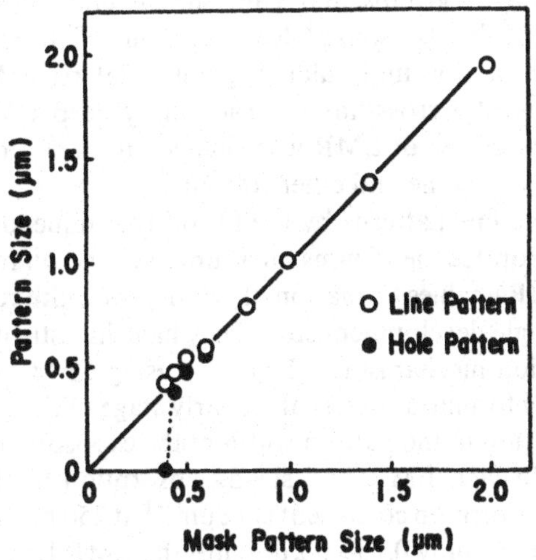

Figure 3.29 Relationship between mask pattern size and fabricated pattern size of SPP resist.[103].

resist became larger at a higher O_2 gas pressure where DC bias voltages drop. These results suggest that the pattern width loss was caused by an oxygen ion sputtering effect during O_2 RIE.

Triple-Layer Process Kawamura *et al.*[109] developed the triple-layer process (photoresist (0.6 μm thickness)/silicon resin (0.2 μm thickness)/novolak photoresist) to achieve 0. 8 μm line and space pattern using an NA 0.35 stepper for volume production.

C. Silylation Coopmans *et al.*[110] have proposed the diffusion enhanced silylated resist "DESIRE" process which was the anisotropic oxygen plasma etching of the nonsilylated resist selective with respect to silylated resist. DESIRE resist is available from UCB-JSR Electronics. Takehara *et al.*[111] investigated the resolution limit of the silylation process in i line lithography. They obtained the result that resolution limit was 0.35 μm in 0.7 μm resist thickness and was not determined by the silylation process and the dry development process.

D. Others Surface Imaging Process Oki Electric Industry and Fuji Chemical Industry groups, and Yamashita *et al.*[112] have developed LMR (Low Molecular weight Resist) for lift-off process. LMR is a NAC-5 ester of a low molecular weight novolak resin (Mw = 1,000). LMR introduced a cross-linking reaction by deep UV irradiation, and the exposed area of LMR was changed to involved for organic solvent, such as ketone and ether solvent.

To form the fine patterns by the lift-off technique, discontnuities between evaporated metal films on a substrate and on resist lines are required. LMR enables formation of submicron width resist patterns through a single development step. They have investigated the overhang formation mechanism of LMR by using SEM measurement. The overhang formation starts at an early stage of development and that no variation in the pattern width of the exposure upper layer is recognized. In fact, LMR had strong absorption in the deep UV region. The absorption coefficient is 12 μm^{-1} at 250 nm, which allows light to penetrate only 0.1 to 0.2 μm into the LMR layer. 0.5 μm line and space patterns have been clearly resolved on an Al substrate. It was unnecessary to change the amount of dose and the developing conditions even when the substrate was changed among Si, SiO_2 and Al. This is due to the fact that there is no appreciable reflection from the substrate because of its high absorption.

3.3.3.3. Image Enhanced Method

A. Contrast Enhanced Layer (CEL) B. F. Griffing and P. R. West[113] found the CEL effect which is a method of improving the contrast of the resist exposure process that could extend the resolution limit of photolithography. The regions of the CEL which are exposed to the highest light intensity of the image are bleached more rapidly than those regions exposed to lower levels of light intensity. Consequently, the ratio of the cumulative energies in the high and low light level regions of the image which transmitted through the CEL is higher than the ratio of incident light levels. Niki *et al.*[114] have studied the CEL effect of new diazonium compounds, according to the simulation. The CEL effect has been calculated by using the A, B and C parameters same as Dill's constant[115]. They obtained the calculated results of CEL and conventional resist profile, assuming that $A = 5\,m^{-1}$, $B = 0.06\,m^{-1}$ and $C = 0.014\,cm^2/mJ$. Furthermore, it was found that CEL effect is mainly determined by the value of the parameter A. Assuming that the required resist contrast is 0.8, the A value of more $3\,\mu m^{-1}$ is necessary to realize the submicron pattern by using AZ-1350J photoresist.

Endo *et al.*[116,117,118,119] have developed water-soluble CEL materials (WSP) for *g*−, *i*− and DUV lithography. The diazonium compounds are decomposited and prepare the nitrogen gas by photo irradiation, and the optical transmittance of residual materials in the films are increases. Pullulan and poly (vinylpyrrolidone) were used as a water soluble layer which has high transmittance and excellent nitrogen gas permeability.

As WSP has a good solubility for alkaline developer, the WSP films are removed during development of resist. The depth of focus latitude has been widened at 0.6 μm patterns and change of pattern width due to the defocusing has been decreased using WSP.

B. Contrast Enhanced Process The PEB "Post Exposure Baking" process has been developed by Walker *et al.*[120]. Ogawa *et al.*[121] investigated the suppression of standing wave curve by using solubility rate of alkaline developer.

They concluded that photodecomposed sensitizer was diffused with PEB process, and reduced the multiple interference effect. Okada *et al.*[122] developed the REL "Resolution Enhanced Lithography" which was deep UV flood exposure at 100°C after imaging. Figure 3.30 shows the REL process. Endo *et al.*[123] proposed the HARD "High Aspect Ratio resist by Alkaline surface Disposal" process which was soaking in alkaline solution before imaging.

3.3.3.4. Image Reverse Process

Tanaka *et al.*[107] investigated the image reverse process of the SPP resist which was composed of an alkali soluble silicon polymer (APSQ) and a NAC-5 photosensitizer. It was known that the SPP resist acts as the positive working after pattern exposure in the near UV region. However, they found that the flood exposure area after the pattern exposure became insoluble for alkali solution. SPP is a dual-mode resist.

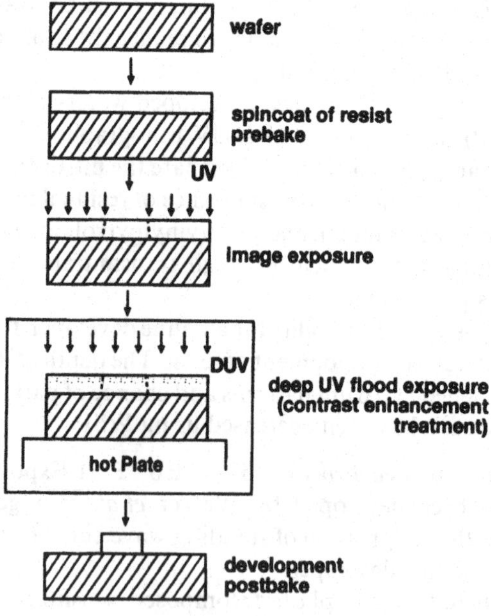

Figure 3.30 REL process flow[124].

3.3.3.5. Developing Enhanced Process

It is important to clarify the developing mechanism to obtain half micron pattern with photoresist.

Yamaguchi *et al.*[124] and Kishimura *et al.*[125] reported the resolution capability dependence on tetramethylammonium hydroxide (TMAH) concentration and discussed the effects on the dissolution characteristics of the photoresist. Based on the these experimental results, they proposed that the most suitable TMAH concentration was 1.5 wt%. Furthermore, Yamaguchi *et al.*[126] investigated the dissolution characteristics of resist in developer with added tetramethylammonium salts (TMA salts). They found that the dissolution rate of the resist was increased by adding TMA salts to alkaline solution and the acceleration effect of the dissolution rate was dependent on the anion size of added salts (the anion effect).

Shimada *et al.*[127] discussed pattern resolution capability improvement by using surfactant in the TMAH developer. They found that the chloride ion in TMAH developer contributed to the protection against sidewall dissolution. Kumagae *et al.*, have investigated the LASER (Lateral and Surface modification for Enhancing Resist contrast) which was carried out by multi-step development along with surface modification. The process sequence of LASER is shown in Fig. 3.31. Minamiyama *et al.*[128] investigated the mechanism of LASER process by using the dissolution measurement. From the results, a thin insoluble layer was formed on both the resist surface and the side wall at the stage of alkali treatment and interruption of the first development, and maintained the resist thickness and profile during the development. The LASER process obtained a steep profile. This process was applied to a bitline poly-Si of 0.4 μm feature size.

3.3.3.6. Dry Developable Resist and its Process

Tsuda *et al.*[129] have designed plasma developable resist which consists of degradable polymer by UV exposure and radical quencher forming compounds.

They chose poly(methylisopropenyl ketone) (PMIPK) as a degradable polymer and 4.4'-diazidobiphenylthioether as a quencher forming compound. Figure 3.32 shows the principal of dry developable resist reaction and dry process flow chart, respectively. This resist

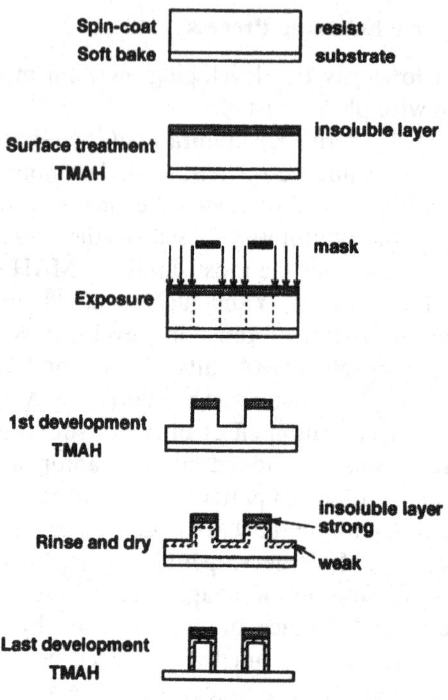

Figure 3.31 Process flow of LASER[128].

had highly dry etch resistant become the excitation energy quenching system was formed in the resist image by the radiation exposure followed by hard baking. Fine pattern of 0.5 μm was obtained by dry developing process where gamma value was 1.5–2.7.

3.3.3.7. Planarization and Anti Reflection Coating

A. Planarization To improve geometry dependent properties, Butherus *et al.*[130] have investigated the spincoating technique by SOG (Spin-On-Glass; Organic Silicon Compounds). It is known that spincoated SOG films crack easily. Ito *et al.*[131] have investigated relationships between the molecular structure and film properties. They proposed the Reactive Glass Stabilization (RGS) which was O_2

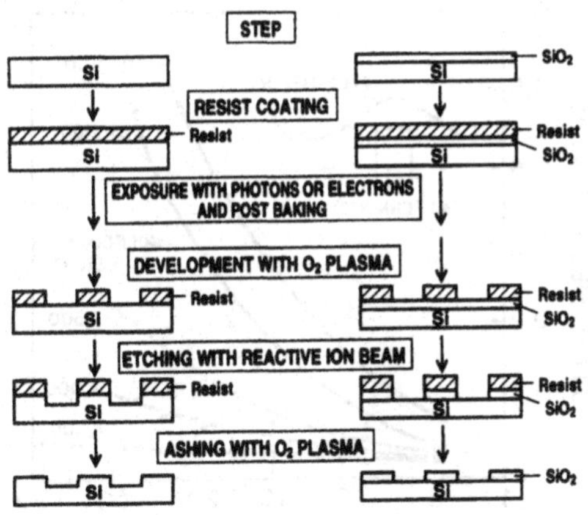

Figure 3.32 Dry development process.[127].

plasma treatment. In the case of SOG treated by RGS, no cracks were found in films. Oikawa *et al.*[132] have developed new polysilphenylenesiloxane resin (SPS) as an interlevel dielectric layer for non-etchback application. SPS films have good resistance to cracking for 2.0 μm thick and heating to 400°C. The 1 μm high topography is planarized for SPS 1.5 μm thick. Measurement of thermal properties clarified that the SPS was not oxidated below 400°C in a oxidative atmosphere. Gokan *et al.*[133] found that the single dispersed low molecular weight polystyrene ($Mw/Mn = 1.06$) was effective in achieving uniform coating .

The low molecular weight polymer ($Mw = 2{,}000$) which was below 300 cp melting viscosity suppressed 0.6 μm initial step height within 0.05 μm (Fig. 3.33). To harden the polymer by deep UV irradiation before etching, this polymer was partly chloromethylated.

B. Anti Reflection Coating Three methods, namely undercoating, overcoating and dye containing resist have been developed for reducing multiple interference effect between the resist film and substrate. This section introduces undercoating and overcoating processes. Tanaka *et al.*[134,135] proposed the ARCOR (Anti Reflection Coating On Resist) process to suppress the linewidth variation for resist thickness deviation. It was found that the suppression effect of the linewidth variation depended on refractive index of ARCOR film (Fig. 3.34).

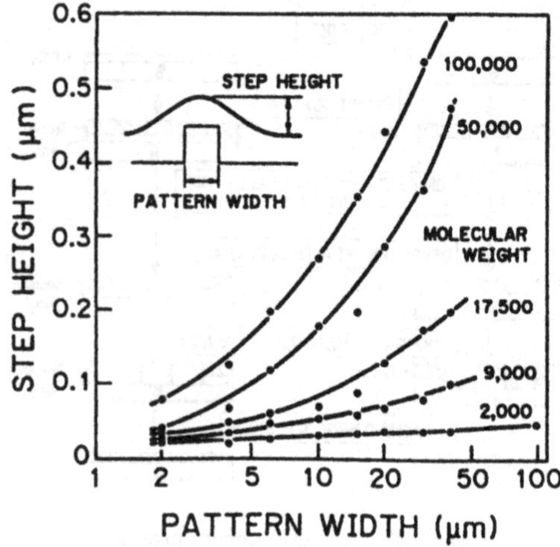

Figure 3.33 Step height after 200°C baking as pattern width for various molecular weight polystyrenes[129].

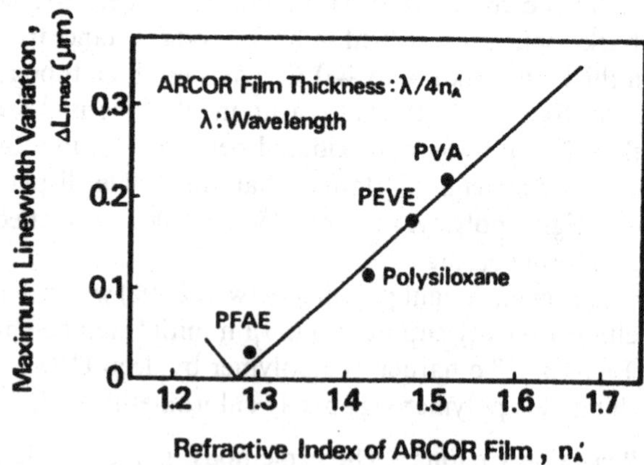

Figure 3.34 Suppression effect of Lmax with he ARCOR method.[134,135].

The linewidth variation for the resist thickness decreased with ARCOR film compared with the conventional process (Fig. 3.35). Koizumi *et al.*[136] investigated the anti reflection overcoating process for KrF lithography.

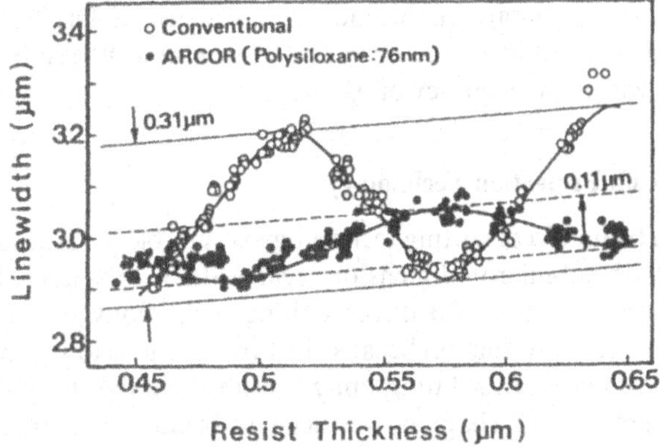

Figure 3.35 Linewidth variation with respect to resist thickness[126].

3.4. EB Lithography

3.4.1 EB Exposure System

3.4.1.1. Gaussian Beam EB Exposure System

Matsuzaka *et al.*[137] and Ohyama *et al.*[138] have developed high speed electron beam lithography system by using variable gaussian optics and a pattern edge process (see Section 3.4.1.4.). This system (HL-700F) was capable of 0.1 μm resolution, 0.04 μm stichting accuracy, 0.04 μm overlay accuracy and 1 wafer/hr throughput.

3.4.1.2. Shaped Beam Technology

Hassel *et al.*[139] developed the JBA-6AIII which has improved throughput, accuracy, data transfer unit and real time shot partitioning function. Sakitani *et al.*[140] and Nakamura *et al.*[141,142] of Hitachi developed variable shaped beam EB system, HL-700D. Hattori *et al.*[143,144,145,146] developed a new rectangular and triangular shaped beam calibration method on the EX-7 EB exposure system[147] which had rectangular first shaping aperture and keyhole-type second shaping aperture to generate triangular beam as well as rectangular beam. Four kinds of triangular shaped beams and rectangular beams of up to 1.6 μm in size ware generated by overlapping the 1st shaping aperture image on the 2nd shaping aperture. They calibrated the beam size within an accuracy of 0.013 μm and the relative beam position within an accuracy of 0.025 μm.

3.4.1.3. Cell Projection Technology

Electron beam direct writing technology is suitable for fabrication of devices with submicron dimensions and ASICS chips in small-scale production. However, EB direct writing technology has not been applied in mass production because its throughput is lower than that of conventional optical lithography. To improve the throughput of EB lithography, the shape of the electron beam was changed from a point beam to a fixed shaped beam and to a variable shaped beam (see Section 3.4.1.2). However, even in a variable shaped beam method, the number of exposure shots is extremely large in the case of a memory pattern, a DRAM or SRAM devices. In order to reduce the shot number, Nakayama *et al.*[148] and Saito *et al.*[149] of Hitachi proposed cell projection EB technology. In a memory pattern, a few simple cell patterns a few μm square are repeated over almost all the chip area. In the proposed technology, this pattern repeatability is utilized.

In a conventional variable shaped beam method, ten shots are needed to exposure the pattern. In contrast, by using cell projection technology, this complicated pattern can be exposed in one shot. However, peripheral circuit pattern of memory device dose not regularity, it is necessary to create the pattern. They have developed EB exposure machine to combined the cell projection method and conventional variable shaped beam method. Figure 3.36 shows the schematic diagram of EB exposure machine. The first aperture image is focused onto the second aperture. The image of the second aperture is demagnified to 1/25 and focused onto the wafer. The maximum beam size on the wafer is 5 μm square. The fabrication of an aperture plate is the one of the key technologies for the EB cell projection. Nakayama *et al.*[149] have tried to make an aperture (Fig. 3.37) from Si single crystal by LSI process technique. They have examined EB exposure by using Si aperture and obtained 0.2 μm minimum feature size SAL 601 resist pattern at 30 KV acceleration voltage. They confirmed that the number of shots was reduced from 3 × 10/10 to

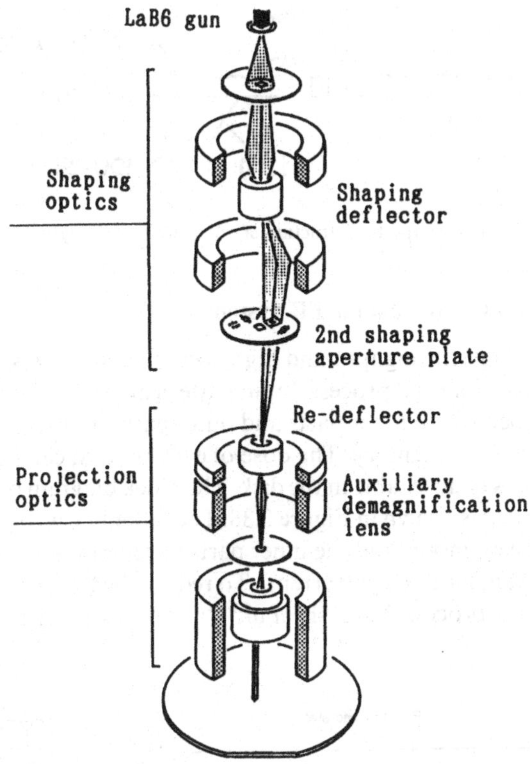

Figure 3.36 Electron optical column in cell projection EB system[143].

3 × 10/8 in the case of 64 Mbit DRAM device. Yasuda *et al.*[150] developed electron beam block exposure system in order to increase the throughput of electron beam direct writing for LSI memory devices. Electron beam is projected to a block of aperture pattern in the stencil mask to change the beam shape. Sakitani *et al.*[151] and Ito *et al.*[152] developed the EB direct-writing system, HL-800D, which adopted a cell projection method and a writing on the fly method at a variable stage speed. The HL-800d has a throughput of 20 wafers/h for a memory pattern and 11 wafers/h for logic type LSI.

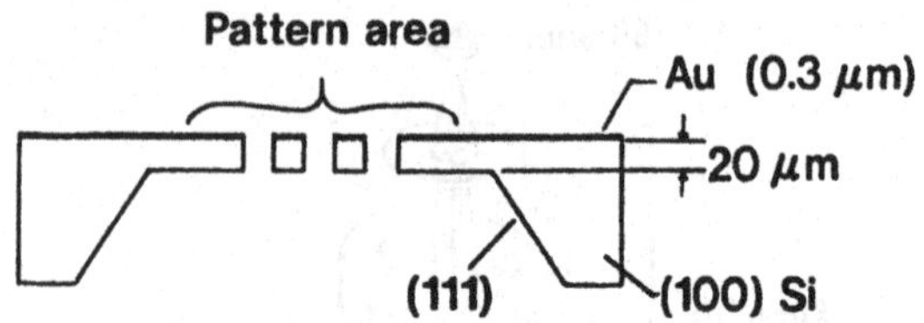

Figure 3.37 Si aperture structure of cell projection EB system[149].

3.4.1.4. Data Conversion for EB System

To achieve high throughput and high accuracy, Matsuzaka *et al.*[153] proposed pattern edge-process. Input pattern data was divided by the framing processor to inner parts and outer parts, and each data was stored in the disk memory. The dose of each pattern can be selected from 64 kinds of dose table in the disk. The block diagram of this data control system is shown in Figure 3.38. The outer line were written in the small beam mode, and the inner parts were written roughly with the large beam mode (high current). To reduce the turnaround in the mask-making process, Magoshi *et al.*[154,155] developed EB data con-

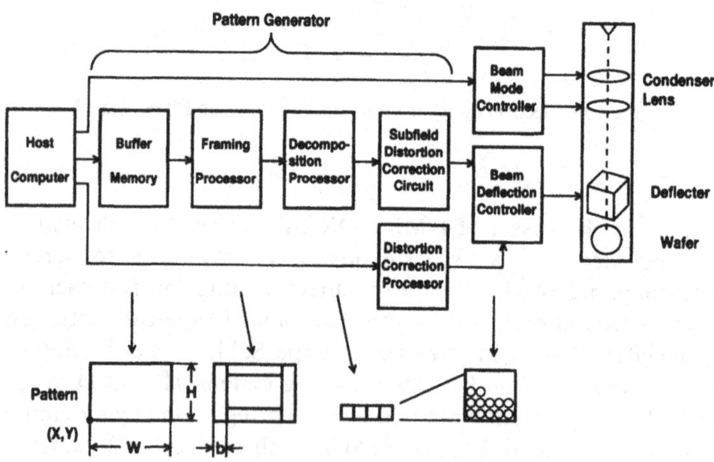

Figure 3.38 Block diagram of pattern edge-processor[153].

version system "VISHAMON" which adopted hierarchical and parallel processing methods. Proximity effect correction is one of most important key technologies in electron beam exposure lithography. This correction method was developed by Parikh[156,157,158] and Owen *et al.*[159]. However, proximity correction methods have a critical problem in that correction time fatally increases with increased integration of the LSI. Abe *et al.*[160,161,162,163] and Yamasaki *et al.*[164] proposed the representative figure method as a means of solving the problem.

This method assigned one simple figure (representative figure) within a region smaller than the backscattering range of the original pattern (Fig. 3.39). The correction calculation time for 1 Gbit DRAM model pattern was reduced to about 1/30 compared with the conventional method.

3.4.2 EB Process

3.4.2.1. Charge Effect Reduction

It was essential to avoid charging effects in EB direct writing for the sub-micron fabrication. To reduce the charge effects, many kinds of materials have been developed. Watanabe *et al.*[165,166] proposed the use of ammonium poly (*p*-styrenesulfonate) (AmSS) as charge reducing films. The pattern deviation of SNR/AmSS bilayer resist process was not found. Tono-oka *et al.*[167] found that a spincoated surfactant layer over the imaging resist can be avoid charge effects. With

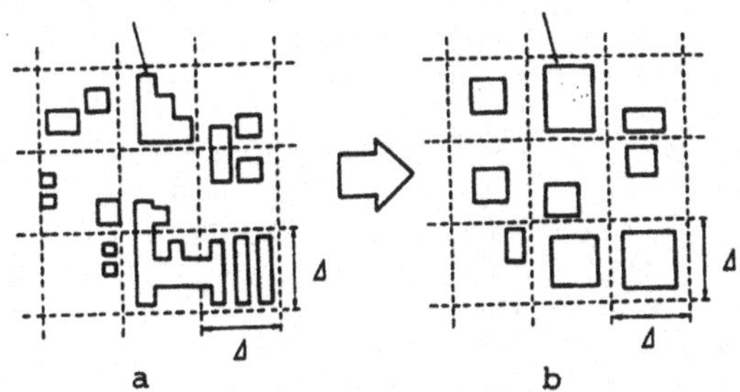

Figure 3.39 Representative figure method. a: IC pattern, b: Treated data by representative figure method[160].

optimum surfactant layer thickness, there was no influence of surfactant layer on resist sensitivity and resolution. The surfactant layer was removed in the imaging resist development process. The registration error was reduced from 1.0 μm to 0.1 μm (2σ) in the tri-level resist of 2.4 μm, containing the 0.12 μm surfactant layer. K. Yano *et al.*[168] developed a novel process of reducing the charging electron beam lithography by using a TCNQ complex and a thermal cross-linkable EB resist(CMR). The CMR developed by Kitakoji *et al.*[169] was insoluble in the solvent after crosslinking by heating at 140 to 190°C. This film can be removed during development of the resist. The steps of the process which are shown in Figure 3.40 adds one step to the conventional resist process. Figure 3.41 shows placement error due to charge formation during electron exposure.

In the case of coating the charge reducing films, the placement error was less than 0.05 μm. The film maintains its ability to reduce charge as long as the film is thicker than 0.05 μm. Hitachi and Showa-Denko group's[170] have developed novel charge reducing materials namely, self-doped organic conducting compounds, poly(alkyl sulfonylated thiophene). It is well known that poly(thiophene) compounds have good conductivity in spite of being organic com-

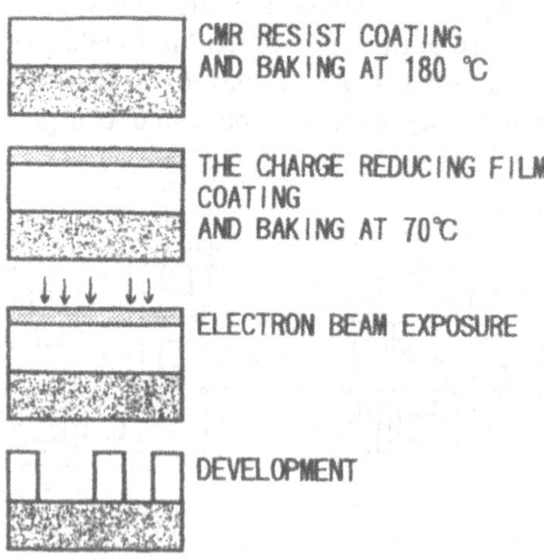

Figure 3.40 The EB process by using charge reducing films[169].

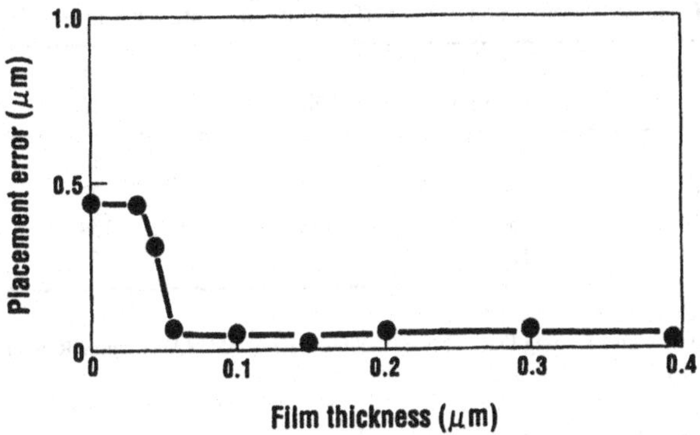

Figure 3.41 Charge reducing film thickness dependence of placement error for 2.0 μm CMR[169].

pounds. They have modified poly(thiophene) by sulfonyl moiety because of these polymer showed unsolved for the water. As a result, they succeeded in obtaining the water soluble charge reducing materials.

3.4.2.2. EB Resist

Tamura *et al.*[171] developed the new positive type electron beam resist having high sensitivity, high dry etching durability and high thermal resistivity. PMMA(poly methylmethacrylate) has a high resolution and is well known to be a standard among EB resists. However, this resist has low sensitivity and no dry etching durability. In order to improve sensitivity of EB, a-methyl groups are substituted for electron withdrawing group, such as chlorine and bromine.

Poly(trifluoroethyl-2-chloroacrylate (EBR-9) resist has high sensitivity, but dry etching durability is lower than that of PMMA resist. They have investigated the homologous series of poly(alkyl 2-cyanoacrylate). They found that dry etching durability of the PCHCA resist was 2.19 times as high as that of PMMA resist. The sensitivity was 1.7 $\mu C/cm^2$ at accelerating voltage of 20 KV, which showed the same sensitivity as poly (butene1-sulfone (PBS) resist (Tab. 3.6).

Using PCHCA resist at 3.2 $\mu C/cm^2$ dose (10 KV) for fabrication by dry etching, the chrome linewidth uniformity was 3σ of 0.034 μm, which was measured in a 11×11 array on 10 mm step. Koyanagi

Table 3.6 Comparison of the performance of positive EB resists.

EB Resist	Sensitivity ($\mu C/cm^2$)	Dry Et'g Durability	Tg (°C)
PMMA	50	1	112
PBS	1.6	0.4	72
EBR-9	1.6	0.49	134
PCHCA	1.7	2.19	152

*Accelerating Voltage: 20KV
**Relative Dry Etching Durability = (Etching Rate of PMMA)/(Etching Rate of Resist).

et al.[172] and Kihara *et al.*[173] have investigated chemically amplified type posi EB resists at same time but independently.

3.4.2.3. EB Resist Process

Matsuda *et al.*[174] have developed a new patterning technique, SIEL (Superficial Image Emphasis Lithography), which can precisely transfer a beam size to a resist and greatly improve the resolution and accuracy of EB lithography. Figure 3.42 shows a schematic of SIEL process. At first in the SIEL process, the uniform concave patterns at the superficial layer of the EB posi resist were formed by wet developing.

The concave depth was achieved by dose control for every feature size. For superficial imaging, the interproximity effect caused by scattered electron was nearly absent for thick resist (2 μm thickness).

These concave patterns were filled up and planarized with a mask material having high resistance to the resist etchant, such as silicone resin based on methylplopylsiloxane. The linewidth was defined by stopping the etchback at halfway of the concave patterns. As a result, linewidth control due to the degradation of the pattern contrast caused by the spread in the incident beam edge slope can be avoided.

They obtained 0.025 μm linewidth pattern by using 0.2 μm beam size at an accelerating voltage of 30 KV. H. Takenaka *et al.*[175] obtained 0.25 m gate electrodes of GaAs FET's by using a two-layer resist system (PMMA/PGMA: (poly (dimethylglutamide)) and lift-off process. K. Sugita *et al.*[176] investigated silylated process of EB lithography.

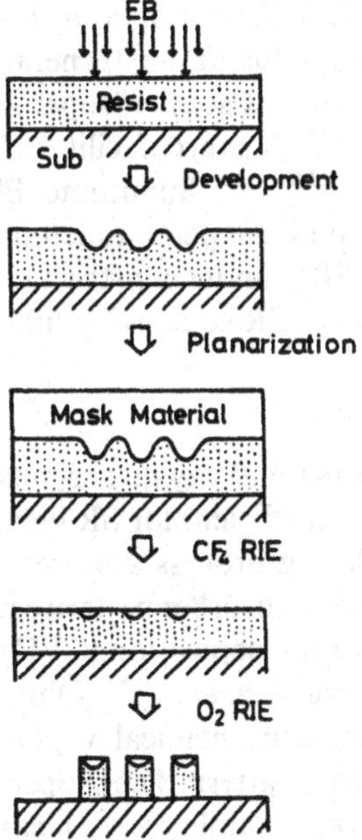

Figure 3.42 Process flow of SIEL[174].

3.5. X-ray Lithography

X-ray lithography includes many technical issues, such as construction of small SR rings, vertical stepper and X-ray mask formation. This chapter mainly outlines how these problems are beingtackled in Japan[177,178].

3.5.1 Source for X-ray Lithography

Recently, compact synchrotron radiation (SR) sources have been developed in Japan for X-ray lithography. Table 5.1 shows SR in Japan. N. Takahashi and SHI (Sumitomo Heavy Industries, Ltd.) Accelerator Research Group[179] have been developing a compact SR light source named AURORA. Takahashi *et al.*[180,181] developed the compact SR source "LUNA" (Lithography Use New Accelerator) for X-ray lithography in producing nextgeneration ULSIs. Kitayama *et al.*[182] built the compact SR source "super ALIS" at NTT is Atsugi R & D Center. The 1 GeV SR source facility at SORTEC Corporation was completed in 1989[183,184]. Sumitomo Electric Industries Ltd. (SEI) have been developing a superconducting SR, called NIJI-III[185]. An 800 MeV compact SR is under construction at Mitsubishi Electric Corp.[186]. Table 3.7 shows SR sources for lithography used in Japan.

3.5.2 X-ray Mask

A. Absorber Absorbers for X-ray masks must have low stress films with a high absorption coefficient for SR light. Gold films which are prepared by electroplating process are used for absorbers. On the other hand an X-ray mask absorber pattern embedded with W into Si grooves by chemical vapor deposition (CVD) has been reported by Chou *et al.*[187] and Mastuhashi *et al.*[188]. Ohta *et al.*[189] fabricated the X-ray mask using tungsten chemical vapor deposition (W-CVD) films for forming absorber pattern. The properties of W-CVD, such as stress, density and thermal stability were measured. They found that the stress can be minimized reproducibly to less than 1×10^8 dyn/cm^2 by controlling the flow rate of WF_6 gas and Ar gas at various substrate temperature and the films stress was thermally stable up to 200°C and the density was 18.5 g/cm^3. Yabe *et al.*[190] proposed to use the DC sputtered W-Ti film for X-ray mask absorber. They found that the stress changes from compressive to tensile with increasing pressure, the stress free W-Ti film was obtained in the region of 1.9–2.1 Pa. The W-Ti film was amorphous. Oda *et al.*[191] investigated the formation of high oriented (b-Ta, (002) plane parallel to the substrate), high purity and high density (16.5 g/cm^3) Ta films. These films were deposited by RF sputtering using Xe rather than Ar as a working gas.

B. Membrane An X-ray mask membrane is required to have high transmittance for soft X-ray, high optical transmittance for accurate alignment, no radiation damage and low tensile stress. Membrane materials developed so far are BN[192], B doped Si[193], LPCVD (low pressure chemical vapor deposition) SiN[194] and LPCVD SiC[195,196,197] and diamond[198]. Ohki *et al.*[198] fabricated the high

Table 3.7 SR in Japan.

	NIJI-III		Super ALIS	LUNA	AURORA	HITACHI	MELCOM
	ETL	SORTEC	NTT	IHI	SHI	HITACHI	MITSUBISHI
Orbit Diameter (m)	15.54	15	16.8		3.14		9.2
Electron Energy (MeV)	600	1000	600	800	650	200	800
Bending Field (T)	4		3.0	1.33	4.34		4.5
Bending Radius (m)	0.5		0.66	2/1.0	0.5	0.6	0.593
Critical Wavelength (nm)	1.2		1.73	2.18	1.02		0.7
Current (mA)	200	200	500	50	300		220
Life Time (H)		50	> 24	> 1	200		> 4
No. of Dipole	4		2		1		2
Radio Frequency (MHz)	154.3		125	178.5	190.86		130
Injection Energy (MeV)	280	40	15	45	150		20–800
Injection Type	Linac	Linac	Linac	Linac	Microtron		Synchrotron

precision X-ray mask (14 × 14 mm) with the bulk-Si etching step in the substrate process (Fig. 3.43) in order to suppress distortion caused by stress in SiN membrane and Ta absorber. A mask-to-mask overlay accuracy of 0.09 μm 3σ for 5 levels was attained with the following distortion control:

(1) The value of the stress SiN membrane must be restricted to within 10×10^4 dyn/cm^2 for Si substrate thickness of 1 mm
(2) The SiN stress should be controlled to be slightly higher than the Ta stress
(3) The Ta stress must be below 2×10^8 dyn/cm^2

They prepared the five X-ray masks with 0.1 μm minimum linewidth patterns: (1) LOCOS, (2) gate, (3) first contact, (4) second contact and (5) Al-wiring of *n*-MOS device. Pattern placement error and the distortion occurring in each process step were measured. From the results, they obtained a mask-to-mask overlay accuracy of less than 0.085 μm 3σ. However, distortions caused by the frame η mounting step showed rather large and uncontrolled values. It was found that low pressure chemical vapor deposition (LPCVD) SiN membrane has high transparency at 638 nm and easily controls stress during deposition[199].

Moreover, the damage-free X-ray mask membrane was required for more than 10^5 exposure shots. Oizumi *et al.*[200,201] investigated the radiation durability of SiN films with the LPCVD method. An SiN membrane with an oxygen concentration below 1% is found to be stable under the X-ray irradiation at a dosage of up to 5 KJ/cm^2. They discussed the damage to SiN membrane based on the results of XPS, FTIR XRD and ESR measurements. Radiation damage is brought about by Si-O bond breaking. Itoh *et al.*[202] found that the Si-N bond scission also causes pattern displacement. Arakawa *et al.*[203] investigated the X-ray irradiation damage mechanism of SiN membrane in 1 bar helium environment in which oxygen concentration was below 10 ppm. The membrane was characterized by XPS, SIMS and ESR. They concluded that the N_2^+ and HeI were prepared by SR irradiation in the He environment, and these species and SR source attacked the membrane surface and the oxygen compounds on it and/or in the environment, thereby enhancing oxidation of the membrane after excitation of the surface oxygen atoms. Kumar *et al.*[204] investigated LPCVD SiN membrane deposited in the temperature range of 900–1000 °C and achieved low tensile stress, 3–5×10^8 dyn/cm^2, and transparency of 95% at 638 nm. SiC have been investigated for X-ray mask membrane by M. Ito[205], H. Luthje[206], M. Kobayashi[207] and M. Yamada[208]. Murooka *et al.*[209] investigated the effect of the addition of HCl to chemical vapor deposited SiC membrane. Marumoto *et al.*[212] investigated the properties of a diamond film made by a hot-filament method with mixture of CH_4 and H_2.

Hasegawa *et al.*[213] reported the simulation of diamond film properties with a view to using the mask membrane for proximity low energy X-ray lithography.

3.5.3 X-ray Resist Process

3.5.3.1. X-ray Resist

Ban *et al.*[214] have developed high resolution X-ray positive resist EXP which utilizes chemical amplification driven by acid-catalyzed decomposition of a *t*-BOC dissolution inhibitor and a novolak/*t*-BOC dissolution inhibitor/triflate onium salt(bis (*p*-*t*-butylphenyl)iodonium triflate :BPIT) three component system.

The sensitivity and resolution of EXP resist were greatly influenced by PEB conditions. They obtained 0.2 μm patterns in a 1.3 μm-EXP resist thickness under the PEB at 65°C for 60 sec. The pattern width remained virtually unchanged during a three-hour holding time between exposure and PEB.

The exposure latitude for ± 10% width change for 0.2 μm holes was 10%.

3.5.3.2. X-ray Resist Process

A. Direct Engraving Process Ichimura *et al.*[215] have examined the direct removal of resist materials by X-ray irradiation as one of the dry processes.

B. Secondary Electron Effect In X-ray lithography, the effects of secondary electron from heavy metal substrates such as gold, molybdenum and tungsten have been examined by Murata *et al.*[216], Betz *et al.*[217] and Clebek *et al.*[218]. The secondary electron effects from silicon and related compounds have been examined using electron cathode type X-ray source[219]. Ogawa *et al.* investigated the effects of secondary electron from Si substrate in SR lithography. It is confirmed that secondary electrons from an Si substrate produce undercuts of 0.1 μm in depth in the replicated resist patterns. The Si KKL Auger electron was proved to be the main cause of this effect. This is ascertained through analysis of many kinds of secondary electrons. Moreover, eliminating the wavelength which excited the Si 1s electron from the exposing SR is one promising way to lessen this effect.

They estimated that the resolution of SR lithography is improved to less than 0.1 μm in the practical wavelength under minimized of the secondary electrons from substrate. Deguchi *et al.* have investigated the effects of secondary electron which were induced by photon or Auger electron[220,221,222].

K. Deguchi *et al.*[223] evaluated photo and Auger-electron scattering effects with the new contact replication method. Small pieces of X-ray absorber pattern, Ta films (0.65–0.85 μm), taken from a conventional X-ray mask, 1.5 μm thick SiN membrane, which are inlaid with positive resist, PMMA, coated on silicon wafer are used as exposure masks. The range of photo- and Auger electron scattering in lateral direction can be derived from the depth of the resist pattern undercut from the absorber pattern edge. The reasons for the penumbra shadow and Fresnel diffraction effects are neglected in the contact printing.

The depth of the undercut increases as the exposure dose increases until it gradually saturates. The relationship between the depth of the undercut and exposure dose can be approximately expressed by

$$\mathrm{Ru} = \mathrm{Rmax}\,\{1 - \mathrm{EXP}[\mathrm{K}(\mathrm{D}/\mathrm{D}_0 - 1]\} \qquad (3.1)$$

where Ru is the depth of the undercut and Rmax is the saturation value of the undercut depth. K is a constant and D is the exposure dose. The *K* value in Eq(3.1) is about 0.4. To investigate the relationship between the range of photo and Auger electron scattering and the incident X-ray wavelength, contact replication was carried out using an electron bombardment X-ray source and a plasma source.

Using an electron bombardment source with Mo rotating target, a 0.54 nm Mo-L/alpha characteristic line (2.3 KeV) contributes mainly to the exposure dose.

The plasma source radiates X-rays ranging from 0.9 to 1.4 nm (peak is 1.2 nm, 1 KeV). The K values in Eq. are about -0.8. The reason for the large K values compared with the SR source seems to be the small distribution of X-ray wavelength.

References

1. Eguchi, K. *et al.* (1988). *Proc. of SPIE* Vol. 922, 335.
2. Matsumoto, K. *et al.* (1989). *Proc. of SPIE*, Vol. 1088, 170.
3. Hirose, R. (1989). *et al.*, *Proc. of SPIE*, Vol. 1088, 178.
4. Nakamura, S. (1990). *et al.*, *Proc. of SPIE*, Vol. 1264, 84.
5. Sugiyama, S. (1988). *et al.*, *Proc. of SPIE*, Vol. 922, 318.
6. Nakase, M. *et al.* (1985). *Proc. of SPIE*, Vol. 537, 160.
7. Nakase, M. *et al.* (1987). *Proc. of SPIE*, Vol. 773, 226.
8. Sasago, N. *et al.* (1986). *IEDM Tech. Dig.*, 316.
9. Ogawa, K. *et al.* (1988). *J. Electrochem. Soc.*, Vol. 135 (9), 2347.
10. Sengupta, U. *et al.* (1990). Proc. of SPIE, Vol. 1264, 486.
11. Sandstrom, R. (1990). *Proc. of SPIE*, Vol. 1264, 505.
12. Lokai, P. *et al.* (1990). *Proc. of SPIE* Vol. 1264, 496.
13. Brimacombe, P. K. *et al.* (1990). *Proc. of SPIE*, Vol. 1088, 416.
14. Furuya, N. *et al.* (1990). *Proc. of SPIE*, Vol. 1264.
15. Saito, K. *et al.* (1989). *Proc. of* 1989 *Intern. Symp. on MicroProcess Conference*, 29.
16. Shimada, Y. *et al.* (1989). *Proc. of* 1989 *Intern. Symp. on Microprocess Conference*, 22.
17. McKee, T. (1989). *Can. J. Phys.* Vol. 63, 214.
18. Wakabayashi, O. *et al.* (1991). *Proc.of SPIE*, Vol. 1463, 617
19. Sasago, M. *et al.*, Extended Abstract, p. 561, (The 37th Spring Meeting, 1989, *The Jpn. Soc. of Appl. Phys.*)
20. Yamashita, K. *et al.*, Extended Abstract, p. 540, (The 39th Spring Meeting, 1991, *The Jpn. Soc. of Appl. Phys.*)
21. Ozaki, Y. (1990). *Proc. of* 1990 *Intern. MicroProcess Conference*, 3.
22. Mutoh, K. *et al.* (1990). *Proc. of* 1990 *Intern. MicroProcess Conference*, 19
23. Fukuda, H. *et al.* (1987). *IEEE Electron Device Lett.*, EDL-8 179.
24. Fukuda, H. *et al.* (1989). *J. Vac. Sci. Technol.*, Vol. B7 (4), 667.
25. Horiuchi, T. *et al.*, Extended Abstract, p. 294, (The 32nd Spring Meeting, 1985, *The Jpn. Soc. of Appl. Phys.*)
26. Fehrs, D. L. *et al.*, KTI Microelectronics Seminar INTERFACE '89 (*KTI Chemicals, Inc.*, San Diego, 1990) p. 217.)

27. Kamon, K. *et al.* (1991). *Proc. of* 1991 *Intern. MicroProcess Conference*, 33.
28. Shiraishi, N. *et al.* (1992). Microlithography World Vol. 1992, (7/8), 7.
29. Fukuda, H. *et al.* (1992). *Digest Papers MicroProcess* '92, 48.
30. Nakagawa, *Mitsui Petroreum Chem. Ind. Technical Review*, (1988, Des., 12)
31. Shibuya, M. Nipon Tokkyo Koho, Shyo 57–62052, 1982, and Japanese Patent number 1441789.
32. Levenson, M. D. *et al.* (1982). *IEEE Trans. Electron Devices*, ED-29, 1828.
33. Levenson, M. D. *et al.* (1984). *IEEE Trans. Electron Devices*, ED-31, 753.
34. Yamakoshi, Y. *et al.* (1986). *Appl. Opt.*, Vol. 25, (6) 928.
35. Somemura, Y. *et al.* (1992). Digest of Papers, 25.
36. Inoue, S. *et al.* (1991). Proc. of 1991 *Intern. MicroProcess Conference*, 22.
37. Watanabe, H. *et al.* (1991). Proc. of 1991 *Intern. MicroProcess Conference*, 28.
38. Hanyu, I. *et al.* (1990). *Proc. of SPIE*, Vol. 1264, 167
39. Terasawa, T. *et al.* (1989). *Proc. of SPIE*, Vol. 1088, 25.
40. Hashimoto, K. *et al.*, Extended Abstract, 474 (*The 37th Spring Meeting* 1990), *The Jpn. Soc. of Appl. Phys.*)
41. Watanabe, H. *et al.*, 474 (*The 37th Spring Meeting* 1990), *The Jpn. Soc. of Appl. Phys.*)
42. Ishiwata, N. *et al.* (1991). *Proc. of SPIE*, Vol. 1463, 423.
43. Ishiwata, N. *et al.* (1991). *Proc. of SPIE*, Vol. 1463, 423.
44. Yanagishita, Y. *et al.* (1991). *Proc. of SPIE*, Vol. 1463, 207.
45. Inoue, S. *et al.*, Proc. of 1991 *Intern. MicroProcess Conferenee*, 22, (1991)
46. Yamanaka, T. *et al.* (1990). *IEDM Technical Digest*, 477.
47. Nakagawa, K. *et al.* (1990). *IEDM Technical Digest*, 817.
48. Imai, A. *et al.*, Extended Abstract, p. 493, (The 51th Fall Meeting 1990), *The Jpn. Soc. of Appl. Phys.*)
49. Watanabe, H. *et al.* (1990). IEDM Technical Digest, 821.
50. Hanyu, I. *et al.* (1991). *Proc. of SPIE*, Vol. 1463, 595.
51. Hanabata, M. *et al.* (1988). Kobunshi Ronbunshu, Vol. 45, (10) 803.
52. Hanabata, M. *et al.* (1989). *ibid.*, Vol. 46 (12), 745.
53. Hanabata, M. *et al.* (1989). *ibid.*, Vol. 46 (12), 753.
54. Hanabata, M. *et al.* (1989). *J. Vac. Sci. Technol.*, Vol.B7 (4), 640.
55. Sugimoto, A. *et al.* (1990). *Proc. of SPIE*, Vol. 1264, 413.
56. Sugimoto, A. *et al.* (1991). *J. Vac. Sci. Technol.*, Vol. B9, (6), 2792.
57. Dill, F. H. *et al.* (1975). *IEEE Trans. Electron Device* Vol. ED-22 (7), 445.
58. Tan, S. *et al.* (1990). *Proc. of SPIE*, Vol. 1262, 513.
59. Uenishi, K. *et al.* (1991). *Proc. of SPIE*, Vol. 1466, 102.
60. Uenishi, K. *et al.* (1992). *Proc. of SPIE*, Vol. 1672, 262.
61. Sato, Y. *et al.* (1989). *Proc. of SPIE*, Vol. 1086, 352.
62. Ichikawa, S. *et al.*, Nihon Tokkyo Koho, Sho-28457, (20 June 1987)

63. Yamaoka, T. *et al.* (1990). *J. Imaging Sci.*, Vol. 34 (2), 50.
64. Nemoto, *et al.* (1992). *Proc. of SPIE*, Vol. 1672, 305.
65. Kajita, T. *et al.* (1991). *Proc. of SPIE*, Vol. 1466, 161.
66. *Proc. of* 1989 *Intern. Symp. on MicroProcess Conferenc*, 10, (1989).
67. Koseki, K. *et al.* (1988). Kobunshi Ronbunshu, Vol. 45, (3), 193.
68. Horiguchi, R. *et al.* (1990). *J. Electrochem. Soc.*, Vol. 137 (11), 3561.
69. Kudo, K. *et al.* (1990). *Proc. of* 1990 *Intern. Microprocess Conference*, 23.
70. Kajimoto, Y. *et al.* (1992). *Proc. of SPIE*, Vol. 1672, 66.
71. Ito, H. *et al.* (1984). ACS Symposium Series, 242, 11.
72. Kawai, Y. *et al.* (1992). Digest of Papers Microprocess '92, 76.
73. Smith, G. H. *et al* U. S. Patent 1973, 3,3779,778.
74. Hayashi, N. *et al.* (1989). *Proc. of* 1989 *Intern. Symp. on MicroProcess Conference*, 186.
75. Hayashi, N. *et al.* (1992). *Abstracts of Intern. MicroProcess Conference*, 74.
76. Ito, H. *et al.* (1988). *J. Electrochem. Soc.*, Vol. 135, 2322.
77. Shiraishi, H. *et al.* (1991). *J. Vac. Sci. Technol.*, Vol. B9, 3343.
78. Hayashi, N. *et al.* (1991). *Proc. of SPIE*, Vol. 1466, 377.
79. Hayashi, N. *et al.* (1991). DENKIKAGAKU, Vol. 59, 1027.
80. Tani, Y. *et al.* (1992). Digest of Papers MicroProcess '92, 78.
81. Onishi, Y. *et al.* (1992). *J. Photopolymer Sci. and Tech.*, Vol. 5 (1), 47.
82. Hayase, R. *et al.* (1993). *J. Photopolymer Sci. and Tech.*, Vol. 6 (4), 495.
83. Buhr, G. *et al.* (1989). *Proc. of SPIE*, Vol. 1086, 117.
84. Kobayashi, E. *et al.* (1992). *Proc. Amer. Chem. Soc.*, Vol. 66, 47.
85. Tada, *et al.*, Extended Abstract, p. 752, (The 38th Spring Meeting, 1990, *The Jpn. Soc. of Appl. Phys.*)
86. Oie, M. *et al.*, Extended Abstract, p. 575, (The 39th Spring Meeting, 1991, *The Jpn. Soc. of Appl. Phys.*)
87. Nakamura, J. *et al.* (1991). *Jpn. J. Appl. Phys.*, Vol. 30 (10), 2619.
88. Nakamura, J. *et al.* (1992). *Jpn. J. Appl. Phys.*, Vol. 31 (12), XX.
89. Ban, H. *et al.* (1991). *J. Vac. Sci. Technol.*, Vol. B9, (6), 3387.
90. Asakawa, K. (1993). *J. Photopolymer Sci. and Tech.*, Vol. 6 (4), 505.
91. Yoshino, H. *et al.* (1992). *Abstract of MicroProcess Conference*, 1992, 82.
92. Nakamura, J. *et al.* (1991). *J. Photopolym. Sci. and Technol.*, Vol. 4, (1).
93. MacDonald, S. A. *et al. Abstract of SPIE's Symposium on Microlithography* p. 180 (3–8 March 1991 San Jose)
94. Naramasu, O. *et al.* (1991). *J. Photopolymer Sci. Technol.*, Vol. 4, 299.
95. Mori, S. *et al.* (1993). *J. Photopolymer Sci. and Tech.*, Vol. 6, (4), 563
96. Kumada, T. *et al.* (1993). *J. Photopolymer Sci. and Tech.*, Vol. 6 (4), 571
97. Endo, M. *et al.* (1988). Kobunshi Ronbunshu, Vol. 45 (10), 771.
98. Kudo, T. *et al.* (1986). *Appl. Phys. Lett.*, Vol. 49, 298.
99. Kudo, T. *et al.* (1987). *J. Electrochem. Soc.*, Vol. 134, 2607.
100. Ishikawa, A. *et al.* (1989). *Proc. of SPIE*, Vol. 1086, 180.
101. Ishikawa, M. *et al.* (1984). *J. Polym. Sci. Polym. Lett.*, Vol. 22, 669.

102. Nate, K. *et al.* (1987). *J. Appl. Polym. Sci.*, Vol. 34, 2445.
103. Tomura, M. *et al.* (1987). *J. Electrochem. Soc.*, Vol. 134, (4), 936.
104. Ueno, T. *et al* (1985). *Proc.of the 4th Technical Conference on Photopolymers in Japan*, 107.
105. Hayashi, N. *et al.*, *Am. Chem. Symp. Ser.*,
106. Tanaka, A. *et al.* (1989). *J. Vac. Sci. Technol.*, Vol. B7, (3), 572.
107. Tanaka, A. *et al.* (1989). *Proc. of 1989 Intern. Symp. on MicroProcess Conference*, 156.
108. Imamura, S. *et al.* (1988). *Proc. of SPIE*, Vol. 920, 291.
109. Kawamura, E. *et al.* (1987). *Proc. of SPIE*, Vol. 773, 89.
110. Coopman, F. *et al.* (1986). *Proc. of SPIE*, Vol. 631, 34.
111. Takehara, D. *et al.* (1990). *Proc. of 1990 Intern. MicroProcess Conference*, 9.
112. Yamashita, Y. *et al.* (1985) *J. Vac. Sci. Technol.*, Vol. B3, (1), 314.
113. Griffing, B. F. and West, P. R. (1983). *IEEE Electron Device Let.*, EDL 4, 14.
114. Niki, H. *et al.* (1985). Extend. Abs. of the 17th Conf. on Sold State Devices and Materials, 361.
115. Dill, H. F., Hornberger, W. P., Hauge, P. S. and Shaw, J. M., (1975). *IEEE Trans. ED*, Vol. ED-22, 445.
116. Endo, M. *et al.* (1988). *J.Vac. Sci. Technol.*, Vol. B6 (2), 559.
117. Endo, M. *et al.* (1988). *J.Vac. Sci. Technol.*, Vol. B6 (5), 1600.
118. Endo, M. *et al.* (1989). *J.Vac. Sci. Technol.*, Vol. B7 (3), 565.
119. Endo, M. *et al.* (1988). Kobunshi Ronbunshu, Vol. 45 (3), 245.
120. Walker, E. J. *et al.* (1975) *IEEE Trans. Electron Device*, Vol. ED-22 (7), 464.
121. Ogawa, S. *et al.*, Extended Abstract, p. 536, (The 35th Spring Meeting, 1988, *The Jpn. Soc. of Appl. Phys.*)
122. Okada, Y. *et al.* (1987). *Proc. of SPIE*, Vol. 771, 61.
123. Endo, M. *et al.*, Extended Abstract, p. 509, (The 35th Spring Meeting, 1988, *The Jpn. Soc. of Appl. Phys.*)
124. Yamaguchi, A. *et al.* (1989). *Jpn. J. Appl. Phys.*, Vol. 28, 2110.
125. Kishimura, S. *et al.* (1988). *J. Photopolymer Sci.*, Vol. 1, (1) 104.
126. Yamaguchi, A. *et al.* (1991). *Jpn. J. Appl. Phys.*, Vol. 30, (1) 195.
127. Shimada, M. *et al.*, *VLSI Symposium, Abstract, July*, 1992, Seattle.
128. Minamiyama, T. *et al.* (1992). *Jpn. J. Appl. Phys.* Vol. 31, 1928.
129. Tsuda, M. *et al.* (1981). *J. Vac. Sci. Technol.*, Vol. 19 (4), 13.
130. Butherus, A. *et al.* (1985). *J. Vac. Sci. Technol.*, Vol. B3 (5), 1352.
131. Ito, S. *et al.* (1989). *Proc. Symposium VLSI Sci. and Tech.*, Vol. 89, 539.
132. Oikawa, A. *et al.* (1990) *J. Electrochem. Soc.*, Vol. 137 (10), 3223.
133. Gokan, H. *et al.* (1988) *J. Electrochem. Soc.*, Vol. 135 (4), 1019.
134. Tanaka, T. *et al.* (1990). *J. Electrochem. Soc.*, Vol. 139 (12), 1390.
135. Tanaka, N. *et al.*, Extended Abstract, p. 293, (The 32nd Spring Meeting, 1985, *The Jpn. Soc. of Appl. Phys.*)
136. Koizumi, T. *et al.* (1992). Digest of Papers MicroProcess '92, 64.

137. Matsuzaka, T. *et al.* (1987). *Proc. of SPIE*, Vol. 773, 234.
138. Ohyama, M. *et al.* (1988). *Proc. of SPIE*, Vol. 923, 246.
139. Hassel, M. *et al.* (1988). *Proc. of SPIE*, Vol. 923, 290.
140. Sakitani, Y. *et al.* (1983). *Hitachi Hyoron*, 65, (7).
141. Nakamura, K. *et al.* (1985). *J. Vac. Sci and Technol.*, Vol. B3, (1), 94
142. Nakamura, K. *et al.* (1986). *Hitachi Hyoron*, 9, (11).
143. Hattori, H. *et al.* (1989). *Proc. of 1989 Intern. Symp. on MicroProcess Conference*, 59.
144. Hattori, K. *et al.* (1987). *Extended Abst. of the 19th SSDM*, 287.
145. Tamamushi, S. *et al.* (1988). *J. Vac. Sci and Technol.*, Vol. B6 (1), 209.
146. Goto, M. *et al.* (1985). *J. Vac. Sci. and Technol.*, Vol. B3 (1), 181.
147. Yoshikawa, R. *et al.* (1987). *J. Vac. Sci. and Technol.*, Vol. B8, (1), 70.
148. Nakayama, Y. *et al.* (1990). *J. Vac. Sci. and Technol.*, Vol. B8, 1836.
149. Saito, N. *et al.* (1990). *Proc. of 1990 Intern. MicroProcess Conference*, 44.
150. Yasuda, H. *et al.* (1991). *Proc. of 1991 Intern. MicroProcess Conference*, 133.
151. Sakitani, Y. *et al.* (1992). *J. Vac. Sci. and* Technol., Vol. B10 (6), 2759.
152. Ito, H. *et al.* (1992). *J. Vac. Sci. and Technol.*, Vol. B10 (6), 2799.
153. Matsuzaka, T. *et al.* (1987). *Proc. of SPIE*, Vol. 773, 234.
154. Koyama, K. *et al.* (1989). *Proc. of 1989 Intern. MicoProcess Conference 64*.
155. Magoshi, S. *et al.* (1992). Digests of Paper MicroProcess '92, 128.
156. Parikh, M. (1979). *J. Appl. Phys.*, Vol. 50, 4371.
157. Parikh, M. (1979). *J. Appl. Phys.*, Vol. 50, 4378.
158. Parikh, M. (1979). *J. Appl. Phys.*, Vol. 50, 4383.
159. Owen, G. *et al.* (1983). *J. Appl. Phys.*, Vol. 54, 3573.
160. Abe, T. *et al.* (1992). *TOSHIBA Rev.*, Vol. 47 (5), 431.
161. Abe, T. *et al.* (1991). *Jpn. J. Appl. Phys.*, Vol. 30, L528.
162. Abe, T. *et al.* (1991). *Jpn. J. Appl, Phys.*, Vol. 30, 2965.
163. Abe, T. *et al.* (1991). *J. Vac. Sci and Tech.*, Vol. B9, 3059.
164. Yamasaki, S. *et al.* (1991). *Jpn. J. Appl. Phys.*, Vol. 30, 3103.
165. Watanabe, *et al.*, Extended Abstract, p. 437, (The Fall Meeting, 1987, *The Jpn. Soc. of Appl. Phys.*)
166. Watanabe, *et al.*, Extended Abstract, p. 552, (The 35th Spring Meeting, 1988, *The Jpn. Soc. of Appl. Phys.*)
167. Tono-oka, Y. *et al.* (1990). *Proc. of SPIE*, Vol. 1263, 199.
168. *Proc. of 1990 MicroProcess Conference*, 147.
169. Kitakoji, T. *et al.* (1979). *J. Electrochem. Soc.*, Vol. 126 (11), 1181.
170. Murai, F. *et al.* (1990). 3rd MicroProcess Conference, 172.
171. Tamura, A. *et al.* (1991). *Proc. of SPIE*, Vol. 1465, 271.
172. Koyanagi, H. *et al.* (1992). *Proc. of SPIE*, Vol. 1672, 126.
173. Kihara, N. *et al.* (1992). *Proc. of SPIE*, Vol. 1672, 194.
174. Matsuda, T. *et al.* (1985). *Appl. Phys. Lett.* Vol. 47 (2), 123.
175. Takenaka, H. *et al.* (1989). *Proc. of SPIE*, Vol. 1089, 132.
176. Sugita, K. *et al.* (1992). *J. Electrochem. Soc.*, Vol. 139, (3), 802.

177. Wilson, M. N. (1992). *Rev. Sci. Instrum.*, Vol. 63 (1), 707.
178. Tomimasu, T. (1992). *Rev. Sci. Instrum.*, Vol.63 (1), 722.
179. Takahashi, N. *et al.* (1988). *Proc. of SPIE*, Vol. 923, 47.
180. Takahashi, M. *et al.* (1992). *Rev. Sci. Instrum.*, Vol. 63 (1), 767.
181. Mandai, S. *et al.* (1989). *Rev. Sci Instrum.*, Vol. 60, 1759.
182. Kitayama, T. *et al.* (1989). *Proc. of SPIE*, Vol. 1089, 159.
183. Kodaira, M. *et al.* (1991). *Proc. of 1991 Intern. MicroProcess Conference*, 71.
184. Awaji, N. *et al.* (1992). *Rev. Sci. Instrum.* Vol. 63 (1), 745.
185. Emura, K. *et al.* (1992). *Rev. Sci. Instrum.*, Vol. 63 (1), 753.
186. Nakanishi, T. *et al.* (1992). *Rev. Sci. Instrum.* Vol. 63 (1), 770.
187. Chou, S. Y. *et al.* (1988). *J. Vac. Sci and Technol.*, Vol. B6, 2202.
188. Mastuhashi, H. *et al.* (1989). *Jpn. J. Appl. Phys.*, Vol. 28, L2309.
189. Ohta, T. *et al.* (1990). *Proc. of 1990 Intern. MicroProcess Conference*, 78.
190. Yabe, H. *et al.* (1992). *Digest of Papers MicroProcess* '92, 14.
191. Oda, M. *et al.* (1990). *Proc. of 1990 Intern. MicroProcess Conference*, 96.
192. Dana, S. S. *et al.* (1986). *J. Vac. Sci. and Technol.*, Vol. B4, 235.
193. Smith, H. I. *et al.* (1973). *J. Vac. Sci. and Technol.*, Vol. 10, 913.
194. Sekimoto, M. *et al.* (1982). *J. Vac. Sci. and Technol.*, Vol. 21, 1017.
195. Yamada, M. *et al.* (1990). *J. Electrochem. Soc.*, Vol. 137, 2231.
196. Luthje, H. *et al.* (1989). *Jpn. J. Appl. Phys.* Vol. 28, 2342.
197. Kobayashi, M. *et al.* (1990). *Microelectronic Eng.*, Vol. 11, 237.
198. Ohki, S. *et al.* (1990). *Proc. of 1990 Intern. MicroProcess Conference*, 68.
199. Sekimoto *et al.* (1982). *J. Vac. Sci and Technol.*, Vol. 21 (4), 1017.
200. Oizumi, H. *et al.* (1990). *Proc. of 1990 Intern. MicroProcess Conference*, 82.
201. Oizumi, H. *et al.* (1990). *Jpn. J. Appl. Phys.*, Vol. 29, 2600.
202. Itoh, M. *et al.* (1991). *J. Vac. Sci. and Technol.*, Vol. B9, 3262.
203. Arakawa, T. *et al.* (1992). *Digest of Papers MIcroProcess* '92, 22.
204. Kumar, R. *et al.* (1992). *Digest Papers, MicroProcess* '92, 10.
205. Ito, M. *et al.* (1991). *J. Vac. Sci. and Technol.*, Vol. B6.
206. Luthje, H. *et al.* (1989). *Jpn. J. Appl. Phys.* Vol. 28, 2342.
207. Kobayashi, M. *et al.* (1990). *Microelectronic Eng.*, Vol. 11, 237.
208. Yamada, M. *et al.* (1990). *J. Electrochem. Soc.*, Vol. 137, 2231.
209. Murooka, K. *et al.* (1991). *Proc. of 1991 Intern. MicroProcess Conference*, 107.
210. Yamashiro, K. *et al.* (1991). *Proc. of 1991 Intern. MicroProcess Conference*, 111.
211. Widischman, H. *et al.* (1990). *J. Appl. Phys.*, Vol. 68, 5665.
212. Marumoto, K. *et al.* (1992). *Digest Papers MicroProcess* '92, 12.
213. Hasegawa, S. *et al.* (1991). *Proc. of SPIE*, Vol. 1465, 145.
214. Ban, H. *et al.* (1991). *J. Vac. Sci. Technol.*, Vol. B9 (6), 3387.
215. Ichimura, S. *et al.* (1983). *J. Vac. Sci. Technol.*, Vol. B1 (4), 1076.
216. Murata, K. *et al.* (1985). *IEEE Trans. Electron Devices*, ED32, (9), 1694.
217. Betz, H. *et al.* (1986). *J. Vac. Sci. Technol.*, Vol. B4, (1), 248.

218. Clebek, J. *et al.* (1987). *Microelectron Eng.*, Vol. 6, 221.
219. Tischer, P. (1987). *Proc. 8th Int. Conf. Electron and Ion Beams Science and Technol.*, 444.
220. Deguchi, K. *et al.* (1987). *J. Vac. Sci. Technol.*, Vol. B5, 551.
221. Deguchi, K. *et al.* (1990). *Jpn. J. Appl. Phys.*, Vol. 29 (10), 2207.
222. Somemura, Y. *et al.* (1992). *Jpn. J. Apply. Phys.*, Vol. 31, 938.
223. Deguchi, K. *et al.* (1990). *Proc. of 1990 Intern. MicroProcess Conference*, 100.

CHAPTER 4

Dry Etching

4.1. Introduction

In the last decade, many new etch technologies have originated from Japanese semiconductor companies. Several of the more important of these technologies are discussed in this chapter. These new technologies are and will be utilized in the production of the ULSI devices up to the 1 gigabit DRAM era. In this chapter, basic etching hardware and process technologies developed in Japan during the past 20 years, and now in widespread use in production lines around the world, are introduced first. These technologies are downstream etching, magnetron RIE and electron cyclotron resonance (ECR) plasma etching. Then, process technologies realized for the magnetron and the ECR systems are discussed. Recent research and development trends respecting etching technologies in Japan are introduced in the last section.

4.2. Basic Etching Hardware and Process Technologies

4.2.1. Downflow Etching

Dry etching technologies employing a low temperature plasma have been rapidly introduced into LSI production lines in the last 20 years, because wet chemical etching processes do not allow fine line engraving to be reproducibly obtained. In particular, reactive ion etching (RIE)[1], utilizing energetic ion bombardment, realized the directional etching feature, and strongly promoted the shrinkage of minimum device feature size. The charged particle bombardment, however, involves the generation of serious radiation damage such as gate oxide breakdown[2].

At the other extreme of dry etching technologies, downflow etching[3], a process carried out using only neutral species, has been used in

LSI manufacturing. Since the etching feature is usually isotropic, downflow etching is not applicable to the engraving of finer patterns. The process, however, is much milder than RIE, making it possible to etch various materials without any radiative damage. Because of this great advantage, downflow etching is attracting renewed interest among LSI manufacturers, and its concept is now being applied to other wafer processing[4-7]. This section shows recent progress in the downflow etching technology.

Reactor Configuration

Figure 4.1 shows a layout diagram of a downflow reactor, which is called a chemical dry etching system (CDE)[8]. The reactor is located far from a discharge tube where a 2.45 GHz microwave is introduced. The wafers are chemically etched by transported long-lived species such as fluorine atoms. Since the charged particle bombardment and the UV light irradiation are eliminated from the reaction chamber, the wafers do not suffer any radiative damage.

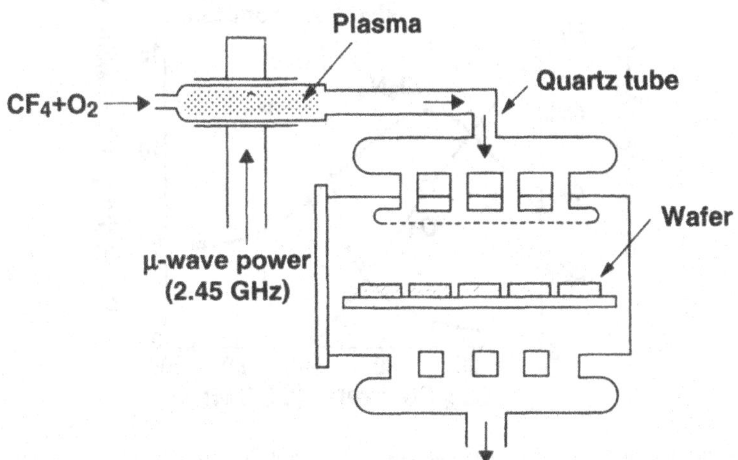

Figure 4.1 Layout diagram of a downflow reactor.

Highly Selective Si_3N_4 Removal on Thin SiO_2 Film

Si_3N_4 is used as a mask material for local oxidation of silicon, LOCOS[9], in LSI manufacturing. Since the underlying SiO_2 film thickness becomes thin to minimize bird's beak length, Si_3N_4 has to be removed with high selectivity to the underlying SiO_2 film. Otherwise, the weakened or thin portion of SiO_2 at the bird's beak corner was etched first by fluorine atoms, which cause the underlying Si substrate etching. This requirement was achieved employing fluorine and chlorine chemistry.

Figure 4.2 shows Si_3N_4 and SiO_2 etch rates as a function of Cl_2 flow rate, where NF_3 flow rate was kept at 30 sccm. SiO_2 etch rate decreases monotonically with increasing Cl_2 flow rate, and becomes zero at 60 sccm Cl_2 flow rate. On the other hand, Si_3N_4 was etched at higher rate even at the high Cl_2 concentration. As a result, the etch rate ratio for Si_3N_4 to SiO_2 becomes high. By adding Cl_2 to NF_3, most fluorine atoms are rapidly converted to interhalogen molecules, FCl, by titration reaction with Cl_2 in the gas phase[10]. The FCl etches

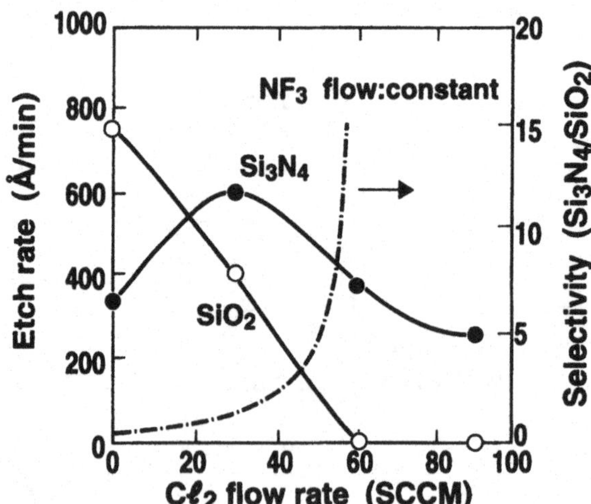

Figure 4.2 Si_3N_4 and SiO_2 etch rates as a function of Cl_2 flow rate, where NF_3 flow rate was kept at 30 sccm (Ref. 4. Hayasaka, *et al.*, Solid State Techonology/April (1988) p. 127).

Si_3N_4, whose chemical bond property is closer to that of Si than SiO_2, while FCl does not react with SiO_2 without any radiative irradiations[11]. Consequently, the infinite selectivity allows Si_3N_4 removal with no Si substrate damage.

Residue-Free Resist Ashing

An O_2 plasma ashing technique employing a barrel reactor has been used to remove the photoresist after RIE or ion implantation. However, the problem of persistent resist-residue in the LSI production line often occurs. It was found to be possible to solve this resist-residue problem by a reaction of fluorine atoms with water vapor[12]. During the reaction of resist surface with oxygen atoms, the inner part of the resist is baked by the heat of reaction[13]. As a result, crosslink reactions such as ester formation occured as oxidation of novolac resins in the posi-type photoresist takes place to produce large molecules. These crosslinked molecules exhibit strong resistivity for the oxidation and remain as persistent residue. The rapid reaction of F and water vapor produces hydrogen fluoride and active oxygen that ashes the resist.

$$2F + H_2O \rightarrow 2HF + O$$

In this ashing technique, fluorine atoms react with resist polymer to extract hydrogen atoms, making the resist polymer weaken and ashed effectively with sufficient oxygen atoms. It was found that the resist after aluminum RIE was etched perfectly at a high rate. However, SiO_2 was not etched at all.

Smoothing Rough Surface

Figure 4.3 shows Si etch rate as a function of O_2 to CF_4 flow rate ratio[14]. Oxide (oxyfluoride) film thickness formed on the Si surface in the course of the etch reaction was also shown. The Si etching with fluorine atoms is clearly suppressed by a large amount of O_2 addition. At the high O_2 flow rate, the etching products are oxidized in the gas phase to form low volatile oxyfluoride. The oxyfluoride is redeposited on the surface, and seems to limit the etching reaction of Si with fluorine atoms.

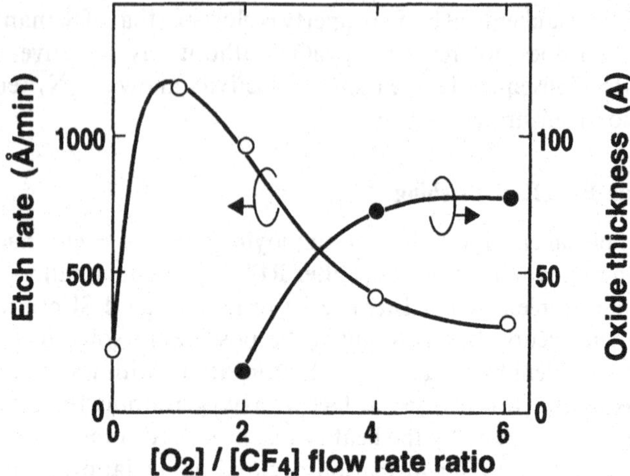

Figure 4.3 Si etch rate and oxide film thickness formed in the course of the etch reaction as a function of O_2 to CF_4 flow rate ratio (Ref. 14).

Generally, the equilibrium vapor pressure for gas phase species is low at a corner with negative curvature, as compared to that with a positive curvature[15]. The oxyfluoride condensed preferentially at the dimpled plane on the rough surface. Consequently, the etching proceeds quickly at a corner with positive curvature along with increasing time, leading to the smoothing of a rough surface. This process can be applied to smooth a rough sidewall of Si trench, and it also can round off a bottom corner with negative curvature.

Future Trend for Downflow Process

In future LSI manufacturing, the downflow process with no radiative irradiation will be used as a damage-free surface treatment such as cleaning, because extremely clean and perfectly controlled surfaces are necessary to produce LSI devices. On the other hand, the energetic beam irradiation, whose energy is minimum where the beam-assisted chemical reaction occurs, enables realization of a directional process much milder than RIE[16]. However, beyond such aspects of practical use, the concept of separated system should be incorporated further in the field of plasma chemistry as simplified research tool.

A more precise understanding of complex phenomena in the plasma is the key for realizing breakthrough processes in nanometer-order precision etch technologies.

4.2.2. Magnetron RIE

High selectivity and critical dimension control are required in dry etch applications for submicron rule devices. High density plasma operated at low pressure is expected to meet these requirements. In the next two sections, we discuss the high density plasma etcher employing a magnetron discharge and an electron cyclotron resonance plasma. Japanese semiconductor manufacturers conceived these systems almost 20 years ago and have subsequently improved them. Recent progress of these two systems is reviewed in following sections.

Magnetron RIE systems which can generate plasma in the $< 10^{-2}$ Torr gas pressure range are promising production tools for etch processes in the near future. These systems have demonstrated high selectivity[17,18] with minimal microloading effects[19]. However, most magnetron etch systems have inherent plasma density non-uniformity due to $\mathbf{E} \times \mathbf{B}$ drift of electrons, which may lead to gate oxide breakdown[20]. It has been reported that gate oxide breakdown is caused by selfbias voltage (Vdc) non-uniformities across the wafer[21].

A new high density plasma system using a dipole-ring magnet (DRM) have been developed to minimize gate oxide degradations[22]. Uniform parallel magnetic fields up to 600 Gauss have been obtained with uniformity extending over an area 300 mm in diameter. A plasma magnetized with the DRM was investigated using gate oxide degradation related to Vdc distribution across the wafer.

Figure 4.4 shows a schematic top view of the DRM configuration. The permanent magnet elements which are made of Nd-Fe-B alloy plates with 300 mm height are assembled in a circle. Each magnet element has a specific magnetized direction and the unidirectional magnetic fields are formed inside the DRM[23]. Except for the magnet assembly, the reactor configuration is similar to the conventional magnetron etcher[18,19,22]. Figure 4.5 shows the magnetic field distributions of a conventional planar shaped magnet (120 Gauss) employed in a magnetron RIE system and of a DRM designed to provide 200 Gauss magnetic field. In the DRM, uniform parallel

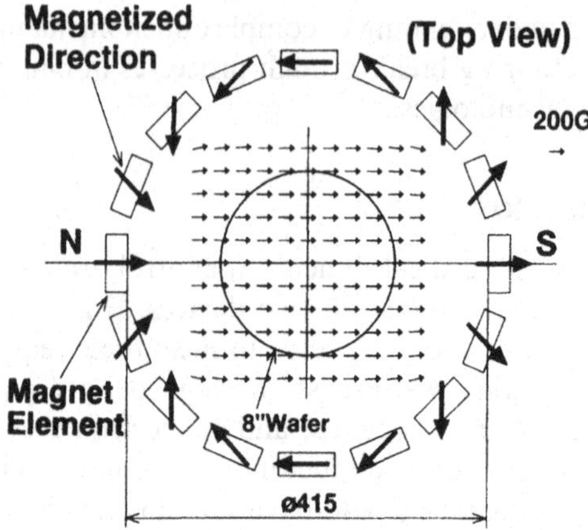

Figure 4.4 A schematic top view of the DRM (dipole-ring magnet) configuration. (Ref. 22 M. Sekine *et al.*, Proc. 14th Symp. Dry Process, Tokyo, 1991 (*Inst. Electr. Eng. Jpn.* Tokyo, 1991) p.99).

magnetic fields of 200 Gauss within ± 5% deviation were measured, with uniform region 250 mm in diameter, as indicated in Figure 4.5(c). The specific arrangement of the magnet elements realizes good uniformity and high magnetic field, and also low magnetic fields outside the DRM.

The planar magnet provided almost parallel magnetic fields except at the wafer edge (Fig. 4.5 (a)), and showed a magnetic field magnitude gradient toward the wafer edge near the N and the S poles, as shown in Figure 4.5 (c). Therefore, the planar magnet forms a mirror field that could confine the electrons in the central portion of the reactor. This plasma confinement is supposed to be one of the reasons for poor etch rate uniformity of the conventional magnetron RIE system without the magnet rotation.

The Vdc distribution across the wafer along the two axes of north (N) to south (S) and east (E) to west (W), as shown in the inset of Figure 4.6, was measured in order to confirm the effects of the uniform parallel magnetic fields, since the nonuniformity of the surface potential causes the gate oxide degradation. Figure 4.6 show the Vdc distributions for the plasmas with the planar magnet and the DRM, respectively. The value of Vdc at the E position was more than 50

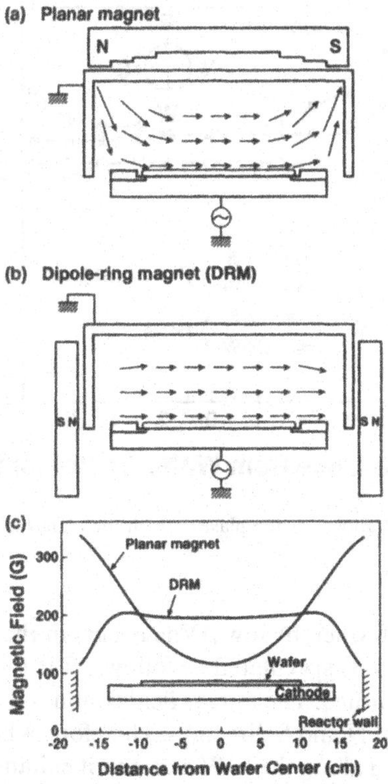

Figure 4.5 Magnetic field distributions for (a) a conventional planar shaped magnet (120 Gauss) employed in a magnetron RIE system and (b) a DRM designed to provide 200 Gauss magnetic field, and (c) magnitude of magnetic fields. (Ref. 22).

V higher than that at the $\overline{\text{W}}$ position for the planar magnet. The maximum Vdc was observed at the east portion. The $\mathbf{E} \times \mathbf{B}$ drift seems to cause non-uniformities in the Vdc along the E-W axis.

For the DRM, the Vdc difference (ΔVdc) between E and W portions was 6.5 V. This difference of Vdc distribution explains why the DRM could reduce gate oxide degradations. The uniform parallel magnetic fields of the DRM do not completely eliminate non-uniformities of the plasma caused by $\mathbf{E} \times \mathbf{B}$ drift. They, however, minimize ΔVdc sufficiently to avoid the damage.

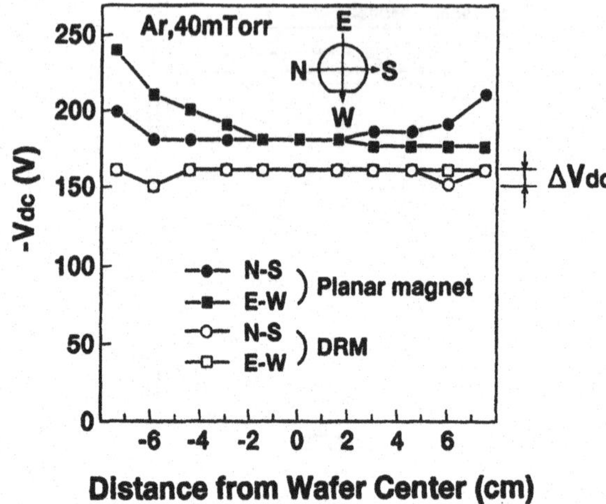

Figure 4.6 Vdc distributions for the plasmas with the planar magnet and the DRM (Ref. 22).

The mechanism whereby low ΔVdc occurs in the DRM plasma is still unknown. It was speculated as follows. For the planar magnet, a mirror field is formed. The mirror field confines the plasma toward the E-W axis from N and S direction. Therefore, a big stream of drift electrons is formed along the E-W axis and it enhances the difference of the plasma density between the E and the W portions. On the other hand, the uniform magnitude of the field in the DRM does not form a mirror field like the planar magnet, and therefore, no plasma confinement occurs. The uniform parallel field would help the electrons to escape to the reactor wall from the higher density plasma region and reduce the plasma density in the W portion. This might facilitate reduction of ΔVdc.

Gate Oxide Degradation Estimate

The gate oxide breakdown was examined using capacitors with an 8-nm thick gate oxide film. The gate electrode was heavily phosphorous doped (n^+) polycrystalline Si (poly-Si) with a thickness of 300 nm. The poly-Si gate was already patterned using chemical dry etching (CDE)[3] without gate oxide degradation due to charged particles. The active thin oxide area was 3×10^{-5} mm^2 and the poly-Si gate covering the whole area of thin oxide was 10 mm^2. Antenna ratio which is defined as the ratio of the gate electrode exposed to plasma to the thin gate oxide area is 3.3×10^5. The sample was exposed to CF_4 plasma at 40 mTorr and RF power density of 2.7 W/cm^2 for 30 sec. Under these conditions, the intention was to estimate the damage during overetching for a process of a via hole etch through an interlayer thick oxide film. After the plasma exposure, a rump voltage test was carried out to check the oxide breakdown. A time-dependent dielectric breakdown (TDDB) test with a constant current stress of 0.01 A/cm^2 was performed for reliability estimations.

The gate oxide breakdown test results for the planar magnet and the DRM are as follows. The magnets were stationary in order to observe the relation of the breakdown and the magnetic bearings. Some breakdowns were observed in the E portion of the wafer for the planar magnet. It is known that gate oxide breakdown is caused by charging due to Vdc non-uniformities across the wafer[6]. The gate oxide breakdown is very sensitive to whether the gate electrode is exposed to the plasma directly and to the antenna ratio. Thus, even with the planar magnet, no gate oxide breakdown was observed for the samples with resist masks over gate electrodes and also for the samples with the antenna ratio below 3×10^4. Furthermore, the antenna ratio of 3×10^5 is two orders of magnitude higher than that for real devices.

On the contrary, no gate oxide breakdown is observed for the system with the DRM. This indicates that the uniform parallel magnetic fields of the DRM minimize Vdc non-uniformities across the wafer and reduce the breakdown damages. A TDDB measurement was also carried out to determine the long-term oxide reliability for the capacitors after the plasma exposures. A reduced gate oxide lifetime was observed for the planar magnet system. There was no observation of lifetime reduction in the case of the DRM. These results indicate that the DRM field realizes lower stress on gate oxide.

To summarize: a high density plasma etching system using DRM has been developed. The uniform parallel magnetic fields of the DRM can generate uniform Vdc distributions across the wafer, which minimizes gate oxide degradation. Higher magnetic fields can enhance the Si etch rate. The DRM's uniform high density plasma makes it an excellent tools for processes requiring high etch rate, high selectivity and precise width control.

4.2.3. Electron Cyclotron Resonance (ECR) Plasma Etching

Two plasma etching methods using microwave excitation were proposed around 20 years ago. One was the CDE mentioned in section 4.2.1. The other was low pressure plasma etching utilizing not only neutral species but also ion bombardments for extreme fine pitch patterning. It is called ECR plasma etching[24,25] or microwave plasma etching[26].

Figure 4.7 shows a schematic of an ECR plasma etching system with optimized complex coils. 2.45 GHz microwave generated in a magnetron resonator is introduced into an etching reactor where a magnetic field of around 875 Gauss is applied by a coil set around the reactor. Electrons in a gaseous discharge move along the electric field of the microwave. Applying the 875 Gauss results in the electron

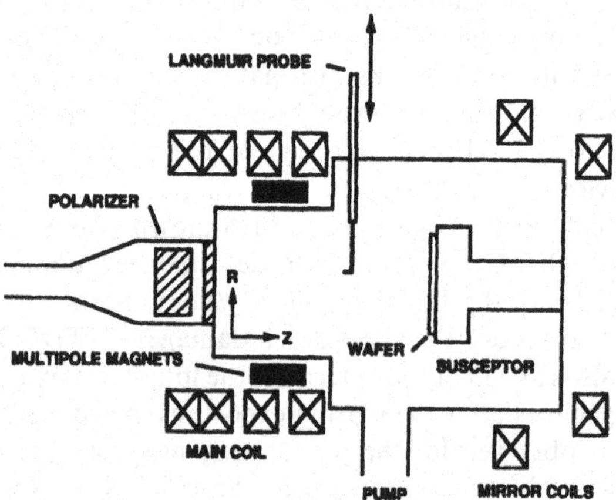

Figure 4.7 A schematic of an ECR plasma etching system with optimized complex solenoid coils and a multipole magnet assembly which generates a circumferential component of magnetic flux and results in a multicusp field. The multicusp field satisfies a magnetohydrodynamic (MHD) stability condition of a plasma. (Ref. 28 N. Fujiwara, H. Sawai, M. Yoneda, K. Nishioka, K. Horie, K. Nakamoto and H. Abe: *Jpn. J. Appl. Phys.*, 30 (1991) 3134).

cyclotron resonance (ECR) phenomenon whereby electrons obtain energy form the microwave very efficiently. A heated electron hits a neutral molecule to decompose or ionize, thereby keeping the plasma. Ionization efficiency in the ECR plasma is 3 to 4 orders higher than for the conventional parallel plate reactive ion etching (RIE) method and easily realizes very high electron density plasma such as $10^{11}-10^{13}\ cm^{-3}$ in low gas pressure region down to 10^{-2} Pa. However, since the microwave power is applied to the electrons in the resonance magnetic field space, it is necessary to design the magnetic field with great precision so as to produce a uniform plasma formation. In order to increase plasma uniformity near a wafer to be etched, the wafer is placed apart from the ECR region. The diffused plasma loses density and this causes lower etch rate and other problems. Magnetic field near the wafer also causes nonuniformity of etch rate distribution. Therefore, some improvement approaches were reported using an optimized magnetic field for uniform and stable discharge with a complex multicoil system[27,28] The optimized complex coils as shown in Figure 4.7 consist of a main coil with four independently controlled solenoid coils and a multipole magnet assembly set outside the discharge chamber to form a multicusp field which satisfies a magnetohydrodynamic(MHD) stability condition of a plasma[29].

In ECR plasma etching, it is necessary for strong anisotropic etching to reduce the ion angular distribution. It is effective for reducing the angular distribution to adopt the multicusp magnetic field, because it satisfies the stable condition of the plasma. Figure 4.8 shows the ion energy distribution when using a hybrid field (Ti = 1.8 eV) and a conventional field (Ti = 5.3 eV). When using a hybrid field, the ion temperature (Ti) was reported to be lower than the case of using a conventional field. The average ion energy is about 20 eV, it is low enough for high selectivity.

Figure 4.9 presents the dependence of the normalized etch rate on the pattern size, when the thickness of photoresist is 1.6 μm. In this figure, the normalized etch rate is defined as the ratio of the etch rate for the specific pattern size to the etch rate for the 20 μm pattern. The microloading effect is smaller when the ion temperature is low as shown in Figure 4.8. It is known that the microloading effect is affected by incident angular distribution of reactive species to a wafer.

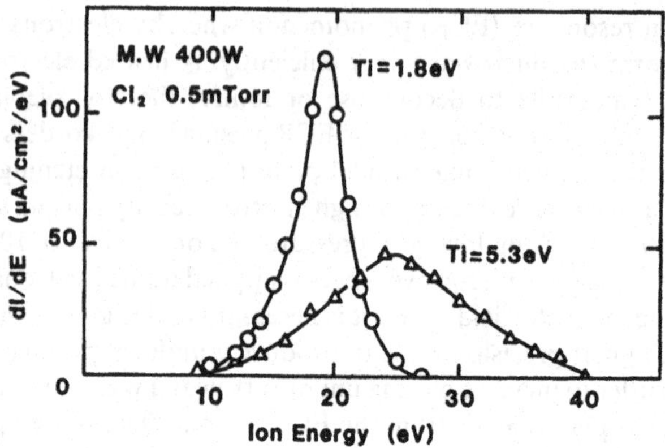

Figure 4.8 Ion energy distribution when using a hybrid field (Ti = 1.8 eV) and a conventional field (Ti = 5.3 eV). (Ref. 29 N. Fujiwara, H. Sawai, M. Yoneda, K. Nishioka, K. Horie, K. Nakamoto and H. Abe: *Jpn. J. Appl. Phys.*, 28 (1989) 2147).

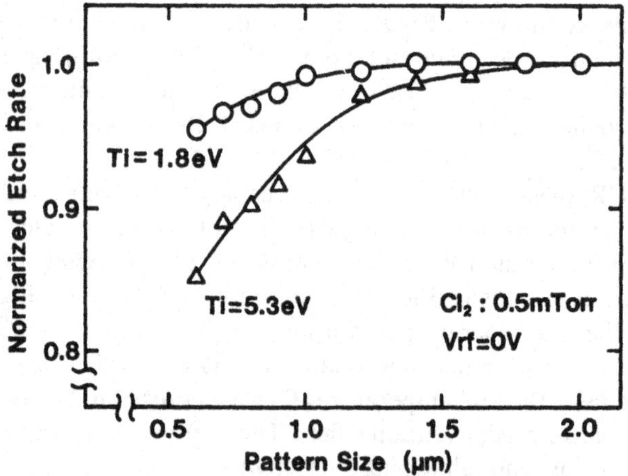

Figure 4.9 Dependence of the normalized etch rate on the pattern size. (Ref. 28 N. Fujiwara, H. Sawai, M. Yoneda, K. Nishioka, K. Horie, K. Nakamoto and H. Abe: *Jpn. J. Appl. Phys.*, 30 (1991) 3134).

Namely, small angular distribution is achieved by reducing ion temperature. Comparing the etched profiles of an isolated single pattern with the above two conditions, there are necks and tails on the pattern sidewall when ion temperature is high. By reducing ion temperature, these distortions disappear and anisotropic profile is realized without applying rf bias.

4.3. Emerging Etching Process Technologies

4.3.1. Low Temperature Etching

The gate oxide thickness of metal-oxide-semiconductor (MOS) transistors become thinner as the minimum feature size of LSIs devices shrinks, and will be reduced to 50 Å in the near future. Therefore, the achievement of a highly selective process in the reactive ion etching (RIE) of gate materials is indispensable for realizing future lower submicron devices. For this purpose, a novel highly selective etching process for phosphorus-doped polycrystalline silicon (n^+poly-Si) has been developed by employing a Cl_2 magnetron plasma at wafer temperatures below O°C[30,31]. The high selectivity of n^+poly-Si against an underlying silicon dioxide (SiO_2) film resulted from a drastic decrease in the SiO_2 etch rate by lowering the wafer temperature. The mechanism of this selective etching of n^+poly-Si over an SiO_2 film at low wafer temperatures is discussed.

Figure 4.10 shows the variations in the n^+poly-Si and SiO_2 etch rates as a function of wafer temperature with and without the magnetic field. The n^+poly-Si etch rates showed almost the same dependence on wafer temperature for with and without the magnetic field. On the other hand, the SiO_2 etch rate in the magnetron plasma dropped drastically below 0°C, in contrast to the etch rate change of SiO_2 in a glow plasma. As a result, the selectivity of n^+poly-Si/SiO_2 reached more than 60 at wafer temperatures below −30°C by the magnetron plasma. The SiO_2 surfaces etched at 25°C and −30°C were analyzed by XPS in order to clarify why the SiO_2 etch rate in magnetron RIE was suppressed at substrate temperatures below 0°C. In a Si2p spectrum obtained from the SiO_2 surface exposed to the Cl_2 magnetron plasma at −30°C wafer temperature, a slight shoulder at a binding energy of 102 – 103 eV was observed besides the Si2p peak (104 eV) due to an Si-O bond. A significant amount of chlorine was also observed on the surface etched at the low temperature. These

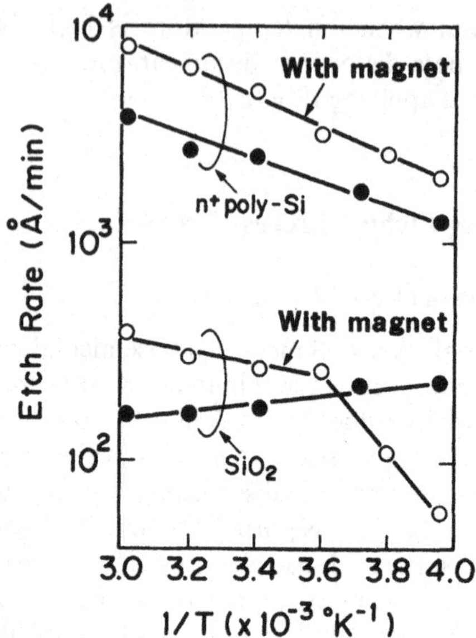

Figure 4.10 Variations in the n^+poly-Si and SiO_2 etch rates as a function of wafer temperature. (Ref. 33 M. Sekine, T. Arikado, H. Okano and Y. Horiike, Proc. 8th Symp. Dry Process (*Inst. Electr. Eng.* Tokyo 1986) p. 42).

results suggest that the SiO_2 surface was covered by etching products, such as $SiCl_x$ $(x = 2, 3)$ and $SiCl_xO_y$ $(x + 2y = 2, 3)$[34].

$SiCl_4$ gas was employed to identify the deposition species, because this gas should provide the same species that were examined by XPS. It was found that n^+poly-Si etching took place even though the wafer temperature was reduced below 0°C, while film formation occurred on the SiO_2 surface. When O_2 gas was added to the $SiCl_4$ plasma, a thicker film was formed selectively on the SiO_2 surface.

Mass analysis was carried out to identify gas phase precursors for film formation in the $SiCl_4$ magnetron plasma. It is revealed that unsaturated SiCl and $SiCl_2$ molecules are precursors for thin film formation and condense preferentially on a cooled SiO_2 surface. In actual etching, etched products that entered into the plasma are efficiently decomposed into unsaturated species such as SiCl and

$SiCl_2$, because of the high decomposition efficiency of the magnetron plasma.

Other materials, Si_3N_4, Al_2O_3, and BaF_2, were exposed to the $SiCl_4$ magnetron plasma in order to investigate the driving force of selective film formation. The etch rates or deposition rates for these materials in the $SiCl_4$ magnetron plasma were measured as a function of substrate temperature. A threshold temperature was defined as the temperature at which deposition began on a material as its temperature was lowered. The threshold temperatures were plotted in Figure 4.11 as a function of the difference in Pauling's electronegativity between two elements in the material. The threshold temperature increased as the difference in SiO_2 electronegativity increased. This means that deposition is likely to occur on the surface of materials that have strong ionic bonds, because ionicity of a chemical bond corresponds to the difference in electronegativity of the elements[35].

A model for selective film deposition can be proposed based on the above results. Unsaturated SiCl and $SiCl_2$ molecules have large dipole moments. Therefore, when polar SiCl and $SiCl_2$ molecules approach a material that also has ionic bonds at the surface, the molecules may be attracted and chemisorbed via dipole-dipole interactions. In other words, Coulomb forces between the dipole

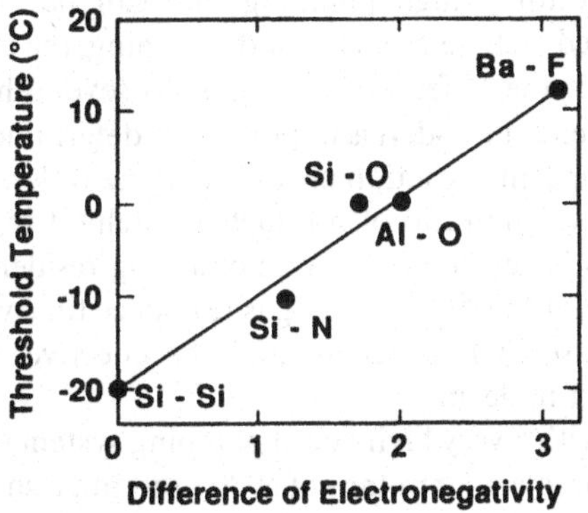

Figure 4.11 Threshold temperatures as a function of the difference in Pauling's electronegativity between two elements in the material. (Ref. 33 M. Sekine, T. Arikado, H. Okano and Y. Horiike, Proc. 8th Symp. Dry Process (*Inst. Electr. Eng.*, Tokyo 1986) p. 42).

molecules and the surface initiate deposition. This adsorption layer acts as a nucleation center for further condensation on a cool surface. No deposition is observed on the poly-Si surface at the same temperature because it does not have ionic bonds that attract the dipolar molecules.

In the actual etching of SiO_2 employing Cl_2 magnetron plasma, the SiO_2 surface is considered to be slightly etched to supply etched products. Some products react with oxygen released from SiO_2, and $SiCl_xO_y$ is formed. The oxychlorides that also have large dipole moments as in SiCl and $SiCl_2$ deposit on the SiO_2 surface. Actually, when O_2 gas was added to Cl_2, a thick selective deposition layer was observed on SiO_2. Once this condensed layer is formed, SiO_2 etching is suppressed, and high selectivity is observed.

4.3.2. High-Rate-Gas-Flow Etching[36]

In order to satisfy complicated requirements in dry etching technologies, to reduce the effect of the etch product which may make the reaction complicated and cause surface reaction via deposition, it is proposed that a low gas pressure discharge with a very high pumping rate, so as to solve the problems posed by the presence of a huge amount of reaction products in the etching reactor.

The necessity for a high pumping rate can be explained with a newly proposed etching model. For dry etching, the etching species fly and collide at the wafer surface and walls several hundred times during the residence period. It is important to determine the timing of the species change into reaction products on the wafer. This depends on the reactivity. The ratio of products to etchant in conventional etching systems is very large because of a long residence time. This model implies that the reduction of gas residence time would provide a drastic increase in the etchant and the effective evacuation of reaction product molecules.

ECR etcher with a very high-speed pumping system was developed using two turbomolecular pumps of 5000 l/sec and a smooth gas flow design. The volume of the reactor was small (70 l). The chamber wall was electrochemically polished and was baked to allow discharge in clean vacuum conditions. The base pressure was 3×10^{-7} Torr. The typical gas flow rate of Cl_2 was 90 sccm at 0.5 m Torr. The shortest residence time obtained was 30 msec at a gas pressure of 0.5 mTorr with a 90 sccm flow rate.

Typical results of high-flow and low-flow ECR etching are shown in Figure 4.12. The increase in the flow rate from 5 to 90 sccm resulted in a drastic increase in the etch rate, The etch rate for crystalline silicon was 1300 nm/min at 0.5 Torr for Cl_2 gas. This rate implies that low gas pressure discharge with a high low rate is applicable to LSI processing. Etching at a low gas pressure was advantageous in terms of etching directionality and low contamination.

To determine the effectiveness of high-flow etching, the optical emissions of discharges were measured for both high-flow and low-flow etching. Figure 4.13 shows Si emission intensity with Cl_2 gas as a function of gas flow rate. The optical emission spectra for Si at 5 sccm and 90 sccm are also shown. The Si peaks of 90 sccm are clearly smaller than those at 5 sccm. Thus, the reaction products are immediately removed from the reactor during high gas flow etching. A simple calculation indicates that the ratio of the number of etching species in the reactor increased by several times with an increase in the

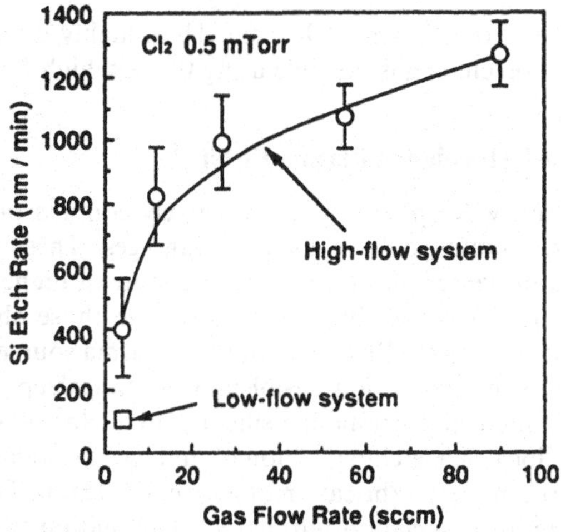

Figure 4.12 Etch rates of Si using high-flow and low-flow ECR etching system as a function of Cl_2 gas flow rate at a constant pressure of 0.5 mTorr (Ref. 36 K. Tsujimoto *et al.*, Proc. Symp. on VLSI Technol. (1992) 46).

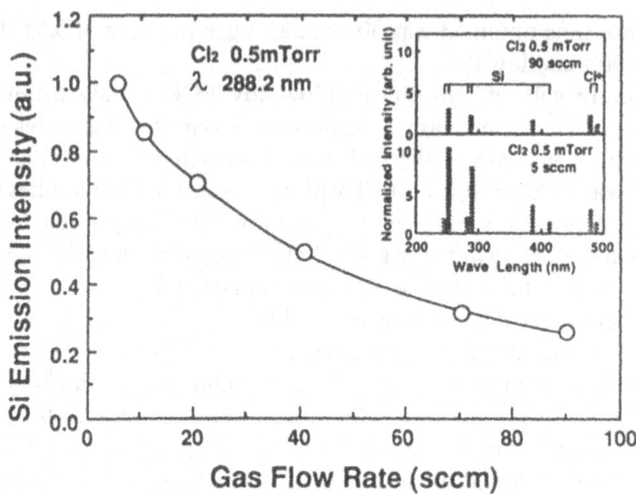

Figure 4.13 Si emission intensity with Cl_2 gas as a function of gas flow rate. The optical emission spectra for Si at 5 sccm and 90 sccm are also shown. (Ref. 36 K. Tsujimoto *et al.*, Proc. Symp. on VLSI Technol. (1992) 46).

gas flow rate from 5 sccm to 90 sccm. Thus, highly directional, low contamination etching is possible using the new high-flow etching.

4.3.3. Pulsed Modulation Plasma Etching[37]

ECR, helicon wave plasma and inductively coupled plasma (ICP) etching are known to have many advantages. These involve the generation of denser plasma at lower pressure, a higher ionization ratio, and more controllable ion energies than those obtainable by reactive ion etching (RIE). However, these plasma sources have been shown to be subject to serious problems respecting deep SiO_2 contact hole and minute polycrystalline silicon gate etchings, such as low selectivity, local side etching[38] "notch" and charge build-up damage in submicron pattern fabrication of less than 0.25 μm. This is due to a high degree of dissociation and charge accumulation on the substrate with higher energy electrons and higher plasma density. Namely, a trade-off still exists between on the one hand, anisotropy and selectivity, and on the other, a high etching rate and charge-free etching process, even with these plasma etching technologies. Thus, a new method for accurately controlling the electron energy (electron temperature) is indispensable to overcome the limitation.

This section discusses a short pulse-time modulated (TM) ECR plasma etching technique that enables a high rate, highly selective, highly anisotropic and charge-free etching using a pulsed discharge in the range of 10 – 20 μsec. A klystron source was used to generate microwaves. The pulse duration (pulse width) and period (interval) were changed from 10 to 100 μsec. The response time for the microwave input was reduced to less than 2 μsec .

SiO_2 etching is performed using fluorocarbon gases in order to deposit a fluoropolymer on the underlying Si to attain a high SiO_2 selectivity to Si. CF_2 radicals are supposed to be a main precursor for polymerization on the Si. However, high density plasma causes a low CF_2 radical density and a large amount of F atoms. Because of its higher dissociation efficiency due to the higher electron density and higher electron temperature. Control of these key species was tried by altering the pulse width. Figure 4.14 shows the dependence of the CF_2

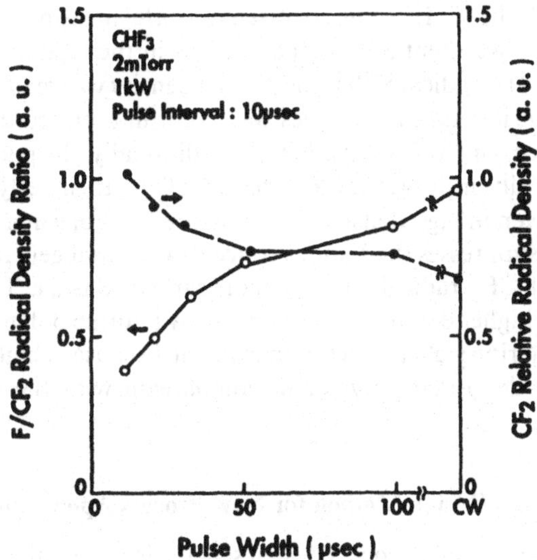

Figure 4.14 Dependence of the CF_2 relative radical density and F/CF_2 density ratio on the pulse width (Ref. 37 S. Samukawa: *Jpn. J. Appl. Phys.*, 33 (1944) 2133).

relative radical density and F/CF_2 density ratio on the pulse width. The pulse interval was fixed at 10 μsec for all conditions. When the pulse width was 10 μsec, a larger amount of CF_2 radicals was generated. By increasing the pulse width, the density of F atoms increased despite the decrease in CF_2 radicals. The electron temperature and electron density in the pulsed discharge and the continuous discharge were examined. It is found that the electron temperature and the plasma density reached a steady state within the first 10 μsec. At the interval, the electron temperature drastically decreases, corresponding to the microwave power. Therefore, the dissociation process progresses at the microwave duration and not at the interval. In other words, the low energy reactions $CHF_3 \rightarrow CHF_2 + F$, $CHF_3 \rightarrow CF_3 + H$, and $CF_2 \rightarrow CF + F$, are not expedited at the beginning of the discharge. Moreover, in a continuous discharge, CF_2 radicals decreased further and F atoms increased, because of the long dissociation processes. Namely, it is suggested that the polymerization and the SiO_2 etching selectivity to underlying Si are improved using an initial discharge of 10 μsec. The SiO_2 etching selectivity and the etching rate as a function of the pulse width for a constant 10 μsec interval of the CHF_3 pulsed discharge are measured. The SiO_2 etching rate was kept almost the same as in the case of continuous discharge. This indicates that the plasma density was maintained, and the ion density and ion energies were kept in a pulsed discharge of 10 – 20 μsec with applied RF biases. Additionally, the pulsed plasma can drastically improve the SiO_2 etch selectivity to underlying Si from 10 to 40, even in high density, low-pressure ECR plasma. The pulsed discharge suppresses the F atom concentration and generates a large amount of CF_2 radicals in the fluorocarbon plasma. Therefore, it achieves a higher deposition rate and a low fluorine polymer, causing a low sputtering yield to ion bombardment, because of high crosslinking of the deposited polymer in comparison with the continuous discharge.

4.3.4. Plasma Design Method for New Process Application

A systematic plasma process design scheme for a self-aligned contact (SAC) hole process was introduced using a mass and energy selected ion beam irradiation tool[39].

A contact hole is etched between the gate electrodes which were protected by an etch stopper such as poly-Si in the SAC technique. SAC can improve a process window for lithography by permitting use of larger hole size or low overlay precision, because the position and size of the contact hole should be defined space between the gate electrode with etch stopper. If the insulator film such as Si_3N_4 can be used as etch stopper, a simpler process without oxidation and related processes is realized. Conventionally, it is hard to get high selectivity between the SiO_2 and Si_3N_4. Thus, a systematic process development was applied to achieve the process control scheme.

In the course of the highly selective etching of SiO_2 over Si_3N_4, fluorocarbon ions were examined with the mass and energy selected ion beam system. Figures 4.15 and 4.16 show etch depth by CFn^+ and C_2F_4 ion beam irradiations on oxide and nitride films. It has been found that the etching yields of SiO_2 and Si_3N_4 increased with increasing the number of F atom. CF_3^+ ion shows high etch rate, but poor selectivity between the oxide and the nitride. CF^+ gave very high selectivity between the films. However, it was found that the etch reaction stops on SiO_2 and Si_3N_4 for larger ion beam dosages. CF_2^+ and $C_2F_4^+$ were most suitable etch species for the highly selective

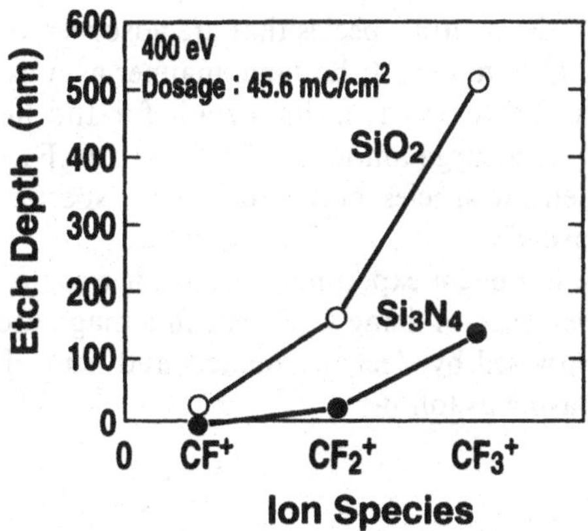

Figure 4.15 Etch depth by CF^+, CF_2^+ and CF_3^+ ion beam (400 eV ion energy) irradiations on oxide and nitride films (Ref. 39 T. Sakai *et al.*, 1993 Dry Process Symposium p. 193).

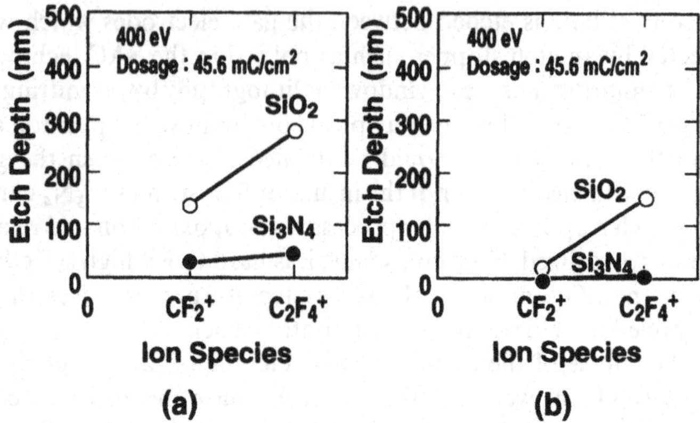

Figure 4.16 Etch depth by CF_2^+ and $C_2F_4^+$ ion beam irradiations on oxide and nitride films, with 200 and 400 eV ion energy. (Ref. 39 T. Sakai *et al.*, 1993 Dry Process Symposium p. 193).

process. At the lower energy CF_2^+ even caused film deposition on the oxide. Thus, it seems preferable to use $C_2F_4^+$ ions with lower energy to realize the high selectivity to the nitride and high etch rate for the oxide. It should also be effective for the high performance process to use CF_2 and C_2F_4 neutral species that are adsorbed on the film and react with the film in almost the same manner as ions upon the ion bombardment. Therefore, it is important for the highly selective process to produce large amounts of CF_2 and C_2F_4 ions with low energy and neutral species and reduce CF_3 species in the wafer processing plasma.

Base on the ion beam experiment results, it was investigated that the plasma chemistry utilizing C_4F_8 gas in a magnetron RIE. C_4F_8 gas was decomposed by electron impacts and neutral species collisions in the plasma as follows.

$$\begin{array}{c} \qquad\qquad\qquad\quad CF_3 \\ \qquad\qquad\qquad\quad \uparrow\ +F \\ C_4F_8 \rightarrow C_2F_4 \rightarrow CF_2 \\ \qquad\qquad\qquad\quad \downarrow\ -F \\ \qquad\qquad\qquad\quad CF \end{array}$$

Of course, many other complicated reaction passes exist. The reaction shown above was the pass most frequently detected by a quadrupole mass spectroscopy (QMS).

The relative amounts of chemical species in the C_4F_8 magnetron plasma were measured by QMS as shown in Figure 4.17(a). C_4F_8 plasma produces C_2F_4 and CF_2 which are preferable species for selective etching. However, it provides a large amount of CF_3 which easily etches nitride and lowers the selectivity. In order to reduce the relative amount of CF_3 and increase those of CF_2 and C_2F_4, it was tried to increase the total gas flow rate so as to decrease residence time of the gas and suppress the decomposition of the gas shown in the above formula. It was also investigated the addition of CO or H_2 gas to scavenge the F atoms to suppress CF_3 formation. Figure 4.17(b) and (c) show the mass spectroscopy of the plasmas with the addition of CO or H_2 gas, respectively. CO addition was found to increase the relative amount of CF species. This might also be effective for selectivity increase because a C/F ratio of total fluorocarbon species increases and that means the condition shift toward higher selective condition to compensate for the effect of the large amount of F radical

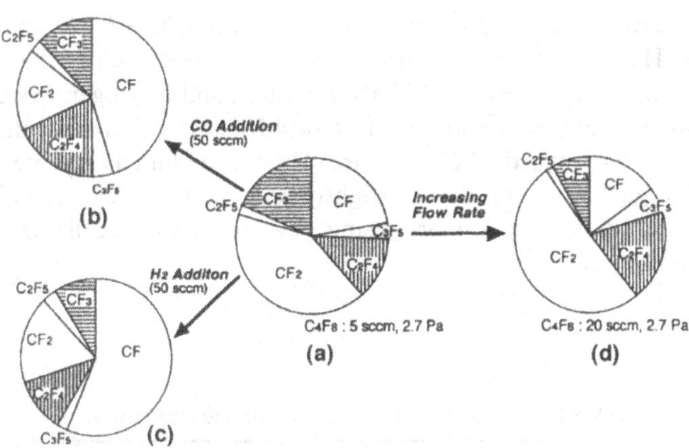

Figure 4.17 Relative amounts of chemical species measured by QMS for (a) in the C_4F_8 magnetron plasma, (b) C_4F_8 + CO plasma, (c) C_4F_8 + H_2 plasma, (d) C_4F_8 plasma with higher flow rate condition. (Ref. 39 T. Sakai *et al.*, 1993 Dry Process Symposium p. 193).

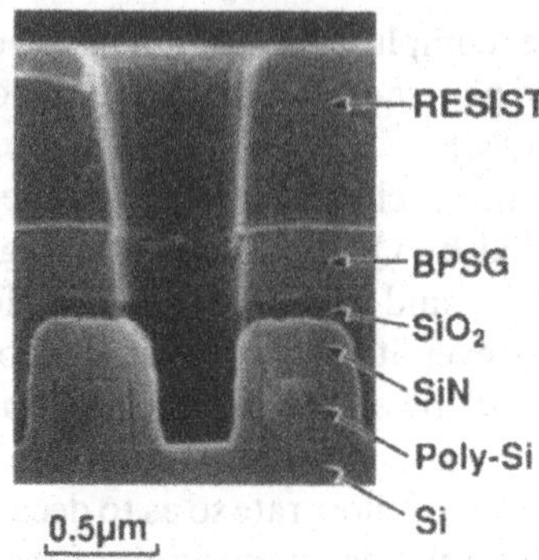

Figure 4.18 Cross-sectional SEM view of etched SAC structure.

in fluorocarbon plasma and is hardly measured by the QMS. H_2 addition also increased C/F ratio of the plasma while decreasing the relative ratios of CF_3 and CF_2. On the other hand, the CO diluted plasma showed increase of preferable species and reduced CF_3. Based on the results shown in Figure 4.17, some conditions were tried in the magnetron RIE as shown in Table 4.1.

The large amount of CO addition successfully realized high selectivity. However, H_2 addition caused less selectivity. A QMS analysis of the H_2 additive plasma during a nitride etching revealed that etch products such as CNH and NH were found and hydrogen works as an etching enhancing species. Figure 4.18 shows a cross-sectional SEM view of etched SAC structure. The nitride film as a protection on the gate was etched very slightly and the C_4F_8/CO chemistry with high flow rate is a promising new process for realizing SAC technology.

Table 4.1 Gas compositions, the flow rate and etch results.

Gas	C_4F_8	C_4F_8+CO	$C_4F_8+H_2$
Flow rate (sccm)	5	10 + 200	10 + 130
Selectivity	5	15	0.5

References

1. Hosokawa, N. *et al.* (1974). *Proc. 6th Int. Vacuum Cong.*, Kyoto, 1973, *Jpn. J. Appl. Phys.*, 13 suppl. 2, Part I. p. 435.
2. Yoshida, Y. *et al.* (1983). *Proc. 5th Symp*, on Dry processes (Inst. Electr. Eng., Tokyo, 1983) p. 4.
3. Horiike, Y. and Shibagaki, M. (1976). *Suppl. Jpn. J. Appl. Phys.*, **15**, 13.
4. Hayasaka, N. *et al.* (1988). Solid State Technology/April, p. 127.
5. Okano, H. *et al.* (1988) *Ext. Abst. Electrochemical Society Spring Meeting*, Atlanta 88–1, p. 159.
6. Nishino, H. *et al.* (1988). *Ext. Abst.* (*The 35th Spring Meeting*, 1988. The Japan Society of Applied Physics and Related Societies) p. 498.
7. Noguchi, S. *et al.* (1987). *Ext. Abst. 19th Conf. on Solid State Devices and Materials*, Tokyo, p. 451.
8. Shibaura Seidakusyo Ltd.
9. Appel, J. A. *et al.* (1970). *Phylips. Res. Repts.*, **25**, 118.
10. Nordine, P.C. *et al.* (196). *J. Chem. Soc. Faraday Trans.*, **172**, 1526.
11. Ibbotson, D. E. *et al.* (1985). *Apple. Phys. Lett.*, **46**, 794.
12. Okano, H. *et al.* (1988). *Ext. Abst. Electrochemical Society Spring Meeting*, Atlanta 88–1 p. 159.
13. Stafford, B. B. *et al.* (1977). Solid State technology/September, p. 51.
14. Nishino, H. *et al.* (1988). *Proc. 35th Annual Meeting of Jpn. Soc. Appl. Phys.*, p. 498. (in Japanese)
15. Swalin, R. A. Thermodyanamicx of Solid (John Wiley & Sons, 191) p. 182.
16. Hayasaka, N. *et al.* (1988). Digest of Papers, *1st Microprocess Conference*, Tokyo p. 114.
17. Sekine, M., Arikado, T., Okano H. and Horiike, Y. (1986). *Proc. 9th Symp. Dry Process*, Tokyo, (*Inst. Electr. Eng. Jpn.*, Tokyo, 1986) p. 42.
18. Oh-iwa, T., Horioka, K., Arikado, T., Hasegawa, I. and Okano, H. (1990). *Proc. 13th Symp. Dry Process*, Tokyo, 1990 (*Inst. Electr. Eng. Jpn.*, Tokyo, 1990) p.105.
19. Hayashi, H., Oh-iwa, T., Tamura, H., Matsushita, M., Hasegawa, I. Horioka K. and Okano, H. (1992). *Proc. 14th Symp. Dry Process*, Tokyo, 1992 (*Inst. Electr. Eng. Jpn.*, Tokyo, 1992) p. 205.
20. Hoga, H. (1991). *Jpn. J. Appl. Phys.*, **30**, 3169.
21. Namura, T. (1989). *Proc. 11th Symp. Dry Process*, (*Inst. Electr. Eng. Jpn.*, Tokyo, 1989) p. 74 . Tsuzuki, K., Tabuchi, S., Banno, T., Kinbara, K., Nakagawa,Y. Tsukada, T. (1993). *J. Vac. Sci. Technol. A*, **11**, 672.
22. Sekine, M. (1991). *Proc. 14th Symp. Dry Process*, Tokyo, 1991 (*Inst. Electr. Eng. Jpn.*, Tokyo,1991) p.99.
23. Halbach, K. (1970). *Nucl. Instr. and Meth.*, **78**, 185. Zijlstra, H., Philips, (1985) **J. Res.**, **40**, 259. Miyata, K. (1990). *COMPEL- The International Journal for Computation and Mathematics in Electrical and Electronic Engineering*, **9**, Supplement A, 115.

24. Matsuo, S. *et al.* (1982). *Jpn. J. Appl. Phys.*, **21**, L4.
25. Matsuo, S. and Kiuchi, M. (1983). *Jpn. J. Appl. Phys.*, **22**, L210.
26. Suzuki, K., Okudaira, S., Sakudo N. and Kanomata, I. (1977) *Jpn. J. Appl. Phys.*, **16**, 1979.
27. Samukawa, S., Suzuki, Y. and Sasaki, M. (1990). *Appl. Phys. Lett.*, **57**, 403. Samukawa, S., Sasaki, M. and Suzuki, Y. (1990). *J. Vac. Sci. Technol.*, B8, 1192. Samukawa, S., Mori, S. and Sasaki, M. (1991) *J. Vac. Sci. Technol.*, A9, 85. Samukawa, S., Nakagawa, Y. and Ikeda, K. (1991). *J. Appl. Phys.*, **30**, 423.
28. Fujiwara, N., Sawai, H., Yoneda, M., Nishioka, K., Horie, K., Nakamoto, K. and Abe, H. (1991). *Jpn. J. Appl. Phys.*, **30**, 3134.
29. Fujiwara, N., Sawai, H., Yoneda, M., Nishioka, K., Horie, K., Nakamoto K. and Abe, H. (1989). *Jpn. J. Appl. Phys.*, **28**, 2147.
30. Arikado, T., Horioka, K., Sekine, M., Okano, H. and Horiike, Y. (1987). *Proc. 48th Annual Meeting of Jpn. Soc. Appl. Phys.*, p. 462 (in Japanese).
31. Horioka, K., Sekine, M., Arikado, T., Okano, H. and Horiike, Y. *Symposium of VLSI Technology*, Digest of Technical papers, p. 81 (San Diego, 1988).
32. Sekine, M., Arikado, T., Okano, H. and Horiike, Y. (1986). Symposium of VLSI Technology, Digest of Technical papers, p.5 (San Diego, 1986).
33. Sekine, M., Arikado, T., Okano, H. and Horiike, Y. (1986). *Proc. 8th Symp. Dry Process* (*Inst. Electr. Eng.*, Tokyo 1986) p. 42
34. Wagner, C.D., Riggs, W. M., Davis, I. E., Moulder, J. F. and Muilenberg, G. E. (1979). Handbook of X-ray Photoelectron Spectroscopy (Perkin - Elmer Corp., Physical Electronics Division, MN).
35. Pauling, L. (1960). The Nature of the Chemical Bond, 3rd ed. (Cornel Univ. Press, 1960) p. 102.
36. Tsujimoto, K., *et al.*, (1992). *Proc. Symp. on VLSI Technol.*, 46. Tsujimoto K. *et al.* (1992). *Proc. 14th Symp. on Dry Process*, 49. Kofuji, N. *et al.*, (1993). *Proc. 15th Symp. on Dry Process*, 67.
37. Samukawa, S. (1944). *Jpn. J. Appl. Phys.*, **33**, 2133.
38. Fujiwara, N., Maruyama, T., Yoneda, M. and Sukamoto, K. *In proceedings of the 15th Dry Process Symposium* (The Institute of Electrical Engineer of Japan, Tokyo, 1993) p. 45.
39. Sakai, T. *et al.*, (1993). *Dry Process Symposium* p. 193.

CHAPTER 5

THIN FILM INSULATOR

5.1. Introduction

Scaling down the feature size of MOS devices will require further reduction of the gate oxide thickness. The thinning ratio of the capacitor dielectric film thickness in dynamic random access memory is suppressed by application of three-dimensional structures such as a trench and a stacked capacitor. MOSFET thin gate insulator thickness, however, has decreased to maintain the scaling rule. Therefore, a lot of attention has to be paid to reliability of the gate oxide. High electric field stress is applied to tunneling oxide in flash EEPROM in order to program with high speed. One of the most serious issues is tunneling oxide reliability. In this chapter, the reliability issues regarding silicon dioxide films, for example, TDDB (time-dependent dielectric breakdown) and leakage current at a trench corner, are described.

5.2. Oxide Breakdown Defect

Thin thermally grown silicon dioxide on single crystal silicon substrate has superior dielectric characteristics, which derive from the wide energy gap (8–9 eV) and the high energy barrier height. Experimentally, however, if the electric field across the silicon dioxide becomes higher than 5 MV/cm, the Fowler-Nordheim tunneling leakage current begins to flow. In addition, if the electric field becomes high enough, for example, higher than 30 MV/cm, some Si-O bonds will be torn apart. This corresponds to a transition of electrons from the valence band to the conduction band. This process, in which an electron penetrates through the energy band gap, is called tunneling. An intrinsic breakdown electric field can be defined as the critical electric field, at which the tunneling probability becomes higher. But, the intrinsic breakdown field has not been clarified experimentally. If the silicon dioxide has some defect, the internal electric field locally increases. And, even though the average electric field is sufficiently lower than the intrinsic breakdown, the oxide locally breaks down. Figure 5.1[1,2] shows a typical breakdown histogram of thin thermally grown silicon dioxide films. In a time zero breakdown test, the MOS capacitors are categorized into three modes by the breakdown electric field, E_{BD}. That is, A, B and C modes. The A mode failure is an initial short, which has the breakdown electric field lower than 1 MV/cm. The B mode failure is a catastrophic breakdown, while the Fowler-Nordheim leakage current of the C mode merely exceeds a judgement value, for example, 1.5 μA, without the oxide breakdown. That is, the C mode is not the breakdown failure. Figure 5.2 shows an oxide thickness dependence of the A mode failure fraction. The A mode fraction increases with decreasing oxide thickness and can be decreased by improving the clean room environment. The A mode is attributed to a pinhole of the oxide films, which stems from

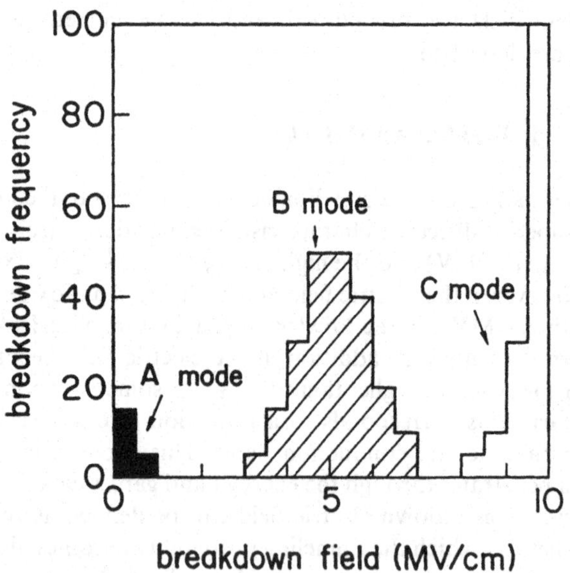

Figure 5.1 Typical oxide breakdown histogram. There are three peaks: A mode (pin hole), B mode(weak spot), and C mode(defect free) capacitors[1].

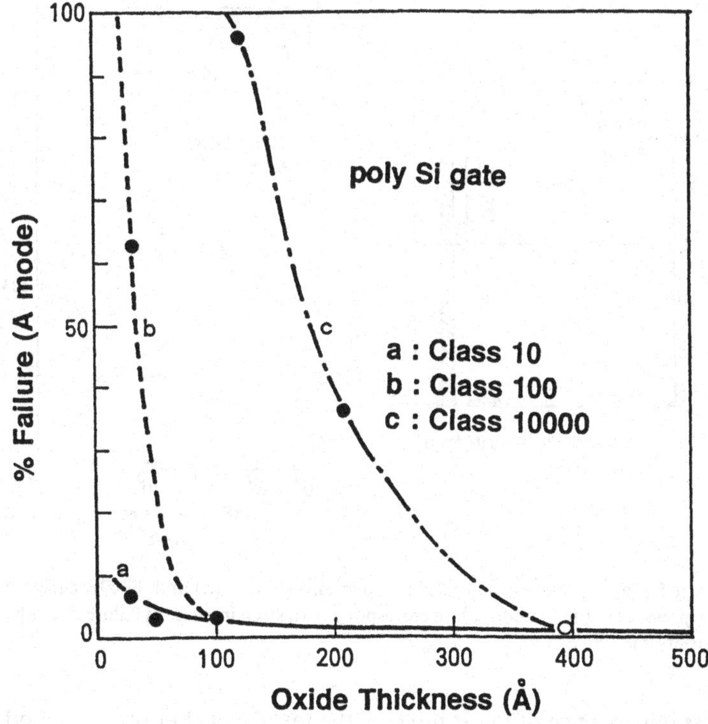

Figure 5.2 Oxide thickness dependence of A mode failure fraction. The A mode failure fraction depends on the sample preparation environment cleanness[1].

a metallic contamination of the silicon surface before the oxidation. It can be considered that main origins of the A mode are particles in the air, water, jigs and so on. The B mode, which has an important responsibility for the time-dependent dielectric breakdown, as shown in Figure 5.3, and the reliability of the MOS devices. In this figure, it can be seen that the "oxide-1" oxide with the B mode failure has an initial steep increase of the TDDB, which is not observed for the "oxide-2" oxide without the B mode. That is, the B mode failure harms the long-term reliability. In Figure 5.4, the B mode failure fractions are shown as a function of the oxide thickness. The failure fraction decreases with decreasing oxide thickness. The oxide thick-

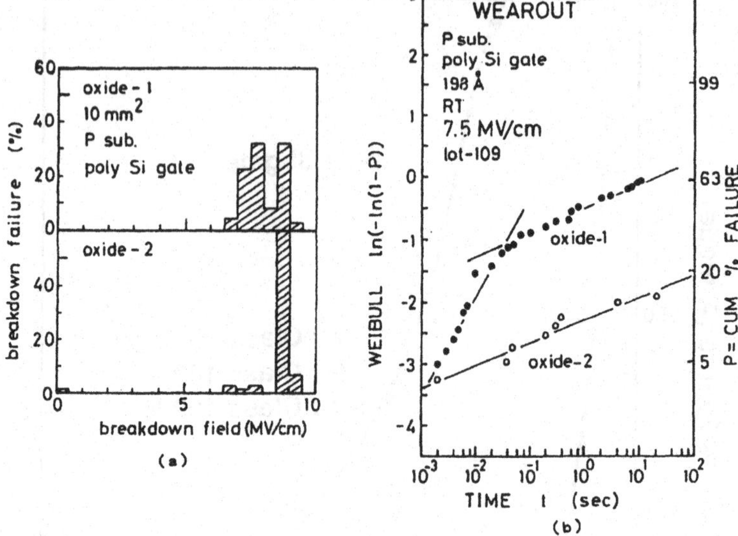

Figure 5.3 Relationship between breakdown distribution (a) and TDDB curve (b). The presence of the B mode failure corresponds to a steep increase of failure fraction in shorter time range[1].

ness dependence of the B mode is the inverse of that of the A mode failure. This fact indicates that the main origin of the B mode failure is different from that of the A mode failure. In Figure 5.4, temperature of sacrificial oxidations prior to the gate oxidation is used as a parameter. Here, the word, "sacrificial", means that the oxide formed during the sacrificial oxidation is removed before the gate oxidation. The B mode failure fraction decreases as the sacrificial oxidation temperature increases. These facts mean that the B mode failure mainly comes from the silicon substrate. The oxygen precipitates (that is, the bulk micro-defect; BMD) in the two silicon substrates which are grown by thermal treatment of 1000°C for 16 hours in N_2 after the formation of the gate electrodes were observed[2]. The B mode defect density of the wafer(a) is about 6 times greater than that of the wafer(b). The oxygen precipitate density in the wafer(a) is more than that in the wafer(b). Additionally, as shown in Figure 5.5, it is found that there is a linear relationship between the B mode defect density

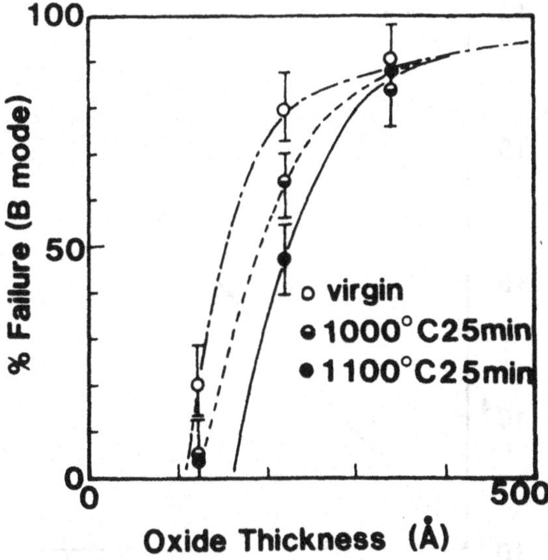

Figure 5.4 Oxide thickness dependence of B mode failure. The failure fraction increases with oxide thickness. This dependence is different from that of the A mode failure[1].

and the BMD density. It can be concluded that the main origin of the B mode oxide defect is the BMD in the silicon substrate. It is known that the BMD is what the super-saturated interstitial oxygen atoms precipitate. Then, it is easy to presume that an outer-diffusion of the interstitial oxygen from the silicon surface by a high temperature annealing in non-oxidized ambient could be effective to decrease the B mode oxide defects. Figure 5.6 shows the breakdown histogram of the thermally grown oxide on the silicon, which is annealed in the non-oxidized ambient at 1200°C for 4 hours. The B mode failure is removed almost perfectly.

5.3. Trench Corner Oxidation

As a feature size decreases, three-dimensional structures, such as the trench capacitor and buried oxide isolation, have been widely exam-

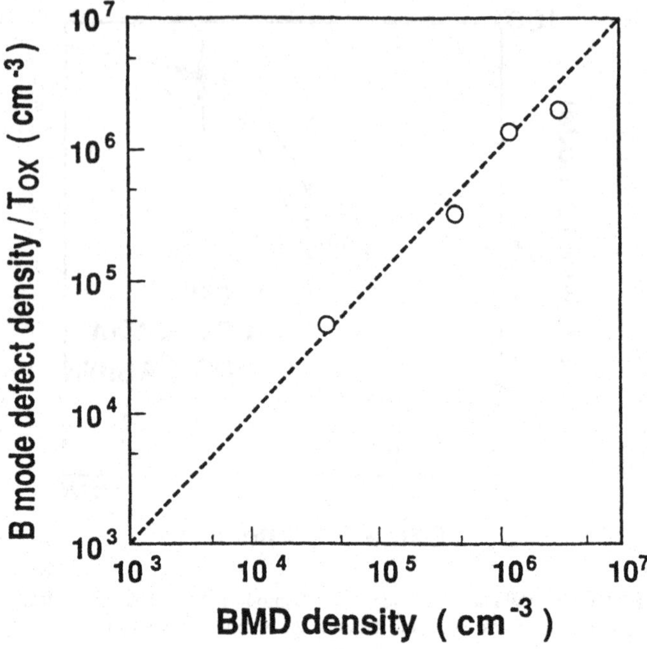

Figure 5.5 B mode defect density vs BMD density. Both densities have a high correlation.

ined. In corner region in these structures, the thermally grown silicon dioxide becomes thinner than that on a plane surface. The electric field also concentrates, making the oxide leakage current increase. In this section, the thermal oxidation controlling the oxide leakage current at convex corner of the trenched silicon surface is described[3].

When the Si crystal converts to the new SiO_2 at the Si-SiO_2 interface, the volume increases by about 2.3 times. This volume increase induces the large compressive stress at the Si-SiO_2 interface, especially, at the Si convex or concave corners. This stress suppresses the oxidation to decrease the oxide thickness and sharpen the convex corner. In order to smoothly round off the convex corner by the thermal oxidation, it is necessary for the above oxidation induced stress to be relaxed. The gate oxide leakage current of the MOS

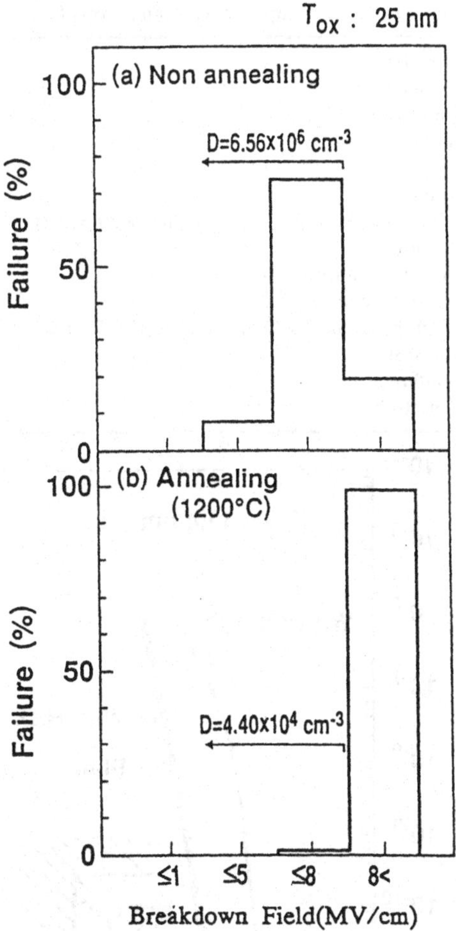

Figure 5.6 High temperature annealing effect for B mode failure.

capacitor on the trenched Si surface is effective for evaluating the rounding-off oxidation.

Table 5.1 is a sample preparation process flow of the trenched MOS capacitors. The rounding-off oxidation condition is examined as a parameter. Figure 5.7 shows the oxide leakage currents as

Table 5.1 Sample preparation process flow.

1) (100) oriented *n* type Si,
2) Wet cleaning treatment,
3) Mask CVD SiO_2,
4) Patterning of Si trenches,
5) SiO_2 RIE,
6) Resist removal,
7) Si RIE; total perimeter length = 50 mm. trench depth = 3 μm,
8) Mask SiO_2 removal,
9) Rounding-off oxidation with various condition,
10) Rounding-off oxide removal,
11) Gate oxide is grown in the dry O_2 ambient at 950°C. oxide thickness = 10 nm,
12) Polysilicon deposition
13) Phosphorus diffusion
14) Pattering of electrodes

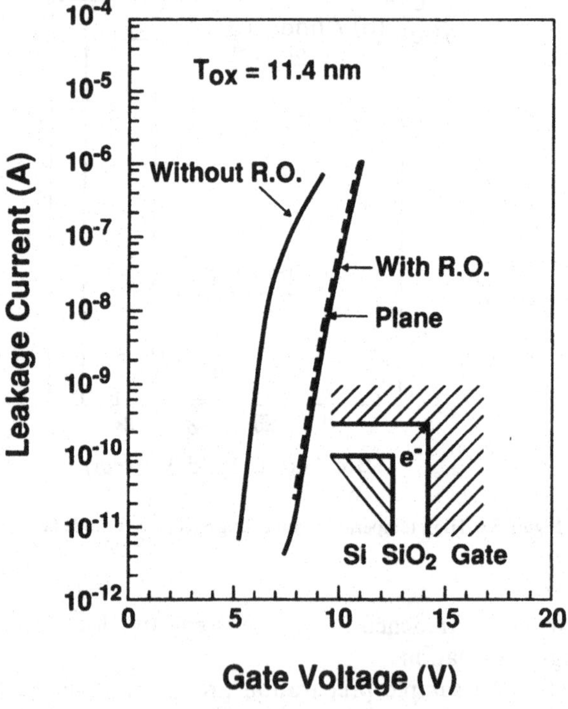

Figure 5.7 I-V Characteristics of three different kinds of MOS capacitors formed on the plane surface, the trenched surface without and with rounding-off oxidation[3].

a function of the gate voltage characteristics for three kinds of the MOS capacitors, that is, on the plane surface, on the trenched surface without the rounding-off oxidation, and on the trenched surface with the rounding-off oxidation. We note that the rounding-off oxidation is effective to reduce the oxide leakage current for the trenched MOS capacitor without the rounding-off oxidation to the level of the plane capacitor. In the following, various conditions of the rounding-off oxidation are examined.

In Figure 5.8, rounding-off oxide thickness dependence on the oxide leakage current is shown. The rounding-off oxidation is per-

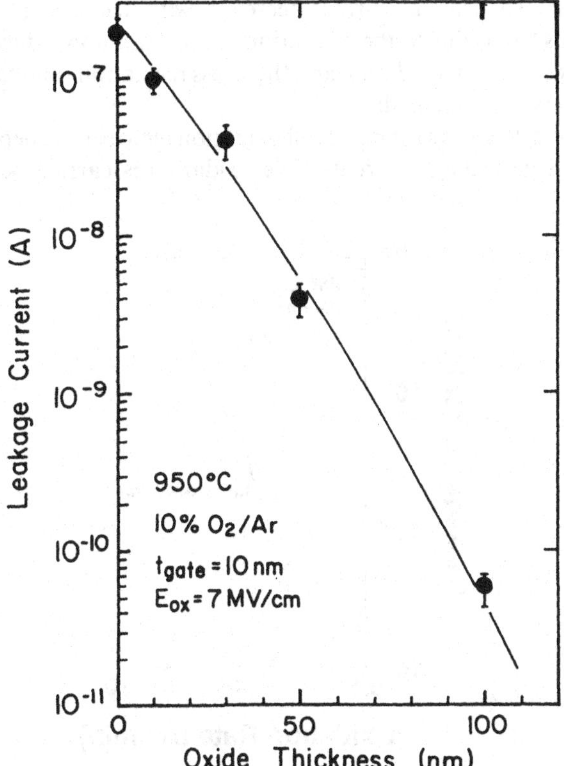

Figure 5.8 Rounding-off oxide thickness dependence of oxide leakage current of trench capacitor in 10% O_2 diluted by Ar[3].

formed in 10% O_2 diluted by Ar at 950°C. The oxide leakage current is measured at electric field of 7 MV/cm. The leakage currents decrease with increasing rounding-off oxide thickness. This dependence reflects the fact that if the oxidation induced stress is sufficiently relaxed, the curvature at the convex corner increases with oxide thickness.

Figure 5.9 illustrates average rounding-off oxidation rate (oxide thickness(= 100 nm)/total oxidation time) dependence of the leakage currents. In this experiment, the rounding-off oxidation is performed in the Ar diluted O_2 at 950°C, where the rounding-off oxide thickness is about 100 nm. The leakage currents are measured at electric field of 8 MV/cm. The leakage current decreases with decreasing oxidation rate. This fact is due to the relaxation of the oxidation induced stress during subsequent oxidation and the stress relaxation simultaneously progresses with the oxidation.

Figure 5.10 shows rounding-off oxidation temperature dependence of the oxide leakage currents. The oxidation is carried out in dry

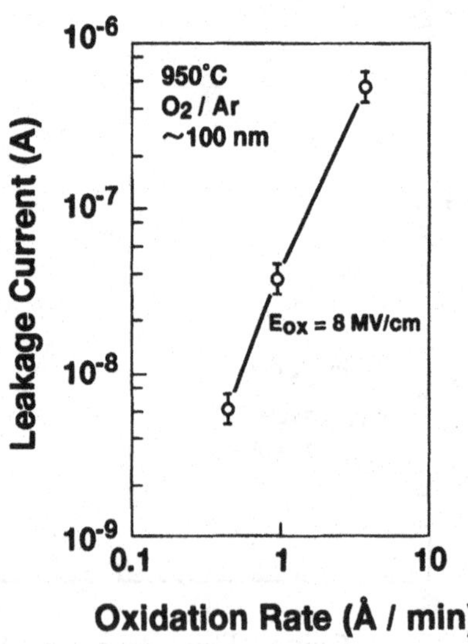

Figure 5.9 Rounding-off oxidation rate dependence of oxide leakage current. Oxidation rate is controlled by dilution of O_2 with Ar gas[3].

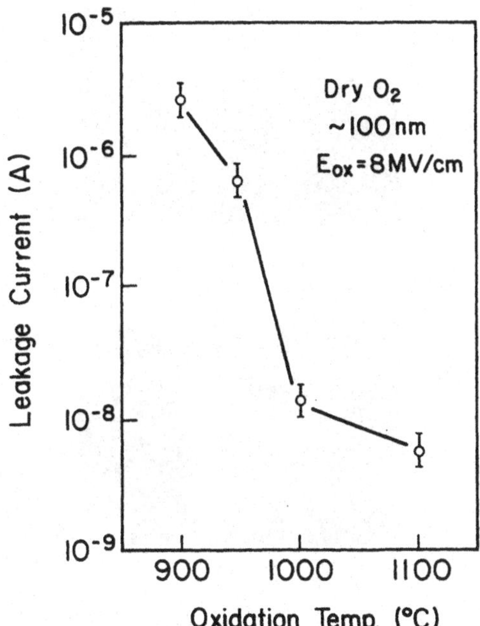

Figure 5.10 Rounding-off oxidation temperature dependence of oxide leakage current[3].

oxygen ambient. The oxide leakage current decreases with increasing oxidation temperature. At 1100°C, the leakage current reaches the same level as that of the plane capacitor. It can be considered that the oxidation induced stress is relaxed enough to uniformly form the oxide at the convex corner.

Figure 5.11 presents cross-sectional scanning electron microscopic photographs (a) and (b) at the convex corner after rounding-off oxidation at 900°C and 1100°C, respectively. These photographs show that the above presumption is a fact. At 900°C, the convex corner is sharpened and the oxide thickness is thinned, while at 1100°C the corner is smoothly rounded off and the uniform oxide thickness is formed.

H_2O molecule inclusion in the oxidation ambient is reported to reduce the viscosity of the thermally grown oxide. Hydroxyl bonds, which are formed by a reaction between H_2O and Si-O bonds, break

(a) 900℃

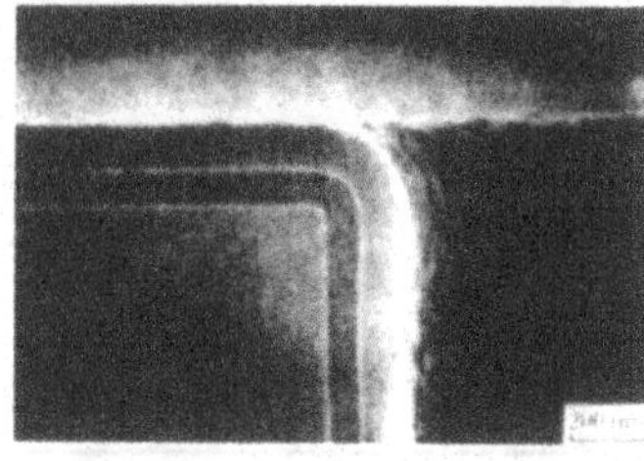

(b) 1100℃

Figure 5.11 Cross sectional SEM photographs of a convex trench corner after oxidation temperature at 900°C and 1100°C[3].

a SiO_2 network. Consequently, the stress relaxation time is reduced. On the other hand, it is well known that H_2O inclusion in the oxidation ambient increases the oxidation rate. Accordingly, it is presumed that there is an appropriate H_2O concentration for the rounding-off oxidation at a given oxidation temperature. In Figure 5.12, the oxide leakage currents for trenched MOS capacitors are plotted as a function of the H_2O concentration in an O_2 ambient for the rounding-off oxidation at 950°C. From this result, it is known that a lower oxide leakage current can be obtained in an O_2 ambient including a few percent of H_2O molecules.

Ratio of the oxidation rate on a flat surface, V_f, and at a convex corner, V_c, is given by,[4]

$$V_c/V_f = (A + 2T_{ox})/[A + 2r_1 \log(r_2/r_1)], \tag{1}$$

where A is ratio of the linear rate constant of the oxidation, B/A, and the parabolic constant, B, respectively. The values r_1 and r_2 are the

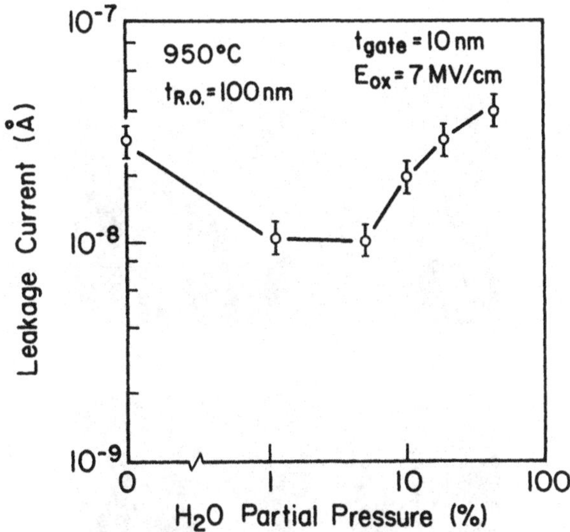

Figure 5.12 Dependence of gate oxide leakage current on H2O partial pressure in O_2 [3].

curvatures of the Si/SiO_2 interface and the SiO_2 surface at the corner, respectively, that is , $r_2 - r_1 = T_{ox}$. In an oxidation condition of the diffusion limit where V_c is larger that V_f, it is presumed that the convex corner is more easily rounded off. For an oxidation of silicon surface with a given structure, an oxidation condition with the smaller A value is more effective to round off the convex corner, considering that Tox is always larger than $r_1 \log(r_2/r_1)$. At 800°C, the B/A for the oxidation in dry $O_2 + NF_3$ ambient is larger by more than twenty times than that in dry O_2 ambient, while both B values are almost the same. That is, the A value in the dry $O_2 + NF_3$ ambient is smaller than that in dry O_2. Halogen atoms have also a possibility to break Si-O bonds and terminate the broken bonds and to more easily release the compressive stress. In Figure 5.13, the cross-sectional structures by the scanning electron microscope of the convex corners after oxidations in (a) the dry O_2 and (b) the $O_2 + NF_3$ ambient are shown. In spite of the lower temperature oxidation of 800°C, it is clear that the rounding-off effect is observed in the $O_2 + NF_3$ ambient. Figure 5.14 shows the rounding-off oxide thickness dependence of the

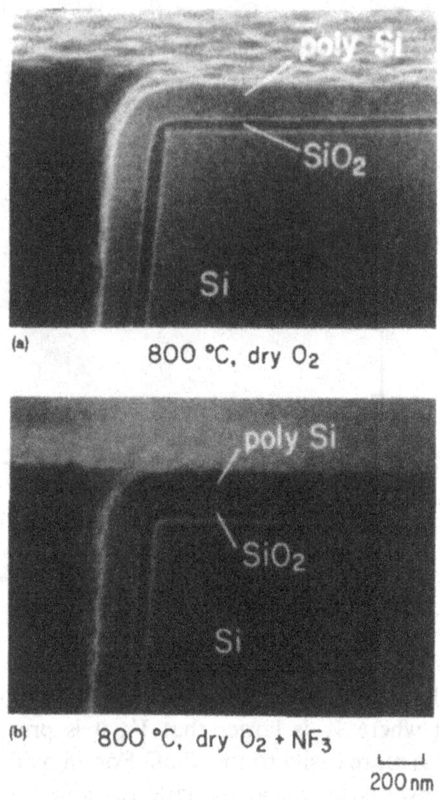

Figure 5.13 Cross sectional SEM images of silicon convex corners oxidized (a)in dry O_2 and (b)in dry $O_2 + NF_3$ ambient[4].

gate oxide leakage current in the dry $O_2 + NF_3$ at 800°C in comparison to the 10% dry O_2 diluted by Ar at 950°C. The rounding-off oxide with thickness of about 50 nm in the dry O_2 with addition of 50 ppm NF_3 gas indicates almost the same rounding-off effect as that of about 100nm in the dry O_2.

5.4. Fatigue Breakdown

Even if the thin oxide has no B mode defect, when the high electric field stress is applied to the oxide for a long time, the oxide is fatigued

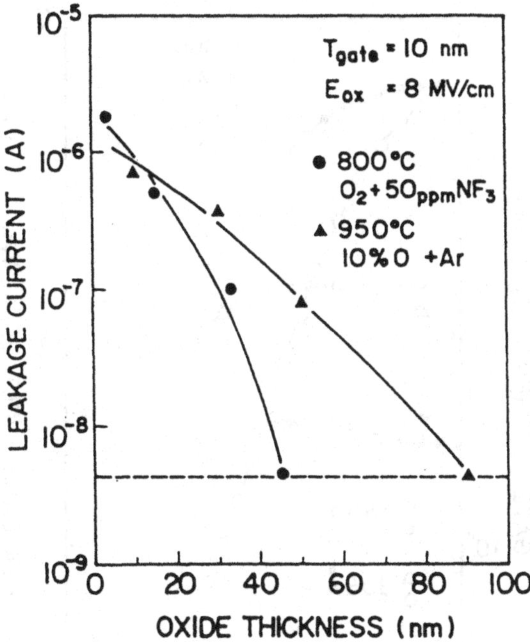

Figure 5.14 Dependence of oxide leakage current for trenched capacitors on rounding-off oxide thickness, in dry O_2 + Ar at 950°C (triangles) and in dry O_2 + NF_3 at 800°C (circles). The dashed line indicates the leak-age current level of a plane capacitor[4].

and at last is broken down. An oxide breakdown mechanism has yet to be clarified. By improving clean technology in Si ULSI processes, the reliable data of thin oxide fatigue breakdown lifetime is led to be obatained. Furthermore, to certainly remove the effect of the B mode defect, the small area MOS capacitors of, for example, 0.015 mm^2 are used.[5]

In the first step, when a high electric field is applied to the oxide, the impact ionization in the oxide occurs. At the same time, the electrons and the holes are trapped in the oxide. As a result, both the oxide leakage current and the flatband voltage shift under the constant voltage stress. Figure 5.15 shows the injected electron number dependence of the leakage current and the flatband voltage for the 15 nm and the 30 nm thick oxides on (100) oriented *p*-type Si. The

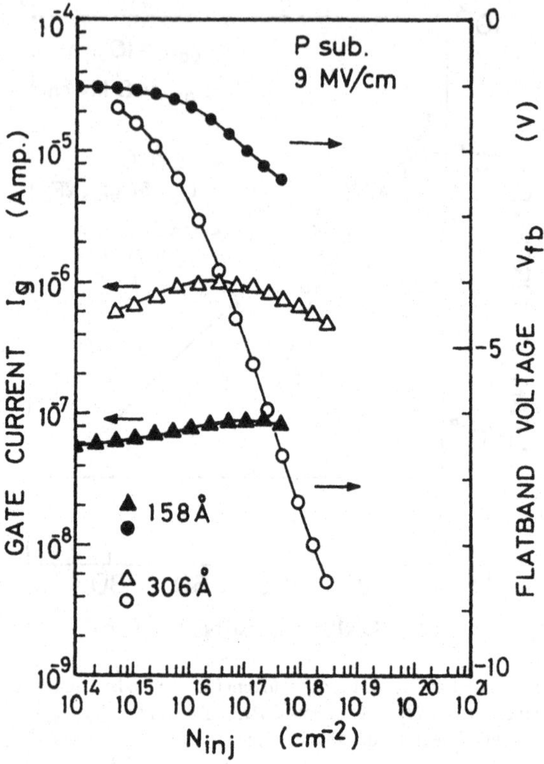

Figure 5.15 Oxide leakage current and flat band voltage shift during high electric field stress application.

negative constant voltage is applied to the gate electrode. It is found that the leakage current increases at once and decreases after reaching the maximum, while the flatband voltage monotonically shifts in the negative direction in the whole experimental range. In the neighborhood of the gate electrode, the electric field in the oxide increases by the effect of the hole trapping and subsequently decreases by the electron trapping. On the other hand, the electric field in the oxide near the Si substrate increases by the hole trapping. From these results, it can be seen that the centroid of the trapped electron distribution deviates from that of the trapped hole distribution. In addition, it is found that the density of the trapped holes for the 15 nm oxide is lower than that for the 30 nm oxide. Under the same electric field stress, the extent of the impact ionization for the 15 nm oxide is smaller than that for the 30 nm oxide.

It can be considered that this charge trapping is closely related to the fatigue of the oxide. Next, the fatigue breakdown charge, Q_{BD}, is defined as a total charge through the oxide during mean time to 50% failure fraction. Figure 5.16 illustrates the fatigue breakdown charge as a function of the stress electric field. The oxide thickness are used as a parameter. The Q_{BD} monotonically decreases with stress electric field. At the same stress electric field, the Q_{BD} increases as the oxide becomes thinner. The stress field-Q_{BD} dependencies approach a characteristic curve as the oxide thickness decreases in the range of the evaluated oxide thickness. The characteristic curve is empirically

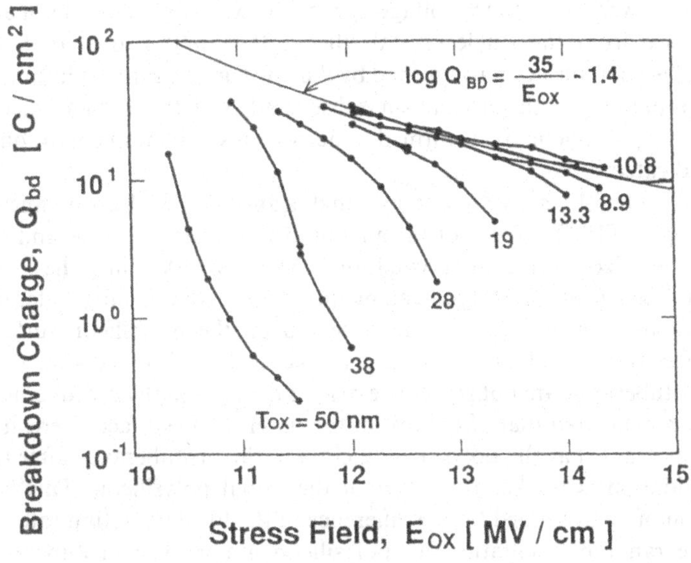

Figure 5.16 Q_{BD} as a function of oxide electric field stress for various oxide thickness. The characteristic curve is represented by Q_{BD}(C/cm^2)%1035$^{5/E_{ox}-1.4\ 5}$.

described by the following equation. That is,

$$Q_{BD}(C/cm^2) = 10^{35}/E_{ox} - 1.4. \quad (2)$$

Where E_{ox} (MV/cm) is stress electric field.

When the oxide is thick, the impact ionization in the oxide is remarkable. If the hole trapping in the oxide is the oxide fatigue, the hole generation by the impact ionization accelerates the fatigue. As the electric field stress increases, the hole generation steeply increases. The electric field dependence of the Q_{BD} is explained like this. And, as the oxide becomes thinner, the impact ionization and the hole trapping are reduced as previously described and the fatigue is suppressed.

5.5. Polysilicon Oxide

The oxide thermally grown from polycrystalline silicon (hereafter called polysilicon) is less reliable in terms of higher leakage current and lower breakdown voltage compared with the oxide thermally grown from the single crystal silicon. It is well known that the polysilicon surface is roughened by the low temperature oxidation. In this paragraph, the mechanism is discussed. And, the leakage current of the polysilicon oxide formed under various oxidation condition is indicated.

Figure 5.17 shows cross-sectional transmission electron microscopic (TEM) images of (a) an initial polysilicon surface and (b) a polysilicon surface after oxidation at 850°C for 500 min[6]. The initial surface is smoothly planarized by the chemical dry etching. After the oxidation, protuberances are observed on the polysilicon surface. After the annealing in nitrogen ambient, it is observed that such protuberances do not grow. The oxide thickness on the protuberance is thinner than that of the rest of the other plane surface. Here, it is important that the polysilicon including the protuberance after the oxidation is thicker than that of the initial polysilicon. This fact cannot be explained by the difference of the local oxidation rates or the random orientations of polysilicon grains. The protuberance growth is explained as followed. The oxidation of the polysilicon surface could lead to the build up of the large compressive stress in the

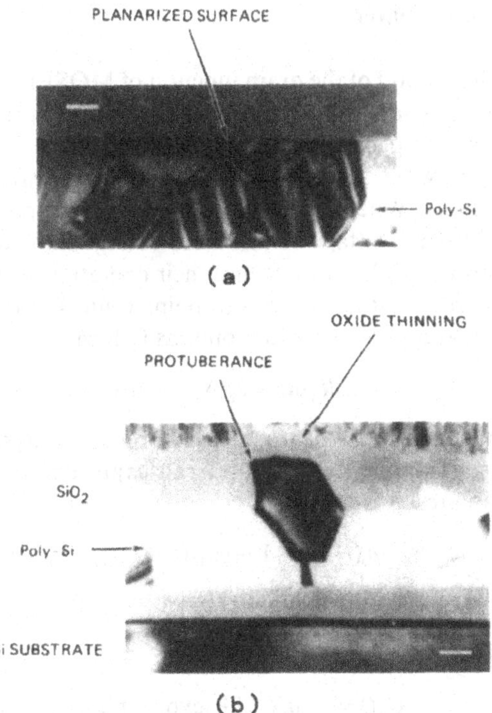

Figure 5.17 Cross sectional TEM images of (a)an initial plane polysilicon surface and (b)a protuberance grown by low temperature oxidation at 850°C for 500 min[6].

polysilicon films. This compressive stress concentrates small grains. The protuberance growth occurs in the case of the smaller grains. This is experimentally confirmed. The compressive stress induces the retardation of the oxide growth as described in paragraph 5.3. As a result of the oxidation retardation, the generation of the interstitial silicon is suppressed at the protuberances. As a whole, it can be presumed that the silicon atom motion from the plane polysilicon-oxide interface to the surface of the protuberances is induced. Then, the protuberances grow more and more.

5.6. Trapping Center

In the neighborhood of the drain junction of MOSFET, high field is induced to give charges high kinetic energy. Some of them can gain enough energy to penetrate the gate oxide. Most of them reach the gate electrode, while some of them are trapped in various kinds of trapping centers. When electrons or holes are trapped in the gate oxide, the flatband voltage or threshold voltage shifts to induce the error operation of ULSIs, or reduce their operation speed.

When the pre-existing electron trapping centers in the oxide trap electrons, the trapping rate equation is as follows

$$dn_t/dt = k_c(N - n_t)\,, \tag{3}$$

Here, n_t is the number of the trapped electrons, N is the total number of the electron trapping centers, k_c is a rate capture constant, t is time. The following result is obtained.

$$n_t(t) = N\{1 - \exp(-t/\tau)\}, \tag{4}$$

$$\tau = 1/k_c. \tag{5}$$

Integrating over the oxide thickness,

$$Q(t) = -qN_t\{1 - \exp(-t/\tau)\}. \tag{6}$$

Here, $Q(t) = \int_0^{T_{ox}} qn_t(t)\,dx$, $N_t = \int_0^{T_{ox}} N dx$, q is electronic charge. When the centroid of the trapped electron distribution is X and the dielectric constant of the silicon dioxide is ε_{ox}, the following relation is obtained.

$$\Delta V_{fb} = -q(X/\varepsilon_{ox})N_t\{1 - \exp(-t/\tau)\}, \tag{7}$$

$$X = \int_0^{T_{ox}} xn_t(t)\,dt/T_{ox}. \tag{8}$$

From the time dependence of the flatband voltage, we can know both a density and a capture cross section of the trapping centers in the oxide.

It has been reported that not only structural defects in the Si-O network such as oxygen vacancy and strained bond but also impurities such as arsine, phosphorus, boron, aluminum and water can become charge trapping centers.

Figure 5.18 shows the typical flatband voltage as a function of injected electron density by the avalanche injection method[7]. The flatband band voltage is measured by using signal with frequency of 1 MHz. The flatband voltage increases in an initial range of the injected electrons. After a maximum, the flatband voltage gradually decreases as the injected electrons increase. The flatband voltage appears to increase again when a large number of electrons are injected. This is called "N-shaped" or "turnaround" behavior. Figure 5.19 shows capacitance-voltage (C-V) characteristics measured at the marked points in Figure 5.18. The C-V characteristics were measured at various frequencies of 1 MHz–83.3 Hz with low amplitude signals. It can be seen that the interface states increase with increasing injected electron density. From these results, it is understood that the N-shaped behavior is the combined result of the electron trapping and the interface generation. That is,

$$\Delta V_{\rm fbt} = |\Delta V_{\rm fb}| + |\Delta V|, \tag{9}$$

here, $\Delta V_{\rm fbt}$ is the real trapped electron density, $\Delta V_{\rm fb}$ is the measured flatband voltage shifts, ΔV is the voltage shift by the generated interface states with longer time constants.

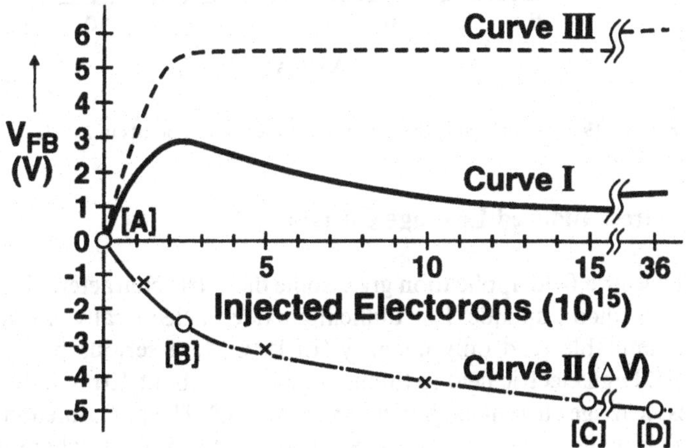

Figure 5.18 Typical flatband voltage shift of avalanche hot electron injection as a function of injected electron number[7].

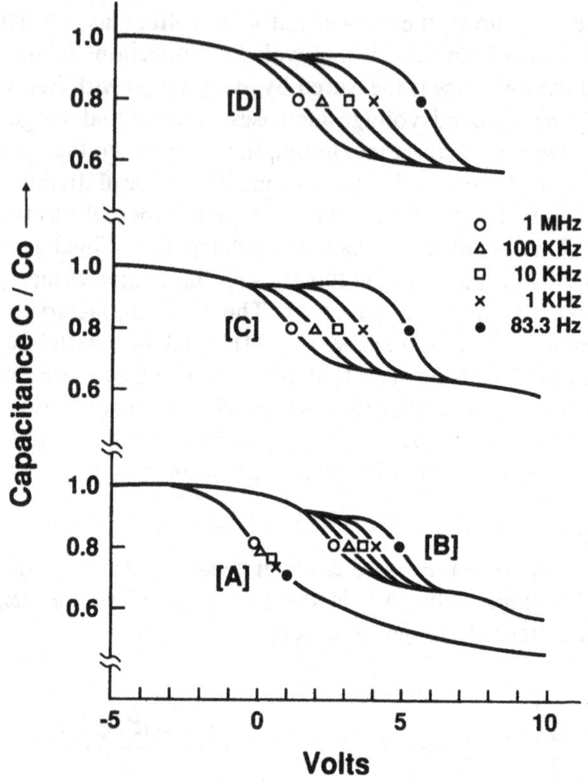

Figure 5.19 C-V characteristics measured at the marked points in Fig. 18[7].

5.7. Stress Induced Leakage Current

High electric field application gives some dielectric characteristics to the thin silicon dioxide. For tunneling oxide in electrically erasable programmable read only memory (EEPROM), a serious problem occurs. High electric field to thinner oxide than about 10 nm induces excess leakage current as shown in Figure 5.20[8]. The phenomenon of stress leakage is clearly observed but only at low field, where the current is enhanced by up to three orders of magnitude. In contrast at high field, only very small changes in the current were observed, of the

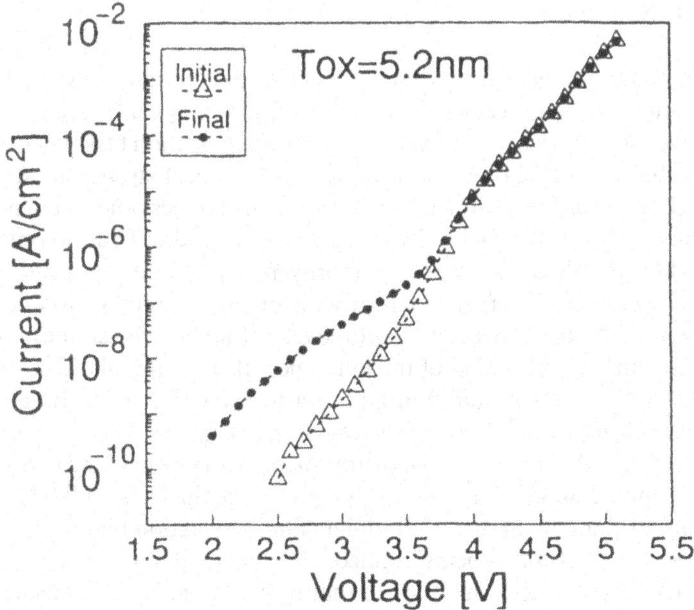

Figure 5.20 The initial I-V characteristics of 5.2nm oxide before stress and finally after stressing for 100 s at 5.6 V[8].

order of a few percent of the initial current. This phenomenon of the stress induced leakage current is distinguished from the current changes by the charge trapping in the oxide as shown in Figure 5.15. Upon stressing the oxide the initial Fowler-Nordheim plot for the stress induced leakage current component is significantly altered. In the low field region an excellent fit to a straight line is obtained but with a greatly reduced gradient. From this gradient, a barrier height is calculated to be a value of 0.94 eV, where in a higher region a value is 2.9 eV. The mechanism of the stress induced leakage current has yet to be clarified. It has been considered that energy levels in the forbidden gap of the oxide are induced by the high electric field to assist electrons tunneling from cathode electrode to anode electrode.

Attention should be paid to this stress induced leakage current because of change of memory data of EEPROM during read operation, which hinders a thinning of tunnel oxide.

5.8. Summary

There are a lot of degradation factors of the oxide quality in the ULSI manufacturing processes. To avoid the degradation, ultra clean processes are necessary. For example, application of multi task machines or cluster tools should be considered. Dynamical stress, radiation, high temperature treatment, surface micro-roughness and so on, may damage to the thin thermally grown silicon dioxides. Thus, to obtain highly reliable oxide, not only improvements of unit processes but also examination of the total process or every process module of a given ULSIs are necessary. Moreover, for highly efficient development, an understanding of the fundamentals of materials, processes and machines is required in addition to the study of degradation mechanisms or reliability of the thin film insulators.

On the other hand, as the integration progresses, thinner oxide will be required. In gigabit class ULSIs, gate oxide thickness will become 5 nm or thinner. As one of candidate films, insulation film with high dielectric constant is being studied. New material films should have a reliability which is superior to that of the thermally grown silicon dioxide.

References

1. Yamabe, K., Taniguchi, K. and Matsushita, Y. (1983). *Proc. Int. Reliability Phys. Sympo.*, p. 184.
2. Yamabe, K. and Taniguchi, K. (1985). *IEEE Trans. J. Solid-State Circuits*, vol. SC-20, 343.
3. Yamabe, K. and Imai, K. (1987). *IEEE Trans. Electron Devices*, vol. ED-34, 1681.
4. Imai, K. and Yamabe, K. (1990). *Appl. Phys. Lett.*, **56**(3), 280.
5. Ozawa, Y. and Yamabe, K. (1991). *Ext. Abs. 1991 Int. Conf. Solid State Devices Mat.*, Yokohama (Japan), 240.
6. Nadahara, S., Shiozawa, J., Imai, K., Suguro, K. and Yamabe, K. (1989). *Appl. Surf. Sci.*, **41**–**42**, 425.
7. Miura, Y., Yamabe, K., Komiya, Y. and Tarui, Y. (1980). *J. Electrochem. Soc.*, **127**, 191.
8. Patel, N. K. and Toriumi, A. (1994). *Appl. Phys. Lett.*, **64**, 1809.

CHAPTER 6

Impurity Doping

6.1. Introduction

Doping of Group III and V elements into semiconductor Si, Group IV element, of integrated circuits substrate is performed to control a threshold voltage of MOS transistor, form a PN junction, lower the resistivity of polysilicon electrodes and the contact with Si and metallic wires, and so on. Doped impurity atoms diffuse during doping thermal treatment and the post thermal treatments such as thermal oxidation and annealing. To realize the small size transistor in ultra large scale integrated circuits (ULSI's), control or suppression of the dopant impurity diffusion is necessary.

At present, the most useful impurity doping technology is energy ion implantation. Impurity distribution is controlled by acceleration energy and dose concentration[1]. One of the recent ion implantation machines realizes the acceleration energy of 2 keV and the dose of 10^{12} ions/cm^2. Given the mechanism of ion implantation, physical damages to the silicon lattice is unavoidable. The ion implantation is accompanied by high temperature annealing, which repairs the physical damage. This high temperature process enlarges the impurity profile.

In addition to the low energy ion implantation technology, the post ion implantation processes are considered. Here, those processes which influence the impurity profile will be discussed.

6.2. Impurity Doping

6.2.1. Ion Implantation

An individual implanted ion undergoes scattering events with electrons and atoms in the silicon crystal, reducing the ion's energy until it comes to rest. A typical ion stops at a distance normal to the surface, called the projected range, R_p. Some lucky ions encounter few scattering events in a given distance in the silicon and come to rest beyond the projected range. Other ions have more than the average number of scattering events and come to rest between the surface and the projected range. The fluctuation in the projected range is ΔR_p. In a first order approximation, the depth profile of stopped ions can be approximated by a symmetric Gaussian distribution function. The concentration of implanted atoms as a function of position is

$$n(x) = n(R_p)\ \exp(-(x - R_p)^2/2\Delta R_p, \qquad (1)$$

where the maximum concentration occurs at $x = R_p$, and ΔR_p is the standard deviation of the distribution. The integral of $n(x)$ gives the dose, ϕ, and the maximum concentration, $n(R_p)$, can be written as

$$n(\delta R_p) = \Phi/(\sqrt{2\pi\Delta R_p}). \qquad (2)$$

A more exact description for the implanted profiles is given by only Pearson-IV solutions. Figure 6.1 shows both the symmetric Gaussian distribution function and Pearson-IV distribution in addition to the measured data points. More information about the Pearson-IV distribution is available in the literature.[2] As shown in Figure 6.1,

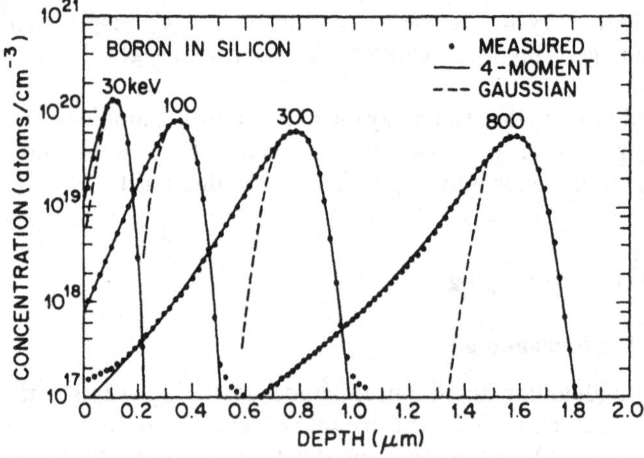

Figure 6.1 Boron implanted atom distribution, with measured data points, and four-moment (Pearson-IV) and symmetric Gaussian curves, (After Hofker, Ref. 2).

a lower energy acceleration gives a shallower as-implanted distribution. The projected range is as a function of the acceleration energy. Arsenic ion lighter than phosphorus ion is implanted in a shallower n^+ region than phosphorus ion. For a shallower p^+ layer, molecular species, BF_2, are practically used. The dissociation of BF_2^+ upon its first atomic scattering event gives a lower energy boron atom. The energy of the boron atoms is $(MB/MBF_2)E_0 = (11/49)E_0$, where MB and MBF_2 are the masses of the boron and BF_2 molecule, respectively, and E_0 is the incident energy of the BF_2 molecule.

Based on Lindhard, Scharff and Schiott (LSS) theory, the implanted ions lose the kinetic energy by electronic and nuclear stopping. The nuclear stopping causes the physical damage to the target silicon crystal, that is, the point defects such as vacancies and interstitial silicons. Light ions (e.g., B_{11}) which enter the surface initially suffer mostly electronic stopping. They gradually lose energy until nuclear stopping becomes dominant. On the other hand, heavy ions (P_{31} or As_{75}) enter the surface and immediately encounter a relative higher fraction of nuclear stopping. They displace a large number of silicon atoms close to the surface.

6.2.2. Doped Silicate Glass

To form a uniform diffused layer at the silicon surface of a three-dimensional structure such as a trench capacitor, not the ion implantation but a doped silicate glasses such as arsenic silicate glass (AsSG) or phospho-silicate glass (PSG) is effective. For a shallower diffused layer formation, AsSG is widely used.[3]

The AsSG film with a uniform thickness can be formed by a low pressure chemical vapor deposition using simultaneous thermal decomposition of tetra-ethoxy-silane (TEOS) and tri-ethoxy-arsine (TEOA) in a standard hot wall type reactor. The AsSG film with a thickness of about 100nm including As atoms of $2 \times 10^{20}\,cm^{-3}$ is typically formed. After isothermal annealing, Figures 6.2 (a) and (b) show As diffusion profiles in AsSG/Si structure with As concentration in AsSG of 2×10^{20} atoms/cm^3 and 1×10^{21} atoms/cm^3, respectively. After 4 hours at 1000°C in nitrogen ambient, the diffused layer with a diffusion depth of 0.13 μm and a surface As concentration of $3 \times 10^{19}\,cm^{-3}$ is realized. This diffusion layer gives us an MOS

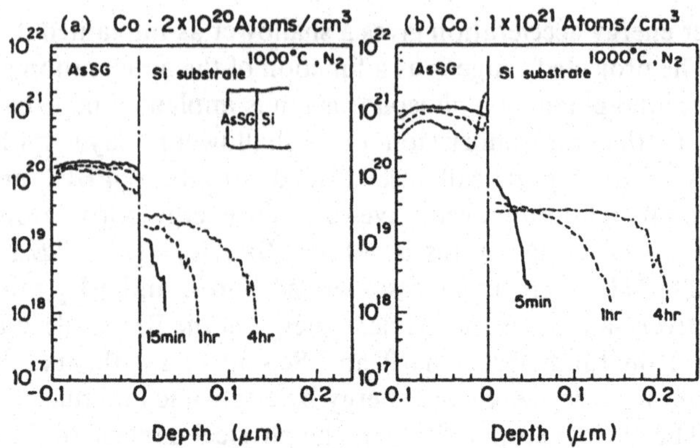

Figure 6.2 As diffusion profiles in AsSG/Si structure with As concentrations of 2×10^{20} cm^{-3} and 1×10^{21} cm^{-3} (After Ref. 2).

capacitor with a sufficiently high inversion capacitance. Note that the arsenic concentration in AsSG of more than 2×10 cm^{-3} at 1000°C is in a supersaturated state in order to precipitate excessive arsenic at the AsSG/Si interface. In the diffusion annealing, the interface of AsSG/Si becomes nucleation sites. This precipitation layer acts as a diffusion barrier to the silicon substrate. Consequently, it is difficult to form an arsenic diffusion layer with a higher total concentration.

6.3. Macroscopic Diffusion Mechanism

6.3.1. Fick's Law

When there is a difference of the impurity concentration in a crystal, the flux of the impurity atoms, J, is proportional to the slope of the impurity concentration, $\delta C/\delta x$. The relation is represented by,

$$J = -D\delta C/\delta x. \tag{1}$$

This is the Fick's first law. Here, x is the distance of the depth diffused. The proportional constant, D, is referred to as the diffusion coefficient.

According to the general form of the transport equation, when no generation and recombination occur,

$$\delta C/\delta t = \delta J/\delta x, \tag{2}$$

where t is time. Substituting eq.(1) to eq.(2), one has

$$\delta C/\delta t = D\,\delta^2 C/\delta x^2. \tag{3}$$

This is Fick's second law of diffusion. Depth profile of impurity atoms in crystal can be obtained by solving the diffusion equation under a given boundary condition. For example, during predeposition the surface concentration, C_s, is kept constant since an infinite amount of the diffusants is available at the wafer surface. That is, in this case the boundary condition that applies to the above diffusion equation is,

$$C(0, t) = Cs. \tag{4}$$

Since the initial condition is,

$$C(x, 0) = 0, \tag{5}$$

the solution to the above diffusion equation is,

$$C(x, t) = Cs\ \operatorname{erfc}\{x/(2\sqrt{Dt})\}. \tag{6}$$

This result is the complementary error function. The total number of dopant atoms, Q, in the crystal is defined by,

$$Q = \int_0^\infty C(x, t)\,dx. \tag{7}$$

For the above case,

$$Q = (2/\sqrt{\pi})\sqrt{Dt}\,Cs. \tag{8}$$

When the value $\sqrt{Dt}$ for drive-in step is much larger than that for predeposition, we can represent the predeposition profile mathematically by a delta function. The impurity concentration distribution after the drive-in step subject to this approximation is given by,

$$C(x, t) = Cs(t)\ \exp(-x^2/4Dt). \tag{9}$$

This is the Gaussian distribution. The surface concentration is,

$$Cs(t) = Q/\sqrt{\pi Dt}. \tag{10}$$

In the above two cases, it is found that the impurity depth profiles are represented by thermal budget, that is, the diffusivity, D, multiplied by time, t.

6.3.2. Thermal Budget

The diffusion of the dopant impurity in silicon is a thermally activated process. The temperature dependence of the diffusivity, D, is described by the Arrhenius equation,

$$D(\text{cm}^2/\text{sec}) = D_0 \exp(-E_a/kT). \tag{11}$$

Here, D_0 is the pre-exponential factor, E_a is the activation energy for the impurity diffusion, k is the Boltzmann's constant ($k = 8.62 \times 10^{-5}$ eV/°C), T is the absolute temperature.

Figure 6.3 shows the diffusivity data for boron and arsenic. The logarithm of the diffusivity plotted versus the reciprocal of the absolute temperature gives a good straight line for both boron and

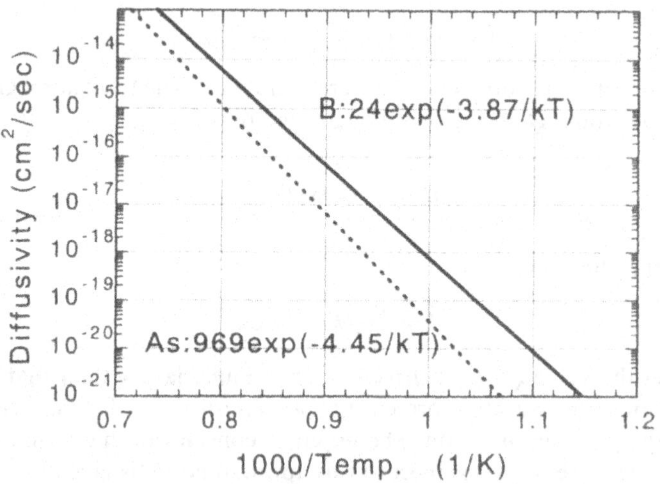

Figure 6.3 Diffusivity data for B and As.

arsenic. In a first order approximation, the impurity profiles after the high temperature treatment are described by the thermal budget, Dt. Even if both the temperature and the time for two diffusion processes are different, if the impurity profiles before the two diffusion processes are the same and the two diffusion processes have the same thermal budget, the impurity profiles after these diffusion processes become approximately the same.

That is, the final impurity profile is determined by the initial impurity profile and the total thermal budget after the impurity doping.

6.4. Microscopic Diffusion Mechanism

6.4.1. Impurity Diffusion and Point Defect

Figure 6.4 shows main three microscopic mechanisms of impurity diffusion. First, in the vacancy mechanism, the atom at the lattice site

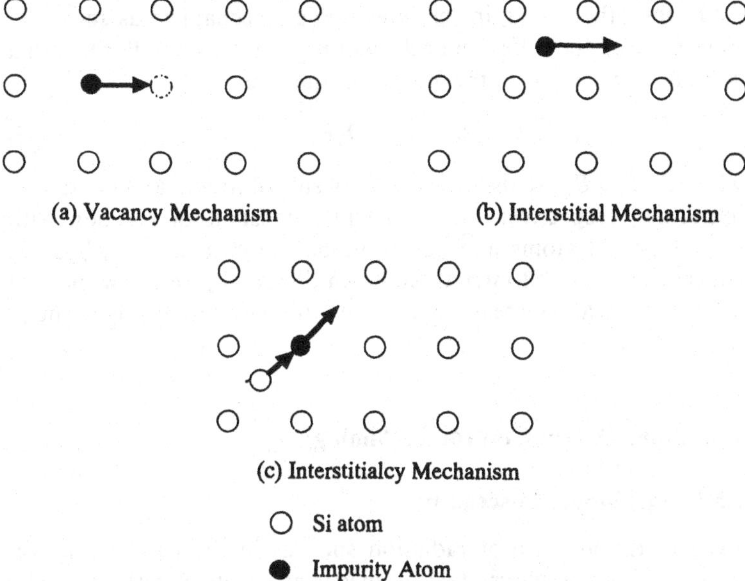

Figure 6.4 Microscopic mechanisms for impurity diffusion.

moves to the vacancy at the neighboring lattice site through the saddle point. Second, in the interstitial mechanism, the atom at the interstitial site rapidly moves through the interstitial site. In the third mechanism, the self interstitial atom kicks out the impurity atom in the lattice site to the next interstitial position. Next, the impurity atom kicks out the neighboring atom in the lattice site to the next interstitial position. This diffusion is called an interstitialcy mechanism. Diffusions of dopant impurities in Si single crystal are mainly attributed to the first or third mechanisms.

In the vacancy mechanism, the diffusion coefficient is represented by the concentration of the vacancy, C_v, and the frequency of attempted jumps, v. That is,

$$D = 3a^2 C_v\, v/16\ \exp(-G_m/kT). \tag{12}$$

Here, ΔG_m is the potential barrier height for the motion of the charged impurities formed by the atoms of crystal, and a is the distance between successive potential barriers. The diffusion coefficient is in proportion to the vacancy concentration.

On the other hand, in the interstitialcy mechanism as shown in Figure 6.4 (c), the diffusion coefficient is given by the self-interstitial concentration, C_i, as in the following equation.

$$D = D_{si} + D_{ii} K_i C_i, \tag{13}$$

where D_{si} and D_{ii} are the diffusivities of substitutional and interstitial impurities, respectively, K_i is the rate constant of reaction with self-interstitial atoms and substitutional impurities, and C_i is the concentration of self-interstitial. From this result, we know that the diffusivity linearly increases with increase of the interstitial concentration.

6.5. Point Defect Control Technology

6.5.1. Equilibrium Concentration

Even in the absence of radiation such as in the case of the ion implantation a single crystal cannot exist in a state of perfection. The lattice vibrations may be represented as a statistical distribution of thermal energy among the atoms of the crystal. In any such distribution, there is a finite probability of sufficient energy to a group of atoms to form a defect in the crystal lattice.

From thermodynamic considerations, one may find that the configuration of defects in the lattice produces the minimum value of the appropriate thermodynamic energy function.

Suppose one has a crystal with n defects of a particular type and N sites available for them. Total Gibbs free energy of the crystal, G, is given by,

$$G = G_0 + n\mathrm{E}_f - \mathrm{TS}_c - \mathrm{TS}_v. \tag{14}$$

Here, G_0 is the Gibbs free energy of the perfect crystal. E_f is the amount by which the internal energy increases when such a defect is introduced and is referred to as the "energy of formation". E_f is the energy which is necessary when the Si atom at the lattice site cuts off four bonds between the neighboring Si atoms and these neighboring atoms are reconstructed. S_c is the change in total entropy associated with the introduction of the n defects and is known as the "configuration entropy". This entropy is,

$$S_c = k \log w = N!/\{n!(N-n)!\}. \tag{15}$$

Using Stirling's approximation, $\log x! \fallingdotseq x \log x$, for large x,

$$S_c = k\{N \log N - n \log n - (N-n) \log (N-n)\}. \tag{16}$$

In addition to the entropy, S_c, the alteration of the vibration disorder, or entropy brought about by the presence of defects, S_v, must be taken into consideration. In the Einstein's model of lattice vibration, the atoms are represented as 3 N independent linear harmonic oscillators and the entropy is,

$$3\,Nk \log\{kT/h\nu\}, \tag{17}$$

Where ν is the natural frequency of the oscillators, given in terms of the Einstein characteristic temperature, ΘE by $h\upsilon = k\Theta E$.

Consider each defect affects the vibration of z neighboring atoms, changing the vibration frequency, on average, to υ'. The entropy of these z atoms will be,

$$3kz \log\{kT/h\nu'\} = 3kz\,[\log\{kT/h\nu\} + \log\{\nu/\nu'\}] \tag{18}$$

Hence, the change in entropy due to the defect is given by the second term. For n defect the total change in entropy, S_v, is,

$$S_v = 3nkz \log\{v/v'\}. \tag{19}$$

For Gibbs Free energy expression, one has,

$$G = G_0 + nE_f - 3nkTz \log\{v/v'\} - kT\{N \log N - n \log n - (N-n)\log(N-n)\}. \tag{20}$$

In equilibrium, n will satisfy $\delta G/\delta N = 0$. From the result for eq. (20), one has,

$$E_f = kT \log[\{(N-n)/n\}\{v/v'\}3Z]. \tag{21}$$

Assuming $N \gg n$, the defect concentration, C_x, is

$$C_x = n/N = \{v/v'\}3z \exp\{-E_f/kT\}. \tag{22}$$

Estimation of the concentrations of the vacancy, C_v, and the self interstitial, C_i, in Si gives the following results, respectively[4].

$$C_v^*(\mathrm{cm}^{-3}) = 2 \times 10^{23} \exp(-2\,\mathrm{eV}/kT), \tag{23}$$

$$C_i^*(\mathrm{cm}^{-3}) = 5 \times 10^{30} \exp(-4.4\,\mathrm{eV}/kT). \tag{24}$$

Figure 6.5 shows the temperature dependence of the equilibrium concentration of the vacancy and the self-interstitial atom. The certainties of these quantities in the temperature ranges given in the figure are at least in the order of a factor of ten.

The single vacancy in silicon is known to exist in at least four charge states: V^+, V^x, V^- and V^{2-}, where + refers to a donor level, x a neutral species, and + an acceptor level. Electron paramagnetic resonance (EPR) measurements and thermally stimulated emission measurements yield the estimated energy levels within the forbidden gap of the silicon. The concentration of each ionized vacancy depends on the Fermi level.

6.5.2. Point Defect Injection

a) Thermal Oxidation

From isotope labeling, in thermal oxidation of silicon surface, a new oxide film generates at the Si/SiO_2 interface. The reaction

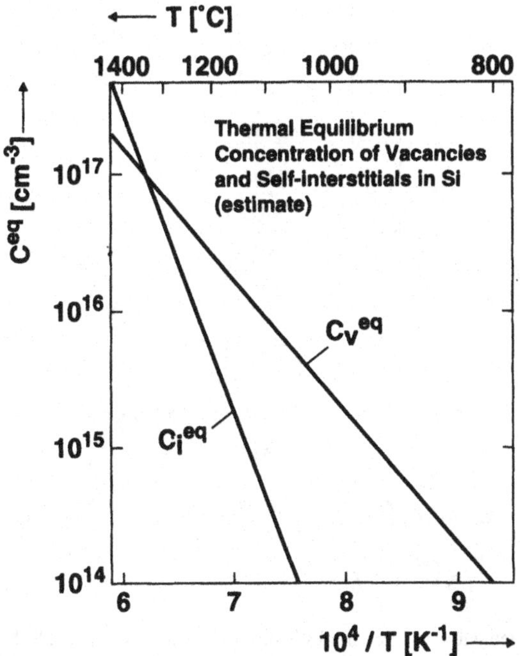

Figure 6.5 Equilibrium concentrations of vacancies, C_v, and of interstitial silicon, C_i (After Ref. 4).

equation is represented as follows.

$$Si + O_2 \rightarrow SiO_2. \tag{25}$$

In this reaction, the volume of the formed SiO_2 film becomes 2.3 times larger than that of the consumed Si. Most of the volume is obtained by movement or deformation of the pre-formed SiO_2 film. At the same time, as is shown in Figure 6.6, one part of silicon atoms can be left oxidized and be emitted as the self-interstitial atom into the bulk silicon or the bulk SiO_2 film, and the vacancies in the silicon can be absorbed as a volume source. Finally, when enough volume is not obtained at the Si/SiO_2 interface, a condensed new SiO_2 film is generated. Contents of both the injected interstitial silicons and the absorbed vacancies depend on the oxidation condition, especially, the oxidation rate.

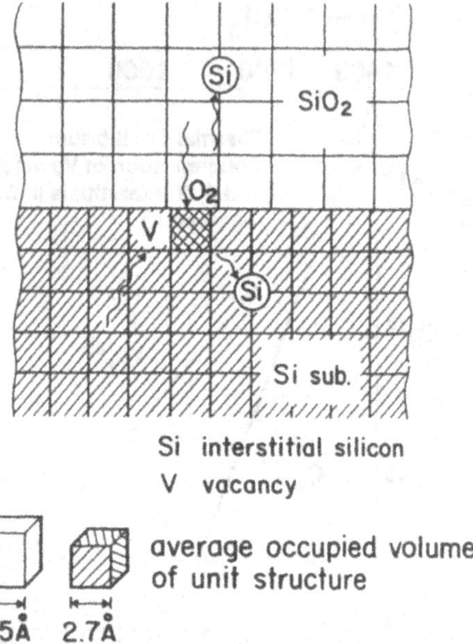

Figure 6.6 Behaviors of interstitial silicons and vacancies near the Si/SiO_2 interface.

In the case of interstitial injection, if there are the origins of stacking faults in the silicon substrate, these trap the injected interstitial atoms and grow to be stacking faults. Accordingly, from observation of the stacking fault growth, the effective injection rate of the interstitial silicon from the Si/SiO_2 interface during oxidation can be estimated. The interstitial silicon concentration, C_i, in the injected region is higher than the equilibrium concentration, C_i^*. Excess interstitial silicons recombine with vacancies during diffusion. Diffusion for both point defects is described as follows.

$$dC_i/dt = D_i\, d^2 C_i/dx^2 + k(C_i^* C_v^* - C_i C_v), \tag{26}$$

$$dC_v/dt = D_v\, d^2 C_v/dx^2 + k(C_i^* C_v^* - C_i C_v), \tag{27}$$

where C_v^* and C_v are the equilibrium concentration and the injected concentration of the vacancy, respectively. In the above equation, the second term in both equations indicates the annihilation point defects by the recombination. Because of high recombination rate, it can be considered that $C_i C_v$ is constant. This makes the application of effective diffusion constant, D_{eff}, possible, which represents the movement of both point defects. That is,[5]

$$dC_x/dt = D_{eff} d^2 C_x/dx^2, \tag{28}$$

$$D_{eff} = 8.6 \times 10^5 \exp(-4eV/kT). \tag{29}$$

Here, x represents vacancy or interstitial silicon. Effective diffusivity is experimentally obtained. The effective diffusivity is higher by a factor of 10^3-10^4 than that of dopant impurities. In larger scale integrated circuits an oxide becomes thinner and the manufacturing process temperature decreases. Let us consider the diffusion length of the point defect, for example, in the case of the oxide thickness of 25nm and 8nm and their process temperatures of 1000 °C and 850 °C, respectively. The oxidation time in the dry oxygen ambient at 1000 °C to form the oxide of 25nm thickness is about 1080 sec, while the oxidation time at 850 °C for 8nm thick oxide is about 2100 sec. The diffusion length of point defect for the former is 7.4 μm, while that for the latter is 0.9 μm. The value of the latter decreases to about an 8th of that of the former. While the concentration of the point defects can be supposed to be uniform in the active region of ULSI's, the depth distribution of the point defects has to be considered in order to precisely control a future device structure with a much smaller size.

Let us call D the instantaneous value by the diffusion coefficient of impurity atom in silicon during oxidation. We can define, D^*, C_i^* and C_v^* as the values which the three parameters take during non-oxidizing thermal treatment at the same temperature. For a given temperature, D^*, C_i^* and C_i^* have the values described above. When both vacancy and the interstitialcy mechanisms are taken into account in the silicon substrate with low dose impurities, the diffusivity is given by,

$$D = D_i^*(C_i/C_i^*) + D_v^*(C_v/C_v^*). \tag{30}$$

Here, D_i^* and D_v^* are the diffusivity for the interstitialcy mechanism and that of the vacancy mechanism, respectively.

Diffusivity enhancement or retardation can be expressed by a ratio, D/D^*. We note that the diffusions of B, P, and As are enhanced whereas that of Sb is retarded.

If we suppose that the diffusivity due to either mechanism (vacancy and interstitialcy) is proportional to the concentration of related point defects both in non-oxidizing and oxidizing atmosphere, ratio D/D^* can be written:

$$D/D^* = f_i(C_i/C_i^*) + (1 - f_i)(C_v/C_v^*), \tag{31}$$

where and f_i is that fraction of the diffusion coefficient which corresponds to the interstitialcy mechanism when silicon is thermally treated in a non-oxidizing ambient, $f_i = D_i^*/D_v^*$. The value, f_i, depends on the impurity species and the diffusion temperature.

Figure 6.7 shows a sample structure of the diffusion experiments. Here, the selective oxidation can progress only in the window region of the Si_3N_4 of the back-side surface of silicon.[6–8] B atoms are doped into the surface side by ion implantation technique and post-anneal-

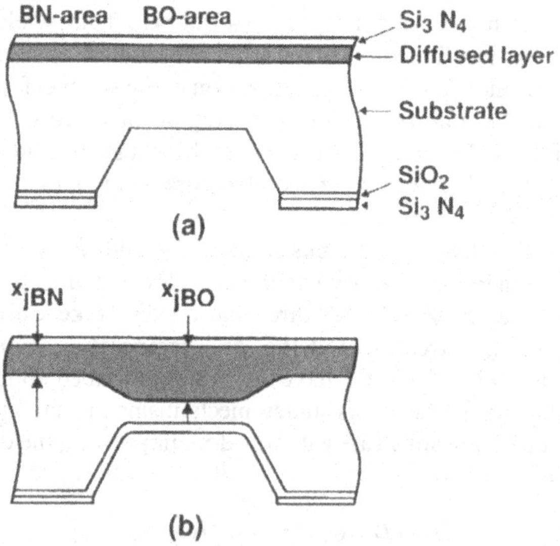

Figure 6.7 Cross sectional view of the samples, (a) after Si etching and (b) after back-side selective oxidation (After Ref. 6).

ing is performed to release crystallographic damage. After selective oxidation, the diffusion length, X_{jBO}, of B in the region which corresponds to the Si_3N_4 windows is larger than that, X_{jBN}, in the region which corresponds to the non-oxidized, Si_3N_4 masked region. In Figure 6.8, the diffusion enhancement values for B, X_{jBO}/X_{jBN}, are plotted as a function of the distance, L, from the oxidizing interface to the silicon surface for various oxidation time. The values, X_{jBO}/X_{jBN}, decrease with L. The phenomenon could be explained as the effect of back-side oxidation. The injected interstitial silicons from the oxidizing interface diffuse in the bulk silicon as they recombine with the vacancies. The decrease with L represents the recombination effect.

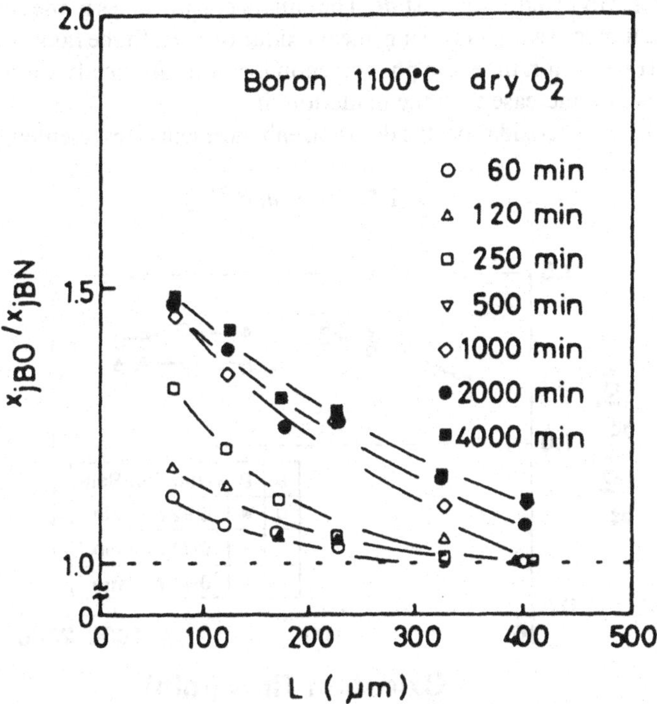

Figure 6.8 Diffusion enhancement values as a function of the distance, L, from the oxidizing interface to the surface for various oxidation time (After Ref. 6).

The range at which X_{jBO}/X_{jBN} reduces to unity increases with oxidation time. This suggests that the interstitial distribution enlarges in the non-steady state within this experimental range. And, B and P doped in the front-side exhibit the same tendency as the above phenomena. That is, it suggests that the diffusion enhancement of both dopant impurities is due to the identical mechanism. In an experiment in which the constant oxidation rate is realized by the pressure increasing oxidation technique, the effect of oxidation rate on the enhanced diffusion has been estimated. Figure 6.9 shows the diffusion enhancement values, X_{jO}/X_{jON}, for the pressure increasing oxidation as a function of the oxidation time. In the longer oxidation time, the values are independent of the oxidation time. In this region, the interstitial supply and the recombination with the vacancies balance to reach a steady state. The enhancement values in the steady state increase with increasing linear oxidation rate. In the range of the short oxidation time, the phenomenon is not in the steady state and the values increase with the oxidation time.

Likewise in oxidation, the diffusion enhancement is represented, by[9],

$$D-D^* \propto (dX/dt)^{0.3} \tag{32}$$

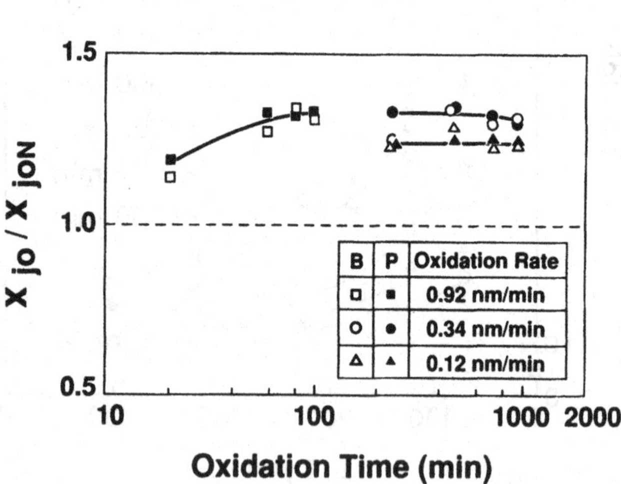

Figure 6.9 Diffusion enhancement for the pressure increasing oxidation as a function of oxidation time (After Ref. 8).

In the B diffusion experiment in the oxidation ambient, the eq. (32) describes the experimental results over the range of this experiment. This, however, cannot explain the results in Figure 6.9. In the above experiment, the CZ silicon substrates were used. There is a difference between CZ and FZ silicon substrate. For both P and B diffusion in the CZ silicon, the diffusion depth ratio, X_{jBO}/X_{jBN}, is almost unity for the back-side oxidation at 1100 °C for 1000 min. This result is explained as an effect of the enhancement by supersaturated interstitials from oxygen precipitate formation. Furthermore, the Si_3N_4 directly covered surface makes the oxidation enhanced diffusion by the back-side oxidation more effective than the SiO_2 covered surface. It can be explained that this result comes from the higher capture rate of the supersaturated interstitials at the Si/SiO_2 interface than that at the Si/Si_3N_4 interface.

Taniguchi *et al.*[10,11] suggested and experimentally examined that when the oxidation rate is low enough, the concentration of the interstitial silicon can become lower than the equilibrium concentration considering the regrowth rate at the Si/SiO_2 interface and the injection rate to the SiO_2 film.

Now, when it is assumed that a θ mole of silicon atoms is ejected as interstitials at the interface, the generation rate of the interstitials, G, is directly proportional to oxidation rate expressed as

$$G = \theta\, dX_0/dt, \tag{33}$$

where X_0 is the oxide thickness. The generated interstitials have three fluxes: 1) J_1 represents the interstitial flux into the oxide which reacts with incoming oxidant, 2) J_2 is the flux arising from the surface regrowth, and 3) J_3 shows the interstitial flux into bulk silicon due to the normal diffusion process. Accordingly, the following relationship exists between these fluxes

$$G = J_1 + J_2 + J_3. \tag{34}$$

Since the relaxation time for the oxidizing system is very short compared to the oxidation time, one can assume steady-state condition in the oxide. At this time, one can also consider that the concentration of the oxidant species should be nearly constant where interstitial diffusion in the oxide is limited only to the interfacial region. Based on these assumptions, the flux J_1 is represented by

$$J_1 = m_l(K_o D_{ol})^{0.5} C_o^{0.5} C_i, \tag{35}$$

where C_o is the oxidant concentration in the oxide near the interface, K_o is the reaction rate of the interstitials due to the first order reaction between the generated interstitials and incoming oxygen in the oxide, D_{ol} is the diffusivity of the interstitials in the oxide, and m_2 is the segregation coefficient, C_{io}/C_i, which is normally larger than one because the enthalpy of formation of the self-interstitial in silicon is much higher than in SiO_2.

Next, J_2 flux is given by

$$J_2 = K_l(C_i - C_i^*), \tag{36}$$

where K_l denotes the surface regrowth rate constant. This equation indicates that the excess interstitials are absorbed when the interstitial concentration, C_i, is higher than C_i^* while the interstitials are generated in the case of the undersaturation of the interstitial silicons.

The third flux, J_3, is expressed as

$$J_3 = -D_i dC_i/dx. \tag{37}$$

Here, D_i is the diffusion coefficient of the interstitial silicon in the silicon substrate. The length of OSF's in the region covered with silicon nitride mask near the LOCOS edge decreases sharply with distance from the oxidation mask edge while the OSF's in the oxidized region show constant length regardless of the distance from the mask edge. This fact reveals that the self-interstitial atom concentration in the oxide is much larger than in the bulk silicon under normal oxidation conditions. Thus, this flux, J_3, is negligibly small, compared with the other terms.

In the Deal-Grove oxidation model, it is assumed that the reaction rate at the interface is proportional to the oxidant concentration. Some experimental results, however, have indicated that the rate constant has sublinear dependence on the oxidant pressure. Thus, the relation between the oxidation rate, $R(= dX_0/dt)$, and the oxidant concentration, C_o, is plausibly expressed as

$$R \propto C_o m. \tag{38}$$

Using eqs. (33)–(38), the normalized concentration of the interstitial silicons at the interface is expressed as a function of oxidation rate by

$$C_i/C_i^* = D_a/D_a^* = (\alpha R + 1)/(\beta R^{1/2m} + 1), \tag{39}$$

where α and β are parameters composed by D_{ol}, K_I, N, K_i and m_I. This equation predicts interstitial undersaturation provided

$$R < R_c = (\beta/\alpha)^{2m/(2m-1)}, \tag{40}$$

where R_c is the critical oxidation rate below which the undersaturation of the self-interstitials can occur and an oxidation retarded diffusion (ORD) for phosphorus can be observed. Actually, ORD of phosphorus has been reported in an experiment at very low oxidation rate, where the oxidation was carried out at 1150 °C for 30 min under an oxygen partial pressure of 0.01 atm.

For relatively large oxidation rate ($\alpha R \gg 1$ and $\beta R^{1/2m} \gg 1$), to which practical oxidation condition corresponds, the equation,

$$D_a/D_a^* \fallingdotseq (\alpha/\beta)R^{1-1/2m}, \tag{41}$$

is obtained. When $m = 0.6$, $D_a/D_a^* \propto R^{0.17}$ which explains a lot of the oxidation rate dependence of OED for phosphorus and boron.

Figure 6.10 shows a comparison between calculated OED results by eq.(39) and experimental results for (100) Si substrate.

b) Nitridation,[12]

Direct nitridation of Si and SiO_2 at high temperature in NH_3 has been investigated. When samples with three different surface region, that is, an area where Si crystal is bare (B area), an area masked with SiO_2 films (O area), and an area masked with double-layered SiO_2–Si_3N_4 films (ON area) as shown in Figures 6.11 (a) are nitrided, junction depths in the three areas are different. In Figures 6.11 (b), typical results for impurity diffusions are illustrated. 1) Enhanced B and P diffusion (retarded Sb diffusion) occur in Si masked with SiO_2 films (O area). 2) An opposite effect is found when nitridation is performed on a bare silicon surface (B area).

Underneath the O area, the oxidation induced stacking faults (OSF's) are observed. From this result, one can suppose that at the Si/SiO_2 interface in the O area the interstitial silicons are generated by

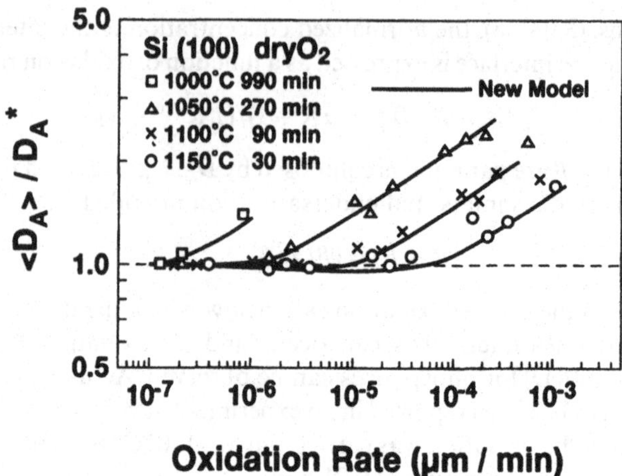

Figure 6.10 Comparison between calculated OED results by eq. (39) and experimental results for (100) Si substrate (After Ref. 11).

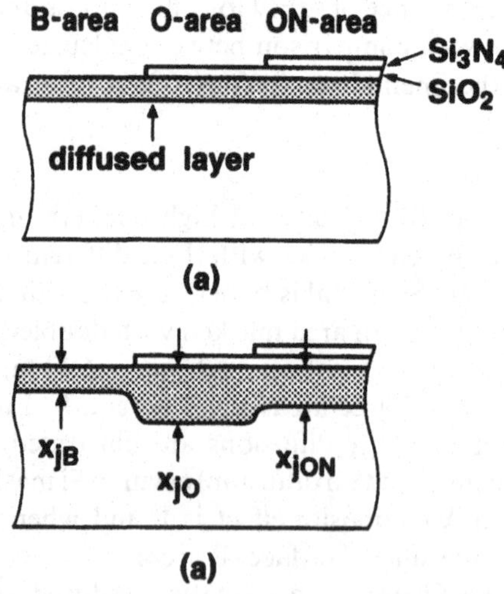

Figure 6.11 Sample structures nitrided in NH_3 gas. And junction depths of three regions are different each other.

the nitridation in the NH_3 ambient. Underneath the B area, the OSF's vanish after the nitridation in the NH_3 ambient. These results can be explained by a model in which the vacancies are generated. Why the nitridation process induces the generation of interstitials (beneath the O area) and of vacancies (on the B area) is not well understood.

c) Ion Implantation[13]

Defect generation by the implantation of ions into silicon is in a direct process of primary and secondary collisions of the ions with the atoms of the host crystal. As radiation damage, a high concentration of point defects occur in the form of interstitials and vacancies. On the other hand, the implanted ions are generally located in electrically inactive sites in the lattice immediately following implantation. Therefore, it is necessary for implantation to be followed by an annealing treatment to serve the two purposes of electrically activating the dopant atoms and reducing the degree of radiation damage in the crystal. In this section, a fast diffusion incidental to the post annealing is discussed.

Figure 6.12 shows the boron profiles for as-implanted (a), after annealing at 800 °C (b), and 1000 °C (c) for 10 sec by SIMS (secondary ion microscopy). In both of (b) and (c), increases of diffusion depth by 0.05 μm are seen. The increases after annealing for 10 sec like this are observed for acceleration energy of both 10 and 20 KeV with a dose of 5×10^{15} cm^{-2} over the range of 700 ~ 1000 °C. It is suggested that the B diffusion can be classified into two stages. The first stage is a very rapid diffusion which takes place within 10 sec. The second stage is the normal diffusion. It is supposed that the rapid diffusion is due to the point defects formed as the radiation damage during ion implantation.

d) Phosphorus Diffusion[14]

In a sample structure the surface of silicon crystal may have an effect on generation or annihilation of point defect. To estimate the effects of point defects on the dopant impurity diffusion, usage of a buried layer of dopant atoms as shown in Figure 6.13 is useful. There are various window sizes for injection of the point defects. In experiments where PSG's (phospho-silicate glasses) are used as a point defect injection source, the junction depth decreases markedly with

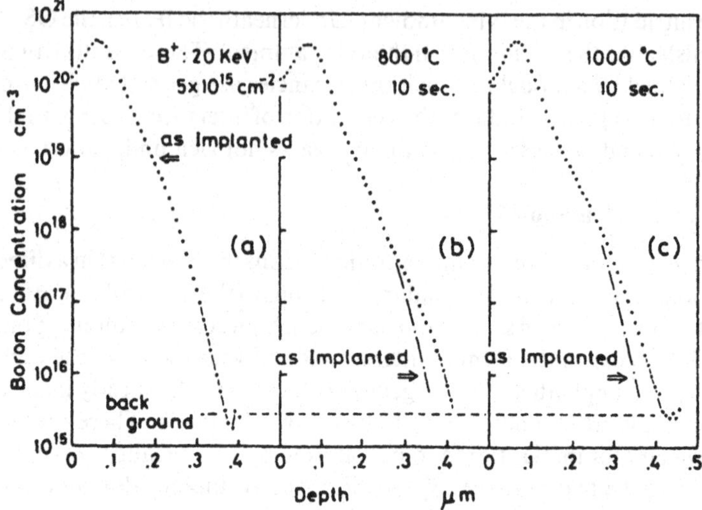

Figure 6.12 Boron profiles for as-implanted, after annealing at 800 °C, and 1000 °C for 10 sec by SIMS (After Ref. 13).

decreasing window area ratio. Figures 6.14 (a) and (b) show in-depth profiles of impurity atoms after annealing at 850°C in Ar ambient. Figure 6.14 (a) is a profile of buried layer underneath diffusion window region, while Figure 6.14(b) is underneath masking region. From these results, diffusivity, recombination rate of point defect and impurity diffusion constant can be measured precisely. The *B* diffusivity is obtained as a function of the injection window area ratio for two buried depths at 750 °C. From slope of fitting curve, one can estimate concentrations of interstitials which reach from the phosphorus diffusion area to the buried layer. From the values, the diffusion coefficients of the interstitial silicon atoms and the recombination rates can be calculated by using a three-dimensional simulator. Figure 6.15 shows the diffusivity of self-interstitial atoms with data from the literature.

e) Silicidation[15,16]

Redistribution of implanted atoms in silicon occurs during silicide formation. When heat treatment for a sample with Pd film on silicon

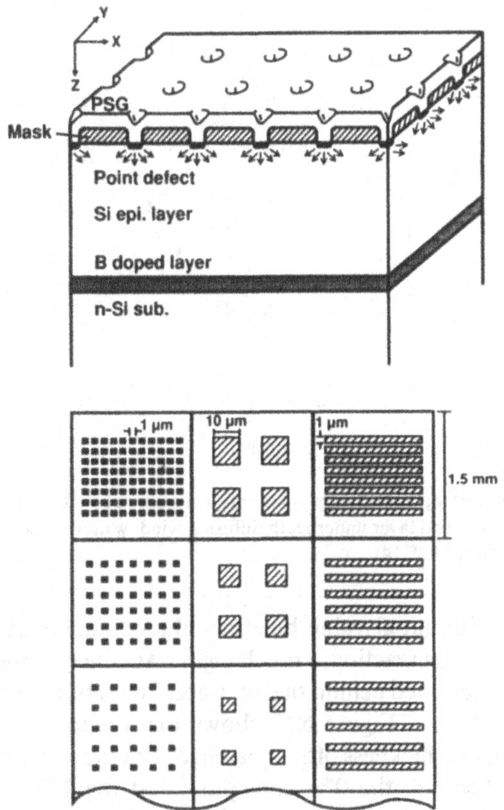

Figure 6.13 Sample structure. Angle-lapped surfaces after the annealing at 850 °C. Arrows indicate junctions of monitor regions (After Ref. 14).

surface after an implantation of As is performed, a high concentration of As atoms is snowplowed by the moving silicide-Si interface into the substrate Si during Pd_2Si formation at 250 °C. Figure 6.16 shows depth profiles of As concentration for the samples without the 900 °C, 30min preannealing (upper) and with the preannealing (lower). The squares, diamonds and triangles represented the distribution after isothermal annealing at 250 °C for 17, 70 and 375 min, respectively. After 17 min annealing, the As concentration near the interface is

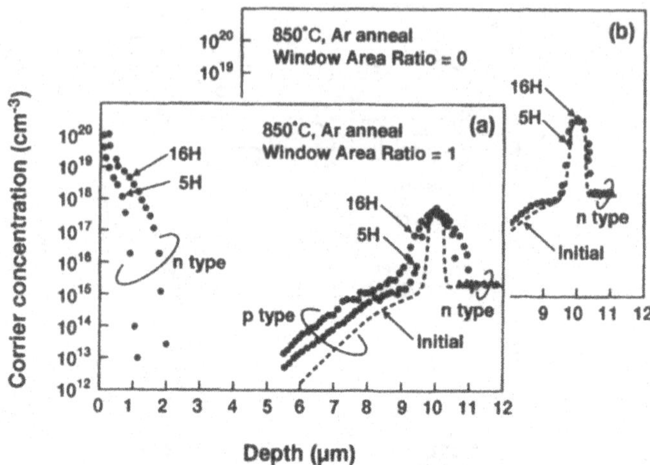

Figure 6.14 Impurity profile changes of monitor regions in 850 °C Ar annealing. (a) In depth profiles of buried layer underneath diffusion window area (area size = 1) and (b) (area size = 0) (After Ref. 14).

higher than the initial value but the values coincide in the deeper region. For 70 min reaction, a much higher As concentration than the initial one is observed behind the interface. The action is completed at 250 °C for 375 min. Figure 6.17 shows the fraction of As in Si as a function of the thickness of Si consumed. The experimental data are all located between the 0 % snowplow and the 100 % snowplow curves. In Figure 6.16, the profiles of 17 min annealing show clearly the snowplow, since their rear position coincides with the initial curves. Some As atoms have redistributed in Si. It is supposed that this snowplow effect, that is, a fast impurity diffusion at a low temperature, occurs as a result of an injection from the silicide/Si interface. The slower growth of Pd_2Si in samples with the 900 °C 30 min preannealing results in a larger amount of snowplow and a deeper penetration of As. Though the preannealing is performed to release radiation damage caused by the ion implantation, how the existence of the crystallographic damage affects the diffusion of the implanted dopant impurity is not clear. From current-voltage characteristics of Pd_2Si/Si contacts with As implantation and snowplow, most of a high concentration of As plowed into Si is electrically active

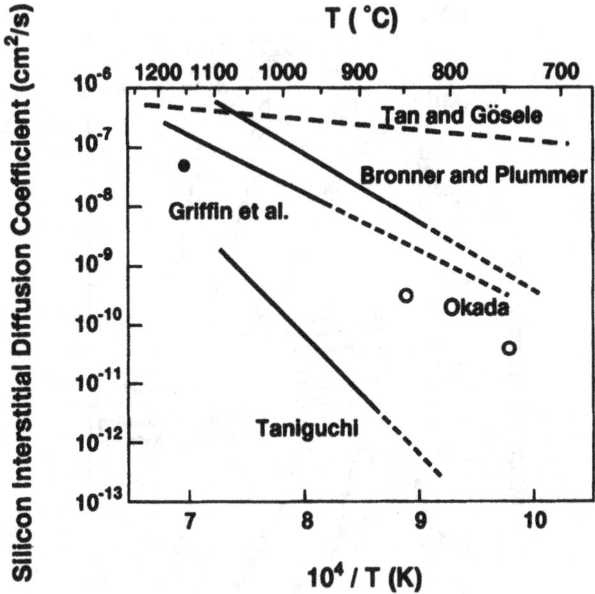

Figure 6.15 Silicon diffusion constants obtained by the 3 dimensional experiments (After Ref.14).

in spite of low temperature annealing of 250°C. The electric activity of the snowplowed As atoms for the samples without preannealing is low and the carrier concentration profiles cannot be obtained because of the high sheet resistivity. It is experimentally confirmed that for the preannealing temperature of about 550 °C, the implanted As atoms become electrically active, while the implanted silicon region is rendered amorphous. This preannealing effect on the activation of the dopant impurity is not yet understood.

6.6. Summary

To form shallow junction for ULSI's, both decreases of an extraneous thermal budget and controls of the point defects in silicon substrate

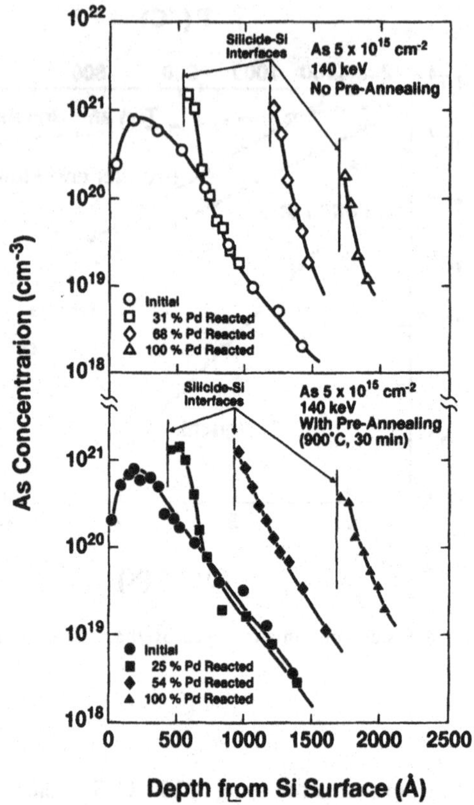

Figure 6.16 Depth profiles of As concentration for the samples without the 900 °C, 30 min preannealing (open symbols) and with the preannealing (solid symbols). The squares, diamonds, and triangles represent the distribution after isothermal annealing at 250 °C for 17, 70, and 375 min, respectively (After Ref. 16).

are examined precisely in addition to shallow doping. Direct observation of the latter has not yet been achieved. In our view, it is also necessary to examine processes other than those indicated in this section.

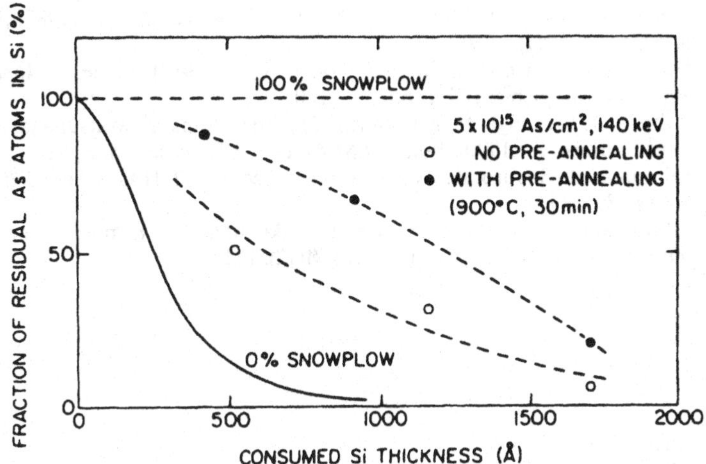

Figure 6.17 Fraction of As remained in Si after the removal of residual Pd and Pd_2Si plotted against the consumed Si thickness. The horizontal dotted line and the solid line represent 100 and 0 % snowplow, respectively (After, Ref. 16).

References

1. Wilson, R. G. and Brewer, G. R. (1973). "Ion Beams with Applications to Ion Implantation", Wiley, New York.
2. Hofker, W. K. (1975). *Philips Res. Repts. Suppl.*, No.8.
3. Tsunashima, Y., Okada, T., Kawaguchi, H., Onga, S. and Yamabe, K. (1989). *Ext. Abs.*, 21st *Conf. Sol. State Dev. Mat.*, Tokyo, p. 181.
4. Tan, T. Y. and Gosele, U. (1985). *Appl. Phys. A*, **37**, 1.
5. Taniguchi, K. and Antoniadis, D. A. (1983). "Defects in Silicon", (The Electrochem. Soc., p. 315.
6. Mizuo, S. and Higuchi, H. (1982). *J. Elecrochem. Soc.*, **129**, 2292.
7. Mizuo, S. and Higuchi, H. (1983). *J. Elecrochem. Soc.*, **130**, 1942.
8. Mizuo, S. and Higuchi, H. (1985). *Appl. Phys. Lett.*, **46**(6), 587.
9. Taniguchi, K., Kurosawa, K. and Kashiwagi, M. (1980). *J. Electrochem. Soc.*, **127**, 2243.
10. Taniguchi, K., Shibata, Y. and Hamaguchi, C. (1989). *J. Appl. Phys.*, **65**(7), 2723.
11. Shibata, Y., Hashimoto, S., Taniguchi, K. and Hamaguchi, C. (1992). *J. Electrochem. Soc.*, **139**, 231.

12. Mizuo, S., Kusaka, T., Shintani, A., Nanba, M. and Higuchi, H. (1983). *J. Appl. Phys.*, **54**(7), 3860.
13. Yamada, K., Kashiwagi, M. and Taniguchi, K. (1983). *Japan. J. Appl. Phys.*, **22**, Supplement 22-1. pp. 157–160.
14.. Okada, T. K., Onga, S., Kawaguchi, H., Mizushima, I., Matsunaga, J. and Yamabe, K. (1990). *Proc. ULSI Process, Elecrochem. Soc.*, 52.
15. Ohdomari, I., Suguro, K., Akiyama, M. and Maeda, T. (1982). *Thin Solid Films* , **89**, 349.
16. Ohdomari, I., Tu, K. N., Suguro, K., Akiyama, M., Kimura, I. and Yoneda, K. (1981). *Appl. Phys. Lett.*, **38**(12), 1015.

CHAPTER 7

Metallization

ULSI technology has produced a variety of electronic devices such as dynamic random access memory (DRAM), static random access memory (SRAM), electrically erasable and programmable read only memory (EEPROM), and logic devices with minimum design rule of 0.35 μm. Up to the present, device feature size has been miniaturized by 67% every three years according to the linear scaling principles[1]. This scaling scenario has been applied for more than 20 years. As for miniaturization of interconnect feature sizes, the interconnect width has been mainly shrunk in order to decrease the interlayer capacitance and increase the interconnects packing desity, while the interconnect thickness has been nearly constant for suppressing the increase in interconnect resistance. As a result, issues in multilevel interconnection technology have been planarization of insulating films and contact plug formation.

However, in the deep submicron regime, the increase in the interconnect induced delay time could be a critical issue in addition to the above-mentioned issues, since the total delay in ULSIs could be dominated by the interconnect feature size (namely the shrinkage of interconnect line/space width and interlayer thickness) will lead to larger interconnect current densities and higher interconnect resistance and capacitance.

In this chapter, issues in multilevel interconnection technology are viewed from the interconnect material and device process development. The most critical problems are as follows.

(1) the increase in the resistance of gate electrodes. (front-end of line)
(2) the increase in the diffusion layer resistance and the contact resistance between metal electrodes and Si substrates. (front-end of line)
(3) the increase in the capacitance between wirings with the scaling of the wiring space. (back-end of line)
(4) the increase in the resistance of global interconnections such as long power lines and bus lines. (back-end of line)

Therefore, low resistivity interconnect materials are required for future front-end and back-end of line interconnect materials, and low permittivity interlayer dielectrics will be required. Morever, since the use of such materials will only reduce the RC delay (the product of resistance and capacitance) by less than one order of magnitude, reverse-scaled interconnects wil be useful for the uppermost metal layer for reducing the interconnect resistance. Thus, a well-balanced design incorporating aspects such as device scaling, good reliability and reduction in performance degrading parasitics, is most significant for future multilevel interconnection technology.

7.1. Gate Electrodes

The first MOSFET was fabricated by using Al gate technology in the mid 1960s. In 1969, the conventional Al gate was replaced by a poly-Si gate which has significant advantages[2]. It features a process in which the poly-Si gate works as a mask for the source and drain formation, thereby inherently giving accurate positioning of the source and drain regions with respect to a gate without any photo-mask aligning steps. This feature inherently results from the thermal stability of Si up to about 1100°C.

On the other hand, since an Al gate cannot endure the entire high temperature processing required for electrical activation of *n*-type or *p*-type dopant impurities, oxidation or anealing, the Al gate must be formed after the source and drain formation with a photo-mask aligning step which is accompanied by the alignment tolerance in positioning the Al gate with respect to the source and drain.

Thus, the implementation of Si gate technology together with advancing photolithography has realized the higher packing density of MOS LSIs. Also, the Si gate technology has easily led to multilevel interconnection in MOS LSIs utilizing the poly-Si as one of the interconnections combined with an overlaying Al electrode as a final metallization. In the 1970 s, the Si gate technology became a main-stream technology to achieve higher packing density MOS devices in the semiconductor industry and this opened the door to the ULSI era.

Refractory metals such as Mo, W and Ta are ideal candidates for LSI interconnects and gate electrodes as far as their low resistivity

((10 ± 5) μΩ·cm) is concerned. However, they are subject to difficulties in the fabrication process, i.e., they are not able to withstand certain chemical reagents and high temperature oxidizing environments including oxygen or water vapor during wafer processing.

As an alternative approach, the use of a refractory metal silicide which has a high compatibility with the silicon gate process and a low resistivity ((100 ± 50) μΩ·cm) has been proposed[3–5].

The traditional interest in refractory metal silicides has been in high temperature applications where the refractory properties of metals have been improved by the introduction of oxidation resistant $MoSi_2$[6]. Silicidation shields metals from gas or chemical corrosion and also protects the refractory metals since a protective SiO_2 layer is formed when silicides are heated in the presence of oxygen[7].

Various silicides have been proposed for the gate material. Among transition metal silicides, $MoSi_2$ and WSi_2 are selected as a good gate material because of high thermal stability, high oxidation resistance, resistance against chemical reagents such as a mixture of sulfuric acid and hydroperoxide solution or chloric acid and hydro-peroxide solution.

In general, silicide resistivity increases with Si composition in the range from MSi_2 to pure Si. Here, M represents metal such as MO and W. On the other hand, oxidation resistance increases with Si composition because of stable SiO_2 formation on the surface. Therefore, the practical composition of silicide is selected in the range from $MSi_{2.5}$ to $MSi_{2.8}$, due to the trade-off between resistivity and oxidation resistance. Since the resistivity of W silicide is about 2/3 of that of Mo silicide, W silicides have become mostly used for gate electrodes in ULSIs.

The gate material trend from 1 M bit DRAM to 1 G bit DRAM is shown in Table 7.1. 256 M and 1 G generation are expectation from presented literature.

Although the gate electrode (word line) is shunted by uppear layer Al wiring, the gate electrode sheet resistivity required from device performance decreases with memory density. The typical resistivity of W silicide, Ti silicide, and W of a W polymetal are 120 ~ 180 μΩ·cm, 20 ~ 30 μΩ·cm[8], 10 ~ 15 μΩ·cm[9]. Here, W polymetal means a $W/WSiN_x$/poly-Si stacked structure. By using this structure, the sheet resistivity less than 2 Ω/□ is easily obtained if the W thickness

Table 7.1 Gate material Trend from M-bit to G-bit DRAM.

Memory Density	1M	4M	16M	64M	256M	1G
Design (μm)	1.2	0.8	0.5	0.35	0.25	0.15
Sheet Resistivity (Ω/□)	20	20	7 ~ 20	5 ~ 10	5 ~ 10	3 ~ 5
Gate Structure	poly-Si	poly-Si	W polycide or poly-Si	W polycide	W polycide or Ti polycide	Ti polycide or W polymetal

exceeds 60–70 nm. Ti silicide and W have one order of magnitude lower resistivity than W silicide. Therefore, Ti polycide or W poly-metal will appear as a low resistivity gate material in near future.

7.2. Source & Drain Contacts

There are three kinds of metal silicide application in LSIs. They are summarized as follows.

(1) Source, drain, and gate of MOSFET
(2) Interconnects such as bit line
(3) Barrier metal or glue layer metal between Al or W interconnects and Si substrate

In the third application, TiN or TiW is usually inserted between an interconnect material and a silicide.

Although the fabrication processes depend on the kinds of applications and specifications, they can be roughly divided into two groups, (a) and (b).

(a) Forming silicide by depositing metal films on Si and annealing for thermal reaction.
(b) Forming silicide by depositing metal-Si alloy films on a substrate and annealing for crystallization or grain growth of silicide.

As a deposition method, sputtering or CVD is commonly used. As an annealing method, there are furnace annealing (FA) and rapid thermal annealing (RTA).

By using the process (a) and selective etching where an unreacted metal is etched while a silicide is not etched, the silicide can be formed only on the Si such as source, drain diffusion area and gate (poly-Si). It is called self-aligned silicide (salicide).

In this section, contact process technology for the source and drain with or without salicide is described.

7.2.1 Barrier Metals

The narrowness of contacts and vias is mainly a result of transistor scaling and the need for higher interconnect packing density. The reason for the continued increase in aspect ratios (depth/width) is that dielectric thickness cannot be reduced along with width because the dielectric that separates the metal wirings cannot be made much thinner without an unacceptable increase in capacitance.

In order to improve the coverage at the bottom of the contact hole and sidewall coverage, TiN and Ti are sputtered by collimation sputtering, LTS (long throw sputtering) or ionized sputtering.

Here, collimation sputtering is a sputtering method by using a collimator which is honeycomb-like shape for filtering sputtered atoms or molecules and directional metal film deposition. LTS is sputtering by expanding the distance between a target and a substrate. Sometimes low pressure (0.02–0.05 Pa) sputtering is combined with LTS for increasing mean free path of sputtered atoms or molecules. Ionized sputtering is based on in-flight ionization of atoms sputtered from commercial magnetron cathodes and then film deposition of the metal ions by means of a sample bias.

CVD TiN is another candidate that also overcomes the conformality problems associated with sputtered TiN film. Metal CVD technology is described in Chapter 8.

7.2.2 Salicide

The salicide process is composed of the following four fundamental processes.

(1) To form a spacer insulator on the sidewall of poly-Si gate by depositiong a CVD Si oxide or nitride combined with anisotropical etching such as reactive ion etching.
(2) To remove an oxide on source, drain and gate.
(3) To deposit (deposition method is usually sputtering) a metal film in a clean vacuum.
(4) To anneal for silicidation.

Salicide structures for both gate and source/drain regions are necessary to reduce the gate resistance of the dual gate CMOS as well as the source/drain resistance. The first pioneering work was carried out by using PtSi[10] and then lower resistivity materials such as C 54-$TiSi_2$[11-13] and $CoSi_2$[14-16] were widely investigated. Table 7.2 (ref. 17) and Table 7.3 (ref. 18) show electrical resistivity and other physical properties of various silicides.

Since Mo or W cannot reduce a native oxide on Si, silicidation reaction is often affected by the native oxide and oxygen incorporated in metal films. For example oxygen originally incorporated in the metal films diffuses to the Si surface and forms SiO_2 during annealing[19-21]. As a result, silicide film thickness becomes non-uniform and the silicide/Si interface becomes rough and high resistivity contact. Similar oxygen pile-up phenomenon is reported for the case where the silicide is deposited on Si substrate and annealing is carried out. The driving force for this phenomenon is explained by chemical potential difference of oxygen between Si and $MoSi_2$[22].

Table 7.2 Silicide phase and resistivity. (ref. 17).

Silicide	Lowest eutectic temperture (°C)	Silicide formation method	Sintering temperture (°C)	Resistivity ($\mu\Omega \cdot cm$)
WSi_2	1440	Cosputtering	1000	~70
$MoSi_2$	1410	Cosputtering	1000	~100
$TaSi_2$	1385	Cosputtering	1000	50 ~ 55
$TiSi_2$	1330	Metal on poly-Si	900	13 ~ 16
$CoSi_2$	1195	Metal on poly-Si	900	18 ~ 20
$NiSi_2$	966	Metal on poly-Si	900	~50
PtSi	830	Metal on poly-Si	600 ~ 800	18 ~ 35

Table 7.3 Physical properties of silicides. (ref. 18).

Silicide	SBH to n-Si (eV)	Formation Temperture (°C)	Melting point (°C)	ΔHf (kcal/mol)	Crystal System	Lattice Constant (Å) a	b	c
$TiSi_2$	0.61 ~ 0.62	600	1540	−32.1	Orthor. (C54)	8.236	4.773	8.523
					Orthor. (C49)	3.620	13.760	3.605
VSi_2	0.654	600	1750	−73.8	Hexag.	4.571		6.372
$CrSi_2$	0.57 ~ 0.57	450	1570	−28.8	Hexag.	4.428		6.363
$ZrSi_2$	0.55	700	1520	−38.1	Orthor.	3.720	14.610	3.670
$NbSi_2$	–	650	1930	−21.9	Hexag.	4.780		6.560
$MoSi_2$	0.55	525	2030	−27.9	Tetrag.	3.200		7.861
$HfSi_2$	0.54	750	1543(Peritectic)	−54.0	Orthor.	3.677	14.550	3.690
$TaSi_2$	0.59	650	2200	−24.0	Hexag.	4.781		6.570
WSi_2	0.65	650	2150	−22.5	Tetrag.	3.212		7.880
$NiSi_2$	0.64 (type A)* 0.78 (type B)*	750	993(Peritectic)	−20.7	Cubic	5.395		
NiSi	0.66	350 ~ 750	990	−20.4	Orthor.	5.233	3.258	5.659
$CoSi_2$	0.64	550	1326	−24.6	Cubic	5.365		
CoSi	0.68	375 ~ 500	1460	−24.0	Cubic (B20)	4.443		
Pt_2Si	0.85	200 ~ 500	1099	−20.7	Tetrag,	3.933		5.910
PtSi	0.87 ~ 0.88	300	1229	−15.8	Orthor.	5.595	5.932	3.603
Pd_2Si	0.71 ~ 0.73	100 ~ 300	1330	−20.7	Hexag.	6.490		3.430
PdSi		850		−13.8	Orthor.	5.599	6.133	3.381

On the other hand, Ti can reduce the native oxide on Si and a Ti silicide film can be formed. However, it is difficult to utilize $TiSi_2$ for deep submicron devices, since narrowing pattern size and thinning film thickness impede the C 49 to C 54 phase transition and accelerate the agglomertion of $TiSi_2$ films. Here, C 49 and C 54 show crystal structure type. Both types have orthorhombic $TiSi_2$ structure, however, lattice constants are different. The density of C 54 structure is 6% higher than that of C 49 structure. Figure 7.1 shows schematic diagram of narrow line effect of $TiSi_2$ resistivity.

In order to improve narrow line effect, preamorphization of Si surface before Ti film sputtering is proposed and about 5Ω/□ is obtained for 0.2 μm in width[23]. On the other hand, $CoSi_2$ and NiSi are reported as a salicide material which has no narrow line effect. Both materials show the sheet resistivity less than 5Ω/□ for pattern size less than 0.15 μm.

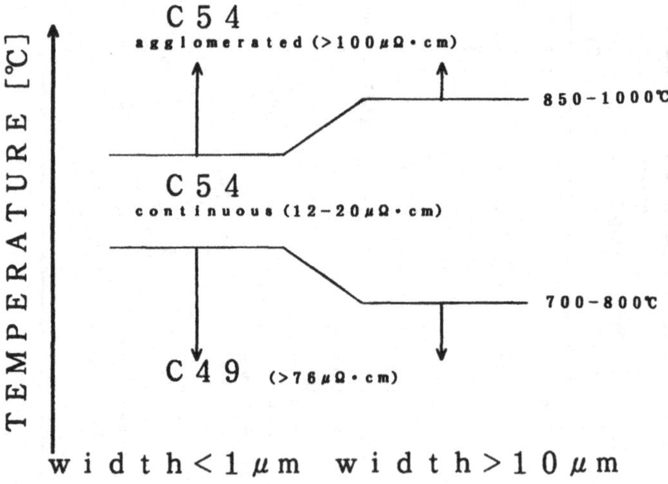

Figure 7.1 Schematic diagram of narrow line effect of $TiSi_2$ resistivity.

7.3. Interconnects

7.3.1 Al Interconnects

Aluminum is the most commonly used interconnect material in ULSIs, since it has many advantages such as low resistivity ($2.6\,\mu\Omega\cdot$cm), adhesion to insulators, chemical stability due to self-passivation by thin Al oxide. However, insufficinet reliability against electromigration (EM) and stress induced migration (SM) has become a more severe problems because of its relatively low self-diffusion activation energy. Therefore, Al is usually deposited by sputering an Al alloy target doped with Cu($\leqslant 0.5$ wt%) or Si($\leqslant 1$ wt%) in order to suppress migration of Al atoms.

An Al/TiN/Ti multilayered structure has been proposed as a means of reliability improvement. A lot of studies have shown that the TiN/Ti underlayer improves the orientation preference of the upper Al layer, but that it degrades Al grain size. As a result, EM and SM lifetimes have been increased to some extent.

Many eleborate studies have clarified that the endurance of interconnects against EM and SM is closely related to the grain structure (grain size distribution, grain orientation, grain boundary structure, etc.). In Al alloy interconnects, the EM mean time to failure (EM-MTF) for interconnects consisting mainly of a grain structure with "triple points" in empirically found to be expressed as

$$\text{EM-MTF} \propto (S/\sigma^2)\cdot \log\,(I_{(111)}/I_{(200)})^3 \tag{7.1}$$

where S, σ, $I_{(111)}$, and $I_{(200)}$ are the median grain size, its standard deviation for a log-normal distribution, and the X-ray diffraction intensity for the (111) plane and for the (200) plane, respectively[24]. On the other hand, SM failures occur thermodynamically (in the sence of miniaturization of excess surface energy) at grain boundaries where two (111) crystal planes encounter each other[25]. In this respect, much interest has centered on how to control the grain structure.

In order to obtain large grains, rapid thermal annealing, laser melting and abnormal grain growth have been proposed[26–32]. On the hand, for controlling grain orientation, metallic underlayers have been proven to play an important role and various methods of forming suitable underlayers have been studied extensively[32–36].

One of the well-known criteria for controlling the grain orientation is to form the interface from a combination of metals with as small lattice mismatch as possible i.e., Al on TiN/Ti[33-35].

It is also reported that Al grows with highly preferred orientation on an amorphous underlayer which has a large surface energy, i.e., Al on Ta-Al[37].

On the other hand, ⟨111⟩ preferred orientation of Al films is affected by the surface roughness of underlying insulators. Figure 7.2 shows FWHM (full width at half maximum) of ⟨111⟩ preference for Al films on rough surface and smooth SiO_2 surface. Smaller FWHM means that Al grains have stronger ⟨111⟩ preference. Amplitude of roughness for the rough SiO_2 surface is 1–10 nm, which is typical roughness of annealed BPSG films. Lower illustration shows the result for Al on the BPSG film planarized by polishing. In this case, the amplitude of BPSG surface rouness is 0.2–0.3 nm as measured by atomic force microscopy.

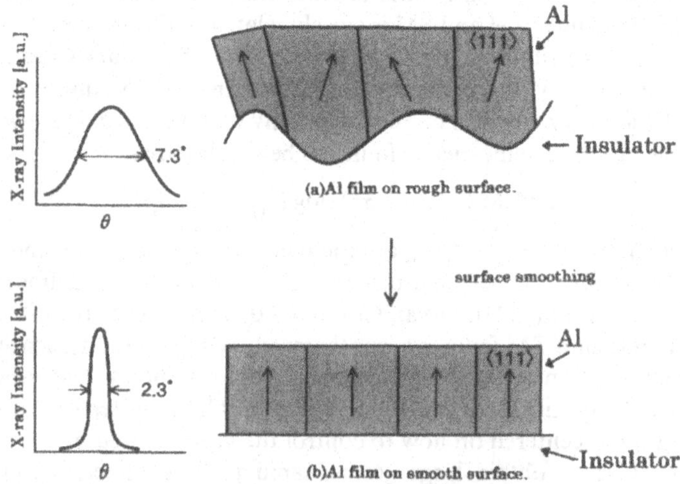

Figure 7.2 FWHM of ⟨111⟩ preference for Al films on rough surfce and smooth surface. ⟨111⟩ angle variations were measured by X-ray diffraction rocking curves. Upper illustration shows Al films on the rough SiO_2 surface, and lower illustration shows Al films on the smooth SiO_2 surface.

However, in these approaches, there exist grain boundaries where vacancy accumulation (void formation) or Al atom accumulation (hillock formation) occurs. Single crystal Al interconnections have excellent endurance against electromigration and stress induced migration[24,38-40]. In most of previous reports, Al single crystal has been formed on single crystal Si substrates. Seeding lateral epitaxial growth of single crystal Al up to about 10 μm in length onto a SiO_2 layer has been also reported by using (100)Si seed[41]. Even if there is no crystal seed, single crystal Al interconnections can be formed in grooves by heating sputtered Al films at temperatures below melting temperature as shown in Figure 7.3[42].

7.3.2 Cu and Other Metal Interconnects

Copper and silver are attractive materials for future interconnections in ULSIs owing to its low bulk resistivity (Cu: 1.68 μΩ·cm and Ag: 1.62 μΩ·cm at room temperature, respectively) and higher reliability against electromigration and stress induced migration compared with aluminum.

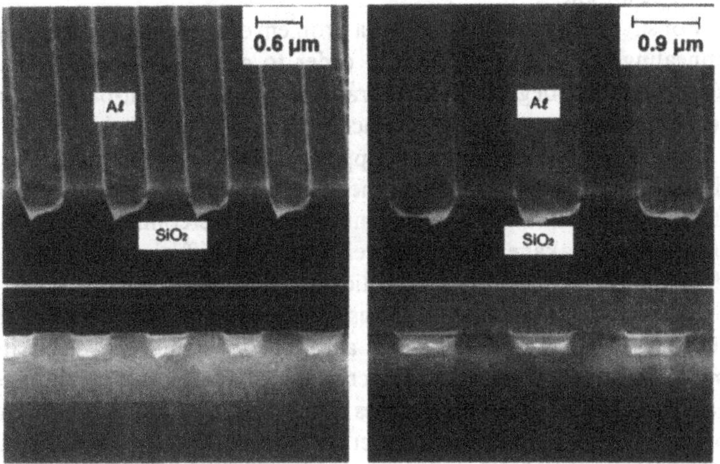

Figure 7.3 SEM micrograph sowing bird's-eye views of the Al film (0.4 μm thick) on substrate with periodic grooves after *in situ* annealing. (ref. 42).

Table 7.4 shows the comparison of physical properties of interconnect materials. As seen in Table 7.4, Cu, Ag, Au, and W have higher melting point compared with Al. Higher melting point means that activation energy for migration is higher than Al. Considering electrical resistivity, Cu and Ag are selected as future interconnect materials.

However, there are several problems in realizing Cu interconnections. One of the serious problems is instability in an oxidizing ambient.

A Cu-Ti (10 wt%) alloy was proposed in order to improve oxidation resistance of Cu[43]. Ti diffuses to the Cu surface and TiN is formed after annealing at 800°C in a nitrogen ambient. High temperature annealing is needed to form the TiN. In the case of a lower temperature, an intermetallic compound Cu_3Ti is formed and the resistivity becomes higher than 2 $\mu\Omega \cdot$cm. A study on a stacked structure such as Ta/Cu/Ta/$TiSi_2$/Si system is described in another report[44]. The sheet resistivity of this structure increased after 600°C annealing. The reason is that Cu turns to its silicide by reacting with both $TiSi_2$ and Si after 600°C annealing.

On the other hand, the resistance to oxidizing ambient processing was improved by Nb self-passivation without causing resistivity increase for Cu[45].

For silver interconnect, there is a problem of agglomeration during annealing or heating process. In order to avoid agglomeration at a few hundred degrees in centigrade, the Ti oxide self-passivation technique was employed and a successful result was obtained[46].

Another important issue in copper or silver metallization in fast diffusion in dielectric layers. The metal diffusion may cause increase in dielectric constant, leakage current between interconnect lines, and pn junction leakage. On the other hand, the diffusion also causes degradation of MOS characteristics, etc. Therefore, reliable barrier metals are indispensable. Various barrier metals are reviewed in reference[47]. TiN is well known as a barrier metal, however, its microstrcture is essentially polycrystalline. Therefore, Cu diffuses easily along TiN grain boundaries at temperatures above 450°C. In order to avoid Cu diffusion, the crystal structure of a barrier metal should be amorphous or defect-free single cryastal. Amorphous barrier metals have been reported effectively suppress Cu diffusion in ULSI processing thermal budget[48,49].

Table 7.4 Comparison of physical properties of interconnect materials.

Mat.	M.P.	ρ	MFP	Oxidation Resistivity	Equi. Partial Pressure of Oxygen	Linear Thermal Expension Coefficient	Young's Modulus	D_o E_a	Deep Level
Al	660°C	2.6 ~ 3 μΩcm	144Å	GOOD	10^{-50} Pa	29 ppm/K	-----	1.7 cm^2/s 1.5 eV	-----
Cu	1083°C	1.68 μΩcm	390Å	BAD	10^{-15} Pa	17 ppm/K	126 GPa	0.35 cm^2/s 2.1 eV	n – type 0.58 ev p – type 0.46 eV
Ag	961°C	1.62 μΩcm	520Å	FAIR	-----	19 ppm/K	75 GPa	0.24 cm^2/s 1.9 eV	n – type 0.78 eV p – type 0.54 eV
Au	1063°C	2.38 μΩcm	-----	GOOD	-----	14 ppm/K	76 GPa	0.091 cm^2/s 1.8 eV	------
a–w	3410°C	5.52 μΩcm	-----	FAIR/BAD	10^{-33} P/a	4.6 ppm/K		> 3 eV	------

Among ternary amorphous alloy barrier metals, $WSi_{0.6}N$ is one of promising candidates as a barrier metal for Cu diffusion at high temperature processing where Cu is melting[50]. Cross-section SEM photograph of double level Cu dual Damascene interconnects are shown in Figure 7.4.

In Cu and Ag metallization, it is rather difficult to make interconnect patterns and many difficulties are encountered in LSI processing. However, recent research shows the possibility of applications of these materials. That is, interconnect patterns can be formed by blanket deposition on grooves followed by chemical mechanical polishing i.e., Damascene method[51–55].

Reliability of these materials is under investigation, but so far only primitive results have been obtained. The results show the Cu has a high activation energy as high as 0.86–1.27 eV against electromigration, twice as high as polycrystalline aluminum and therefore, more reliable interconnections can be made by using Cu.

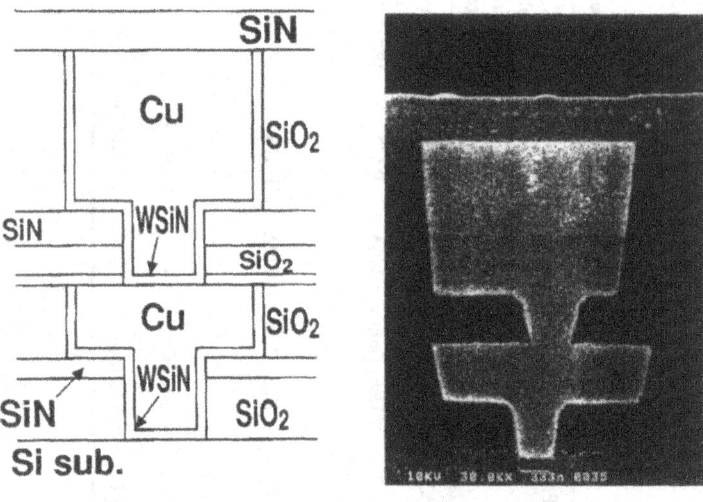

Schematic diagram SEM photograph

Figure 7.4 Cross-sectional view of double-level Cu inlaid interconnections with simultaneously filled via-plug. (ref. 50).

7.3.3 Planarization by CMP

Chemical mechanical polishing (CMP) is fast becoming the technology of the dacade. In early CMP processes, no reliable endpoint monitoring system existed so the duration of the wafer polish was calculated from a monitor wafer rate and measurements from previously polished patterned wafers. Wafers often required repolish to get within the target thickness. The ability to monitor remaining oxide thickness of a patterned wafer during CMP now allows the user to stop at the remaining thickness without repolishing, thus improving throughout and process window. *In situ* endpoint monitoring compensates for the decline in polishing rates and can provide early detection in nonuniformities as they occur[56].

The current economic conditions facing the semiconductor industry are driving the move to advanced process technologies in ULSIs. Recent CMP systems have a rotating head and a circular platen for mechanical abrasion. Future systems provide a variety of new features from extra platens for two-step polishing and increased throughput to *in situ* end-point monitoring. Typically, CMP uses orbital mechanics. However, some of the machines introduced a linear track system.

One of the primary driving forces for the CMP of either dielectrics or metals is the need to adhere to the focal budget dictated by the depth-of field limitations associated with nex generation deep UV lithography tools.

Damascene structures have been evaluated during the last decade in an attempt to circumvent some of the problems associated with extending subtractive etch techniques down into the deep submicron regime. The combination of Damascence metal interconnects and chemical mechanical polishing of dielectrics has resulted on SRAM and DRAM circuits[57,58].

7.4. Summary

M-bit to G-bit metallization technology is reviewed in this chapter. There is some trends in gate, source and drain formation. Gate material changes from W polycide to Ti polycide or W polymetal structure in DRAM. In logic devices gate metallization can be carried out simultaneously with source and drain by $TiSi_2$ or $CoSi_2$, that is, salicide. For high speed devices, the source and drain are metallized by the salicide. Interconnect material changes from polycrystalline Al to highly oriented aluminum/barrier metals. Extreme case is a single crystalline Al. Cu is one of the promising candidates as future interconnections, especially, as grobal interconnections. Low permittivity insulators are also important and they are described in Chapter 8.

References

1. Dennard, R. H., Gaensslen, F. H., Yu, H. N., Rideout, V. L., Bassous, E. and Leblanc, R. (1974). *IEEE Trans.* SC-9, 256.
2. Vadasz, L. L., Grove, A. S., Rowe, T. A. and Moore, G. E. (1969). *IEEE Spectrum*, **6**, 28.
3. Mochizuki, T., Shibata, K., Inoue, T. and Ohuchi, K. (1978). *Jpn. J. Appl. Phys.*, **17**, suppl. 17–1, 37.
4. Crowder, B. L. and Zirinsky, S. (1979). *IEEE J. Solid State Circuits*, SC-14, 291.
5. Murarka, S. P. (1979). *IEEE IEDM Tech. Dig.*, 454.
6. Cherniak, G. B. and Elliot, A. G. (1964). *J. Am. Ceramic Soc.*, **47**, 136.
7. Berkowitz-Mattuk, J. B. and Dils, R. R. (1965). *J. Electrochem. Soc.*, **112**, 583.
8. Murarka, S. P., "Silicides for VLSI Applications" (Academic Press, New York, 1983), p. 1.
9. Akasaka, Y., Suehiro, S., Nakajima, K., Nakasugi, T., Miyano, K., Kasai, K., Oyamatsu, H., Kinugawa, M., Takagi, M., Agawa, K., Matsuoka, F., Kakumu, M. and Suguro, K. (1995). *Proc. of V-MIC* 95, Santa Clara, (*IEEE*, New York), p. 168.
10. Shibata, T., Hieda, K., Sato, M., Konaka, M., Dang, R. L. M. and Iizuka, H., *IEEE J. Solid State Circuits, SC-17* (1982) 161.
11. Ting, C. Y., Iyer, S. S., Osburn, C. M., Hu, G. J. and Schweighart, A. M., (1982). *ECS Proc. 1st Int. Symp. VLSI Sci. Technol.*, **82-7**, 224.
12. Lau, C. K. (1983). *Ext. Abstracts of the Electrochem. Soc.*, **83-1** (San Francisco, CA, p. 569.
13. Iyer, S. S., Ting, C. Y. and Fryer, P. M. (1985). *J. Elecrochem. Soc.*, **132**, 2240.
14. Lucchese, C. J. (1982). *ECS Proc. 1st Int. Symp. VLSI Sci. Technol.*, **82-7**, 232.
15. Van den Hove, L., Wolters, R., Maex, K., De Keersmecher, R. and Declerck, G. (1987). *IEEE Trans. Electron. Devices*, ED-34 554.

16. Morgan, A. E., Broadbent, E. K., Delfino, M., Coulman, B. and Sadana, D. K. (1987). *J. Electrochem. Soc.*, **134**, 925.
17. Winnerl, J. (1994). *Semiconductor international*, **17**, 81.
18. Suguro, K. and Kunishima, I. (1995). *Hyoumen-Kagaku* (Japanese), **16**, 2.
19. Cappelletti, P., Mori, F., Pignatel, G., Ferla, G., Nava, F. and Ottaviani, G. "Semiconductor Silicon 1981" ed. by Huff, H. R., Kriegler, R. J. and Takeishi, Y. (Electrochem. Soc., Pronceton, 1981) p. 608.
20. Nava, F., Majni, G., Cantoni, P., Pignatel, G., Ferla, G., Cappelletti, P. and Mori, F. (1982). *Thin Solid Films*, **94**, 59.
21. Iwata, S. and Yamamoto, N. (1981). *41st Japan Applied Physics Soc. Fall Meeting*, p. 716.
22. Suguro, K., Yamada, K., Mochizuki, T. and Kashiwagi, M. "Layered Structures and Interface Kinetics" edited by Furukawa S. (KTK Scientific Publishers, Tokyo, 1985) p. 297.
23. Kikkawa, T. and Sakai, I. *MRS Symposium Proc.*, **402** (Boston, MA, 1995) p. 199.
24. Vaidya, S. and Sinha A. K., (1981). *Thin Solid Films*, **75**, 253.
25. Kaneko, H., Hasunuma, M., Kawanoue, T., Kahanawa, Y., Sawabe, A., Komatsu, S. and Miyauchi, M. (1990). *in Proc. of the 28th Annual International Reliability Physics Symposium*, New Orleans, (IEEE) p. 194.
26. Gangulee, A. and D'Heurle, F. M. (1972). *Thin Solid Films*, **12**, 399.
27. Mayer, N. M., Hoffmann, H. and Schafer, A. (1982). *Thin Solid Films*, **91**, 241.
28. Thompson, C. V. (1985). *J. Appl. Phys.*, **58**, 763.
29. Wong, C. C., Smith, H. I. and Thompsonm C. V. (1986). *Appl. Phys. Lett.*, **48**, 335.
30. Frost, J. J. and Thompson, C. V. (1988). *J. Electron. Mater.*, **17**, 447.
31. Frost, H. J., Thompson, C. V. and Walton, D. T. *Acta Metall. Mater.*, **38** 1455.
32. Longworth, H. P. and Thompson, C. V. (1991). *J. Appl. Phys.*, **69**, 3929.
33. Nakasaki, Y., Minamihaba, G., Itow, H. and Suguro, K. (1995). *J. Appl. Phys.*, **77**, 2454.
34. Kageyama, M., Tetsudam, H., Hashimoto, K. and Madokoro, A., (1991). *IEICE Tech. Rep.*, SDM-180 25.
35. Shibata, H., Ikeda, N., Murota, M., Asahi, Y. and Hashimoto, K. (1991). *In Symposium on VLSI Technology*, Digest of Technical Papers, Oiso, 1991 (Business Center for Acad, Soc. Japan), p. 33.
36. Mitsuzuka, T., (1992). *Jpn. J. Appl. Phys.*, **31**, L1280.
37. Toyoda, H., Kawanoue, T., Hasunuma, M., Kaneko, H. and Miyauchi, M. (1994). *In Proc. of the 32nd Annual International Reliability Physics Symposium, San joe,* (IEEE, New York) p. 178.
38. Hummel, R. E. (1989). *In Proc. of the 27th Annual International Reliability Physics Symposium,* (IEEE, New York) p. 207.
39. Hasunuma, M., Kaneko, H., Sawabe, A., Kawanoue, T., Kohanawa, Y., Komatsu, S. and Miyauchi, M. (1989). *Proc. of the IEEE IEDM* , p. 677.

40. Shingubara, S., Nakasaki, Y. and Kaneko, H. *Ext. Abst. of the 22nd Conf. on Solid State Device and Materials* (Sendai, 1990) p. 251.
41. Kusuyama, K., Nakajima, Y., Murakami, Y. and Yamaguchi, H. (1991). *Ext. Abst. of the 52nd Japan Society of Applied Physics*, Autumn Meeting, p. 720.
42. Wada, J., Suguro, K., Hayasaka, N. and Okano, H. *Jpn. J. Appl. Phys.*, **32** (1993) 3094.
43. Hoshino, K., Yagi, H. and Tsuchikawa, H. *In Proc. of the 6th Int. IEEE VLSI Multilevel Interconnection Conference*, Santa Clara, CA, 1989 (IEEE, New York, 1989) p. 226.
44. Chang, C.-A. and Hu, C.-K. (1990). *Appl. Phys. Lett.*, **57**, 617.
45. Itow, H., Nakasaki, Y., Minamihaba, G., Suguro, K. and Okano, H. (1993). *Appl. Phys. Lett.*, **63**, 934/
46. Iijima, T., Ono, H., Nishiyama, N., Ushiku, Y., Hatanaka, T. and Iwai, H. *Ext. Abst. of the 1993 Int. Conf. on Solid State Devices and Materials* (Chiba, 1993) p. 183.
47. Wang, S. Q. MRS Bulletin, November (1994) 30.
48. Reid, J. S., Kolawa, E., Ruiz, R. P. and Nicolet, M.-A. (1993). *Thin Solid Films*, **236**, 319.
49. Iijima, T., Shimooka, Y. and Suguro, K. *Mat. Res. Soc. Proc. eds.* Demczyk, B. G., Garfunkel, E., Clemens, B, M., Williams, E. D. and Chuomo, J. J. (1995). **355**, (Mat. Res. Soc., Pittsburgh), p. 459.
50. Minamihaba, G., Iijima, T., Shimooka, Y., Tamura, H., Kawanoue, T., Hirabayashi, H., Sakurai, N., Ohkawa, H., Obara, T., Egawa, H., Idaka, T., Kubota, T., Shimizu, T., Koyama, M., Ohshima, J. and Suguro, K. (1996). *Jpn. J. Appl. Phys.*, **35**, 1107.
51. Luther, B., White, J. P., Uzoh, C., Cacouris, T., Hummel, J., Guthrie, W., Lustig, N., Greco, S., Greco, N., Zuhoski, S., Agnello, P., Colgan, E., Mathad, S., Saraf, L., Weitzman, E. J., Hu, C. K., Kaufman, F., Jaso, M., Buchwalter, L. P., Reynolds, S., Malinowski, C., Horkans, J., Deligianni, H., Harper, J., Andricacos., P. C., Parazczak, J., Pearson, D. J. and Small, M. (1993). *Proc. VLSI Multilevel Interconnections Conf.*, Santa Clara, CA (IEEE, New york,) p. 15.
52. Abe, K., Harada, Y., Hashimoto, K. and Onoda, H. (1994). *Ext. Abstracts of the 1994 Int. Conf. and Sold State Device and Materials*, Yokohama (Business Center for Academic Soc. Japan, Tokyo,) p. 937
53. Gelatos, A. V., Ngunen, B.-Y., Perry, K., Marsh, R., Peschke, J., Filipiak, S., Travis, E., Bhat, N., La, L. B., Thompson, M., Saaranen, T. and Tobin, P. J. (1995). *on VLSI Tech. Digest*, Kyoto (Business Center for Academic Sec. Japan, Tokyo,) p. 25.
54. Ueno, K., Ohto, K. and Tsunenari, K. *Symp. on VLSI Tech. Digest*, Kyoto (Business Center for Academic Soc. Japan Tokyo, 1995) p. 27.
55. Hirabayashi, H., Kaneko, H., Hayasaka, N., Higuchi, M., Mase, Y. and Ohshima, J. in *Ext. Abstracts of the 42nd Spring Meeting*. Tokai University, 1995 (The Japan Society of Applied Physics and Related Societies), **2**, 811.

56. DeJule, R. Semiconductor International (November, 1996) p. 88.
57. Wang, J.-F., Sethuraman, A. R., Cook, L. M., Kistler, R. C. and Schwartz, G. P. *Semiconductor International* (October, 1995) p. 117.
58. Misawa, N., Ohba, T. and Yagi, H. MRS Bulletin (August, 1994) p. 63.

CHAPTER 8

Chemical Vapor Deposition (CVD)

8.1. Introduction

CVD of various materials has been studied with a view to application in VLSI fabrication. Polycrystalline silicon and SiO_2 CVD using SiH_4 have been used widely in Kbit-scale devices. The aspect ratio of surface topography of Mbit-scale ULSI devices, such as grooves between metal wire, contact and via holes, has been increasing with shrinkage of device size and increasing the number of metal layers. The topography with high aspect ratio is detrimental to high resolution lithography and interconnection reliability. Planarization of device surface is indispensable for realizing small feature size devices, notably for fabricating multilevel interconnection. To overcome these problems, CVD of metals and insulators have been developed in the expectation that it would realize film deposition with superior step coverage. In this chapter, the CVD technologies for polycrystalline silicon , metals and insulator which were developed for application to Mbit-scale device processes and research efforts for Gbit-scale ULSI processes are reviewed.

8.2. CVD of Polycrystalline Silicon

Polycrystalline silicon has been used widely in VLSI devices, for example, for the gate and capacitor electrode, for diffusion sources, and for interconnection wire. Many applications of polycrystalline Si require controllable doping to reduce resistivity. Doping needs additional processes which require high temperature, namely more than 900°C. However, given the need for shrinkage of device size, lower process temperature is required because of fabrication of shallower junctions. To avoid extra processes and high temperature diffusion processes, *in situ* doping by CVD has been developed.[1-5] SiH_4 have been used as a source gas and PH_3, AsH_3 and B_2H_6 were used as doping gases. The addition of PH_3 and AsH_3 was reported to reduce the deposition rate, while B_2H_6 increased the rate[6]. PH_3 and AsH_3 were considered to adsorb easily on the surface, which prevents SiH_4 chemisorption on the surface leading to reduction of the deposition rate. B_2H_6 was considered to promote SiH_4 decomposition on the surface or in the gas.

Recently, CVD using Si_2H_6 instead of SiH_4 as a source gas has been developed to reduce process temperature and to obtain low resistivity polycrystalline silicon[4,5]. Kobayashi *et al.*, reported *in situ* doping to polycrystalline Si by CVD using $PH_3 + Si_2H_6$ at temperature below 550°C. They obtained resistivity of 0.7 mΩcm after annealing the film at the low temperature of 650°C[4]. Shiozawa *et al.*, reported CVD of *in situ* B doped amorphous Si using $B_2H_6 + Si_2H_6$ at temperature of 350°C[5]. And they obtained poly-Si with low resistivity of 1.7 m Ω cm after annealing the deposited amorphous Si at 600°C[5] as shown in Figure 8.1.

The shrinkage of feature size of DRAMs is required to introduce a complex capacitor structure (see chapter 2). H. Watanabe *et al.*, proposed a new capacitor structure formed on rugged poly-Si surface to increase capacitor area for 64 M and larger DRAMs[7,8]. In this technology, poly-Si was deposited at 550°C, which is the transition temperature of the film structure from amorphous to polycrystalline. Applying the rugged poly-Si surface, they obtained storage capacitance twice that of a capacitor formed on an even surface.

8.3. CVD of Metals

8.3.1 W CVD

One of the most serious problems in Mbit VLSI metallization was wiring reliability. Poor step coverage of PVD (physical vapor deposition) Al caused open failures at the contact and via holes. To solve this problem, W plug technologies have been developed intensively using blanket CVD with good step coverage or selective CVD. And after 16Mbit DRAM, thermal CVD of W has been used widely for VLSI fabrication as a plug formation method.

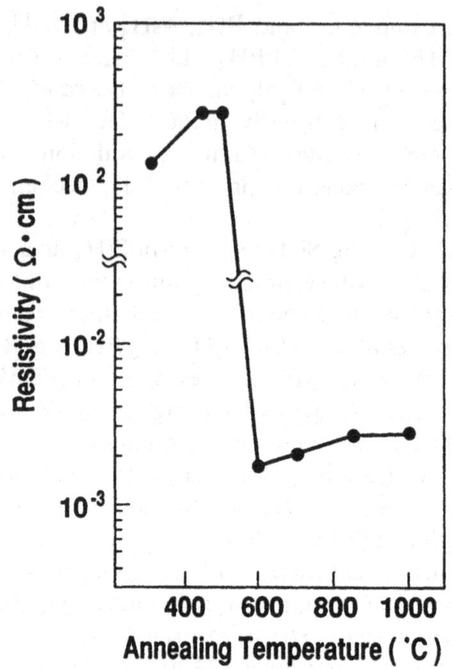

Figure 8.1 Resistivity of B doped poly-Si deposited by LP-CVD using $Si_2H_6 + B_2H_6$ at deposition tepmerature of 350°C as a function of annealing temperature after deposition[5].

Many semiconductor manufacturers in Japan have been using the blanket W CVD for plug formation[9,10]. The problems to which blanket W CVD is subject are poor adhesion between underlayer and roughened surface morphology. Usually, underlayer film such as TiN is required to obtain good adhesion, and $WF_6 + H_2$ chemistry is used because H_2 reduction thermal CVD can achieve smoother surface than SiH_4 reduction at typical CVD temperature of ~450°C, which is a critical temperature to use in Al multilevel interconnection. Blanket W CVD at low temperature using SiH_2F_2 reduction process was proposed[11]. In this technology, conformal CVD at a temperature of less than 400°C was achieved.

An etch back process is needed to form W plug by using blanket W CVD. And a conformal underlayer CVD technology is also the key to achieving good step coverage of W CVD in the future, because aspect ratio of contact and via holes increases with the shrinkage of device size.

Selective W CVD was expected to be a promising plug formation technology because it does not require underlayer film and etch back processes, thereby meeting the need for reduction of process steps in ULSI fabrication. Therefore many workers studied selective W CVD for a long time[12-31]. In the early stage of developing W selective CVD, the H_2 reduction process using $WF_6 + H_2$ chemistry was studied. In the H_2 reduction process, the deposition temperature of $>450°C$ is required to obtain high deposition rate for practical use. And this high temperature deposition causes encroachment of Si, which is a serious problem because it leads to increasing junction leakage[13]. To solve these problems, the SiH_4 reduction process was proposed[19,20,21]. Figure 8.2 shows an SEM photograph of surface after plug formation by selective W CVD using SiH_4 reduction process(a) and after Al wire formation(b). In the SiH_4 reduction process, selective CVD was achieved at a temperature of less than 300°C with a deposition rate of 1.0 µm/min[23]. Also, the Si_2H_6 and Si_3H_8 reduction processes were investigated[19]; however, Si inclusion in W film increased in these processes.

In spite of the many studies of selective W CVD, it was not used widely because practical application at production lines was subject to many problems concerning the surface control process. Selective W CVD strongly depends on surface condition, and control of surface condition is the key to achieving CVD without selectivity breakdown, which caused shorts of Al wiring in the upper layer of the W plug, thereby reducing device production yields.

Some surface treatments were reported to achieve reliable W CVD having good repeatability, selectivity and electrical properties such as low contact resistance. *In situ* $NF_3 + H_2$ dry cleaning[24], BCl_3 RIE[25,31], dimethylhydrazine treatment[26], etc. are reported as surface treatment. These treatments were reported to improve selectivity. It was considered that surface contamination such as native oxide was removed by the *in situ* pre-treatment and control of surface chemical bonds. SiCl and SiOCl formed on SiO_2 by BCl_3 RIE were considered to improve selectivity[25].

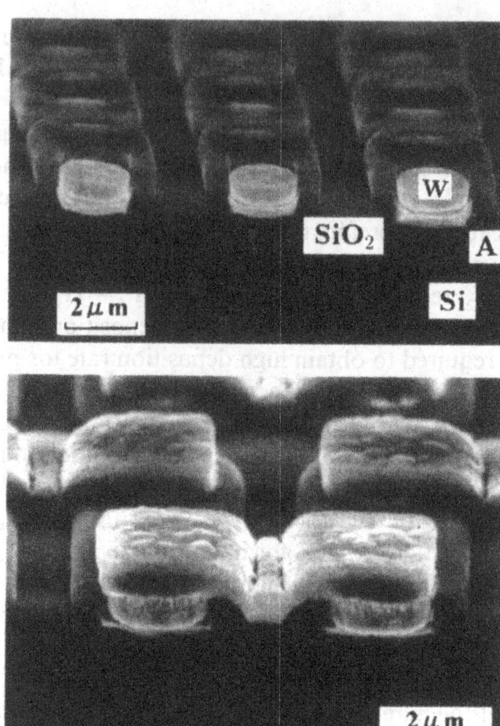

Figure 8.2 SEM photograph of CVD W plug formed by selective CVD using $SiH_4 + WF_6$, Upper photograph shows Wplug on Al wire(a), and lower shows Al/W plug/Al structure(b).

In the case of contact hole filling by selective W CVD, W should be grown on various materials such as n^+-Si, p^+-Si and WSi_2. $TiSi_2$ buffer layer covered with various materials before W selective CVD was proposed to control deposition condition between various materials[27]. This technology has been using in 16 Mbit DRAM, 0.5 μm logic and larger ULSI in combination with BCl_3 RIE pre-treatment. The mechanism of selective W CVD has also been studied extensively. Ito *et al.*, proposed WF_6 dissociation in view of the fact that electron transfer from substrate is the origin of selective CVD[29] as shown in Figure 8.3. Kobayashi *et al.*, investigated reaction products by FT-IR

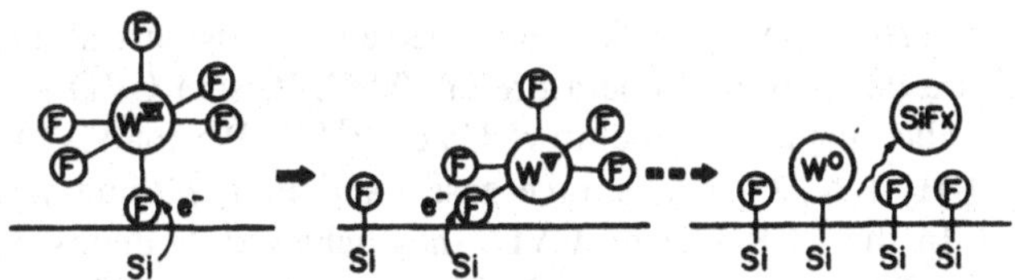

Figure 8.3 Mechanism of W CVD; WF6 decomposition promotos due to electron transfer from substrate[29].

during selective CVD, and they consider $SiHF_3$ to be the main product for selective CVD in the $WF_6 + SiH_4$ reaction system[30,31].

8.3.2 TiN CVD

TiN is widely used for various purposes for example, as a barrier layer to prevent reaction between metal and silicon interface and a glue layer for blanket CVD W, because it is chemically and thermodynamically stable. Conventionally, TiN is deposited by reactive sputtering. However, in sub micron ULSI processes, aspect ratio of contact and via holes become higher, so that sputtering is not available to form conformal TiN film in the holes with high aspect ratio.

Some techniques to improve step coverage of reactive sputtering have been studied, such as collimated sputtering[32] and long through sputtering[33]. However, improvement of step coverage of PVD is subject to inherent limitation, and so TiN CVD with good step coverage is being studied extensively for future VLSI devices. In the first stage, thermal CVD of TiN with $TiCl_4$ and NH_3 as source gases was studied[34–36]. However, in the TiN CVD using $TiCl_4$ and NH_3, the deposition temperature was more than 600°C to decrease Cl incorporation to less than 1% in the film, and this temperature is too high for practical use in Al multilevel interconnection. To decrease deposition temperature, several methods were investigated, which were applying new reducting gases, plasma CVD and new source gases.

Suzuki *et al.*, reported achievement of TiN CVD at a temperature of less than 500°C by using dimethlhydrzine ($(CH_3)NHNH_2$) with

$TiCl_4$ as a reducing gas[37]. They obtained a low resistivity film of 90 μ Ω cm at a deposition temperature of 500°C. Plasma CVD has also been studied for low temperature CVD[38,39,40]. Plasma CVD using $TiCl_4 + H_2 + N_2 + Ar$ as source gases, and ECR plasma were reported. In the ECR plasma CVD, they achieved Ti deposition by using the $TiCl_4 + H_2$ system, which cannot be achieved by thermal CVD. And the Ti/TiN sequential CVD made it possible to form low resistivity ohmic contact between n^+ and/or p^+ Si and Ti/TiN.

Cl incorporation is the crucial issue respecting CVD using $TiCl_4$. These CVD methods mentioned above could reduce Cl incorporation to less than 1%. However, it was observed that Cl out-diffusion during annealing in a metallization process leads to degradation of reliability due to metal corrosion, substrate erosion, etc. To eliminate Cl incorporation, CVD using metal-organic(MO) gases such as tetrakis-dimethylamino-titanium (TDMAT), tetrakis-diethylamino-titanium (TDEAT), and biscyclopentadienyl-titanium diazide ($Cp_2Ti(N_3)2$; $Cp = C_5H_5$) whose molecules do not include Cl, were investigated[41,42,43]. In these methods, TiN film was formed at a temperature of less than 500°C; however, the resistivity of the film was higher than that by $TiCl_4$, because these films include much carbon. To reduce carbon is an important subject regarding the improvement of film quality in MO CVD. Although TiN CVD has yet to be applied at production lines, the advent of Gbit-scale ULSIs will increase the need for this technology. Thus, great effort are required to solve the above-mentioned problems, so as to bring TiN CVD into practical use.

8.3.3 Al and Cu CVD

Conventional Al film formation has been done by using sputtering technology. New sputtering technologies were developed, namely directional sputtering, such as a collimated sputtering[32], long through sputtering[33] and high temperature sputtering[44], called reflow sputtering, to improve step coverage of sputtered Al. It was confirmed that the W plug method helps to improve interconnection reliability. However, W plug formation needs complex process steps such as W CVD and recess. And recently it was reported that W/Al interface degraded interconnection reliability for future high current density operation, which is expected to increase with decreasing device size[45,46]. Recently, "Dual Damascene" technology was proposed to be an atractive technology for future multilevel interconnection, which had monolithic Al plug and interconnection metallization[47]. This technology is expected to solve the problems of interconnection with W plug, and which will need Al deposition with good step coverage in future.

Al CVD has been studied since the mid-1980s in Japan[48,49]. It was reported that selective and blanket CVD were achieved by LP-CVD using various MO source gases such as triisobthylaluminum (TIBA)[50,51], dimethylaluminum hydride (DMAH)[52,53] and trimethylaluminum (TMA)[54]. Al film can be deposited at the low temperature of less than 400°C. And in selective CVD using DMAH, single crystal Al was obtained on Si(100) surface[51,52]. It was confirmed that single crystal Al has excellent reliability[55]. However, it was difficult to form single crystal Al on amorphous insulator such as SiO_2, that were required in an actual ULSI fabrication.

The issues regarding Al CVD were development of doping method of additive such as Cu, of precursors to allow reliable CVD process and of control of a texture of the film to improve migration resistance. Moreover, the development of process tools is also key issue to use Al CVD for mass production. Many efforts to use Al CVD in actual ULSI devices should be made for Gbit generation.

Recently, multilevel interconnection is said to limit device performance due to RC delay of the interconnection, which increases with decreasing device size[56]. To decrease RC delay, the introduction of low resistivity metals such as Cu, Ag and Au are required for ULSI interconnection. Cu has been expected to be most promissing material for future interconnection. However, fine pattern delineation of Cu by RIE is difficult, because Cu make it difficult to form volatile materials by the reaction of active species such as halogen gases. And in Gbit- scale VLSI, the plug material should be same as the interconnection material as well as Al dual damascene wire. Therefore, the damascene method is being studied to form wiring[57]. In these studies, Cu film formations by thermal CVD are being investigating intensively. In Cu CVD, most studies were carried out by using metal-organic(MO) source gases such as β-diketonate compound[58-64]. Cu film resistivity of less than 2 $\mu\Omega$cm were obtained by Cu CVD at deposition temperature of less than 300°C. Figure 8.4 shows the

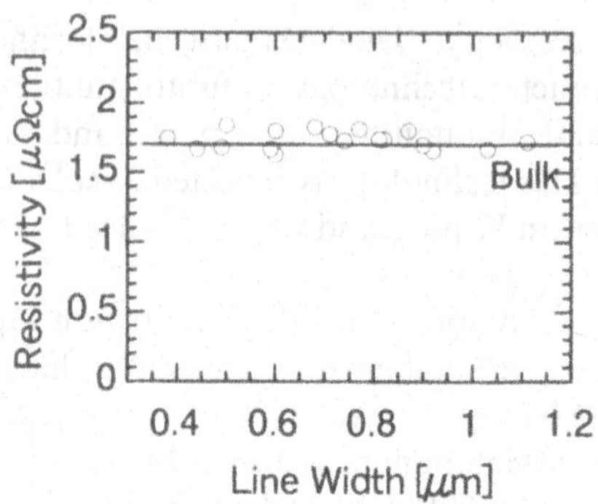

Figure 8.4 Resistivity of Cu wire as a function of the width of wire; Cu were deposited by the LP-CVD using Cu (hfa)(tmvs) at deposition temperature of 200°C[64].

resistivity of Cu wires formed by thermal CVD using Cu(hfa)(tmvs)[64]. Use of Cu for VLSI interconnections involve many issues, for example, suppression of Cu diffusion and Cu recess method to form damascene wire. These issues have to be solved to develop Cu interconnection as well as developing CVD method.

8.4. CVD of Insulators

CVD of the insulators which were used in multilayer interconnection have been studied extensively in the Mbit scale VLSI generation. The step coverage and decreasing deposition temperature of the insulator CVD were of great interest in that generation. In this section, first, we present thermal CVD and plasma CVD of the insulators for multi-layer interconnection developed for Mbit scale VLSI. And next, we present the CVD of new materials such as low dielectric constant and high dielectric constant insulators which are developing for Gbit-scale ULSI devices.

8.4.1 Thermal CVD

SiH_4 has been widely used to form silicon oxide and silicon nitride. However, the film deposited using SiH_4 had poor step coverage, which caused several problems, namely void formation in the gap of metal wires, thinning of the metal at the step on the insulator, etc. These affected production yield and device reliability. To overcome these problems, tetraethylorthosilicate (TEOS or tetraethoxysilane) was introduced as a source gas of SiO_2 CVD[66-69]. The highly conformal coating of SiO_2 from TEOS can be achieved by pyrolytic LPCVD between 650°C and 750°C at pressure between 700 and 900 mTorr. Deposition rate of about a few tenths of A/min was obtained, depending on the deposition parameters such as temperature, pressure and TEOS flow rate. The formation of conformal deposition is considered to be due to low sticking coefficients of precursors which are considered to be oxidized species of TEOS such as TEOS dimer[70].

Pyrolytic LPCVD of TEOS cannot be used on Al interconnection layer because CVD temperature is too high to use. Therefore, this CVD is applied at below Al interconnection[67]. And it was reported that As-doped SiO_2 (AsSG) was formed for diffusion source on sidewall in the Si trench using TEOS and TEOA (triethoxyarsine) by LP-CVD reactor[71]. AsSG with high As concentration of $10^{20}-10^{21}$ atoms/cm^3 was obtained with a conformal step coverage.

Thermal CVD using TEOS-O_3 gases was reported to form SiO_2 at low temperature of between 350°C and 450°C[67,68]. And conformal film formation and flow shape profile of the CVD film were also confirmed in this CVD[69]. These results indicated that TEOS-O_3 CVD has a large capability for multilevel interconnection dielectric formation method, therefore many studies were carried out in Japan[67-69,72,73]. The experimental result of device application for sub-micron ULSI and its capability were reported[67,74]. The flow shape profile is considered to be due to liquification of deposition precursor on the surface[67]. Surface liquification model was first proposed by CVD using reaction between TMS (tetramethylsilane) and plasma excited oxygen gas at low temperature of −40°C[75]. In this experimental system, deposition rate increases with decreasing deposition temperature, and at low temperature of less than −25°C step coverage changes drastically to flow-like shape as shown in Figure 8.5. This change of step coverage depending on deposition temperature was considered to be due to liquification of deposition precursor on the surface. Matsuura *et al.*, also reported the CVD

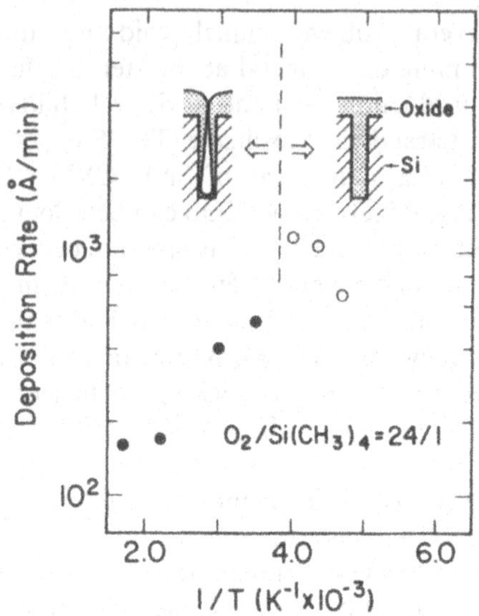

Figure 8.5 Deposition rates as a function of deposition temperature for TMS + plasma excited oxygen CVD[75].

method whose step coverage was flow shape by thermal CVD reactor using SiH_4 and H_2O_2 at room temperature[76].

The issue of TEOS-O_3 CVD is that CVD characteristics strongly depend on surface such as surface material and condition[77,78]. For example, Figure 8.6 shows the deposition rate of SiO_2 using TEOS-O_3 CVD on SiO_2 and Si. Deposition rate on Si is found to be larger than that on SiO_2. This is considered to be due to chemisorption of reaction product on the surface which prevents chemisorption of deposition precursors[67,77,78].

BPSG (borophosphosilicate glasses) is the most common material used as an intermetal dielectric below Al interconnection because this allows smoothing of the device typography by glass flow at high temperature of up to 850°C. BPSG is also obtained using TEOS, O_3 and doping gases such as TMP(trimethylphosphate) and TMB (trimethylborate)[79,80]. It was reported that TEOS-O_3 based BPSG CVD had good step coverage and reflow characteristics and achieved

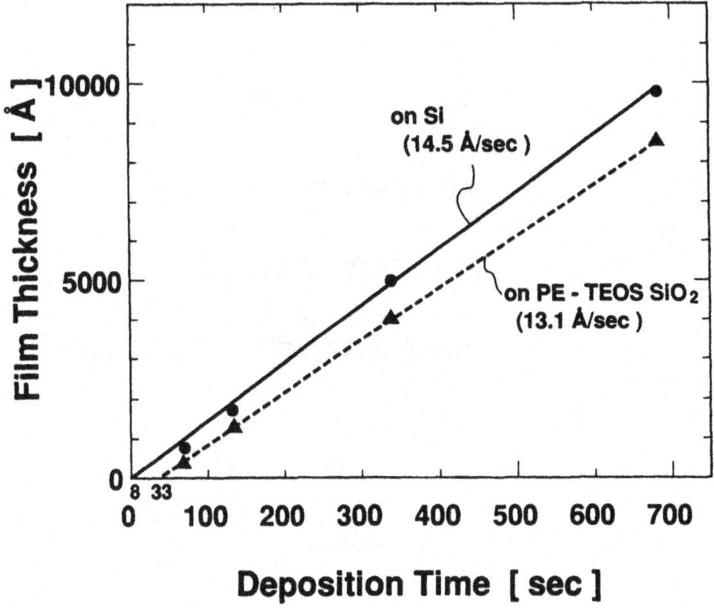

Figure 8.6 Film thicknesses as a function of deposition time for TEOS + O_3 CVD on Si and SiO_2.

sub-micron gap filling. These technologies have been introduced in actual ULSI.

8.4.2 Plasma CVD

ECR (electron cyclotron resonance) plasma CVD was studied intensively in Japan because it was able to deposit high quality SiO_2 at low temperature of less than 300°C[81-86]. It was expected to be the CVD for forming dielectrics of sub-half micron interconnection system. This low temperature CVD allows decreasing thermal stress of Al interconnection to suppress stress migration of Al wire[87] as shown in Figure 8.7. SiH_4 and O_2 were used as a source gases for SiO_2 deposition in ECR plasma CVD. Two types of ECR plasma CVD methods were reported. In one type the substrate was floats[81,84] and in the other RF bias is applied to the substrate(bias-ECR)[82,83]. In the

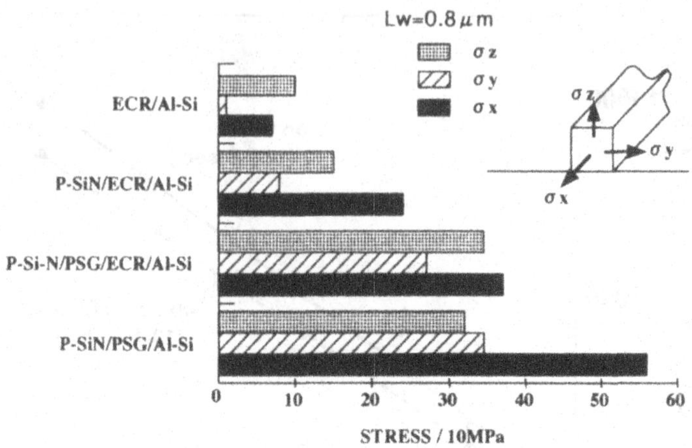

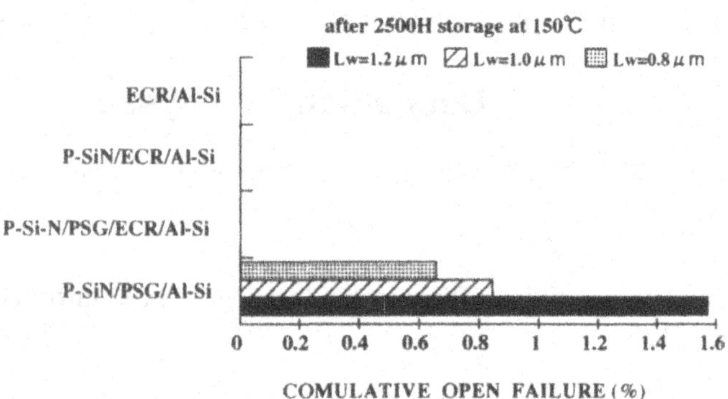

Figure 8.7 Three dimensional stress measured by X-ray diffractometry in Al wire and comulative open failure after stress test for various passivation films; In the case of ECR plasma CVD passivations, higher reliabilities were obtained because deposition temperature was lower than other CVD methods[87].

case of substrate floating, step coverage of the film was controlled by the plasma condition. And it was reported that step coverage was improved to bring ECR position close to the substrate[84]. In the case of bias-ECR plasma CVD, sputter etching occurred on the surface during deposition, leading to successful gap filling without void formation between metal wires[82]. It was reported that the SiO_2

produced by bias-ECR plasma CVD has high resistance against water diffusion[88]. Therefore, it was applied to the underlayer film of TEOS $-O_3$ CVD SiO_2 which includes water to prevent water diffusion to transistor region. SiON film was also deposited by bias-ECR plasma CVD and reported to have excellent film quality[86].

TEOS also came to be used for plasma CVD in Mbit scale ULSIs because the step coverage of the CVD film was superior to SiH_4 plasma CVD by a parallel plate plasma CVD reactor[89,90] as shown in Figure 8.8. However, complete planarization cannot be achieved only by TEOS plasma CVD (TEOS PE-CVD), and therefore, other methods for planarization were used with TEOS PE-CVD , such as etch back method and SOG(spin on glass) coating. Now, TEOS PE-CVD is being applied in actual ULSI fabrication. The major concern regarding TEOS based CVD film is H_2O and OH inclusion in the films, which leads to degradation of process reliability due to

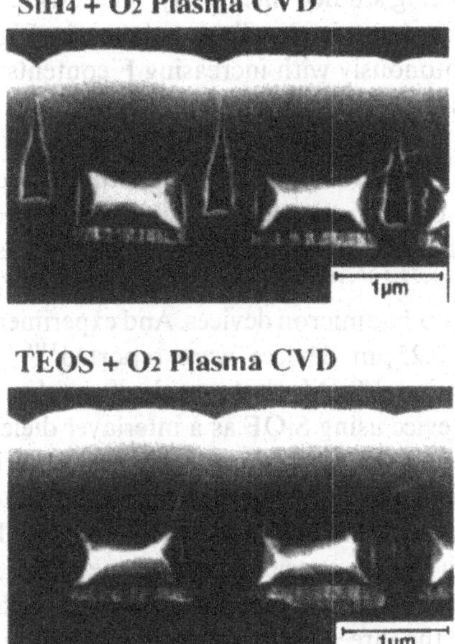

Figure 8.8 Step coverages of $SiH_4 + O_2$ and TEOS $+ O_2$ plasma CVD.

metal corrosion and hot-carrrier-induced degradation of MOS-FET[88,91]. Great efforts are needed to overcome this problem so that TEOS based CVD can be used for Gbit-scale VLSI.

8.4.3 Low Dielectric Constant and High Dielectric Constant Insulator CVD

Multilevel interconnection is becoming increasingly important for fabricating high-performance ULSIs such as MPU[56,92]. Regarding multilevel interconnections of deep sub-micron devices, the strong demands for interlayer dielectrics is low dielectric constant, because, RC delay, which is considered to limit operation speeds of ULSIs, depends on dielectric constant of interlayer dielectrics[56]. Several materials have been studied with a view to their formation by using CVD, such as SiOF(Fluorine doped SiO_2)[93-104] SiBN[105] etc. Recently, SiOF formed by plasma CVD is considered to be a promising material as a low dielectric constant insulator for sub-half micron devices, and is being studied intensively. Dielectric constant of SiOF depends on F contents in the film as shown in Figure 8.9[99]. That decreases monotonously with increasing F contents. Dielectric constant of 2.7 was obtained at F content of about 12 at %. However, it was found that water absorption in SiOF increased with increasing F contents and the resistance to water absorption depended on CVD method[99]. Low dielectric constant of 3.3 was obtained without water absorption by using high density plasma CVD such as a helicon wave excited plasma[94,99,100,106]. SiOF is being applied for the development of actual sub-halfmicron devices. And experimental results of its application to 0.25 μm devices were reported[106,107]. Figure 8.10 shows cross sectional SEM photograph of the developed sub-half-micron ULSI device using SiOF as a interlayer dielectric.

The shrinkage of the minimum feature size of DRAM creates a strong requirement for high dielectric constant material for capacitor cell, such as Ta_2O_5, $SrTiO_3$ and $(BaSr)TiO_3$(see Ref. in Chap. 2). Recently, $(BaSr)TiO_3$ is considered to be one of the most promising materials for future DRAM cells, because of its high dielectric constant. However, the three-dimensional capacitor should be formed to realize 1Gbit DRAM and beyond even if $(BaSr)TiO_3$ is used. Therefore, CVD for $(BaSr)TiO_3$ is studied extensively[108-111]. Metal or-

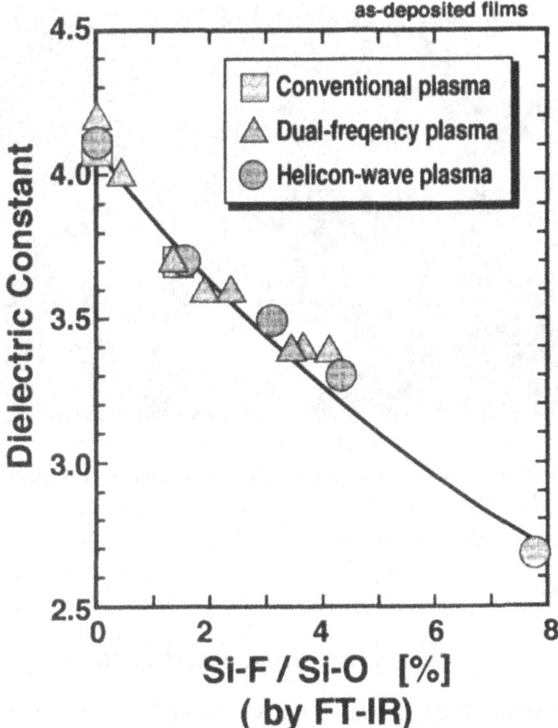

Figure 8.9 Dielectric constant of plasma CVD SiOF films as a function of F content of the film[100].

ganic compounds such as β-diketonate compounds of Ba, Sr and Ti are used as a CVD source gases. Typical CVD temperature is between 400°C–600°C for thermal CVD, and dielectric constant of about 200–400 was obtained. 1Gbit DRAM capacitors of 25–30 fF/cell in capacitor area of less than 0.15 μm^2 were achieved[108,109], and it was indicated in the reports that CVD $(BaSr)TiO_3$ was a promising material for future DRAM capacitors. It is important to develop CVD apparatus, including an MO source gas supply system, so as to be able to use CVD $(BaSr)TiO_3$ film in mass production of future DRAMs.

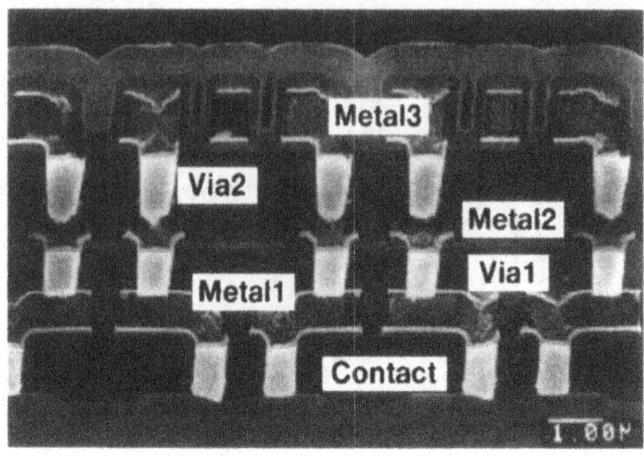

Figure 8.10 Cross sectional SEM photogrph of sub-half-micron logic device using SiOF as a interlayer dielectrics[107].

Reference

1. Murota, J. (1982). *ECS Fall Meeting* (1982) Extended Abstract 82–2 p. 363.
2. Nakayama, S., Yonezawa, H. and Murota, J. (1984). *Jpn. J. Appl. Phys.*, **23**, p. L493.
3. Nakayama, S., Kawashima, I. and Murota, J. (1986). *J. ECS*, **133**, p. 1721.
4. Kobayashi, T., Iijima, S., Aoki, S. and Hiraiwa, A. (1988). *Extended Abstracts of the 20th Conf. on Solid State Device and Materials (SSDM)* (The Japan Society of Applied Physics), pp. 57–60.
5. Shiozawa, J., Kasai, Y., Mikata, Y. and Yamabe, K. (1992). *Extended Abstracts of the 24th Conf. on SSDM* (The Japan Society of Applied Physics), pp. 410–412.
6. Adams, A. C. (1983). "VLSI TECHNOLOGY" Edited by S. M. Sze (McGraw-Hill Book Company,) Chap.3 p. 93.
7. Watanabe, H., Aoto, N., Adachi, S., Ishikawa, T., Ikawa, E. and Terada, K. (1990). *Extended Abstracts of the 22nd (International) Conf. on SSDM* (The Japan Society of Applied Physics), pp. 873–876.
8. Watanabe, H., Tatsumi, T., Niino, T., Sakai, A., Adachi, S., Aoto, N., Koyama, K. and Kikkawa, T. (1991). *Extended Abstracts of the 23rd (International) Conf. on SSDM* (The Japan Society of Applied Physics), pp. 478–480.

9. For Example; see Nikkei Microdevices, No. 66 (Dec. 1990) p. 80.
10. Ohba, T. (1992). "Advance Metallization for ULSI Application" Edited by V. V. S. Rana, R. V. Joshi and I. Ohdomari (Material Research Society, Pittsburgh, Pennsylvania), p. 25.
11. Goto, H., Kobayashi, N. and Homma, Y. (1991). *Extended Abstracts of the 23rd (International) Conf. on SSDM* (The Japan Society of Applied Physics) pp.183–185 & Goto, H., Kobayashi, N. and Homma, Y. "Advance Metallization for ULSI Application" Edited by Joshi, R. V. and Ohdomari, I. (1992). (Material Research Society, Pittsburgh, Pennsylvania), p. 135.
12. Moriya, T., Shima, S., Hazuki, Y., Chiba, M. and Kashiwagi, M. (1983). *IEEE International Electron Device Meeting* (IEDM), *Tech. Digest*, pp. 550–553.
13. Moriya, T., Yamada, K., Tsunashima, T., Nakata, R. and Kashiwagi, M. (1983). *Extended Abstracts of the 15th Conf. on SSDM* (The Japan Society of Applied Physics), p. 225.
14. Moriya, T., Yamada, K., Shibata, T., Iizuka, H. and Kashiwagi, M. (1983). *Symp. on VLSI Technology, Digest of Tech. Paper*, p. 96.
15. Itoh, H., Nakata, R. and Moriya, T. (1983). *IEEE IEDM*, *Tech. Digest*, p. 606.
16. Itoh, H., Moriya, T. and Kashiwagi, M. (1987). *Solid State Tech.*, **30**, p. 80.
17. Ohba, T., Ohyama, Y., Inoue, S. and Maeda, M. (1987). "Tungsten and Other Refractory Metals for VLSI Application □" Edited by E. K. Broadbent (Material Research Society), p. 59.
18. Shioya, Y., Maeda, M. and Yanagida, K. (1986). *J. Vac. Sci. & Tech.*, **B4**, p. 1175.
19. Ohba, T., Inoue, S. and Maeda, M. (1987). *IEEE IEDM*, *Tech. Digest*, p. 213.
20. Kotani, H., Tsutsumi, T., Komori, J. and Nagao, S. (1987). *IEEE IEDM*, *Tech. Digest*, p. 217.
21. Nishiyama, A., Ushiku, Y., Kunishima, I. and Itoh, H. (1988). *Symp. on VLSI Technology*, Digest of Tech. Paper, Abstr. No. 10–2.
22. Sekine, M., Kakuhara, Y., Yamazaki, K. and Murao, Y. (1991). *Proc. of 8th International IEEE VLSI Multilevel Interconnection Conf.*, p. 335.
23. Itoh, H., Moriya, T., Shima, S., Nakata, R. and Kashiwagi, M. (1989). "Handoutai Kenkyu" Edited by J. Nishizawa (Kogyochosakai) p. 113 in Japanese.
24. Hara, T., Suzuki, T., Misawa, N., Ohba, T. and Furumura, Y. (1990). *Proc. 11th International Conf. Chem. Vapor Deposition*, Edited by K. E. Spear and Cullen, G. W. (Electrochemical Society, Pennington, N. J.), p. 441.
25. Tamaru, T., Iwata, S., Kobayashi, N. and Tokunaga, T. (1990). *Proc. of Symp. on Dry Process*, (The Institute of Electrical Engineers of Japan, Tokyo Japan), p. 51.

26. Ohba, T., Furumura, Y. and Tsuchikawa, H. (1992). "Advance Metallization for ULSI Application" Edited by Rana, V. V. S., Joshi, R. V. and Ohdomari, I. (Material Research Society, Pittsburgh, Pennsylvania), p. 211.
27. Itoh, H. and Mori, K. (1995). *Proc. of Advance Metallization and Interconnection System for ULSI Applications* in 1995 (Japan Sessin, Tokyo), p. 78.
28. Sekine, M., Kakuhara, Y., Yamazaki, K. and Murao, Y. (1992). "Advance Metallization for ULSI Application" Edited by Rana, V. V. S., Joshi, R. V. and Ohdomari, I. (Material/Research Society, Pittsburgh, Pennsylvania), p. 255.
29. Itoh, H., Kaji, N., Watanabe, T. and Okano, H. (1991). *Jpn. J. Appl. Phys.*, 30, No. 7, pp. 1525–1529.
30. Kobayashi, N., Goto, H. and Suzuki, M. (1990). *Extended Abstracts of the 23rd International Conf. on SSDM* (The Japan Society of Applied Physics, Tokyo), p. 865.
31. Kobayashi, N., Goto, H. and Suzuki, M. (1991). *J. Appl. Phys.*, **69**, p. 1013.
32. Joshi, R. V. and Brodsky, S. (1992). *Proc. of 9th International VLSI Multilevel Interconnection Conf.*, p. 253.
33. Motegi, N., Kashimoto, Y., Nagatani, K., Takahashi, S. Kondo, T., Mizusawa, Y. and Nakayama, I. (1995). *J. Vac. Sci. and Technology*, **B13**(4), 1906.
34. Yokoyama, N., Hinode, K. and Homma, Y. (1989). *J. Electrochem. Soc.*, **136**, p. 882.
35. Yokoyama, N., Hinode, K. and Homma, Y. (1991). *J. Electrochem. Soc.*, **138**, p. 190.
36. Mori, K., Akazawa, M., Iwasaki, M., Ito, H., Tsukamoto, K. and Akasaka, Y. (1991). *Extended Abstracts of the 24th International Conf. on SSDM* (The Japan Society of Applied Physics, Tokyo), p. 210.
37. Suzuki, T., Ohba, T., Furumura, Y. and Tsutikawa, H. (1992). *IEEE IEDM Tech. Digest*, p. 979.
38. Akahori, T., Tanihara, A. and Tano, M. (1991). *Jpn. J. Appl. Phys.*, **30**, No. 12B, p. 3558.
39. Akahori, T., Murakami, T. and Morioka, Y. (1993). *Proc. 10th International VLSI Multilevel Interconnection Conference (VMIC)* p. 405.
40. Miyamoto, T., Kawashima, A., Kadomura, S. and Aoyama, J. (1995). *Proc. 10th International VLSI Multilevel Interconnection Conference (VMIC)*, p. 195.
41. Ikeda, K., Maeda, M. and Arita, Y. *Symp. on VLSI Technology, Digest of Tech. Papers*, (Honolulu, 1990), p. 61.
42. Eizenberg, M., Littau, K., Ghanayem, S., Mak, A., Maeda, Y., Chang, M. and Shiha, A. K. (1994). *Appl. Phys. Lett.*, **65**, p. 2416.
43. Sekiguti, A., Jimba, H., Kim, S. W., Yoshimura, T., Watanabe, K., Mizuno, S., Hasegawa, S., Okada, O., Takahashi, N. and Hosokawa, N.

Proc. of Advance Metallization and Interconnection System for ULSI Applications in 1995 (Japan Sessin, Tokyo, 1995), p. 72.
44. Liu, R., Cheung, K. P. and Lai, W. Y. C. (1989). *Proc. 4th International VLSI Multilevel Interconnection Conference (VMIC)*, p. 329.
45. Tao, J. *et al.* (1992). *Proc. of 30th International Reliability Process Symp.*, p. 338.
46. Hu, C. K., Ho, P. S. and Small, M. B. (1992). *J. Appl. Phys.*, **72**, p. 291.
47. Kaanta, C. W., Bombardier, S. G., Cote, W. J., Hill, W. R., Kerzykowski, G., Landis, H. S., Poindexter, D. J., Pollard, C. W., Ross, G. H., Ryan, J. G., Wolff, S. and Cronin, J. E. (1991). *Proc. of 8th IEEE VLSI Multilevel Interconnection Conference (VMIC)*, p. 144.
48. Ito, T., Sugii, T. and Nakamura, T. (1982). *Symp. on VLSI Technology, Digest of Tech. Papers*, p. 20.
49. Amazawa, T. and Nakamura, H. (1986). *Extended Abstracts of the 18th Conf. on SSDM* (The Japan Society of Applied Physics, Tokyo), p. 775.
50. Amazawa, T., Nakamura, H. and Arita, Y. (1988). *IEEE IEDM Tech. Digest*, p. 442.
51. Kobayashi, T., Sekiguchi, A., Hosokawa, N. and Asamaki, T. (1988). *Jpn. J. Appl. Phys.*, **27**(9), p. L1775.
52. Masu, K., Tsubouti, K., Hiura, Y., Matano, T. and Mikoshiba, N. (1991). *Jpn. J. Appl. Phys.*, **30**(1A), p. L56.
53. Shinzawa, T., Sugai, K., Kishida, S. and Okabayashi, H. (1990). *Proc. of Mat. Res. Soc. VLSI V.* (MRS, 1990), p. 377.
54. Masu, K., Sakurai, J., Shigeeda, N., Tsubouti, K., Mikoshiba, N., Takeuti, Y. (1988). *Extended Abstracts of the 20th Conf. on SSDM* (The Japan Society of Applied Physics, Tokyo) p. 573.
55. Hasunuma, M., Kaneko, H., Sawabe, A., Kawanoue, T., Kohanawa, Y., Komatsu, S. and Miyauchi, M. (1989). *IEEE IEDM Tech. Digest*, p. 677.
56. Ushiku, Y., Kushibe, H., Ono, H. and Nishiyama, A. (1990). *Proc. of 7th IEEE VLSI Multilevel Interconnection Conference (VMIC)*, p. 413.
57. Luther, B., White, J.F., Uzoh, C., Cacouris, T., Hummel, J., Guthrie, W., Lustig, N., Greco, S., Zuhoski, S., Agnello, P., Colgan, E., Mathad, S., Saraf, L., Weitzman, E. J., Ho, C. K., Kaufman, F., Jaso, M., Buchwalter, L. P., Reynolds, S., Smart, C., Edelstein, D., Baran, E., Cohen, S., Knoedler, C. M., Malinowski, J., Horkans, J., Deligianni, H., Harper, J., Andricacos, P. C., Paraszczak, J., Pearson, D. J. and Small, M. (1993). *Proc. of 10th VLSI Multilevel Interconnection Conference (VMIC)*, p. 15.
58. Hazuki, Y., Yano, H., Horioka, K., Hayasaka, N. and Okano, H. (1989). *Proc. of the 11th Symp. on Dry Process* (The Institute of Electrical Engineerings of Japan, Tokyo), p. 173.
59. Awaya, N. and Arita, Y. (1989). *Symp. on VLSI Technology, Digest of Tech. Paper*, p. 103.
60. Awaya, N., Ohno, K., Sato, M. and Arita, Y. (1990). *Proc. of 7th IEEE VLSI Multilevel Interconnection Conference (VMIC)*, p. 254.

61. Arita, Y., Awaya, N., Ohno, K. and Sato, M. (1990). *IEEE IEDM Tech. Digest*, p. 39.
62. Awaya, N. and Arita, Y. (1991). *Symp. on VLSI Technology, Digest of Tech. Paper*, p. 37.
63. Misawa, N., Kishii, S., Ohba, T., Arimoto, Y., Furumura, Y. and Tsutikawa, (1993). *Proc. of 10th VLSI Multilevel Interconnection Conference (VMIC)* p. 353.
64. Kajita, A., Kaneko, H. and Hayasaka, N. (1995). *Proc. of The 17th Symp. on Dry Process* (The Institute of Electrical Engineerings of Japan, Tokyo) p. 123.
65. Becker, F. S., Pawlik, D., Anzinger, H. and Spitzer, A. (1987). *J. Vac. Sci. & Tech.*, **B5**(6), p. 1555.
66. Kotani, H. and Matsui, Y. (1991). "Handoutai Kenkyuu **36**" Edited by Nishizawa, J. (Kougyo-chosakai, 1991) p. 189 (in Japanese).
67. Maeda, K. and Sato, J. (1971). *Extended Abstract of Electrochem. Soc. (ECS) Spring Meeting* No. 9, p.31.
68. Nishimoto, Y., Tokumasu, N., Furuyama, T. and Maeda, K. (1987). *Abstracts of the 19th Conf. on SSDM* (The Japan Society of Applied Physics, Tokyo), p. 447.
69. Kotani, H., Matsuura, M., Fujii, A., Genjou, H. and Nagao, S. (1989). *IEEE IEDM Tech. Digest*, p. 669.
70. Sorita, T., Shiga, S., Ikuta, K., Egashira, Y. and Komiyama, H. (1993). *J. ECS* **140**(10), p. 2952.
71. Tsunashima, Y., Nakao, T., Todori, K. and Yamabe, K. (1990). *Abstracts of the 22nd Conf. on SSDM* (The Japan Society of Applied Physics, Tokyo), p. 445.
72. Adachi, M., Okuyama, K., Tohge, N., Shimada, M., Sato, J. and Muroyama, M. (1994). *Jpn. J. Appl. Phys.*, **33** PART 2(3B), p. L447.
73. Homma, T., Suzuki, M. and Murao, Y. (1993). *J. ECS.*, **140**(12), p. 3591.
74. Kishimoto, K., Suzuki, M., Hirayama, T., Ikeda, Y. and Numasawa, Y. (1992). *Proc. of 9th VLSI Multilevel Interconnection Conference (VMIC)*, p. 149.
75. Noguchi, S., Okano, H. and Horiike, Y. (1987). *Abstracts of the 19th Conf. on SSDM* (The Japan Society of Applied Physics, Tokyo), p. 451.
76. Natsuura, M., Hayashide, Y., Kotani, H., Nishimura, T., Iuchi, H., Dobson, C.D., Kiermasz, A., Beekmann, K. and Wilby, R. (1994). *IEEE IEDM Tech. Digest*, p. 117.
77. Matsuura, M., Kotani, H. and Abe, H. (1990). *Abstracts of the 22nd Conf. on SSDM* (The Japan Society of Applied Physics, Tokyo) p. 239.
78. Fujino, K., Nishimoto, Y., Tokumasu, N. and Maeda, K. *J. ECS.* **138**, (1991) p. 550 and Fujino, K., Nishimoto, Y., Tokumasu, N. and Maeda, K. *J. ECS.* **139**(6), p. 1692.
79. Ikeda, Y., Numasawa, Y. and Sakamoto, M. (1989). *NEC Research & Development* No. 94, p. 1.

80. Kotani, H., Matsuura, M. and Nagao, S. (1989). Semiconductor World (Press Journal, Tokyo) No.11, p. 81 (in Japanese).
81. Matsuo, S. and Kiuchi, M. (1983). *Jpn. J. Appl. Phys.*, **22**(4), p. L210.
82. Machida, K. and Oikawa, H. (1985). *Abstracts of the 17th Conf. on SSDM* (The Japan Society of Applied Physics, Tokyo), p. 329.
83. Machida, K. and Oikawa, H. (1986). *J. Vac. Sci. & Tech.*, **B4**, p. 1986.
84. Fukuda, T., Suzuki, K., Mochizuki, Y. Ohue, M., Homma, N. and Sonobe, T. (1988). *Abstracts of the 20th Conf. on SDM* (The Japan Society of Applied Physics, Tokyo), p. 65.
85. Fukuda, T., Ohue, M., Homma, N., Suzuki, K. and Sonobe, T. *Jpn. J. Appl. Phys.*, **28**(6), p. 1035.
86. Ishikawa, H. and Murao, Y. (1994). *Proc. of 11th VLSI Multilevel Interconnection Conference (VMIC)*, p. 67.
87. Hazuki, Y., Ushiku, Y., Matsuda, T. and Kashiwagi, M. J. (1989). IEICE (The Institute of Electronics, Information and Communication Engineers) J.72-c-□ p. 312 (in Japanese).
88. Shimoyama, N., Machida, K., Murase, K. and Tsuchiya, T. (1992). *Symp. on VLSI Technology, Digest of Tech. Paper*, p. 94.
89. Kawai, M., Matsuda, M., Miki, K. and Sakiyama, K. (1988). *Proc. of 5th IEEE VLSI Multilevel Interconnection Conference (VMIC)*, p. 419.
90. Musaka, K., Mizuno, S. and Hara, K. (1993). *Abstracts of the 25th Conf. on SSDM* (The Japan Society of Applied Physics, Tokyo) p. 510.
91. Takayanagi Takagi, M., Yoshii, I. and Hashimoto, K. (1992). *IEEE IEDM Tech. Digest*, p. 703.
92. Hashimoto, K. and Shibata, H. (1992). *Symp. on VLSI Technology, Digest of Tech. Paper*, p. 53.
93. Nishiyama, Y., Nakata, R., Hayasaka, N., Okano, H. and Sato, A. (1993). *Extended Abstract of The 40th Spring Meeting* (Japan Society of Appl. Phys. and Related Societies, 1993) No. 2, p. 799 (in Japanese).
94. Hayasaka, N., Nishiyama, Y., Miyajima, H., Tomioka, K., Nakata, R. and Okano, H. (1993). *Proc. of the 15th Symp. on Dry Process* (The Institute of Electrical Engineerings of Japan, Tokyo), p. 163.
95. Usami, T., Shimokawa, K. and Yoshimaru, M. (1993). *Abstracts of the 25th Conf. on SSDM* (The Japan Society of Applied Physics, Tokyo), p. 161.
96. Fukada, T. and Akahori, T. (1993). *Abstracts of the 25th Conf. on SSDM* (The Japan Society of Applied Physics, Tokyo), p. 158.
97. Usami, T., Shimokawa, K. and Yoshimaru, M. (1994). *Jpn. J Appl. Phys.*, **33** Part1(1), p. 408.
98. Homma, T. and Murao, Y. *IEEE IEDM Tech. Digest.* (1991). p. 289.
99. Homma, T., Yamaguti, R. and Murao, Y. (1993). *J. ECS.*, **140**(3), p. 687.
100. Miyajima, H., Katsumata, R., Hayasaka, N. and Okano, H. (1994). *Proc. of the 16th Symp. on Dry Process* (The Institute of Electrical Engineerings of Japan, Tokyo) p. 133.

101. Katsumata, R., Miyajima, H., Nakasaki, Y. and Hayasaka, N. *Proc. of the 17th Symp. on Dry Process* (The Institute of Electrical Engineerings of Japan, Tokyo) (1995) p. 269.
102. Aoki, R., Hayasaka, N., Nishiyama, Y., Miyajima, H., Nakasaki, Y. and Okano, H. (1994). *Extended Abstract of The American Vacuum Soc. 41st National Symp.*, p. 230.
103. Fukada, T. and Akahori, T. (1995). *Proc. of First International Dielectrics for VLSI/ULSI Multilevel Interconnection Conference (DUMIC)*, p. 43.
104. Matsuda, T., Shapino, M. J. and Nguyen, S. V. (1995). *Proc. of First International Dielectrics for VLSI/ULSI Multilevel Interconnection Conference (DUMIC)*, p. 22.
105. Maeda, M., (1990). *Jpn. J. Appl. Phys.*, **29**(9), p. 1789.
106. Anand, M. B., Matsuno, T., Murota, M., Shibata, H., Kakumu, M., Mori, K., Ohtsuka, K., Takahashi, M., Kaji, N., Kodera, M., Itoh, H., Nagata, M. and Aoki, R. (1994). *Proc. 11th International VLSI Multilevel Interconnection Conference (VMIC)*, p. 15.
107. Oyamatsu, H., Kasai, K., Matsunaga, N., Igarashi, H., Yamaguchi, T., Asamura, T., Azuma, A., Shibata, H., Kinugawa, M. and Kakumu, M. (1995). *IEEE IEDM Tech. Digest*, p. 705.
108. Kawahara, T., Yamamuka, M., Yuuki, A. and Ono, K. (1994). *Fall Meeting of MRS*, I2–6.5.
109. Yuuki, A., Yamamuka, M., Makita, T., Horikawa, T., Shibano, T., Hirano, N., Maeda, H., Mikami, N., Ono, K., Ogata, H. and Abe, H. (1995). *IEEE IEDM Tech. Digest*, p. 115.
110. Yamamichi, S., Lesacherre, P-Y., Yamaguchi, H., Takemura, K., Sone, S., Yabata, H., Sato, K. and Tamaru, T. (1995). *IEEE IEDM Tech. Digest*, p. 119.
111. Eguchi, K. and Kiyotoshi, M. (1995). *Extended Abstract of The 42nd Spring Meeting* (Japan Society of Appl. Phys. and Related Societies, 1995) No. 2, p. 389 (in Japanese).

CHAPTER 9

Crystal Technology

9.1. Introduction

A semiconductor device like ULSI (ultra large scale integration) and so on, has become the key to modern industry and its importance has been growing more and more. Most of devices have been produced by using the silicon wafers as substrates. The mono-crystalline silicon has many advantageous characteristics for device technology, such as a thermal stability, a simple formation of oxide as an insulator, precise controllability of electrical type (p or n), and so on. In addition, the silicon single crystal can be easily produced in large diameter. These are reasons why the silicon wafer has been used in semiconductor industry.

The silicon wafer used for semiconductor industry is cut from a dislocation free single crystal ingot, which is grown by Czochralski (CZ) method or float zone (FZ) method. The dislocation free crystal had been first developed by the FZ method.

9.2. Silicon Crystal Growth Technology

9.2.1 Crystal Ingot Growth Method

(1) *Float zone (FZ) method* The basic principle of FZ method is shown in Figure 9.1. A polycrystalline silicon ingot as a raw material is molten from the ingot end in vacuum or argon gas atmosphere by radio induction heating. A rotating mono-crystalline Si seed is touched to the molten silicon and pulled down with moving the molten zone to polycrystalline region. The dislocation-free crystal can be obtained by applying a Dash's necking technique[1]. Dislocations would be introduced into the seed crystal by the thermal shock when the seed touches to the molten silicon. Then, the dislocations are driven out from the crystal during the process making the seed slender

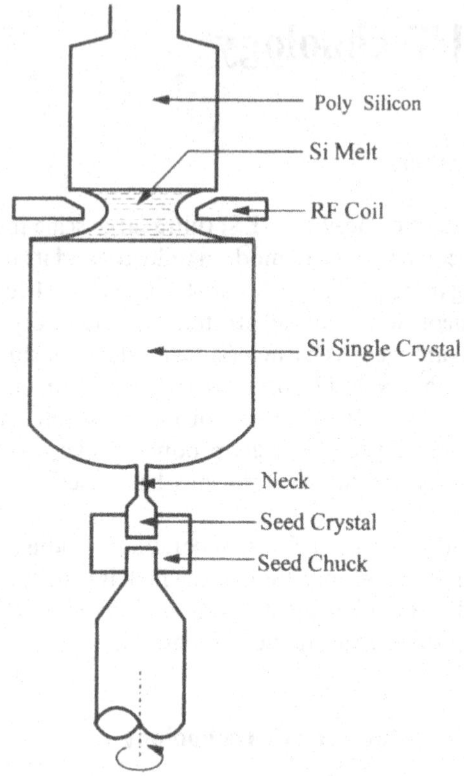

Figure 9.1 Schematic drawing of FZ method.

about 2–4 mm (Dash's necking technique) and growing the crystal to a couple of cm. After that, the crystal shoulder is formed and the dislocation-free crystal is grown with large diameter.

Since the crucible is not necessary in FZ method, it is possible to obtain the crystal with very high purity and/or uniform doping. However, it is difficult to grow the large diameter crystal in FZ method, because the large crystal must be held by the slender seed. The present FZ technology can produce the crystal with a diameter of 150 mmϕ or smaller, but has not achieved that with a diameter of 200 mmϕ or larger. Therefore, the FZ silicon crystal is mainly used for the device that requires the uniform high resistivity substrate, that is, the substrate for neutron transmutation doping.

(2) *Czochralski (CZ) method* The CZ method was a single crystal pulling technique proposed by Czochralski[2]. Figure 9.2 shows schematic drawing of the CZ method. A poly-silicon is molten in a quartz crucible heated by surrounding carbon heater. A seed crystal is dipped into the melt and is slowly pulled up. Both the seed crystal and the crucible are rotating during crystal pulling. The Dash's necking procedure is applied to make the crystal dislocation free in the initial stage of seed pulling.

In the semiconductor industry, a substrate crystal wafer becomes larger and larger, because of the device productivity improvement

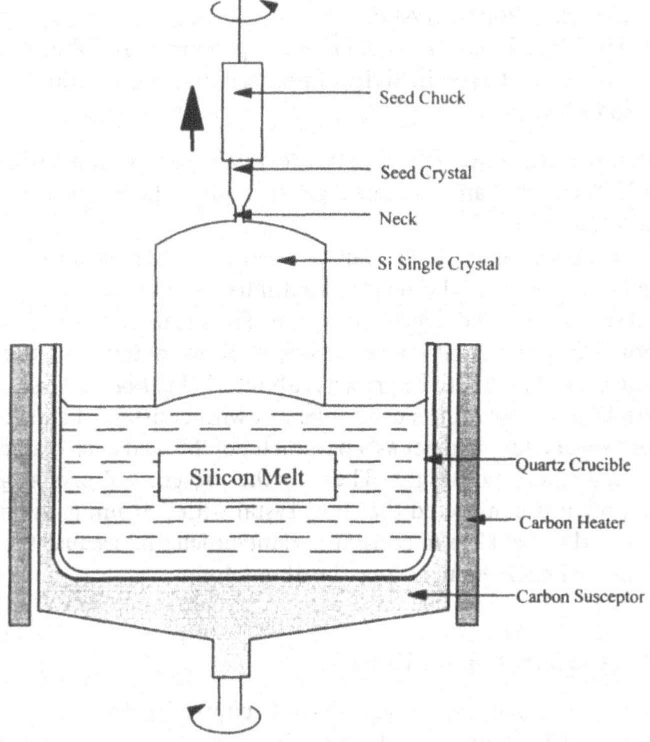

Figure 9.2 Schematic drawing of CZ method.

and cost down. Nowadays, the wafer with 300 mm in diameter is going to be used in ULSI (Ultra Large Scale Integration) industry. Since the CZ method is suitable technology to grow a large diameter crystal, most of the substrate crystals used in semiconductor industry are grown by CZ method. Therefore improvement of CZ crystal quality is one of the most important subjects for the semiconductor industry.

(3) *Large diameter crystal* The CZ silicon crystal is mainly used as the substrate crystal in the semiconductor industry, nevertheless the purity of CZ crystal is lower than that of the FZ crystal. That is because

(1) CZ crystal has a high mechanical strength because of high oxygen concentration in crystal.
(2) The large diameter crystal is easily produced by CZ method and promising the productivity improvement in semiconductor device industry.

In the present, most of the substrate crystals have 200 mm in diameter, and 300 mm in diameter of next generation crystal has reached world wide consensus.

The limitation for large diameter depends on the shear strength of seed neck, because the slender seed must support the heavy crystal and seed neck is the slenderest region. The shear strength of silicon is about 20 kg/mm2[3]. If the seed neck is 4 mm in diameter, the maximum crystal weight to be grown is about 250 kg. Figure 9.3 shows the correlation between the crystal length with constant diameter position and crystal diameter as a parameter of the seed neck diameter for the 250 kg crystal weight. Then, in the present CZ crystal growth method, it is considered that the crystal with 300 mm in diameter is bounded to be 0.9 m in constant diameter length, because the maximum seed neck diameter may be about 4mm.

9.2.2 Impurity Control Technology

(1) *Dopant* The crystal resistivity is controlled by doping the III impurity (B, Al etc.) for *p*-type or the *V* impurity (P, As, Sb etc.) for *n*-type. The doped impurity is incorporated into the crystal depending

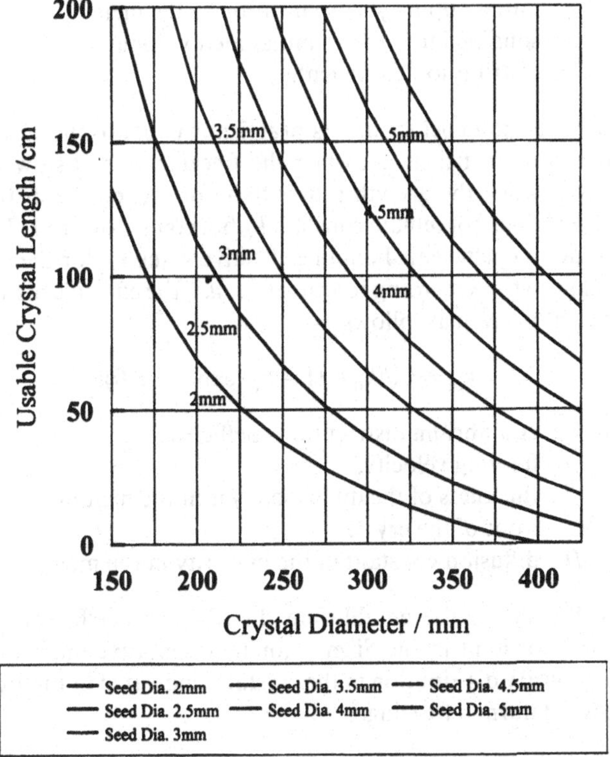

Figure 9.3 Dependence of maximum usable crystal length on second neck diameter.

on a distribution coefficient k at the interface between the melt and the solid. The distribution coefficient k is different from 1 for nearly all impurities, then the resistivity fluctuates in both axial and radial direction. In the case of normal freezing, Pfann[4] indicated that the axial distribution of the impurity in the crystal is given by the following equation.

$$C/C_0 = k(1-g)^{k-1} \tag{9.1}$$

where C; impurity concentration incorporated into the crystal at the freezing interface.

C_0 ; initial impurity concentration in the melt.
g ; solidified fraction to initial melt volume.
k ; distribution coefficient.

The distribution coefficient k is practically equal to the equilibrium distribution coefficient k_0, when the freezing rate is slow enough. However, when the growth rate is finite or higher, the distribution coefficient does not remain constant k_0 but comes toward 1. Then, the distribution coefficient should be effective value k_{eff} for the practical crystal growth. According to Burton *et al.*[5], the effective distribution coefficient is given as follows.

$$k_{eff} = k_0/(k_0 + (1 - k_0)\exp(-vd/D)) \tag{9.2}$$

where k_0; equilibrium distribution coefficient,
v; freezing velocity,
d ; thickness of the diffusion layer in the melt in front of the crystal,
D ; diffusion constant of the impurity in the melt.

Table 9.1 shows the equilibrium distribution coefficient and the diffusion constant in the Si melt for representative impurities. The axial impurity distribution in the crystal is indicated in Figure 9.4 for the case of normal freezing.

Table 9.1 Properties of impurities in silicon.

Element	Distribution Coefficient k_0	Maximum solid solubility (atoms/cm^3)	Diffusion melt coefficient in the (cm^3/sec)
Boron	0.8	1×10^{21}	2.4×10^{-4}
Aluminum	0.002	2×10^{19}	7.0×10^{-4}
Gallium	0.008	4×10^{19}	4.8×10^{-4}
Indium	0.0004	4×10^{17}	6.9×10^{-4}
Carbon	0.07	3.5×10^{17}	2.0×10^{-4}
Nitrogen	0.0007	5×10^{15}	
Phosphorus	0.35	1.3×10^{21}	2.3×10^{-4}
Arsenic	0.3	1.8×10^{21}	3.3×10^{-4}
Antimony	0.023	7×10^{19}	1.5×10^{-4}
Oxygen	1.4	2×10^{18}	3.3×10^{-4}

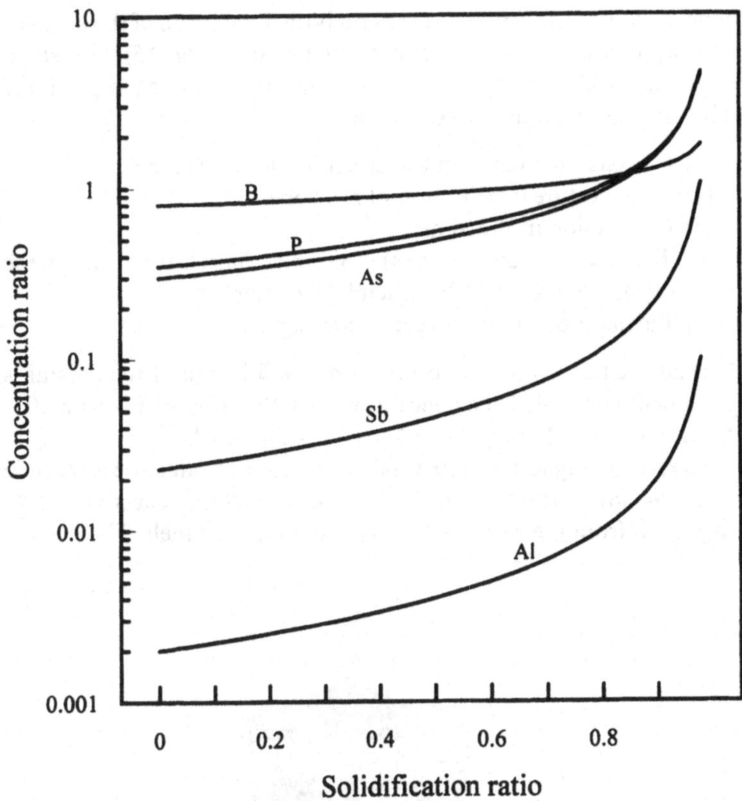

Figure 9.4 Bopant concentration as a function of solodification ratio.

(2) *Light element impurities* Since the CZ crystal pulling needs the quartz crucible, the quartz is dissolved into the melt and oxygen as an impurity is incorporated into Si crystal. The oxygen, which is the impurity with the highest concentration, is supersaturated in the crystal at a temperature used in device manufacturing process. The supersaturated oxygen become the origin of micro defects, such as oxide precipitates, dislocations and so on, induced by heat treatments. The controls of oxygen concentration and distribution are the most important subjects in the CZ crystal. The oxygen concentration depends upon that in the melt in front of the crystal. And the

concentration in the melt depends on both dissolution of the crucible and vaporization of oxygen from Si melt surface (Fig. 9.5). Therefore, in order to control the oxygen concentration in the crystal the following factors must be controlled.

(1) Contact area between the crucible and the Si melt.
(2) Temperature distribution of hot zone.
(3) Convection in the Si melt.
(4) The free surface area of the Si melt, that is, the ratio of the crystal diameter to the crucible diameter.
(5) Partial pressure of oxygen in atmosphere.

Nowadays, the oxygen concentration in full length of the crystal is practically controlled at a concentration in the range of $5 - 10 \times 10^{17}$ atoms/cm^3 with fluctuation $\pm 1 \times 10^{17}$ atoms/cm^3.

The second highest impurity is carbon. Both a heater and a crucible susceptor are made of carbon. The carbon, which reacts with SiO vaporized from the melt surface, is taken into the melt. The carbon

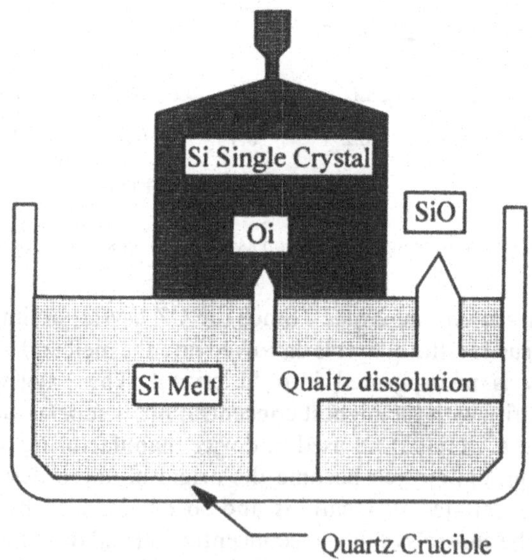

Figure 9.5 Mechanism of oxygen introduction into Si crystal.

atoms acts as nucleus for oxygen precipitation and induce many detrimental effects for LSI devices. Therefore, the carbon concentration in the crystal must be decreased. The decrease of carbon concentration is practically carried out by controlling the gas stream not to incorporate the CO gas into the melt. The carbon concentration in the CZ crystal is suppressed to be lower than 1×10^{16} atoms/cm^3.

Other impurities besides oxygen and carbon in the crystal are boron, aluminum, transition metals and so on. These impurities, which come from the impurities in the crucible, row material polysilicon and contamination during crystal growth procedures, are ultra trace, because the distribution coefficients are very low. However, some of them have fatal effects on the devices even in the ultra trace, then the greatest care for contamination control must be taken in the crystal growth.

(3) *Oxygen control*: Magnetic field applied crystal growth
The melt convection plays the important roll for the incorporation of impurities in CZ crystal growth. In order to suppress the convection, magnetic field is applied the Si melt. This growth method is called MCZ (magnetic field applied Czochralski[6]). Since the Si melt is conductive, the force against the melt flow is generated according to Lenz's low when the magnetic field is applied to the melt. This practically corresponds to the increase of viscosity. According to Hoshi *et al.*[6] the effective viscosity coefficient ν_{eff} is expressed as follows.

$$\nu_{eff} = (\mu H D)^2 \sigma / \rho \tag{9.3}$$

Where H; Strength of applied magnetic field
σ; Magnetic permeability of Si melt
μ; Electric conductivity of Si melt
ρ; Density of Si melt
D; Diameter of the crucible

For example, if the magnetic field with strength $H = 2000$ G is applied to the Si melt in the transverse direction, the effective viscosity coefficient becomes over 10^6 times of that without magnetic field and the melt convection is almost perfectly suppressed. As the solid-liquid interface comes to stable, the growth striation is also suppressed and the oxygen concentration can be controlled in wide range. In addition, it is possible to grow the crystal faster because of suppression of the temperature fluctuation. The comparison between CZ and MCZ method is summarized in Table 9.2.

Three directions are proposed in the applied magnetic field. Those are vertical direction, horizontal direction and cusp field that is combination of vertical and horizontal field. Since the vertical convection can not be suppressed by the vertical field, the oxygen concentration of radius distribution is widely scattered. Therefore, the horizontal magnetic field[6] and the cusp magnetic field[7] are practically used in the semiconductor industry.

9.3. Crystalline Defect Control

9.3.1 Defect in as-Grown Crystal

Since the Dash's necking technology has been applied in crystal growth, the crystal has not large defects such as dislocations but micro defects in both CZ and FZ crystals.

The micro defects, which make shallow pits not corresponding to dislocation pits after defect etching, have been firstly observed in FZ crystal[8]. The micro defects are named as "Swirl defects" from the defect distribution emerged. The swirl defects are classified in A-defect and B-defect from a defect decoration analysis of Cu and Li[9]. Both the Cu and Li are decorated on the A-defect and only Cu is decorated on

Table 9.2 Comparison between CZ and MCZ method.

Item	CZ	MCZ
Temperature stability at crystal growth	~ 10	< 0.1
Growth striation	Complex	Simple and weak
Resistivity controllability		
Average (W-m)	0.001 ~ 100	0.001 ~ 1000
Deviation s (%)	±5%	±3%
Oxygen concentration controllability		
Average (aoms/cm^3)	$5 \sim 10 \times 10^{17}$	$1 \sim 12 \times 10^{17}$
Lifetime t (msec)	< 200	< 1000

the B-defect. The A-defect is recognized to be an interstitial type dislocation loop from the observation by electron microscope. According to Foll *et al.*[10] the B-defect is a complex of interstitial silicones, which are generated at the solid-liquid interface when the melt is solidified. The complex is formed at the impurity carbon as nucleus.

The swirl defect generation depends on the growth rate as shown in Figure 9.6[11]. Both the A- and B-defect are suppressed at a growth rate lower than 0.2 mm/min or higher than 5 mm/min because of out diffusion or freezing of interstitial Si, respectively. However, the growth rate becomes much higher, another defect which is considered as aggregations of vacancies called D-defect, is generated.

The as-grown CZ crystal has also micro defects. When the CZ wafer is etched by Secco's etching solution for about 30 min. or longer, shallow pits called flow pattern defects are emerged[12]. When the wafer is soaked into alkaline cleaning solution SC – 1 ($H_2O_2 + NH_4OH + H_2O$), tiny pits, called COP (Crystal originated particle)[13] or SMD (Surface micro defect)[14], appear on the mirror surface. This defect is correlated with the defect of thin oxide formed on the wafer[14]. In addition, it is recognized that the as-grow Si crystal has the defects of about 10 nm in diameter, when the inner part of the crystal is observed by IR tomography[15]. The behaviors of the defects

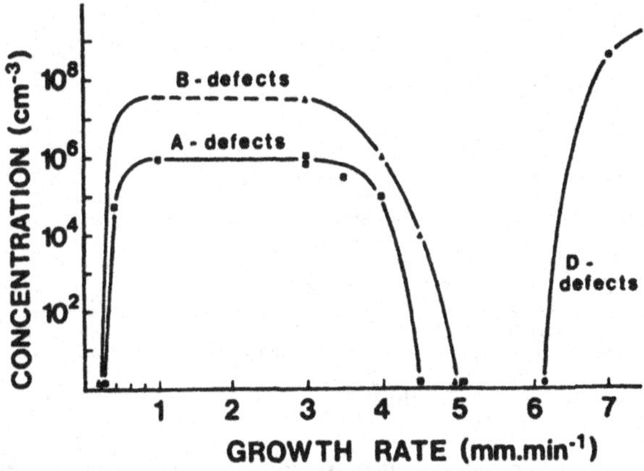

Figure 9.6 Dependency of defect type and density in FZ crystal on growth rate[11].

and those effects on the device performance, which have not been clear yet, are important subjects for both the crystal science and the industry.

9.3.2 Thermally Induced Defect

(1) *Bulk micro defect* Since the CZ Si crystal has oxygen supersaturated, the many micro defects are induced by heat treatments in device manufacturing process. The oxygen atoms occupy the interstitial sites in as-grown crystal. The supersaturated oxygen are precipitated during heat treatments and oxides (SiO_2) are generated in the bulk. Therefore, the precipitated oxygen increases with the increase of initial oxygen concentration, as shown in Figure 9.7[16].

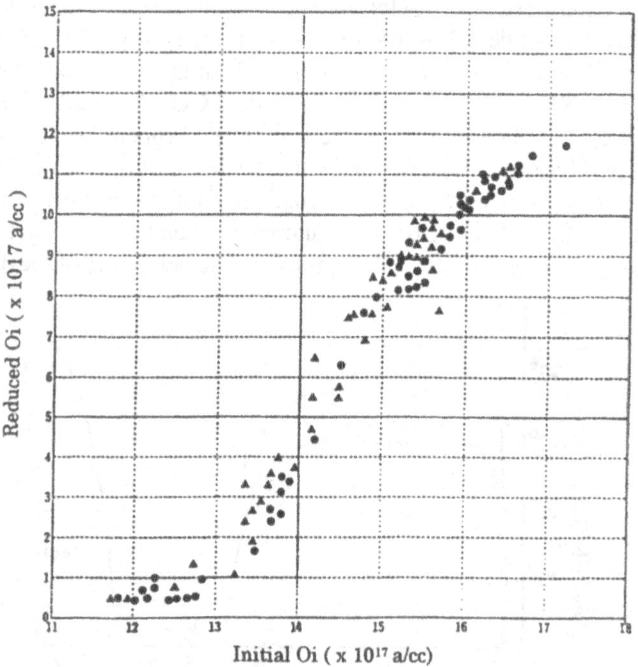

Figure 9.7 Correlation between initial oxygen content and reduced oxygen content. (Heat treatment; 650C,3H + 780C, 3H + 1000C,16H, Oxygen content is converted by ASTM; F121-'83)

When the Si atoms is transformed to the SiO_2 precipitates, its volume increases about twice. Then, secondary defects, such as dislocations, stacking faults and so on, are induced in the bulk. All of these defects including the oxide precipitates are generally called BMD (bulk micro defect). The BMD has different characteristics and behaviors depending on temperature of heat treatment. The BMD behaviors are summarized in Table 9.3.

At around 450C, silicon-oxygen complex, which forms donor state, is generated. The donor is called oxygen donor or thermal donor (TD). The origin of thermal donor is considered to be more than six kinds of SiO_x ($x = 3 \sim 8$)[17]. The thermal donor disappears by heat treatment at a temperature around 650°C, that is called a donor killer process. And a prolonged heat treatment at that temperature induces the other kind of donor called new donor (ND)[18]. The new donor is considered to be owing to tiny SiO_2 precipitates and the behavior is different from that of thermal donor. The tiny precipitates, which are induced at a temperature between 600°C and 800°C, act as nuclei for oxygen precipitation at higher temperature. And the tiny precipitates sometimes associate dislocation dipoles elongated to ⟨110⟩ direction. The precipitate are formed in heterogeneous nucleation mechanism at a site of carbon[19] or other impurities.

When the heat treatment is carried out at a temperature between 800°C and 1100°C, platelet precipitates and punch-out dislocations

Table 9.3 Characteristics of BMD induced by heat treatment at various temperature.

Temp. (deg.C)	400	600	800	1000	1200
Oxide Precipitate		μμ ppt (Cosite)	Platelet (Cristobalite)	(Amorphous)	Polyhedron
Nucleus	SiO_x ($x = 3–8$)	Nucleation (Heterogeneous, Carbon)		Large Nucleus (Vacancy)	
Density	Exponentially decrease as temperature increase				
Secondary defect		Dislo. dipole		Punch-out Dislo.	Stacking fault
Electrical	Thermal Donor	New Donor		Recombination Center	

to ⟨110⟩ direction from the precipitates are induced. Extrinsic type stacking faults in the bulk are often observed in addition to the punch-out dislocations. The precipitates, which have various shapes from platelet to dendrite[20], are presumed to be amorphous SiO_2 or cristobalite. These precipitates and dislocation loops have powerful ability to capture harmful impurities, that is well known as intrinsic gettering.

When the heating temperature is higher than 1100C, octahedron or polyhedron precipitates are induced. The precipitates are amorphous SiO_2 and the shape is defined by interior oxidation of silicon crystal lattice. That is, the precipitate habit plane is correspond to silicon [111] plane which is the slowest plane of oxidation. The octahedral precipitate is called negative crystal.

The BMD has high performance for gettering of harmful impurity. However if the BMD is induced in a device active area, some detrimental influences, such as junction leak or pattern edge dislocation generation and so on, is suffered. Therefore, it is very important in ULSI manufacturing to control the BMD distribution in depth direction. The BMD generation is dependent not only on oxygen concentration but also on oxygen precipitation nucleus, that is induced by thermal history during crystal growth and pre-heating. It must be necessary to design the thermal history through the process from crystal growth to heat treatment in ULSI manufacturing, especially temperature range from 550 to 800°C, which is effective to the nucleus formation.

(2) *OSF (Oxidation induced stacking fault)* The representative defect induced by oxidation is OSF (Oxidation induced stacking fault). The OSF, which is extrinsic type defect, is formed by excess interstitial silicones supplied by the oxidation. The OSF is generally generated at the site of surface damage induced by wafer manufacturing process, device manufacturing process such as ion implantation, RIE (Reactiveion etching) etc., surface contamination and so on. In addition, the OSF is generated at the position of BMD which appears on the surface. That is, the OSF generation is closely related with both the surface in-homogeneity as nucleation site and the concentration of interstitial silicon at the surface region.

The OSF growth and shrinkage depend on the diffusion coefficient and solubility of interstitial silicon and the quantity of interstitial silicon supplied. The observed length of OSF l is empirically denoted as follows[21].

$$l = AP_o m_t n \exp(-Q/kT) \tag{9.4}$$

where T; oxidation temperature, t; Oxidation time
P_o; Oxygen partial pressure, Q; activation energy 2.3eV,
k; Boltzmann constant A; Constant

It was reported that m in the formula (9.4) is a number between 0.28 and 0.5 increasing with the temperature increase and n is around 0.5 to 0.9 decreasing with temperature[21]. There is a critical temperature over which the OSF is not observed as shown in Figure 9.8[22]. At a temperature higher than the critical temperature, the interstitial silicon generated by oxidation is quickly spread out in the bulk, then the OSF is not formed.

Recently as the crystal diameter becomes large, the OSF is often generated a circular position in high density. The dense OSF's are called ring OSF. The ring OSF is correlated with the distribution of point defects introduced during crystal growth process[23]. The ring position shifts to outer position with increase of the growth rate. The suppression of ring OSF is generally performed by increasing the growth rate and driving the ring position out of the crystal.

9.3.3 Defect Control Technology; Gettering

In order to keep the device active region clean enough, a technology, which restricts the defect generation far from the device active region, has been developed. This technology is called gettering. The gettering technology is categorized in EG (extrinsic gettering) and IG (intrinsic gettering).

(1) *EG; Extrinsic gettering* The EG is the method applying various damages intentionally introduced by processing or stress induced by thin film covered on the wafer back surface. Detrimental impurities are captured at the defects or in the film. Table 9.4 indicates the EG technologies proposed until now. From the region forming the gettering centers, the EG is classified in two categories as BSG (Back

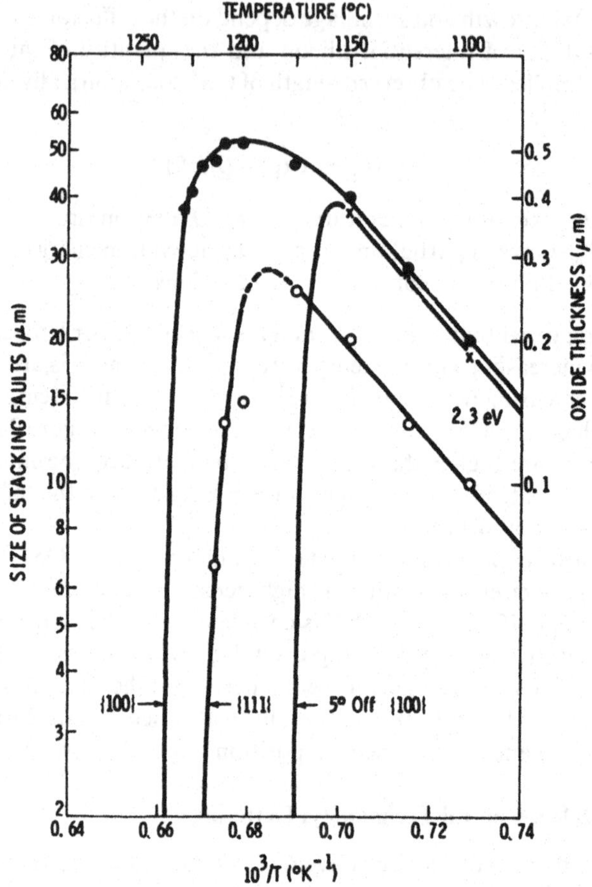

Figure 9.8 Oxidation temperature dependence of OSF size[22].

side gettering) and FSG (Front side gettering). The EG is applied in two stages in the device manufacture industry. One is method called POGO (Pre-oxidation gettering of the other side), that is applied in the initial wafer, and the other is IPG (In process gettering) applied in the device manufacturing process. The representative POGO and IPG technologies used in the industry are sand blast or poly silicon

Table 9.4. Extrinsic gettering method.

Method	Gettering source	Effects	Operation	Ref.
Abrasion	Mechanical damage SF on back surface	OSF suppression I-V characteristics	POGO	a)
Sand blast	Mechanical damage SF on back surface	OSF suppression I-V characteristics	POGO IPG	b)
ISS (Impact sound stressing)	Mechanical damage SF on back surface	OSF suppression Lifetime	POGO	c)
Lapping	Mechanical damage SF on back surface	OSF suppression Lifetime	POGO	d)
Laser irradiation on back surface	Dislocation loop	OSF suppression I-V characteristics	POGO IPG	e)
Ion Implantation on back surface	Small dislocation loop Amorphous layer	OSF suppression I-V characteristics	POGO IPG	f)
Poly Si deposition	Interface stress Grain boundary	OSF suppression Heavy metal	POGO	g)
Si3N4 deposition	Film stress	OSF suppression I-V characteristics	POGO IPG	h)
Excess diffusion	Dislocation network Chemical binding	OSF suppression Heavy metal	IPG	i)

POGO: Pre-Oxidation Gettering of the Other side, IPG: In Process Gettering
a) D. Pomerantz : *J. Appl. Phys.*, **38** (1976) 5020
b) Asai and Ushio: Ohyobutsuri, **48** (1979) 140 (in Japanese)
c) G. H. Schwuttke: IBM TR-22 (1976) 1997
d) E. J. Mets : J. Electrochem. Soc., 112 (1965) 420
e) Y. Hayahuji, T. Yanada and Y. Aoki: *J. Electrochem. Soc.*, 128 (1981) 1975
f) H. J. Geipel and W. K. Tice: *IBM J. Res. Develop.*, **24** (1980) 310
g) R. A. Craven and G. K. Fraundorf: *Ext. Abst. 164th ECS Meeting.* (1983) #303
h) P. M. Petroff, G. A. Rozgonyi and T. T. Sheng: *J. Electrochem. Soc.*, **123** (1976) 565
i) G. A. Rozgonyi, P. M. Petroff and M. H. Read : *J. Electrochem. Soc.*, **122** (1975) 1725

deposition on the back surface and phosphorous diffusion from the back surface, respectively.

(2) *IG; Intrinsic gettering* The IG method uses the BMD's induced during heat treatments as gettering centers. The IG ability, that is correlated with to the BMD density, is strongly dependent on the oxygen concentration in the wafer and the heat sequence in the device manufacturing process. The IG technologies proposed is summarized in Figure 9.9[24]. Two step heat treatments as shown in Figure 9.9 (c), which are high temperature and low temperature heat treatments, are

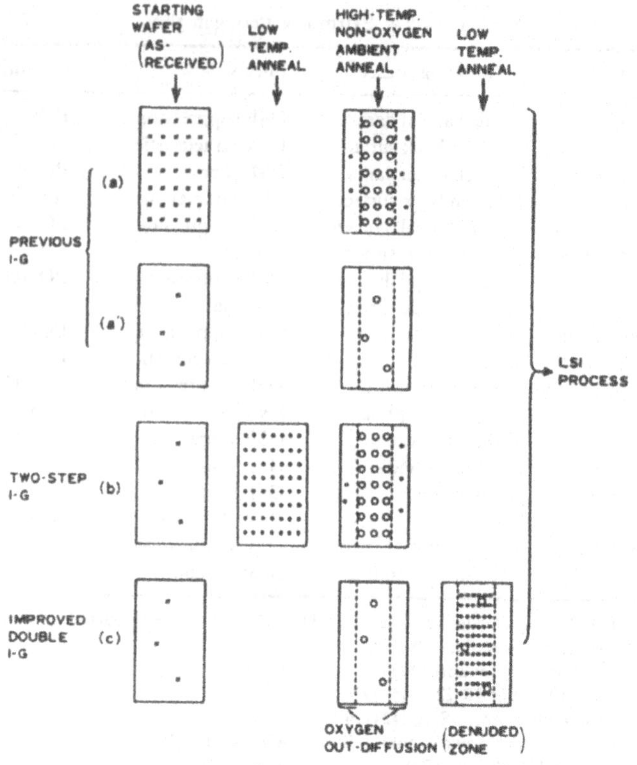

Figure 9.9 Thermal process of IG method[24].

commonly used in the industry. The interstitial oxygen is out-diffused from the near surface region in the first high temperature heat treatment over 1100C. In the following heat treatment at low temperature between 600 and 800°C, the nuclei for oxygen precipitation are formed. And during the heat treatments in the device manufacturing process, the BMD as gettering center is induced in interior of the wafer and the device active region near the surface becomes defect free. The defect free region is called denuded zone.

The gettering is powerful technology for contamination control. If the contamination is perfectly suppressed in the process, the gettering could not be necessary or may affect the worse influences on the device performance because of the defect introduction intentionally. However, the present process has some contamination, then the gettering is the important technology in the device manufacturing process.

9.3.4 Improvement of thin gate oxide integrity

As gate oxide of MOS device is formed by oxidation of the silicon wafer surface, the gate oxide integrity (GOI) is strongly dependent on the wafer surface quality as well as cleanness of oxidation process[25]. Typical retention field distribution of thin gate oxide is shown in Figure 9.10. The distribution is classified in three mode, A, B and C. The A mode, which has a retention field lower than 1MV/cm, indicates the initial short. Main origin of A mode is a particle adhered on the wafer during oxidation. The C mode has higher retention field than 8 MV/cm and comes to a judgment current without dielectric breakdown in the measurement.

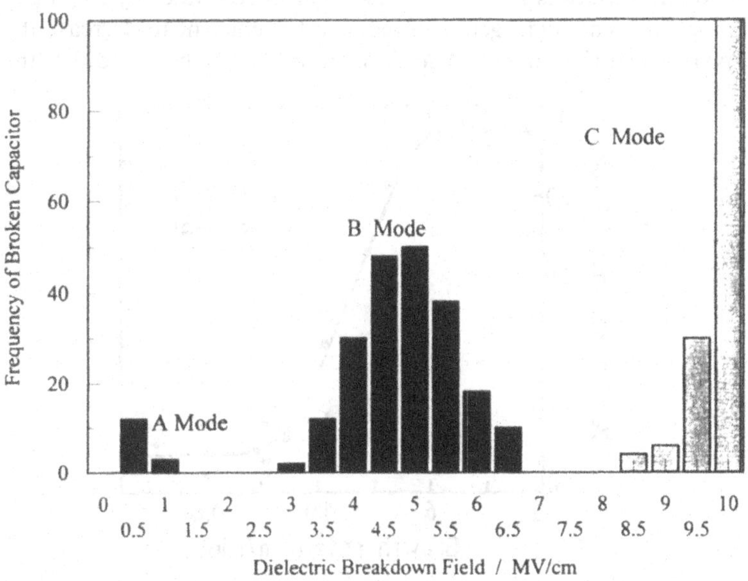

Figure 9.10 Dielectric breakdown field distribution of the capasitor with thin oxide.

The B mode, which has the retention field between 1 MV/cm and 8 MV/cm, corresponds to a weak spot. The B mode distribution is dependent on the crystalline wafer surface quality. Figure 9.11[26] shows the C mode ratio, that is nearly equal to 1-B mode ratio, as a function of crystal growth rate. It is clear that the C mode ratio increases as the growth rate decreases. The origin of B mode is considered to be the BMD emerged on the surface[27] or the COP (Crystal Originated Particle). The COP density shows almost one to one correspondence to the oxide defect density calculated from the B mode distribution as shown in Figure 9.12[14].

In order to improve the GOI, both the COP and the BMD near the surface must be decreased. It has been founded that the wafer annealed in hydrogen ambient at a high temperature decreases the defect near the surface and improves the GOI[28]. The wafer annealed in hydrogen ambient is called HAI wafer (hydrogen annealed IG wafer). Figure 9.13 shows the GOI mode distribution in the wafer before and after hydrogen annealing[29]. This is because the oxygen near the surface is perfectly diffused out of the wafer by hydrogen annealing. The hydrogen as a reductant is efficient to decrease the oxygen near the surface. In addition, it has been recognized that the

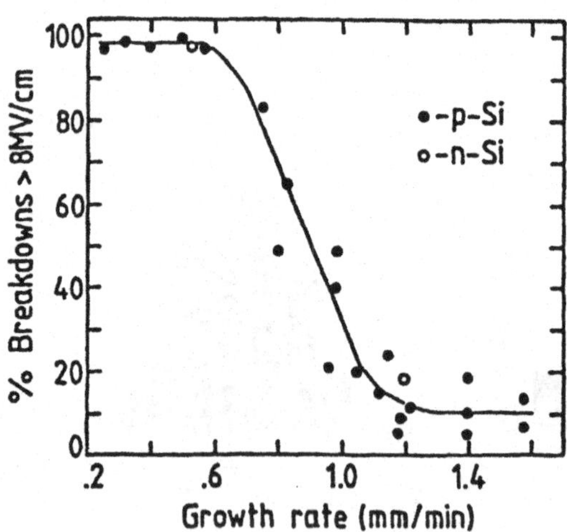

Figure 9.11 Ratio of gate oxide breakdown failure as a function of crystal growth rate[26].

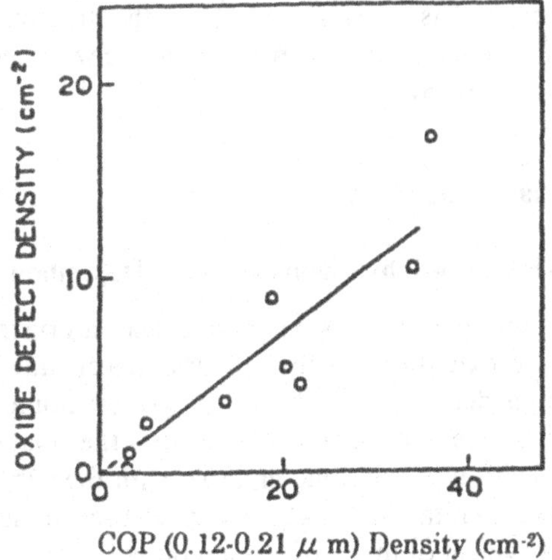

Figure 9.12 Correlation of COP density and oxide defect density[14].

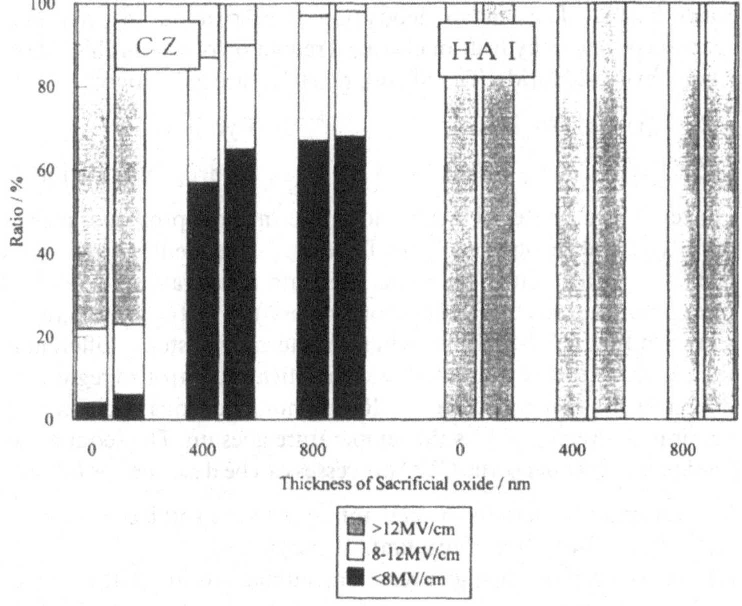

Figure 9.13 GOI distribution of CZ wafer and HAI wafer. GOI distribution are shown as a function of sacrificial oxide thickness.

hydrogen anneal has powerful effect on the suppression of OSF generation[29]. The HAI wafer is being watched with keen interest as a high quality substrate.

9.4. Epitaxial Wafer

9.4.1 Epitaxial Growth by Chemical Vapor Deposition

Epitaxial growth is a process which produces a crystal-graphically oriented film as extension of substrate oriented crystal. The epitaxial growth is considered in two basic categories: homo-epitaxy and hetero-epitaxy. The homo-epitaxial growth is the crystal-graphically oriented deposition of the same material with the substrate, that is, A on A. Silicon epitaxial growth, which is used in semiconductor industry, is a typical example of homo-epitaxy.

Silicon epitaxial film is usually grown by chemical vapor deposition (CVD) method. The source gas, that is silane or chlorosilane, is flowed with hydrogen carrier gas on the mono-crystalline silicon wafer heated. The silicon deposition is carried out by pyrolysis reaction of silicon hydride or chemical reduction of silicon chloride or silicon hydro-chloride. The overall reactions are as follows.

$$SiH_4(v) \rightarrow Si(s) + 2H_2(v) \quad ; \text{Pyrolysis}$$

$$SiCl_4(v) + 2H_2(v) \rightarrow Si(s) + 4HCl(v) \quad ; \text{Hydrogen reduction}$$

However, as a matter of fact, various intermediate products, such as $SiCl_2$ etc., are recognized. Growth rate is dependent on the many factors such as source gas, flux, substrate temperature, crystalline orientation and so on. The effect of temperature on the growth rate is shown in Figure 9.14. The growth rate determining step is different in three temperature regions, that is, kinematically controlled region (A), mass transfer controlled region (B) and homogeneous nucleation in vapor phase region (C), as the temperature goes up. The sequence of fundamental events in the CVD processes can be described as follows.

(1) diffusion of reactants in stagnant layer to the surface;
(2) surface adsorption of reactants at the surface;
(3) events, such as chemical reaction, surface motion, lattice incorporation, etc.;

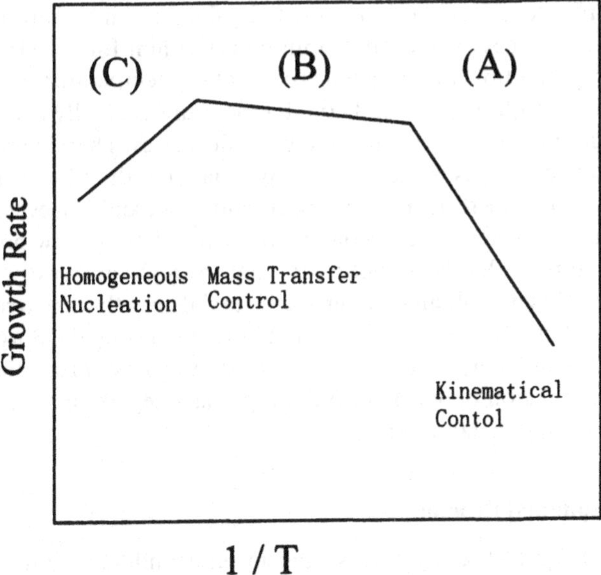

Figure 9.14 Temperature dependennce of epitaxial grown mechanism.

(4) desorption of products from the surface;
(5) diffusion of products away from the surface.

The slowest event is the rate-determining step. In the kinematically controlled region (A) at low temperature, the growth rate R is strongly dependent on temperature T according to following Arrhenius's equation;

$$R = A\exp(-E_a/kT) \tag{9.5}$$

where E_a : Activation energy, A : constant, k : Bortzmann' s constant.

In the mass transfer controlled region (B), the growth rate is controlled by the reactant diffusion through the stagnant layer to the substrate. That is, the growth rate is not particularly dependent on the temperature but on the concentration of source gas flow. Thus the epitaxial growth is conventionally carried out in this region, because the growth rate control is fairly easy.

In order to control both the resistivity fluctuation by auto-doping and the thickness variation of thin epitaxial film for ULSI in sub-micron generation, the epitaxial growth at low temperature (<900C) is strongly required. The epitaxial temperature generally goes down as the number of chlorine in source gas decreases. Then the SiH_4 or Si_2H_4 as source gas is used for the epitaxial growth at low temperature. It is possible to achieve the high quality epitaxial film even at low temperature, when the epitaxial growth carried out in low pressure. For example, it has been reported[30] that the high quality crystalline epitaxial film was obtained when the epitaxial growth was carried out at 826°C in pressure as low as 25torr by using dichlorosilane (SiH_2Cl_2) as source gas. In addition, it was recognized that the transition region of boron auto-doping is as steep as about 40nm in a p on p+ epitaxial wafer.

9.4.2 Epitaxial Reactor

Most of the epitaxial reactors used in semiconductor industry are vertical type and barrel type, which are schematically shown in Figure 9.15 and Figure 9.16, respectively. The vertical type reactor has a carbon susceptor coated with SiC and RF induction coil under the susceptor. The substrate wafer is heated through the susceptor heated by the RF induction coil. The epitaxial growth is carried out by rotating the susceptor and by introducing the source gas from the upper part. The epitaxial film is obtained in very uniform thickness. However, the crystalline defect such as slip tends to be easily induced, because the wafer is warped heating from back surface. This tendency is more remarkable as the wafer diameter becomes larger.

In the barrel type reactor, the substrate wafer is supported by leaning on the susceptor with polyhedron structure and heated from the front surface by heating lamps. Then, the slip is hard to be induced even in the wafer with large diameter. The most of epitaxial wafers for MOS devices are produced by using the barrel type reactors. However, throughput becomes the worse as the wafer diameter the larger, then the cost-up of the epitaxial wafer is unavoidable. This is fatal for the epitaxial wafer use in semiconductor industry.

For the technology keeping the high throughput for the wafer with large diameter, a single wafer processing epitaxial reactor has been

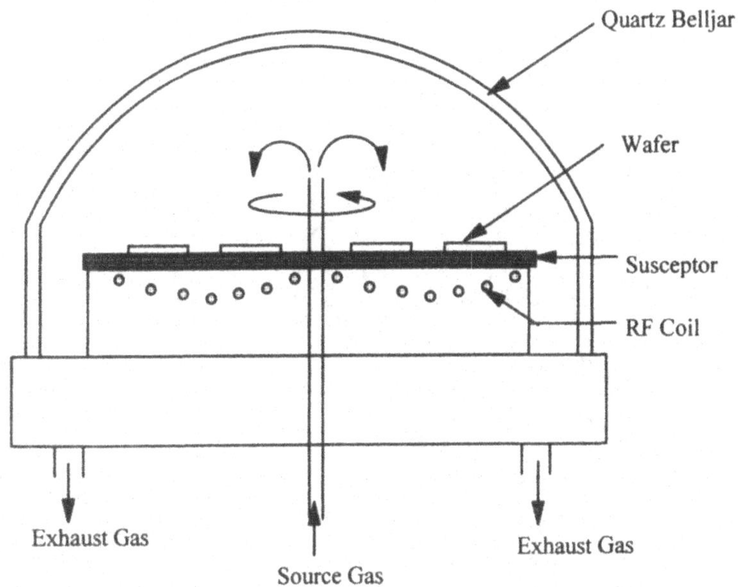

Figure 9.15 Shematic drawing of vertical type reactor.

developed[31]. Figure 9.17 shows the schematic drawing of single wafer epitaxial reactor. The rotated substrate wafer is heated from both surfaces by heating lamps. The source gas is flowed along the front surface, then the uniform epitaxial layer is obtained. Besides, the single wafer processing epitaxial reactor, in which the substrate wafer is rotated at a great rate, has been developed[32]. It is reported that the growth rate notably goes up and the thickness uniformity improves, when the substrate is rotated over 1000 rpm. This is because the laminar flow of source gas is efficiently formed on the substrate when the rotation rate is high enough.

9.4.3 Selective Epitaxial Growth

When the silicon substrate surface is partly covered by SiO_2 layer, it is possible to grow the epitaxial film only on the silicon substrate but not on the SiO_2 layer. This is called selective epitaxial growth (SEG).

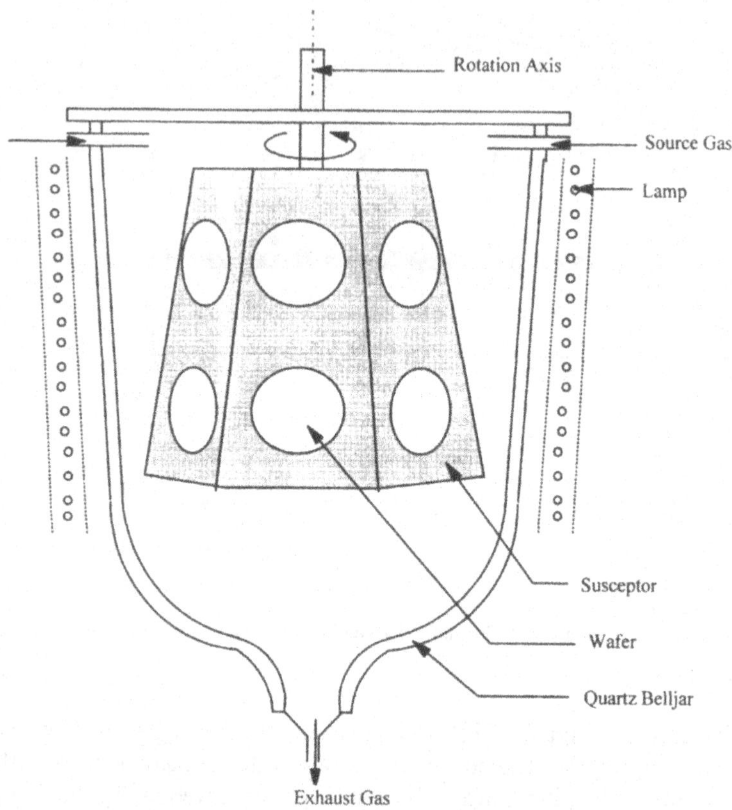

Figure 9.16 Shematic drawing of cylinder type reactor.

The SEG is carried out by flowing the source gas with HCl gas in low pressure on the wafer with partly SiO_2 layer[33]. The nuclei formed on the SiO_2 layer are perfectly removed by etching effect of HCl gas and the monocrystalline silicon film is consequently formed only on the bare silicon substrate. When the HCl flow rate increases, good selectivity can be obtained but the growth rate goes down. On the contrary, if the HCl flow rate decreases, the growth rate increases but the selectivity is degraded. Therefore, the gas flow ratio of HCl to source gas must be carefully adjusted in order to achieve the high performance SEG. The SEG is expected for application to the

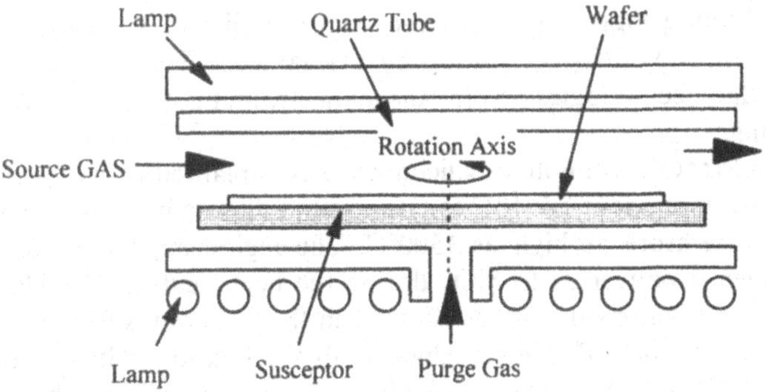

Figure 9.17 Shematic drawing of cylinder type reactor.

sub-micron ULSI, however, there are many problems, such as the defect introduced at the interface between silicon and SiO_2, the facet growth of epitaxial layer and so on. These problems must be overcome for the SEG use in the ULSI fabrication process.

9.5. SOI Technology

9.5.1 SIMOX Technology

Since the silicon thin film formed on insulator film, that is called SOI (silicon on insulator), is electrically separated with the substrate, the SOI has following various merits for the devices.

(1) High endurance against high voltage.
(2) Low parasitic capacitance.
(3) High endurance to cosmic ray. Soft error free.
(4) Substrate bias effect free.

Then, the SOI wafer is applied for a high voltage device and a radiant ray resist device. That is expected for the application of next generation devices which are high speed and/or low power.

Regarding manufacturing of SOI film, a re-crystallization depending on a beam anneal using laser or electron beam and horizontal epitaxial technology were firstly investigated. However it was difficult to obtain a high quality mono-crystal thin film in a wide area. At present, SIMOX (Separation by IMplanted OXygen) and wafer bonding technologies become the main stream in SOI film manufacturing.

In SIMOX technology, silicon wafer is implanted by oxygen ions with a dose about 1×10^{18} ions/cm^2 and followed heat treatment at a temperature as high as 1300°C. The region supersaturated by oxygen is converted to SiO_2 during the heat treatment[32]. Thin Si layer remains on the buried SiO_2, then the SOI film is formed. And a thickness of SOI film gets thick as an acceleration voltage is high. Since the buried oxide is formed by the implanted oxygen, the oxide uniformity depends on control of ion implantation. The oxide thickness is restricted less than several % in the plane distribution. However, in order to form SOI layer by re-growth of a layer damaged by ion implantation, defects can easily survive in SOI layer. In addition, there is the case that a crystal Si is left inside the buried oxide layer. The perfection of SOI layer is the most important problem in SIMOX technology.

Recently, a method to perform oxidation after forming the SOI film by SIMOX was developed to obtain the thick uniform buried oxide, and the SOI quality is improved.

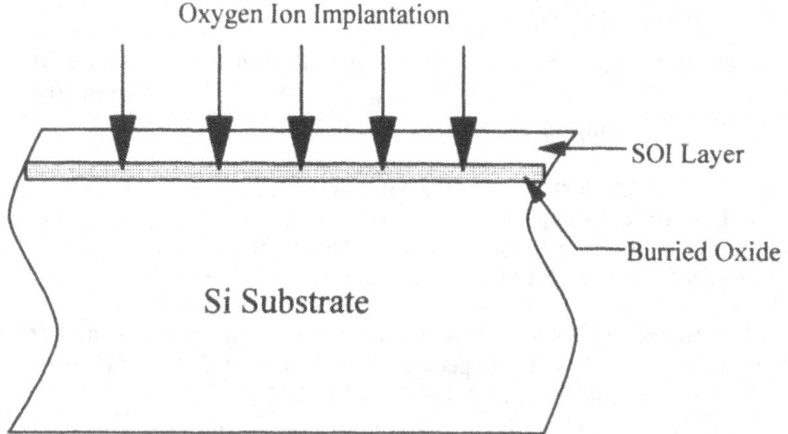

Figure 9.18 SOI layer formation by SIMOX method.

9.5.2 Wafer Bonding

Wafer bonding is the method that two wafers, covered by oxide film, are adhered closely each other and applied the heat treatment at a temperature higher than 800°C[33]. The SOI layer is manufactured by lapping and chemi-mechanical polishing the one side of the bonded wafer. It is practically possible to control the SOI film as thick as about 1 micron by polishing method. However, it is difficult to produce the thinner SOI film by polishing, that is required for the highly integrated devices. Thin film processing technology, applying the plasma etching, has been recently developed and it is possible to obtain the uniform SOI layer with 0.1 micron thickness. The uniformity of the SOI layer is quite high and thickness fluctuation is restricted lower than 10% (Fig. 9.19). The crystal quality of SOI layer produced by wafer bonding method is considered to be same as that of bulk Si and defect free. Then the bonded SOI wafer is expected for the application to the next generation devices.

9.6. Hereafter Subject of Crystal Technology

9.6.1 Micro Defect

Silicon crystal technology at semi conductor industry is advanced the development considering it as a purpose to make "what is the most

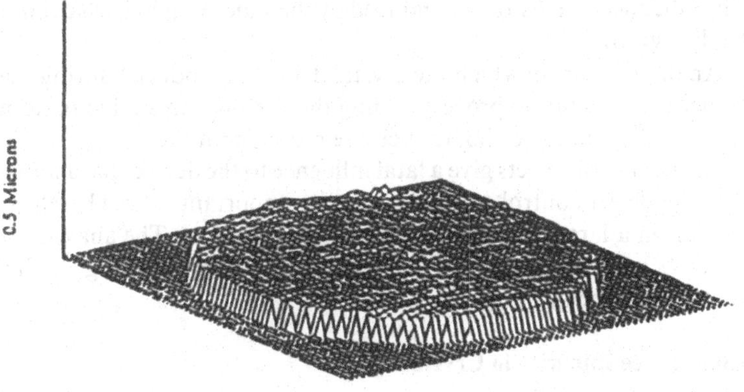

Figure 9.19 Thickness uniformity of SOI layer produced by wafer bonding method[36].

suitable crystal for a device" clear. This purpose should not change for the crystal development in future. Especially, the micro defect control, considering oxygen behavior, is taken as the important task. An unsettlement problem remains much in respect of origin of micro defect generation, though the majority got clear.

Electrical charge quantity to manage in the device decreases as the device scaling low getting minute. Then, the ultra micro defect, that has not influence on the conventional device, cannot be disregarded. In order to control the ultra micro defect, it is indispensable to develop the control technology of nucleus such as vacancy clusters and other trace impurities. In addition, as a micro-roughness has an influence on the device characteristics, the micro-roughness control has become an important subject for the device. The controls of surface micro defect and surface uniformity is a significant task more and more in the as-grown and heat treated wafer, even to control the micro-roughness.

9.6.2 Crystal Stress

A tendency to large diameter silicon wafer is still strong in the semiconductor industry. This is because keeping the high productivity in the high integration device whose chip size becomes lager. Taking account of DRAM, the wafers with 200 mm and 300 mm in diameter are required for 16 M to 64 M and 256 M to 1G, respectively. The influence of a distortion induced by the wafer weight itself cannot be disregarded.

An oppotunity, in which the crystal defects are induced during the device manufacturing process adding the thermal stress, fine pattern stress and so on, is getting to increase more and more.

As the crystal defects give a fatal influence to the device characteristics, the defect control technology is the important task. Therefore, a stress in a large diameter wafer must be analyzed. The analysis of stress behavior during heat treatment and manufacturing of fine pattern is especially important task.

9.6.3 Trace Impurity in Crystal

Concerning to impurity in the silicon crystal, a behavior of light elements especially oxygen has been investigated. Other impurities, such as metals, have not been studied enough because those impurities are very small amount and there is no suitable analysis method. The metallic impurities, which have sever influence on the device performance even in trace, must be studied in detail hereafter. Especially, new analysis method for trace impurities should be developed.

References

1. Dash, W. C. (1958). *J. Appl. Phys.*, 29, 736.
2. Czochralski, J. (1977). *Z. Phys. Chemie* 92, 219.
3. Kim, K. M. and Smetana, P. (1990). *J. Cryst. Growrh* 100, 527.
4. Pfann, W. G. (1952). *Trans. AIME* 194, 747.
5. Burton, J. A., Prim, R. C. and Slichter, W. P. (1953). *J. Chem. Phys.*, 21, 187.
6. Hoshi, K., Suzuki, T., Okubo, Y. and Isawa, N. *Semiconductor Silicon* 1981 C. S. Pennington, 1891) p. 811.
7. Hirata, H. and Hoshikawa, K. (1989). *J. Cryst. Growth*, 96, 747 Kobayashi, S., Fujiwara, H., Fujiwara, T., Kubo, T., Inami, S., Okui, M., Miyahara, S., Akashi, Y., Kuramochi, K., Tsujimoto, Y. and Okamoto, S., Semiconductor Silicon 1994, (E.C.S., Pennington, 1994) p.58.
8. Abe, T., Sumizo, T. and Murayama, S. (1986). *Jpn. J. Appl. Phys.*, 5, 458.
9. de Kock, A. J. R. and Boonen, P. G. T. (1973). 44, 2816.
10. Foll, H., Gosele, U. and Kolbesen, B. O. (1977), *J. Cryst. Growth* 40, 90.
11. Bradshow, S. E. and Goorissen, J. (1980). *J. Cryst. Growth*, 48, 514.
12. Yamagishi, H., Fusegawa, I., Fujimaki, N. and Katayama, M. *Sym. Advanced Science and Tehnology of Silicon Materials* (JSPS, Kona, Hawaii, 1991) p. 83.
13. Ryuta, J., Morita, E., Tanaka, T. and Shimanuki, Y. (1990). *Jpn. J. Appl. Phys.*, 29, L1947.
14. Miyashita, M., Fukui, H., Kubota, A., Samata, S., Hiratsuka, H. and Matsushita, Y. *Ext. Abst. Sol. Stat. Dev. and Mat.* (*Jpn. Soc. Appl. Phys.*, Yokohama, 1991) p. 568.
15. Hourai, M., Sano, M., Sumita, S., Miki, S. and Shigematsu, T. (1992). *Proceedings of 20th Symp. on ultra clean tecnology* (UCS, Tokyo, 1993) p. 176.
16. Takiguchi, R., Monma, Y., Hirohuji, Y. *Ultra Clean Technology*, 4, 251.
17. Suezawa, M. and Sumino, K. (1984). *Phys. Stat. Solid*, (a) 83, 235.
18. Kanamaori, A. and Kanamori, M. (1979). *J. Appl. Phys.*, 50, 8095.
19. Matsushita, Y., Kishino, S. and Kanamori, M. (1980). *Jpn. J. Appl. Phys.*, 19, L101.
20. Aoki, S. (1993). *Mat. Transaction, JIM*, 34, 746.

21. Murarka, S. (1977). *J. Appl. Phys.*, 48, 5020.
22. Hu, S. M. (1975). *Appl. Phys. Lett.*, 27, 165.
23. Habu, R., Tomiura, A. and Harada, H. (1994). *Semiconductor Silicon* (The Electrochem. Soc., Pennington, 1994) p. 635.
24. Nagasawa, K., Matsushita, Y. and Kishino, S. (1980). *Appl. Phys. Lett.*, 37, 622.
25. Yamabe, K., Taniguchi, K. and Matsushita, Y. *Pro. Symp. Defect in Silicon* (E.C.S., Pennington, 1983) p.629.
26. Tachimori, O., Sakon, T. and Kaneko, T. *7th Kesshou Kougaku Symp., JSAP* (Jpn. Soc. Appl. Phys., 1990) p. 27 (in Japanese).
27. Hisatomi, K., Matsushita, Y., Watanabe, M., Kashima, H. and Kashiwagi, A. (1991). *Abst. 38th Spring Meet. Jpn. Soc. Appl. Phys. and Related Soc.*, 30p-ZL-9/I (in Japanese).
28. Matsushita, Y., Wakatsuki, M. and Saito, Y. *Ext. Abst. 18th Int. Conf. Sol. Stat. Dev. and Mat.* (Jpn. Soc. Appl. Phys., Tokyo, 1986) p. 529.
29. Samata, S., Numano, M., Amai, T., Matsushita, Y., Kobayashi, H., Yamamoto, Y., Kawaguchi, Nadahara S. and Yamabe, K. *Pro. Symp. Degradation of Elect.* Devices due to Device Operation as well as Crystalline and Process-induced Defects (EC.S., Pennington, 1994) p. 101.
30. Borland, J. O., Schmidt, D. N. and Stivers, A. R. *Ext. Abst. 18th Int. Conf. Sol. Stat. Dev. and Mat.* (Jpn. Soc. Appl. Phys.,Tokyo, 1986) p. 53.
31. Robins, M. and Lawrence, H. (1988). *5th Int. Symp. Semicon. Processing*, p. 1.
32. Sato, Y., Ohmine, T. and Saito, Y. *Pro. 12th Int. Symp. Chemical Vapor Deposition* (E.C.S., Pennington, 1993) p. 141.
33. Tanno, K., Endo, N., Kitajima, H. and Tsuya, H. (1982). *Jpn. J. Appl. Phys.*, 21, L564.
34. Izumi, K. *et al.* (1980). *Jpn. J. Appl. Phys.*, 19, Supplement 19-1, p. 151.
35. Lasky, J. B. (1986). *Appl. Phys. Lett.*, 48, 78.
36. Mumola, P. B. *SEMI-JEIDA Joint Tech. Symp.* July (1993).

CHAPTER 10

Process and Device Simulation

10.1. Introduction

TCAD (Technology CAD) tools such as process/device simulators are expected to accelerate device development by starting from pre-optimized transistor structures and process flows. These tools are now widely used in most semiconductor companies, and without them, it is almost impossible to design semiconductor devices' fabrication conditions, for example, ion-implantation doses for threshold control, thermal budget to realize shallow junctions and so on.

To scale down device feature size, complex device structures such as trench memory cells are introduced using new process technologies. From the physical-model point of view, device size miniaturization requires simulation programs to solve more complicated and memory intensive equations with a lot of unknown variables such as hydrodynamic carrier transport equations and non-equilibrium point defect models of dopants. Moreover, at least two-dimensional (hopefully three-dimensional) process, topography, device simulations are expected to be run on a mid-range workstations. To realize this, efficient data structures, robust and stable numerical methods for solving non-linear systems and fast linear equation solvers are indispensable. From the user's point of view, integration of individually developed tools with sophisticated graphical user interfaces is important.

As a result of continuing efforts to verify the validity of TCAD software through intensive physical model developments and their model parameter calibrations the predictability of process/device simulators is being confirmed. Recently, new approaches have been tried in order to solve so called "reverse problems" such as identifying two-dimensional dopant profiles in small size MOSFETs by using TCAD tools, and analyzing limitation of MOSFET miniaturization by fluctuating device structures.

In this chapter, topics of process and device modeling and simulation field, reported mainly by Japanese company and organization, are reviewed.

10.2. Process Simulation

Process simulation programs are designed to reproduce semiconductor device structures including dopant distributions by solving numerical models corresponding to each fabrication step such as ion-implantations, oxidation, diffusion, etching and deposition. Its primary function has been considered to simulate dopant profile to predict electrical characteristics. However, with the increasing complexity of device structures, need for predictions concerning device topology and for simulation of thermal stress during thermal processes are increasing. In this section, after a brief introduction of the diffusion model, some process simulation programs are reviewed.

10.2.1. Dopant Diffusion in Silicon

In 1974, Yoshida *et al.*, proposed that phosphorous diffuses through the combination with vacancy pair and explained kink profile in high dose region[1]. In accordance with their proposal, point defects have been considered to cause various anormalous diffusion phenomena. From the modeling point of view, significant progress is achieved through the understanding of many kinds of anormalous diffusion such as oxidation enhanced diffusion[2,3], oxidation retarded diffusion[4], and anormalous pile-up of arsenic under nitrogen ambient[5,6], by introducing the reaction between point defects (i.e., interstitial silicon and vacancy) and dopant atoms. Currently, diffusion of dopant atoms like boron, phosphorous, and arsenic is considered to occur through interaction with point defects[7]. Here, we call this model as pair-diffusion model. Baccus *et al.* succeeded in reproducing dopant profiles previously reported, by using non-equilibrium pair-diffusion model with unified parameter sets[8]. Figure 10.1 shows the comparison of measurement and simulation of boron($10^{21}/cm^3$) and arsen ($10^{19}/cm^3$), where "standard model" without point defect fails to reproduce both tail profiles. In the following, the model used by Baccus *et al.*, will be explained.

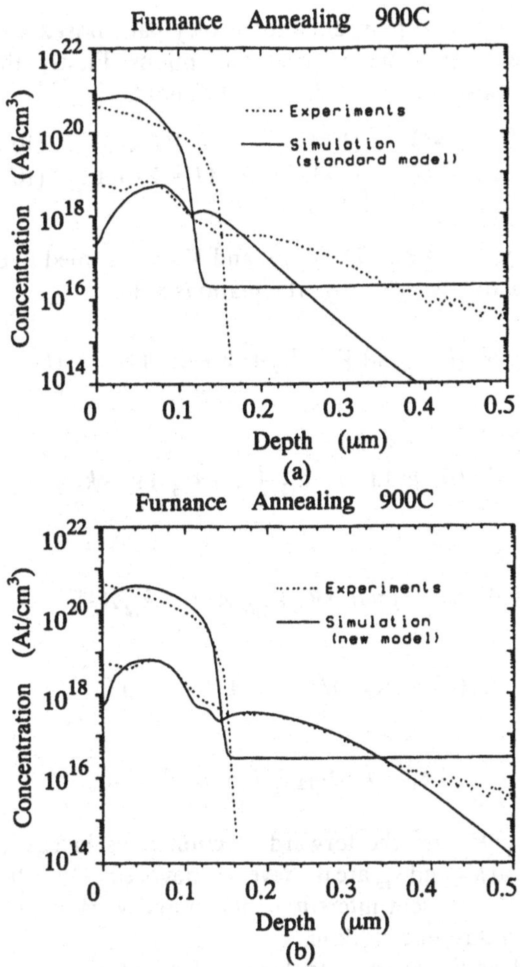

Figure 10.1 Simulated arsenic and boron profiles in the case of 900°C furnace annealing and comparison with experimental results (SIMS); (a): standard model, (b) pair diffusion model[8].

Hereafter, for simplicity, A, X, I, V represent (concentration of) dopant atom at substitutional site, point defect, interstitial silicon, vacancy, respectively, AX, AI, AV represent dopant point defect pair, dopant-interstitial pair, dopant-vacancy pair. Based on Hu's diffusion model[9], they made three assumptions. Firstly, the following reactions exist between A, I, V, AI, AV, holds:

$$I + V \leftrightarrow O \quad (10.1.1) \qquad A + V \leftrightarrow AV \quad (10.1.2)$$
$$A + I \leftrightarrow AI \quad (10.1.3) \qquad AI + V \leftrightarrow A \quad (10.1.4)$$
$$AV + I \leftrightarrow A \quad (10.1.5)$$

Secondary, not A but AI, AV, I, and V are assumed to diffuse. This means the following transport equations hold,

$$\frac{\partial V}{\partial t} = -\operatorname{div}(D_V \cdot \operatorname{grad} V) - k_{f2} A \cdot V + k_{r2} AV - k_1 (I \cdot V - I^* \cdot V^*) \tag{10.1.6}$$

$$\frac{\partial I}{\partial t} = -\operatorname{div}(D_I \cdot \operatorname{grad} I) - k_{f3} A \cdot I + k_{r3} AV - k_1 (I \cdot V - I^* \cdot V^*) \tag{10.1.7}$$

$$\frac{\partial AV}{\partial t} = -\operatorname{div}(D_{AV} \cdot \operatorname{grad} AV) + k_{f2} A \cdot V - k_{r2} AV \tag{10.1.8}$$

$$\frac{\partial AI}{\partial t} = -\operatorname{div}(D_{AI} \cdot \operatorname{grad} AI) + k_{f3} A \cdot I - k_{r3} AI \tag{10.1.9}$$

$$\frac{\partial A}{\partial t} = k_{r2} AV + k_{r3} AI - (k_{f2} A \cdot V + k_{f3} A \cdot I) \tag{10.1.10}$$

where, k_{f2}, k_{f3} are the forward reaction rates in eqs. (10.1.2) and (10.1.3), and k_{r2} and k_{r3} are the reverse ones of eqs. (10.1.2) and (10.1.3). I^* and V^* represent interstitial silicon and vacancy concentration under equilibrium condition.

Actually, point defects and dopant point defect pairs have charged states, and in the case of donor atom, concentration of AX is the sum of negative charged AX^- and neutral AX^0. Their third assumption is that all charged species, such as negative charged vacancy V^-, are in equilibrium with the neutral species. This allows us to express concentration of charged species by using neutral species by the following equations:

$$V^- = (n/n_i) \cdot V^0 \cdot \exp\{(E_i - E_{V-})/(kT)\} = \delta^- (n/n_i) V^0$$

As a result, in the case of donor atom, the following equation is obtained for vacancy dopant pair.

$$\frac{\partial AV}{\partial t} = \frac{\partial AV^0}{\partial t} + \frac{\partial AV^-}{\partial t} = \left(1 + K\frac{n}{n_i}\right) \cdot \frac{\partial AV^0}{\partial t}$$

$$= \mathrm{div}(D_{AV^0} \cdot \mathrm{grad}\, AV^0 + D_{AV^-} \cdot \mathrm{grad}\, AV^-$$

$$- \frac{q}{kT} D_{AV^-}\, AV^- \,\mathrm{grad}\, \phi) + GR_{AV}$$

$$= \mathrm{div}\left(D_{AV^0}\left(1 + \frac{D_{AV^-}}{D_{AV^0}} K \frac{n}{n_i}\right) \mathrm{grad}\, AV^0\right) + GR_{AV} - \frac{K}{n_i} AV^0 \frac{\partial n}{\partial t} \tag{10.1.11}$$

where, GR_{AV} is generation of AV pairs, grad ϕ is electric field. Similarly, we get the following equation for AI.

$$\frac{\partial AI}{\partial t} = \mathrm{div}\left(D_{AI^0}\left(1 + \frac{D_{AI^-}}{D_{AV^0}} K' \frac{n_i}{n}\right) \mathrm{grad}\, AI^0\right) + GR_{AI} - \frac{K'}{n_i} AI^0 \frac{\partial n}{\partial t} \tag{10.1.12}$$

Note that conventional diffusion equation model proposed by Fair, modulation of diffusivity due to point defects is expressed as follows[10],

$$D_{\mathrm{eff}} = h\left(D_0 + D_- \frac{n}{n_i} + D_+ \frac{n_i}{n}\right), \text{ where } h = 1 + \frac{1}{\sqrt{1 + 4(n_i/n)}}$$

If we consider $\partial A/\partial t = \partial AI/\partial t + \partial AV/\partial t$ and combine (10.1.11) and (10.1.12), similar terms including n/n_i, n_i/n appear. This means that the non-equilibrium pair-diffusion model is a kind of generalization of the conventional diffusion model.

Several pair-diffusion models have been proposed and these models are expected to predict or explain reverse short channel effect of MOSFET threshold voltage(RSCE), which is quite important phenomena to be considered in designing lower sub-micron MOSFET devices, and also deteriorates quantitative predictability of process simulators. By using two-dimensional process/device simulators, Hane *et al.*, have shown that binding energy between boron and interstitial silicon is a key parameter to reproduce measured RSCE of nMOSFET results quantitatively[11]. Figure 10.2 shows the effect of binding energy between boron and interstitial silicon on MOSFET threshold voltage shift.

10.2.2. Oxidation Model

In order to increase packing density, many field isolation structures with smaller bird's beak has been proposed. To optimizate these structures and to reduce leak current, fabrication process should be optimized to reduce stress near SiO_2/Si interface. However, it is very difficult to measure the stress distribution by non-destructive manner. Stress simulation, with calibrated model parameters, is the only tool available to analyze microscopic stress distribution.

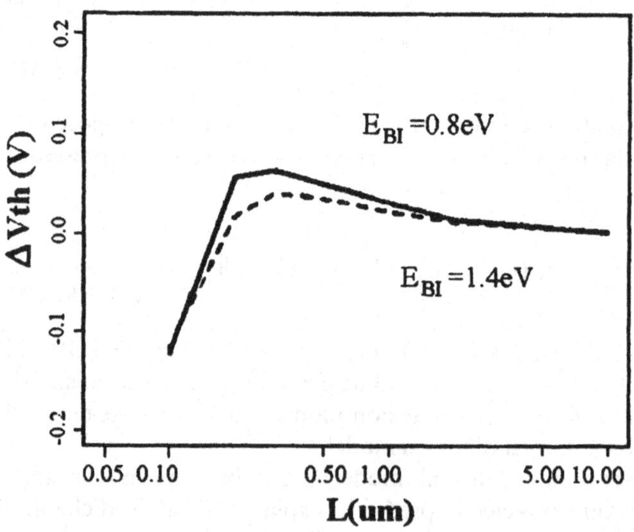

Figure 10.2 Two dimensional calculation results for the reverse short channel effect with different boron silicon-interstitial binding energy EBI[11].

Chin *et al.*, proposed two-dimensional oxidation model to simulate LOCOS structure[12]. They assumed SiO_2 layer to be an incompressive viscous flow, and oxidant diffuses in SiO_2 layer toward SiO_2/Si interface where it is consumed by chemical reaction. Matsumoto *et al.*[13] and Isomae *et al.*[14] proposed visco-elastic oxidation model independently. silicon dioxide is considered to be modeled by using incompressive viscous flow in high temperature and by using visco-elastic material below 950 °C.

In both cases, oxidant concentration is modeled by using Laplace equations,

$$\operatorname{div}(D \cdot \operatorname{grad} C) = 0 \tag{10.1.13}$$

with the following boundary conditions:
Along the Si/SiO_2 interface:

$$-D \operatorname{grad} C = k C \tag{10.1.14}$$

Si/SiN interface and the end of analysis region:

$$n \operatorname{grad} C = 0 \tag{10.1.15}$$

SiO_2/air interface:

$$n D \operatorname{grad} C = h(C^* - C) \tag{10.1.16}$$

where, C is concentration and D is effective diffusivity of oxidant, respectively, k is surface reaction rate, and n is normal vector. Diffusivity and surface reaction rate are modeled as functions of stress and surface orientation, and surface tension at the oxide is introduced to determine P at the free oxide surface.

In the incompressive viscous flow model, creeping flow equations and continuous equations are solved[12] to obtain pressure P and oxidation flow velocity v.

$$\mu \nabla^2 v = \operatorname{grad} P \tag{10.1.17}$$

$$\operatorname{div} v = 0 \tag{10.1.18}$$

And in the case of the visco-elastic model, the following equilibrium equation and stress-strain relation equation are used:

$$\frac{\partial\sigma_{xx}}{\partial x}+\frac{\partial\sigma_{xy}}{\partial y}+\frac{\partial\sigma_{xz}}{\partial z}=0,\quad \frac{\partial\sigma_{yx}}{\partial x}+\frac{\partial\sigma_{yy}}{\partial y}+\frac{\partial\sigma_{yz}}{\partial z}=0,$$

$$\frac{\partial\sigma_{zx}}{\partial x}+\frac{\partial\sigma_{zy}}{\partial y}+\frac{\partial\sigma_{zz}}{\partial z}=0,$$

$$\sigma_{ij}(t)=G_{ijkl}(\tau)\cdot\varepsilon_{kl}(0)+\int_0^t G_{ijkl}(t-\tau)\cdot\frac{\partial\varepsilon_{kl}(\tau)}{\partial t}d\tau \qquad (10.1.19)$$

where, relaxation tensor G_{ijkl} is modeled as

$$G_{ijkl}(t)=\{K(t)-(2/3)\mu(t)\}\,\delta_{ij}\,\delta_{kl}+\mu(t)(\delta_{ik}\,\delta_{jl}+\delta_{il}\,\delta_{jk}) \qquad (10.1.20)$$

where δ_{ij} is Kronecker's delta, $K(t)$ and $\mu(t)$ correspond to bulk modulus and shear modulus for elastic materials. Figure 10.3 shows the thinning of SiO_2 film thickness at convex and concave corner in silicon trench structures by Umimoto *et al.*[15] They showed that the thinning at concave corner and concave are caused by the stress-dependent surface reaction rate and stress-dependent oxidant diffusion, respectively.

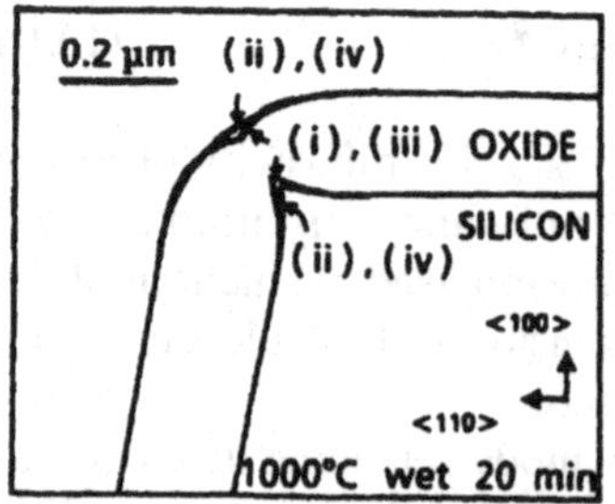

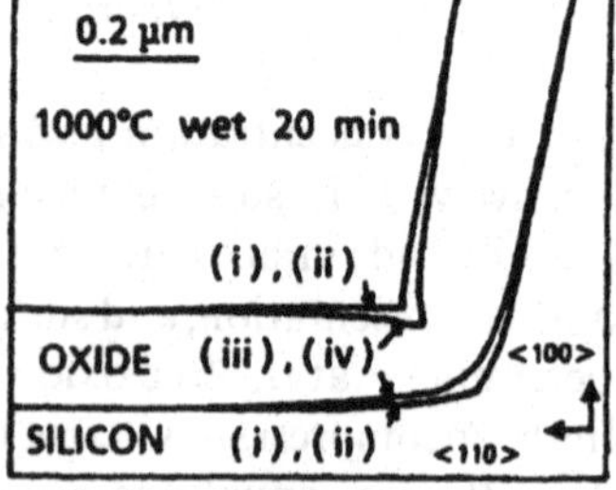

Figure 10.3 Comparison of convex corner oxidation simulation (left) and concave oxidation (right). Simulations are performed by changing surface reaction rate (ks) model, oxidant diffusion coefficient (Dox) model and oxide viscosity (μ ox) model. Case (i) ks depends on stress, (ii) ks and μox depend on stress, (iii) ks and Dox depend on stress, (iv) ks, μ ox and Dox depend on stress[15].

The incompressive viscous flow model was also applied to simulate a shape of BPSG (Boron Phosphorous Silicate Glass) film by Umimoto[16]. Figure 10.4 shows the comparison of BPSG coverage at the step corner.

10.2.3. Topological Simulation

Simulation of cross-sectional device structure is usually modeled by using a string model in which the cross section of each material layer is expressed by polygons. However, to representation and handle three-dimensional (3D) device topology efficiently, many problems must be solved. In SAMPLE-3D[17], a 3D topography simulator developed at U.C.B., triangle patches are used to express material interfaces and surfaces. However, this approach includes very complicated geometrical operation codes. Figure 10.5 shows an typical simulation result of etching and deposition, in which, you can see many triangle elements representing material surfaces.

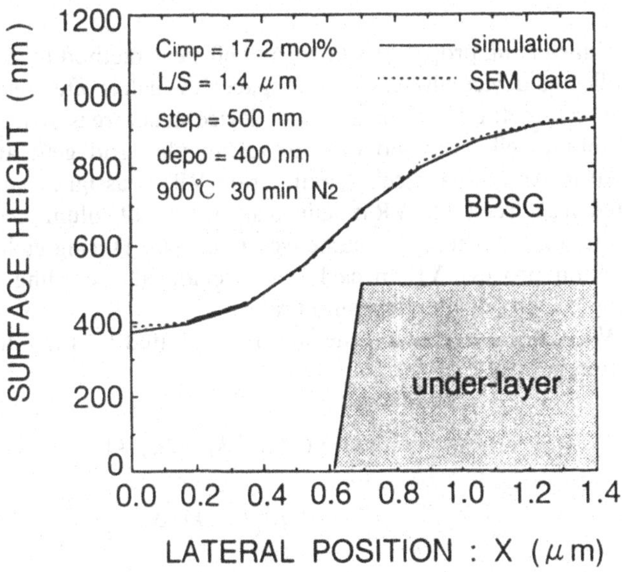

Figure 10.4 Comparison of BPSG surface profile in the line structure[16].

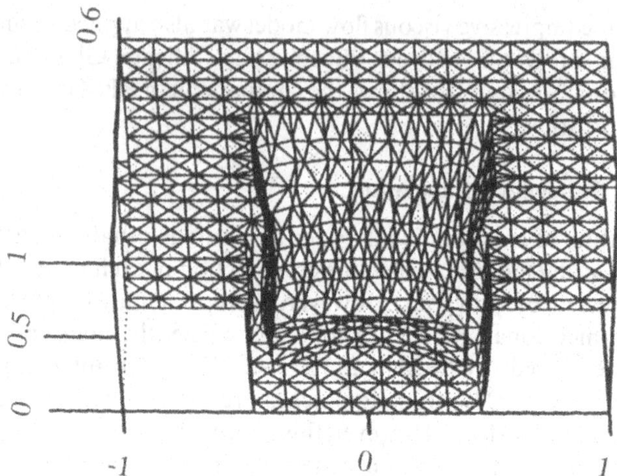

Figure 10.5 Examples of etching by using SAMPLE-3D. Numbers in the figure are coordinate in micron[31]

Fujinaga *et al.* proposed a novel and efficient method to simulate complicated device surfaces in a 3D space[18], which is often refered to as the "cell-method". In this method, device structure is divided into small cubic cells corresponding to rectangular grid generated by simulator. And in each cell, Volume rate (VR) is assigned, and calculated in each cell. The VR is defined as the ratio of volume occupied by some material to cell volume (see Fig. 10.6). During etching or deposition process, VR in each cell is changed according to the etching velocity or film deposition rate.

A VR $C(i, j, k)$ at each time step is calculated by the following equation.

$$C_m^{(n+1)}(i,j,k)\cdot V(i,j,k) = C_m^{(n)}(i,j,k)\cdot V(i,j,k) + R_m^{(n)}(i,j,k)\cdot \Delta t^{(n)} \tag{10.1.21}$$

$$C_t^{(n)}(i,j,k) = \sum_m C^{(n)}(i,j,k)/c_{m0} \tag{10.1.22}$$

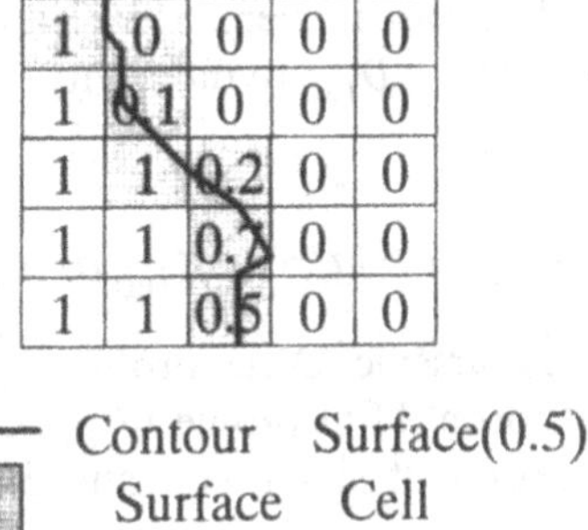

Figure 10.6 Schematic figure of cell, volume rate and interface[18].

where, superscript represents time step, c_m is volume-rate, c_{m0} is density of m-th material, $V(i, j, k)$ is cell volume, $R_m(i, j, k)$ is flux rate of m-th material across the cell surface and $C(i, j, k)$ is material density. At the end of a simulation, VR is averaged on each grid point, and equi-contour surfaces on which VR = 0.5 is generated. The equi-contour surface on which material A's VR = 0.5 is considered to be A's surface. Using this method, they simulated various photoresist patterns after development process and etched silicon surface within a reasonable computation time (several minutes in 15MIPS machine)[19].

10.2.4. Process Simulation in Three-Dimensional Spaces

To meet the needs for analysis of three-dimensional(3D) effects, such as dopant density lowering at convex corner of small diffusion layer and thinning of LOCOS isolation layer at convex field-corner, several 3D process simulators have been developed[16]. From modeling point of view, it is very interesting to simulate the 3-dimensional effect using the most general and complicated physical model, such as non-equilibrium pair-diffusion model. However, the CPU time will be prohibitively long for such a high-end model. And a qualitative analysis of 3D effect sometime provides enough insight, and in this case it is not necessary to use very accurate models.

In SMART-P, developed by Umimoto *et al.*, a simple models for explaining oxidation enhanced diffusion (OED) and transient enhanced diffusion (TED) are implemented. They introduced the additional terms ΔD_{OED} and ΔD_{TED} to diffusivity,

$$D = D_{\mathrm{N}} + \Delta D_{\mathrm{OED}} + \Delta D_{\mathrm{TED}}$$
$$= f_{\mathrm{I}} D_{\mathrm{i}} ((C_{\mathrm{I}} - C_{\mathrm{I}}^{\mathrm{eq}})/C_{\mathrm{I}}^{\mathrm{eq}}) + K_{\mathrm{TED}} D_{\mathrm{i}} \exp(-t/\tau) \qquad (10.1.23)$$

And they obtained arsenic OED profile in the drain region of nMOSFET, and boron TED profile in pMOS drain. Figure 10.7 shows the comparison of simulation and SIMS measurement of boron profile.

From the software point of view, in order to realize 3D process simulators with advanced physical models designed to simulate submicron devices, much innovative work is necessary. In particular, adaptive tetrahedral-element generation algorithm, which can generate properly shaped tetrahedral-elements for moving boundary problems and also for the problems including very thin layers in it. And stable discretization method algorithm for non-linear drift-diffusion equation and efficient linear equation solver are also indispensable.

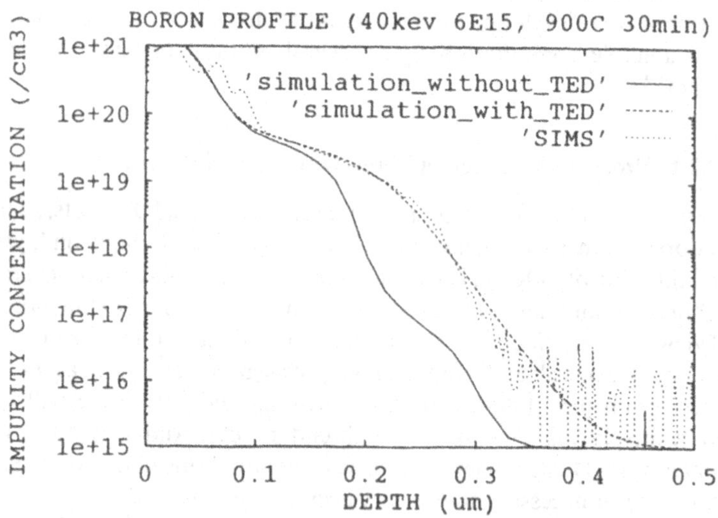

Figure 10.7 Drain profile of boron for *n*-channel MOSFET[15].

Moreover, to improve such a big and complicated system, an object-oriented programming approach seems to be indispensable.

10.3. Device Simulation

Many semiconductor companies have been developing in-house device simulators during the last decade. They are used 1) to analyse small geometry effects such as short channel effect on threshold voltage, 2) to optimize device structures with numerous design parameters such as LDD-MOSFET, 3) to understand and reduce "single event upset" phenomena such as alpha-particle induced soft-error and latch-up of CMOS structure, 4) to study the limitation of MOSFET miniaturization, and 5) to optimize device structures by analysing performance sensitivity to process parameter variations.

In this section, review of carrier transport models in standard device simulators such as mobility, intrinsic carrier concentration and band-gap narrowing effect are presented.

10.3.1. Physical Model

Compared with process simulation models, there are fewer variations of carrier transport models for standard device simulation. This seems to be the result of the relative simplicity of the interaction mechanism with the background material (silicon crystal) and another carrier. Actually, in the case of modeling carrier transport in polysilicon and amorphous silicon many unresolved models such as carrier trap density and thermoionic emission at the grain boundary, dominate device performance.

10.3.2.1. Drift Diffusion Model and Hydrodynamic Model

Many conventional device simulation programs solve drift-diffusion model in which, electron and hole current flow are assumed to be the summation of the two components. The first component is proportional to the gradient of carrier density and the second component is in proportional to a product of electric field and carrier density. These current components can be derived from Boltzmann's transport equation[20]. Electric field is determined by the electric potential which satisfies Poisson's equation. So, the basic equations of drift diffusion model are

$$\mathrm{div}(\varepsilon \cdot \mathrm{grad}\,\psi) = -q(n - p + N_A - N_D) \tag{10.2.1}$$

$$\partial n/\partial t = -\mathrm{div}(J_n/(-q)) + GR_n \tag{10.2.2}$$

$$\partial p/\partial t = -\mathrm{div}(J_p/q) + GR_p \tag{10.2.3}$$

$$J_n = -q\mu_n \,\mathrm{grad}\,\psi + D_n \,\mathrm{grad}\, n \tag{10.2.4}$$

$$J_p = q\mu_p \,\mathrm{grad}\,\psi + D_p \,\mathrm{grad}\, p \tag{10.2.5}$$

where, suffix n and p represent that the models are related to electron and hole, respectively, ψ is electric potential (in eV), n and p are electron and hole density, J is current vector, D is diffusivity, GR is carrier generation velocity and μ is mobility.

In order to consider carrier energy transport which is of great interest for sub-micron MOSFETs, Boltzmann transport equation are multiplied by square of carrier velocity (i.e., v^2), and integrated in whole space- and velocity-components to get the following hydrodynamic equations.

$$(\partial c_n/\partial t) + \mathrm{div}\,(c_n u_n) = (\partial c_n/t)_{coll} \tag{10.2.6}$$

$$(\partial p_n/\partial t) + u_n(\mathrm{div} p_n) + (p_n \nabla) u_n = (-1)^n q c_n E - \mathrm{grad}\,(c_n k T_n) + (\partial p_n/\partial t)_{coll} \tag{10.2.7}$$

$$(\partial w_n/\partial t) + \mathrm{div}(u_n w_n) = (-1)^n q c_n (u_n E) - \mathrm{div}(u_n c_n k T_n) - (\partial w_n/\partial t)_{coll} \tag{10.2.8}$$

$$\text{where, } p_n = m_n c_n u_n, \tag{10.2.9}$$

$$w_n = (3/2) c_n k T_n + (1/2) m_n c_n u_n^2 \tag{10.2.10}$$

and subscript n denotes carrier type (1 for electron 2 for hole), c is carrier density, u is carrier velocity, p is carrier momentum, w is carrier energy, E is electric field and T is carrier temperature. The collision terms $(\partial p_n/\partial t)_{coll}$ and $(\partial w_n/\partial t)_{coll}$ are often approximated by using momentum and energy relaxation time τ_{pn} and τ_{wn}, as follows.

$$(\partial p_n/\partial t)_{coll} = -p_n/\tau_{pn} \tag{10.2.11}$$

$$(\partial w_n/\partial t)_{coll} = (w_n - w_{n0})/\tau_{wn} \tag{10.2.12}$$

A simplified hydrodynamic model can be obtained by neglecting convection term in the eqn. (10.2.7) and neglecting the kinetic energy term in eqn. (10.2.8). When we assume steady state, $O(u_n^2) \ll 1$ and isothermal condition, left-hand side of eqn. (10.2.7) vanishes and the drift diffusion current equation is obtained. This means that the hydrodynamic model is a generalization of the drift diffusion model.

Hydrodynamic and simplified hydrodynamic models are used to analyse hot carrier injection and velocity overshoot effect on channel current in lower submicron devices. Matsuzawa *et al.* have shown that velocity overshoot effect in a nearly-intrinsic channel SOI device is pronounced and large channel current is expected[21]. Figure 10.8 shows the electron velocity distribution along the channel region of *n*-type SOI MOSFET, in which electron velocity exceeds saturation velocity (about 10^7 cm/s). They have also shown the hot carrier injection at the back side gate can degrade device reliability.

10.3.1.2. Reconsideration of Physical Models and Parameter Calibration

In order to predict device performance accurately, parameter values even for basic physical models should always be reconsidered critically. Great care should be taken when extracting a parameter value from measured data, because measured data includes many complicated relationship with a lot of physical models. Shigyo *et al.* proposed the novel mobility model considering the difference of minority carrier and majority carrier scattering by Coulomb forces[22]. Green has shown that n_i, a widely used intrinsic carrier concentration value is not correct[23]. Table 10.1 shows basic physical parameter values after Shigyo. Shigyo *et al.* proposed an improved band-gap narrowing model based on a correct n_i[24]. By using the new band-gap narrowing model and their mobility model, they succeeded in reproducing measured bipolar transistor current and $I_c - f_T$ characteristics accurately[26].

Model predictability is the key requirement to ensure the usefulness of TCAD·technology and its successful application to actual device design. Only the accuracy of a TCAD tool helps engineers to decide which technologies to select. And in such a situation, global models are needed to make it possible for simulators to predict device

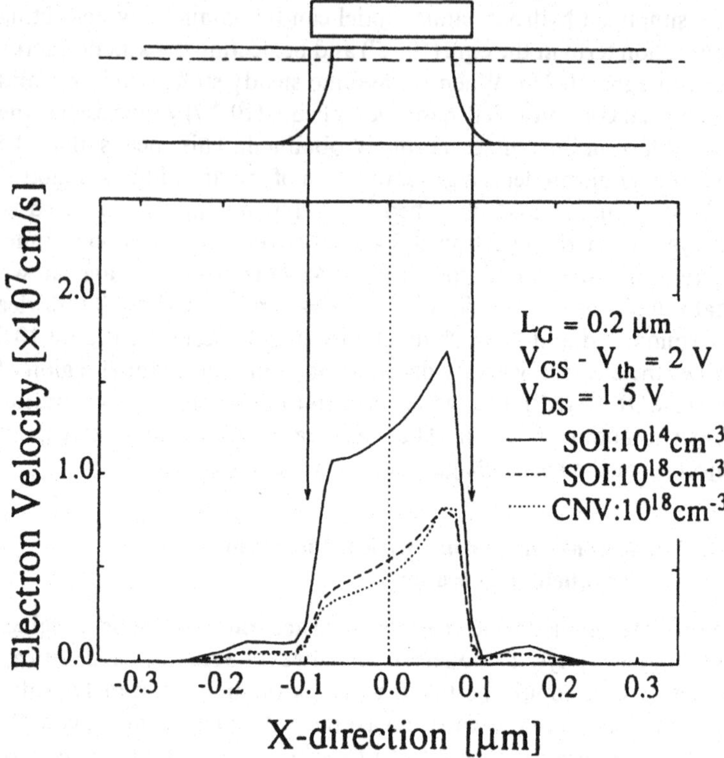

Figure 10.8 Electron velocity distribution along Si/SiO_2 interface of different boron concentration *n*-type SOI MOSFET. 'CNV' means the simulation result of bulk device[21].

Table 10.1 Intrinsic carrier density and related parameters of silicon.

	$n_i(cm^{-3})$	$Nc(cm^{-3})$	$Nv(cm^{-3})$	Eg(eV)
A. S. Grove	1.45E10	2.8E19	1.04E19	1.11
S. M. Sze	1.45E10	1.8E19	1.04E19	1.12
M. A. Green	1.08E10	2.86E19	3.10E19	1.1242

performance accurately even outside the range of current technologies. The examples mentioned above are a kind of global modeling. Ideally, global modeling can also be achieved by using *ab-initio* modeling. However these modelings are too complex for application to actual devices. Therefore, in another approach, local models should be considered to achieve the required accuracy. Since the relevant physics and chemistry are not clear, the model parameters should be considered to be an object to be fitted to the available data. This approach works well within a limited range of process conditions. Masuda demonstrated that relative drain current error of 0.85 % is achieved by using an optimized parameter set[27].

10.3.3. Simulation System

There are many simulation softwares and many device engineers find it difficult to master them. Kato *et al.* proposed a unified user interface system for two-dimensional process simulator and device simulator[28]. Figure 10.9 is their system configuration, in which basic concept of virtual device fabrication is included. In this system, they consider that both unified graphical user interface and unified interchange data format are important. As shown in Figure 10.9, simulations start after defining the cross section by using mask data and end with the display of current-voltage characteristics. In more advanced

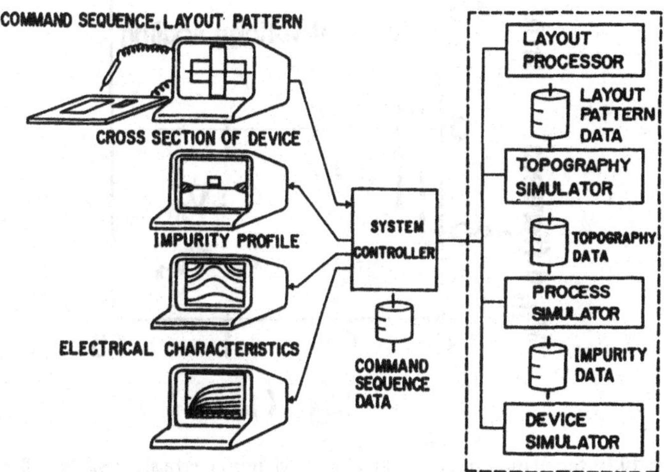

Figure 10.9 Configuration of integrated process and device simulation system[28].

system, statistical analysis tool of device performance, parameter extraction tool for circuit simulation program, and other software tools are integrated[27].

The extension of these idea is a virtual fabrication which is expected to contribute the acceleration of device development schedules.

10.3.4. Some Application Examples

Generally, simulation provides not only insights into objects such a carrier flow but also answers "What if?" questions, and the latter is one of the most useful functions provided the model is valid.

Nishinohara *et al.* reported the effect of microscopic dopant fluctuation on MOSFET threshold voltages (V_{th})[30]. Their motivation was to find a limitation to MOSFET miniaturization and they focused on uncontrollable deviations of a device parameters, namely a fluctuation of dopant distribution in a nMOSFET channel region. They put dopant density grid by grid by using Poisson distribution random number generator. According to their analysis, as expected, standard deviation of V_{th} increases as channel length decreased. Figure 10.10

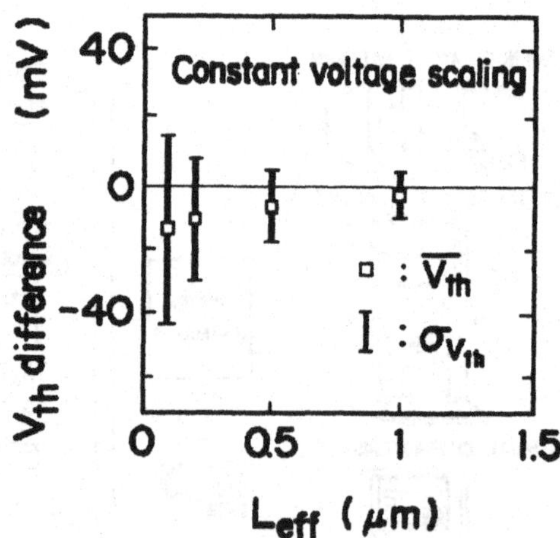

Figure 10.10 Simulation results of standard deviations (vertical bars), the difference between average threshold voltages with and without dopant fractuation effect (rectangle marks)[30].

shows the standard deviations (vertical bars) and difference of average threshold voltages (V_{th}) with and without dopant fluctuation effect (rectangle symbols) as a function of channel length. And what is interesting is that average V_{th} decreased compared with the non-fluctuated simulation result. They explain this by using a simple one-dimensional model and consider this phenomenon to be attributed to the asymmetric effect of doping density deviations on V_{th}.

10.4. Conclusion

There are several ways for TCAD technologies to go. The one is to develop a physical model hierarchy including a so called *ab*-initio models to get backgrounds of microscopic insights for fundamental processes which, at present, are modeled only phenomenologicalty. Another way is to be integrated with a so called ECAD (Electronic CAD) system designing tools, like mask-pattern layout and timing simulation software, to reduce device designing cycle.

References

1. Yoshida, M., Arai, E., Nakamura, H. and Terunuma, Y. (1974). *J. Appl. Phys.*, **45**, 1498.
2. Collard, and Taniguchi, (1986). *IEEE Trans. on Electron Devices*, **ED-33**(10), 1454–1462.
3. Okada, T. K., Kambayashi, S., Onga, S., Mizushima, I., Yamabe, K. and Matsunaga, J. (1990). *Tech. Digest of Int. Electron Device Meeting*, 733–736.
4. Mizuno, T., Okamura, J. and Toriumi, A. (1994). *IEEE Trans. ED*, **41**(11), 2216–2221.
5. Aoki, N., Kanemura, T. and Mizusawa, I. (1994). *Appl. Phys. Lett.*, **64**(23), 3133–3135.
6. Aoki, N. and Nakamura, M. (1995). *Technical Report of IEICE*, VLD95-56, ED95-77, SDM95-117, pp. 23–30.
7. Fahey, P. M., Griffin, P. B. and Plummer, J. P. (1989). *Review of Modern Physics*, **61**(2), 289–384.
8. Baccus, B., Wada, T., Shigyo, N., Norishima, M., Nakajima, H., Inou, K., Iinuma, T. and Iwai, H. (1992). *IEEE Trans ED*, **ED-39**(3), 648–661.
9. Hu, S. M., Fahey, P. and Dutton, R. W. (1983). *J. Appl. Phys.*, **54**(12), 6912–6922.
10. Shaw, D. (1975). *Phys. Status Solidi B*, **72**, 11.

11. Hane, M., Rafferty, C. S., Ikezawa, T. and Matsumoto, H. (1996). *SISPAD '96*, pp. 15–16.
12. Chin, D., Oh, S. Y., Hu, S. M., Dutton, R. W. and Moll, J. L. (1983). *IEEE Trans. on Electron Devices*, **ED-30**, 744.
13. Matsumoto, H. and Fukuma, M. (1985). *IEEE Trans. Electron Devices*, **ED-32**, 132.
14. Isomae, S., Yamamoto, S., Aoki, S. and Yajima, A. (1986). *IEEE Electron Device Lett.*, **EDL-7**, 368.
15. Umimoto, H., Odanaka, S. and Nakao, I. (1989). *IEEE Trans. on CAD*, **CAD-10**(7), 330–332.
16. Umimoto, H., Odanaka, S. and Gohda, A. (1995). "3-Dimentional Process Simulation" pp. 30–56, Springer-Verlag.
17. Neureuther, A. R., Wang, R. H., Helmsen, J. J., Sefler, J. E., Scheckler, E. W., Gunturi, R. and Winterbottom, R. (1995). "3-Dimentional Process Simulation" pp. 57–76, Springer-Verlag.
18. Fuijinaga, M., Kotani, N., Kunikiyo, T., Oda, H., Shirahata, M. and Akasaka, Y. (1990). *IEEE Trans. ED*, **ED-37**(10), 2183–2192.
19. Fujinaga, M. and Kotani, N. (1995). "3-Dimentional Process Simulation" pp. 1–29, Springer-Verlag.
20. Selberher, S. (1984). "Analysis and Simulation of Semiconductor Devices," Springer-Verlag, Wien, New York, pp. 11–20.
21. Matuzawa, K., Takahashi, M., Yoshimi, M. and Shigyo, N. (1992). *IEICER Trans. Electron.*, **E75**(12), 1477–1483.
22. Shigyo, N., Tanimoto, H., Norishima, M. and Yasuda, S. (1990). *Solid State Electron.*, **33**(6), 721–731.
23. Green, M. A. (1990). *J. Appl. Phys.*, **67**, 2944.
24. Shigyo, N. (1996). *J. Applied Phys.*, **65**(12), 1276–1277.
25. Shigyo, N., Konishi, N. and Satake, H. (1992). *IEICE Trans. Electron.*, **E75**(2), 156–160.
26. Shigyo, N. and Niitsu, Y. (1993). *IEEE Trans. ED*, **40**(11), 2087–2089.
27. Masuda, H. (1995). "Simulation of Semiconductor Devices and Processes" **6**, 408–415, Springer-Verlag.
28. Kato, K., Shigyo, N., Wada, T., Onga, S., Konaka, M. and Taniguchi, K. (1987). *IEEE Trans. ED*, **34**(10), 2049–2058.
30. Nishinohara, K., Shigyo, N. and Wada, T. (1992). *IEEE Trans. ED*, **39**(3), 634–639.

CHAPTER 11

SOI Technology

11.1. History of SOI Technology

In recent years, SOI (silicon-on-insulator) technology has attracted more attention than ever before because of its numerous unique features which are suitable to proliferating multimedia applications. In terms of its low-capacitance structure, SOI devices are seemingly identical to SOS (silicon-on-sapphire) devices. However, SOI devices differ from SOS counterparts in their high quality of material, various advantages ranging from low-power but high-speed operation, soft-error hardness, easy isolation, to capability to build 3D circuits and so on. Historically, SOI or SOS became a focus of attention whenever bulk silicon devices faced formidable obstacles. In the SOS era, *i.e.*, from the 70's to the beginning of the 80's, it was difficult to achieve high-speed operation with bulk silicon devices. However, bulk silicon technology eventually overcame this problem by simply down-scaling the device dimensions. In the early 80's, on the other hand, severe difficulty was encountered in overcoming photolithography's resolution limit of around 1 μm, which made the future of two-dimensional integration quite opaque. In Japan, this motivated the initiation of a national project to study 3D-IC (Three-Dimensional Integrated Circuits)[1,2], in which laser or e-beam annealed SOI technology was intensively studied. It turned out, however, to be possible to circumvent photolithography's limitation by using a shorter wavelength of the light source or the incorporation of a large numerical aperture lens in a step-and-repeater system, which resulted in a very prosperous LSI industry with respect to submicron devices.

In the 90's, in view of the mounting demand for low-power computer systems for portable multimedia applications, it is becoming clear that bulk silicon devices are not always appropriate for low-power devices. This is because bulk silicon MOSFETs suffer from various parasitic capacitances and degraded performance which become noticeable at a low supply voltage. Moreover, as the device dimension is reduced to the deep submicron region, a number of problems which are considered to be critical and fundamental begin to appear. These are limit in LOCOS isolation, difficulty in shallow junction formation, degraded mobility due to high doping in the channel region and so on. In dynamic RAMs, on the other hand, memory cell structures are becoming increasingly complicated to ensure memory data in read/write operations or maintain soft-error immunity, making the fabrication process long and difficult. Furthermore, the ever-increasing investment required to implement new processes is imposing a heavy burden on ULSI manufacturers.

Studies of SOI devices have revealed that SOI technology is capable of coping with these problems, which is the reason why SOI is once more in the limelight in the 90's. The following chapters review the development of SOI technology in Japan, focusing on the topics of thin-film SOI-MOSFETs, development of SOI processes, SOI substrate technology, and its ULSI applications.

11.2. Thin-film SOI Structure

In the early 80's when the study of SOI technology began, it was common to build SOI MOSFETs on relatively thick (typically around 500–800 nm) SOI films. This was presumably due to the historical legacy of SOS, or process reasons respecting recrystallization of polycrystalline Si, which needed a thick film to suppress overheating of silicon. Due to such thick SOI films, SOI devices suffered severely from floating-body effects. That is, minority carriers tend to accumulate in the SOI substrate, giving rise to electrically unstable effects, such as the kink effect[3] or the current-overshoot effect[4]. These problems hamper an accurate prediction of the drain current for static and dynamic circuits, making accurate circuit design difficult. Additionally, crystal quality of SOI material was inferior to what is currently available, so that the application of SOI devices were limited to certain specialized areas such as radiation-hardened equipment.

In the latter half of the 80's, however, it became clear that thinning an SOI film to less than the maximum depletion width (Fig. 11.1)

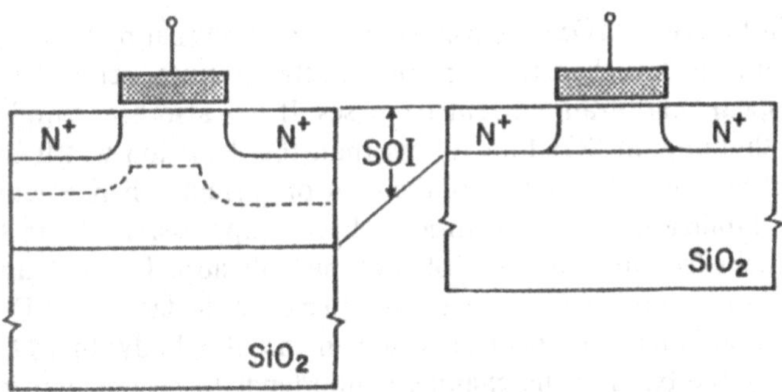

Figure 11.1 Structure comparison of a thin-film (fully-depleted (FD)) SOI MOSFET (right) and a conventional thick-film (partially-depleted (PD)) SOI MOSFET (left)[5–7].

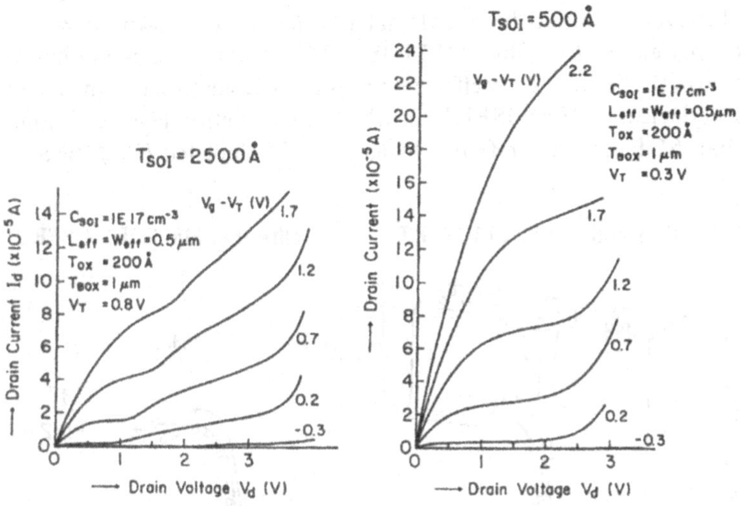

Figure 11.2 Simulated current-voltage characteristics in a thick-film SOI MOSFET (left) and a thin-film SOI MOSFET (right)[7].

brings about a number of improvements[5–7]. This type of device is referred to as a fully-depleted (FD) SOI MOSFET. Figure 11.2 shows the simulation results for Id–Vd characteristics for 0.5 μm channel-length SOI-MOSFETs for a thick-film SOI MOSFET (left) and a thin-film SOI MOSFET (right). It can be seen that by thinning an SOI film to less than the depletion width (100 nm, here), the kink disappears and drain current increases. It has also been confirmed that thinning an SOI film to less than the depletion width brings about not only elimination of the kink or current enhancement but also stabilization of the transient effect[9], suppression of the short channel effect, improvement of subthreshold slope factor[10], and so on. These improvements are a consequence of the fact that FD-type devices eliminate the neutral region in the SOI body. In FD type devices, the band in the channel region tends to become flat in the vertical direction, which makes the potential in the SOI body entirely elevated for holes, as shown in Figure 11.3. Flatness of the band diagram in the SOI region also brings about a decrease in the vertical electric field as well, which leads to enhancement of low-field mobility. However, it should be noted that the drain breakdown voltage is decreased in a thin-film SOI MOSFET[11], which is also a manifestation of the floating body effect remaining in FD devices. In contrast to FD devices, SOI MOSFETs in which the depletion layer is thinner than SOI films are referred to as partially-depleted (PD) devices.

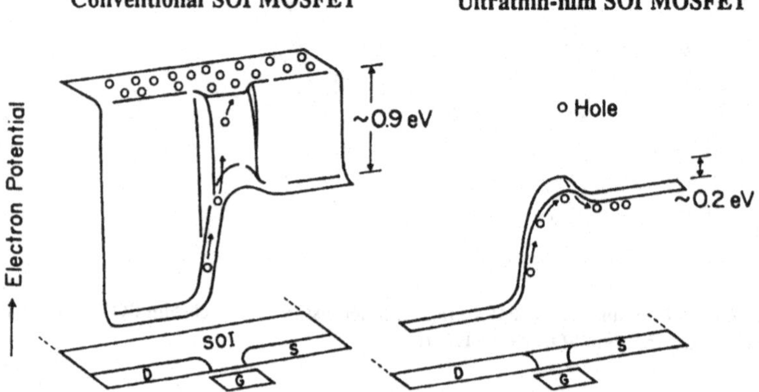

Figure 11.3 Schematic explanation of kink elimination in FD device. Potential and hole flow in a thick-film (PD) SOI MOSFET (left) and a thin-film (FD) SOI MOSFET (right) are shown. In an FD SOI MOSFET, holes generated at the drain flow to the source and recombine with electrons[7].

Although FD devices exhibit various advantages, they suffer from narrow process window for threshold voltage adjustment[12], which can bring about larger scattering in the threshold voltage due to SOI film fluctuation. The required SOI thickness for an FD device in 0.25 μm design rule is, for example, approximately 40 nm, which is rather too thin, considering the ability of state-of-the-art SOI substrate technology or possibility of increased contact resistance. In PD devices, however, the floating-body effect is still severe and hampers normal operation of LSI circuits, as already mentioned. The floating-body effect has long been discussed as the critical issue in SOI device technology, since it severely affects the device operation whichever type of SOI MOSFETs are used. To suppress the floating-body effect, hole absorption by a field-shield structure (shown in the last section), reducing parasitic bipolar gain by forming a SiGe layer in the source region (Fig. 11.4)[13], reducing the lifetime of minority carriers by Ar implantation in the source[14], and so on have been proposed.

At any rate, the SOI thickness which is commonly used in device fabrication has become typically around 100 nm, which is very thin compared with the thick SOI used previously. SOI substrate technologies have been developed targeting this thin-film structure, as shown in the next section.

11.3. SOI Substrate Technology

To meet the requirement of a thin-film structure, various SOI material technologies have been proposed and developed. Especially, SIMOX (Separation by Implanted Oxygen) and bond-and-etch SOI (BESOI) technology have been developed as two major technologies, both of which have high crystal quality as well as high potential for mass production. Izumi *et al.* of NTT found in 1978 that implantation of oxygen into a silicon substrates led to the formation of high quality silicon-dioxide[15]. However, early experiments showed that SIMOX substrate suffered from crystal defect density as high as 10^9 cm^{-2} which mostly originated from threading dislocations. However, it was found in 1987 that high-temperature annealing as high as 1300 °C[16-18] as well as elevating temperature during implantation up to more than 550 °C brings about drastic lowering of defect

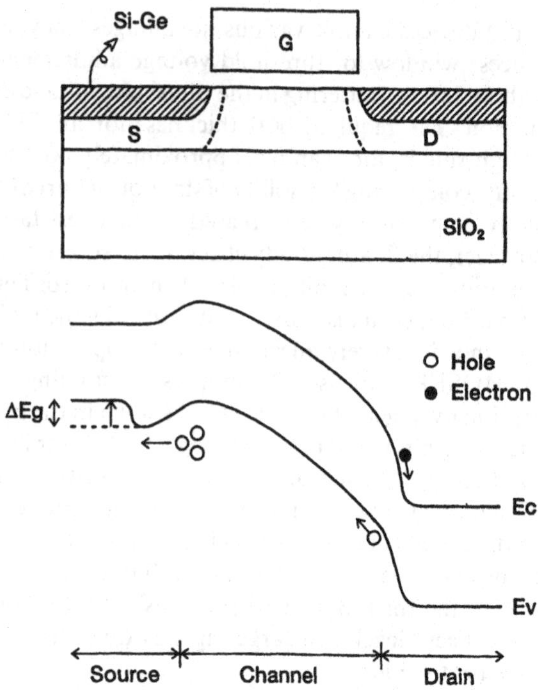

Figure 11.4 A SiGe source structure to suppress the floating-body effect. The narrow bandgapped SiGe layer absorbs excess holes in the channel[13].

density down to approximately 10^6 cm^{-2}. Moreover, in 1989, Nakashima *et al.*, of NTT found that lowering the oxygen dose resulted in a more drastic decrease in defect density[19]. Figure 11.5 and 6 show that the defect density decreases as the oxygen dose decreases and the high-quality oxide layer was found to be realized at the dose window of 4×10^{17} cm^{-2}. It should be noted that the defect density under this condition is as low as 10^2–10^3 cm^{-2}. In addition, it should be noted that lowering the oxygen dosage is advantageous in terms of increasing wafer throughput. In 1994, moreover, Nakashima *et al.* of NTT also presented that the buried oxide can be further thickened by additional oxidation at high temperature[20]. This oxidation also improves the roughness at Si/SiO_2 interface as well as decreasing the

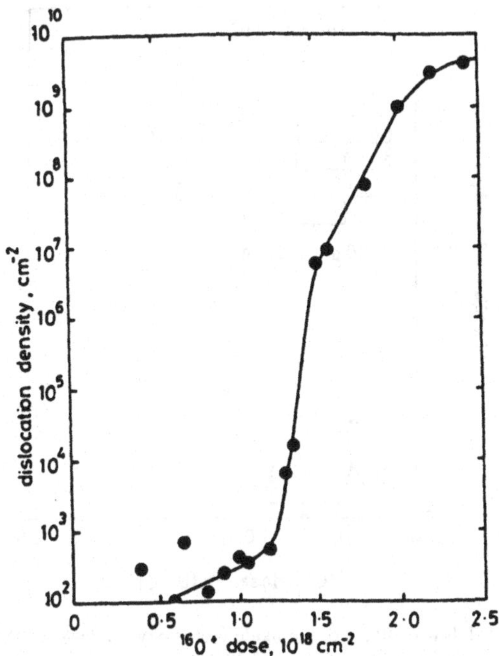

Figure 11.5 Dislocation density of superficial silicon film in SIMOX as a function of oxygen dose. The implantation condition was 180 kV at 550 °C. High temperature anneal at 1300 °C in Ar-O_2 mixture was carried out for 4 hours. The defect density drastically decreased to 10^2–10^3 cm^{-2} as the oxygen dose decreased[19].

pin-hole density in the buried oxide. Today, commercially available SIMOX wafers have the SOI thickness uniformity of less than 5%. So far, a number of LSIs have been fabricated using SIMOX wafers.

On the other hand, BESOI technology has made great progress as well. It has been well known that when water-containing surfaces of two polished silicon wafers are contacted, they make a hard contact which cannot be separated even at room temperature. It has been experimentally proved that elevating temperature to more than 1000°C ensures much tighter contact[21,22]. SOI substrates can be obtained by thinning one of the two wafers down to a few microns or

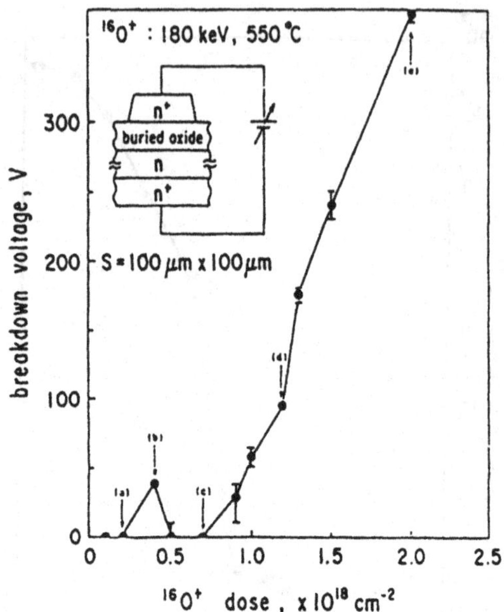

Figure 11.6 Breakdown voltage of the oxide versus oxygen dose in SIMOX technology. At the dose window of 4×10^{17} cm^{-2}, high-quality silicon dioxide is formed[19].

below. Although wafer bonding technology is advantageous in terms of its high crystal quality and the potential for high throughput, the critical issue was thickness control of an SOI layer. The limitation of SOI-thickness control by conventional mechanical grinding and polishing processes is approximately +/− 0.1 µm. To achieve a thin-film SOI layer usable for ULSI applications, a variety of methods have been proposed[23–25].

In 1992, Mumola *et al.*, of Hughes Danbury Optical Systems reported that computer-controlled plasma-etching can be used to obtain 100 nm +/- 5% range SOI thickness[26]. This process is called PACE (Plasma Assisted Chemical Etching). In the PACE process, the thickness variation of conventional ground-and-polished SOI films are measured in advance and SOI films are thinned by scanning a plasma nozzle while controlling the duration time depending on the measured thickness variation. Figure 11.7 shows 58 nm thickness SOI film with variation of less than 5%.

In Japan, Tanaka *et al.*, of Fujitsu fabricated 60 nm thick SOI MOSFETs using a LOCOS oxide stopper, in 1991 (Fig. 11.8)[27]. Nishihara *et al.*, of Sony also utilized an oxide stopper to obtain a buried capacitor cell structure (Fig. 11.9)[28]. In 1994, Yonehara *et al.* of Canon reported that a 100 nm thick SOI structure can be fabricated by epitaxial growth on a porous silicon[29]. In France, on the other hand, in 1995, SOITEC/LETI reported in 1995 the "Smart Cut" process in which a silicon surface layer is peeled off and transferred to another wafer by implanting hydrogen into silicon and bonding wafers[30], as shown in Figure 11.10. The Unibond wafer made by Smart Cut is reported to have film-thickness uniformity of less than 5%.

11.4. Application to ULSI Circuits

Using SOI substrates, a number of LSI fabrications have been reported. Aiming at high-speed, low-voltage applications, Kado *et al.*,

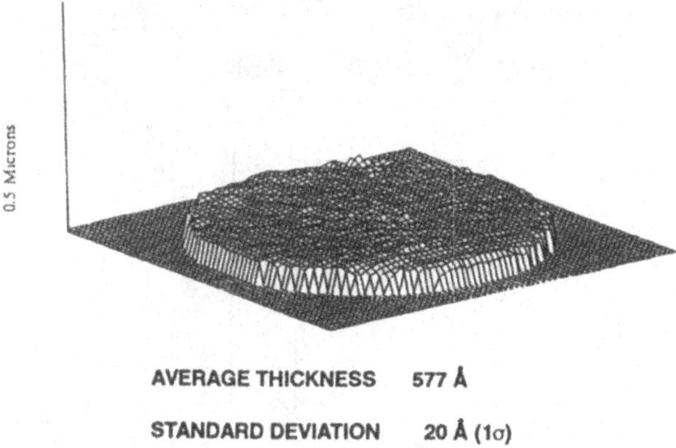

Figure 11.7 SOI thickness variation in a plasma-thinned bonded SOI wafer. Thickness variation of less than 5% has been achieved for 577 Å thickness[26].

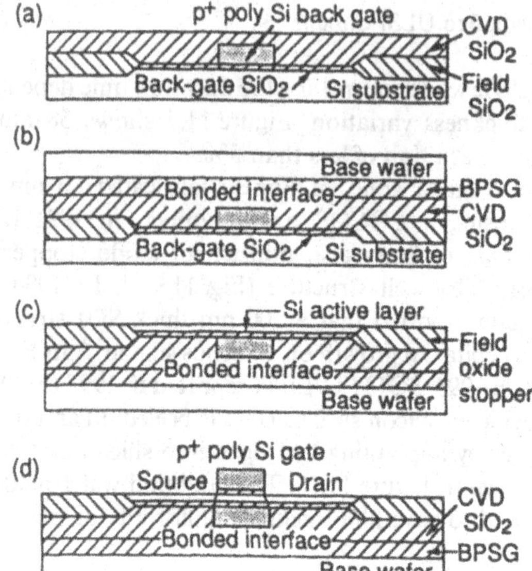

Figure 11.8 Fabrication process of a dual gate MOSFET. Field oxide acts as a polish stopper[27].

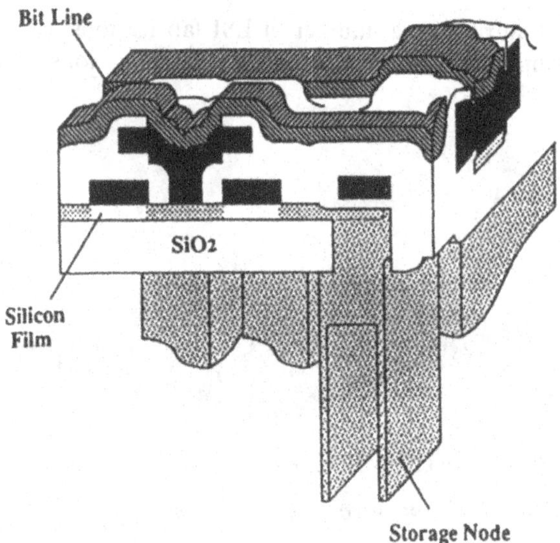

Figure 11.9 Schematic view of buried capacitor cell. SOI film is made by polish stop by field oxide[28].

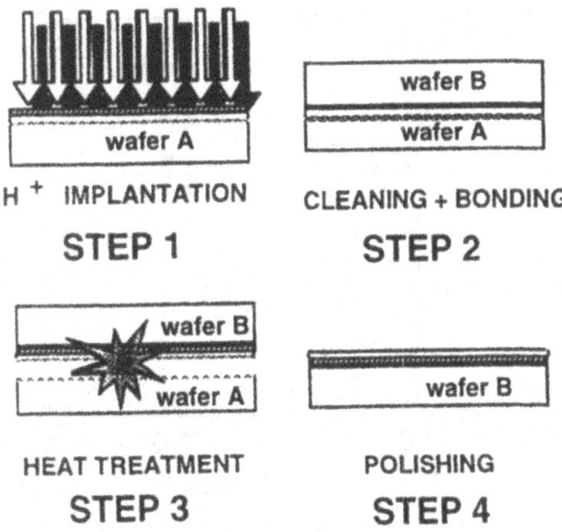

Figure 11.10 Process flow of Smart Cut. Hydrogen is implanted through oxide to form a damaged layer in wafer A. Only surface layer of wafer A is peeled off and transferred to wafer B by bonding and heat treatment[30].

of NTT have reported that a prescaler made on a SIMOX substrate operates at a frequency of 1 GHz under 1 V power supply and at a power consumption as low as 1 mW, as shown in Figure 11.11[31]. The performance of a SIMOX device was much better than that by BiCMOS or GaAs devices, which have been conventionally used in portable communication systems. Yamaguchi *et al.*, of Mitsubishi reported that 16-bit multiplier made on a SIMOX substrate operated at a speed 30% higher than bulk silicon devices as shown in Figure 11.12[32]. Inoue *et al.*, of Mitsubishi reported that they fabricated 256 k SRAM which operated to as low as 1.2 V in a stable manner, as shown in Figure 11.13[33]. As for DRAM applications, Gotou *et al.*, of Fujitsu reported that 64k DRAM made on bonded SOI wafers has much higher soft error immunity than bulk silicon DRAM with a thinned SOI film, as shown in Figure 11.14[34]. Suma *et al.*, of Mitsubishi also reported that SOI-DRAM fabricated on SIMOX substrates are practically soft-error free, as shown in Figure 11.15[35]. They reported that SOI DRAM is advantageous in terms of drastic reduction in cell capacitance as compared with bulk silicon

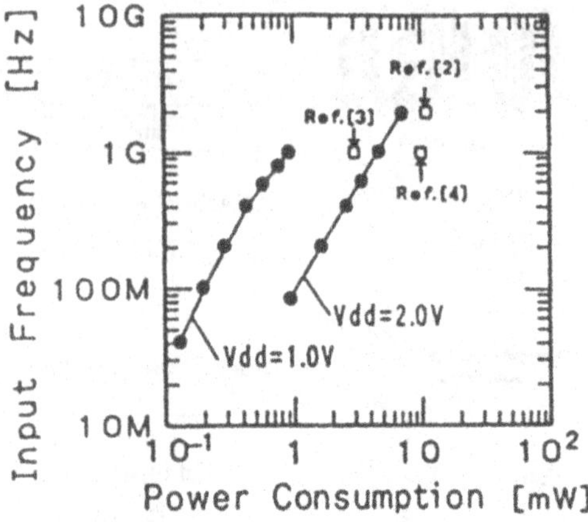

Figure 11.11 Relation between input frequency and associated total power consumption in a prescaler made on a SIMOX. Power consumed in the output buffer with a 2.7 pF external load is included[31].

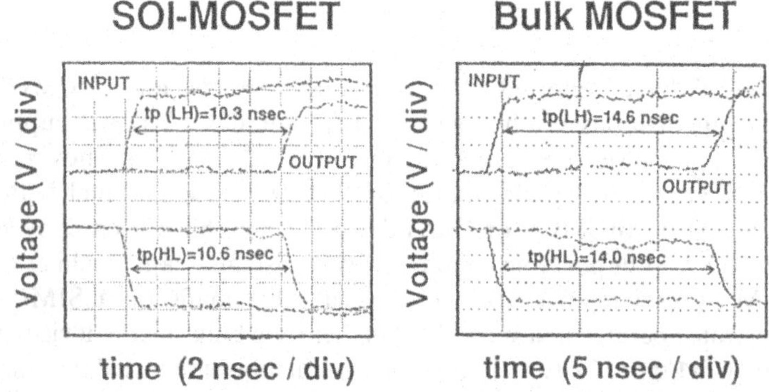

Figure 11.12 Comparison of waveforms of a 16 bit multiplier for SOI-MOSFET (left) and bulk MOSFET (right). In an SOI-MOSFET, 30% higher operation speed has been achieved[32].

DRAMs[36]. They also proposed a field-shield structure to avoid the floating-body effect, as shown in Figure 11.16. Tanigawa *et al.*, of NEC reported in 1994 that the retention time in SOI DRAMs is six

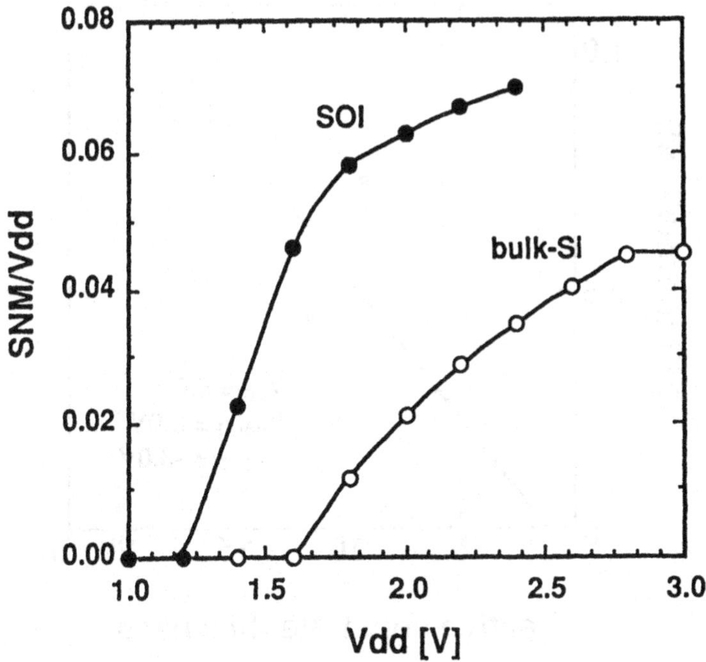

Figure 11.13 Comparison of signal noise margin (SNM) in an SRAM cell for SOI MOSFET (solid circle) and bulk MOSFET (open circle). In an SOI MOSFET, SRAM cell operates in a stable manner to as low as 1.2 V[33].

times longer than that of bulk silicon DRAMs[37]. It should be noted that in 1995, Samsung in Korea demonstrated a fully-working 16M DRAM chip by using a SIMOX substrate[38]. But at the same time, it was pointed out that the gate oxide integrity of SOI substrates including SIMOX and BESOI is still inferior to that of bulk silicon. In 1995, Nakamura et al. of Fujitsu reported reversed stacked capacitor (RSTC) cell structure by wafer bonding using a LOCOS oxide as an etch stopper[39]. In 1996, Ino *et al.*, of NTT reported a 300k-gate gate-array which was fabricated using 0.25 μm rule on a SIMOX substrate[40]. Toshiba reported that the supply voltage can be reduced to well below 0.5 V by a gate-to-SOI body connected structure. They

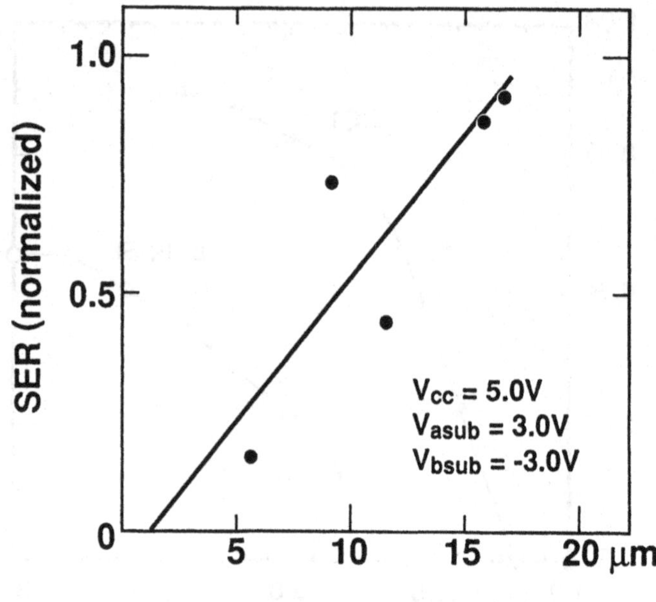

Figure 11.14 Dependence of soft-error rate (SER) on active substrate (SOI) thickness. DRAM is made on BESOI substrate. Vertical axis shows SER normalized by an averaged SER of several conventional DRAMs[34].

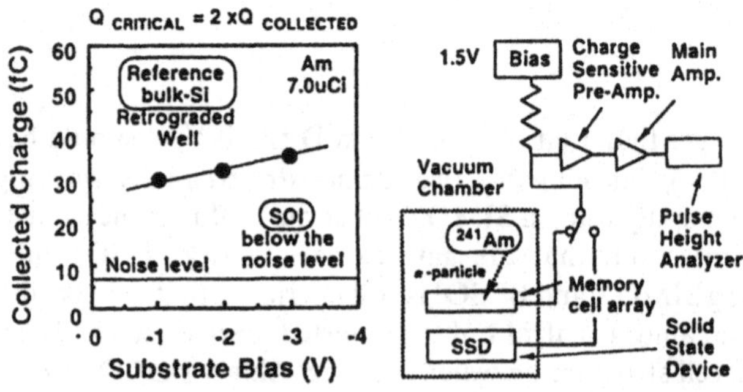

Figure 11.15 Collected charge in a memory cell active area on SOI film/bulk-Si substrate measured by a charge-sensitive amplifier and statistical measurement system (right). In an SOI-DRAM, the collected charge is below the detection limit[35].

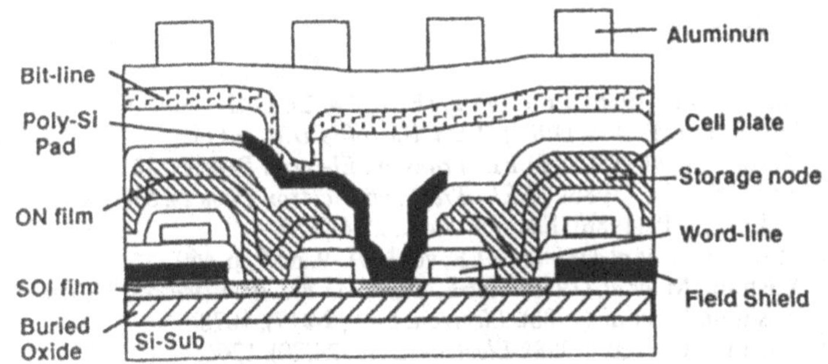

Figure 11.16 Schematic cross-sectional view of SOI-DRAM cell having a field shield structure. Excess holes in the channel are absorbed to the field area[36].

also predicted that the sophisticated circuit design can reduce the power-delay product by a further one order of magnitude compared with that of conventional SOI circuit[41].

11.5. Summary

We have witnessed rapid progress of SOI technology in the present decade. A thin-film SOI MOSFET has become a major structure to realize the high performance required of recent ULSIs. SOI material technology has also made noticeable advancement where SIMOX and BESOI have grown as practical technologies. Using these substrates, various LSIs ranging from low-power logic, gate array, to memory have been fabricated. Considering the trend in the 90's toward personalized multimedia computer systems, SOI technology is very attractive from viewpoints of low power consumption, high-speed operation, and low cost. All the indications are that it will not be long before SOI technology will be used as a conventional technology, just as bulk silicon technology has been until now.

References

1. Akasaka, Y. (1986). *Proc. of the IEEE*, **74**(12), 1703.
2. Nishimura, T. *et al.* (1987). *Tech. Dig. of IEDM*, p.111.
3. Kato, K. *et al.* (1985). *IEEE, Trans. on Electron Devices*, **32**(2), 458.
4. Kato, K. *et al.* (1986). *IEEE, Trans. on Electron Devices*, **33**(1), 133.
5. Colinge, J. P. (1986). *Electron. Lett.*, **22**(4), 187.
6. Sturm, J. C. *et al.* (1988). *IEEE*, vol.EDL-9, no.9, p. 460.
7. Yoshimi, M. *et al.* (1989). *IEEE, Trans. on Electron Devices*, **36**(3),493.
8. Yoshimi, M. *et al.* (1988). *Electron. Lett.*, **24**(17), 1078.
9. Hazama, H. *et al.* (1988). *Electron. Lett.*, **24**(20), 1266.
10. Colinge, J. P. (1986). *IEEE*, vol.EDL-7, no.4, p. 244.
11. Yoshimi, M. *et al.* (1990). *IEEE, Trans. on Electron Devices*, **37**(9), 2015.
12. Su, L. T. (1995). *Ext. Abst. of the 1995 Int. Conf. on SSDM*, Osaka, p. 542.
13. Yoshimi, M. *et al.* (1994). *Tech. Dig. of IEDM*, p. 429.
14. Ohno, T. *et al.* (1995). *Tech. Dig. of IEDM*, p. 627.
15. Izumi, K. *et al.* (1978). *Electron. Lett.*, **14**(18), 593.
16. Jaussaud, C. *et al.*, *Appl. Phys. Lett.*, vol.46, 1985, p.1064.
17. Celler, G. K. *et al.*, Hemment, P. L. F., West, K. W. and Gibson, J. M. (1986). *Appl. Phys. Lett.*, **48**(8), 532.
18. Jaussaud, C. *et al.*, Margail, J., Stoemenos, J. and Bruel, M. (1988). *Proc. of Mat. Res. Soc. Symp.*, **107**, 17.
19. Nakashima, S. *et al.* (1990). *Electron. Lett.*, **26**, 1647.
20. Nakashima, S. *et al.* (1994). *Proc. of IEEE SOI Conf.*, p. 71.
21. Sinbo, M. *et al.* (1986). *J. Appl. Phys.*, **60**(8), 2987.
22. Lasky, J. B. *et al.* (1985). *Tech. Dig. of IEDM*, p. 684.
23. Abe, T. *et al.* (1990). "Silicon on Insulator Technology and Devices", edited by Schmidt, D. N. (Electrochem. Soc., Pennington).
24. Abe, T. *et al.* (1991). *Tech. Abst. of 1st International Symposium on Wafer Bonding*, Science, Technology, and Applications, ECS Fall Meeting, Arizona, USA, p. 703.
25. Arimoto, Y. *et al.* (1993). *J. of the Electrochem. Soc.*, **140**(4), 383.
26. Mumola, P. B. *et al.* (1992). *Proc. of IEEE SOI Tech. Conf.*, p. 152.
27. Tanaka, T. *et al.* (1991). *Tech. Dig. of IEDM*, p. 683.
28. Nishihara, T. *et al.* (1992). *Tech. Dig. of IEDM*, p. 803.
29. Yonehara, T. *et al.* (1994). *Appl. Phys. Lett.*, **64**(16), 2108.
30. Bruel, M. (1995). *Electronics Letters*, **31**(14), 1201.
31. Kado, Y. *et al.* (1992). *Tech. Abst. of Symposium on VLSI Circuits*, p. 44.
32. Yamaguchi, Y. *et al.* (1993). *IEEE Trans. on Electron Devices*, **40**(1), p. 179.
33. Inoue, Y. *et al.* (1993). *Proc. of IEEE SOI Tech. Conf.*, p. 94.
34. Gotou, H. *et al.* (1987). *Tech. Dig. of IEDM*, p. 870.
35. Suma, K. *et al.* (1994). *Tech. Abst. of ISSCC 94*, p. 138.
36. Eimori, T. *et al.* (1993). *Tech. Dig. IEDM*, p. 45.

37. Tanigawa, T., Yoshino, A., Koga, H. and Ohya, S. (1994). *Tech. Dig. of Symp. on VLSI Tech.*, p. 37.
38. Kim, H-S. *et al.* (1995). *Dig. of Symp. on VLSI Tech.*, p. 143.
39. Nakamura, S. *et al.* (1995). *Tech. Dig. of IEDM*, p. 889.
40. Ino, M. *et al.* (1996). *Digest of IEEE ISSCC*, p. 86.
41. Fuse, T. *et al.* (1996). *Digest of IEEE ISSCC*, p. 88.

Index

Other titles in the Japanese Technology Reviews series

Volume 29

TFT/LCD: Liquid-Crystal Displays Addressed by Thin-Film Transistors

Toshihisa Tsukada

Volume 30

Charge-Coupled Device Technology

Shigeyuki Ochi, Tetsuya Iizuka, Masaharu Hamasaki, Yasushi Sato, Tadakuni Narabu, Hideshi Abe, Yoshiaki Kagawa and Keiji Kato

Printed in the United States
by Baker & Taylor Publisher Services